VIRGINIA DOMESTIC RELATIONS
CASE FINDER

Brien A. Roche

*Member of Virginia
and District of Columbia
Bars*

THE MICHIE COMPANY
Law Publishers
CHARLOTTESVILLE, VIRGINIA

PREFACE

This book is a compendium of cases dealing with domestic relations issues. Its purpose is much the same as the *Virginia Torts Case Finder*. Although my practice is more focused in the tort area than the domestic relations area, I have found that the writing of this book has made me more sensitive to the breadth of issues in domestic relations litigation. Hopefully it will assist you in addressing those issues.

TABLE OF CONTENTS

CHAPTER 1

MARRIAGE

CHAPTER 2

TERMINATION OF THE MARRIAGE

CHAPTER 3

CHILDREN

CHAPTER 4

SUPPORT—CHILD AND SPOUSAL

CHAPTER 5

PROPERTY DISTRIBUTION

CHAPTER 6

MISCELLANEOUS

CHAPTER 7

EVIDENCE

§ 7-8. Witnesses.

CHAPTER 8

PROCEDURE

CHAPTER 1

MARRIAGE

§ 1-1. Bigamous Marriages.

See Va. Code § 18.2-362 et. seq. and cases cited.

See Va. Code § 20-38.1 prohibiting certain marriages such as bigamous marriages and marriages among certain relatives.

1940—*Adkins v. Commonwealth,* 175 Va. 590, 9 S.E.2d 349.

> Unmarried person who married another, knowing that person already to be married, may be convicted of aiding and abetting commission of bigamy.

1937—*Farewell v. Commonwealth,* 167 Va. 475, 189 S.E. 321.

> Essential element is second marriage of person who already has living consort. Either second unlawful marriage or cohabitation after second marriage must occur in this State to give courts jurisdiction.

1921—*Corvin v. Commonwealth,* 131 Va. 649, 108 S.E.2d 651.

> Divorce obtained by fraud or without proper jurisdiction will not relieve man of bigamy if he subsequently remarries.

1871—*Bird v. Commonwealth,* 62 Va. 800.

> In this bigamy prosecution, witness testified to fact that marriage had been solemnized in usual and customary manner in another state by person duly authorized to celebrate rights of marriage, and that parties thereafter lived together as husband and wife. This was held to be sufficient evidence of valid marriage.

1867—*O'Neale v. Commonwealth,* 58 Va. 582.

> Admissions of party and his acts are competent evidence to prove marriage without producing record or witness present at marriage.

§ 1-2. Ceremonial Marriages.

See Va. Code § 20-13 requiring that every marriage in this State shall be under license and solemnized in manner herein provided.

1

§ 1-3. Cohabitation.

1963—*Colley v. Colley,* 204 Va. 225, 129 S.E.2d 630.
>As used in venue statute, word cohabit means having dwelt together under same roof with more or less permanency and does not signify having of sexual relations as it does in some other statutes. As such, it was error to dismiss complaint on grounds that party had last had sexual relations in different county.

1962—*Ware v. Ware,* 203 Va. 189, 123 S.E.2d 357.
>Wife alleged that husband resumed cohabitation with her pending divorce suit, which under general rule, would have justified her in not appearing to make defense in belief that suit had been abandoned. Her evidence did show that husband continued to take his meals at home, made voluntary payments for support of herself and their child and named her as his wife and beneficiary in insurance policies. He testified however that he acted solely from affection for child and that marital relations had not been resumed. Court found in his favor.

1954—*Anderson v. Anderson,* 196 Va. 26, 82 S.E.2d 562.
>Husband and wife cohabited after entry of temporary decree. This was held to be sufficient to bar merger into final decree. Such acts, however, might not be sufficient to abrogate property settlement agreement.

1951—*Roberts v. Pace,* 193 Va. 156, 67 S.E.2d 844.
>Mere casual cohabitation between husband and wife after divorce a mensa unaccompanied by resumption of normal married life together or reasonable explanation for their failure to do so is not sufficient to show reconciliation. Cohabitation in this case was spasmodic and as such does not constitute reconciliation even though parties may have intended to effect reconciliation.

1919—*Reynolds v. Adams,* 125 Va. 295, 99 S.E. 695.
>Presumption of marriage from cohabitation, apparently matrimonial, is one of strongest presumptions known to law. This is especially true in case involving legitimacy. This presumption can be repelled only by most cogent and satisfactory evidence. Cohabitation and repute do not constitute marriage. They are only evidence tending to raise presumption of marriage.

1899—*Eldred v. Eldred,* 97 Va. 606, 34 S.E. 477.
>Presumption of marriage from cohabitation, apparently matrimonial, is very strong, especially where legitimacy is involved; and this presumption can only be overcome by cogent and satisfactory proof.

§ 1-4. Common Law Marriages.

1953—*Patterson v. Anderson,* 194 Va. 557, 74 S.E.2d 195.
>Plaintiff claimed to be legitimate offspring of common law marriage in D.C. No common law marriage established in view of fact that her

mother had married twice without attempting to divorce her alleged common law husband, her mother made no claim to his estate and further mother testified she was never married to him.

1923—*Vanderpool v. Ryan,* 137 Va. 445, 119 S.E. 65.
Common law marriage is void. Law presumes marriage between man and woman when they live ostensibly as husband and wife and are received and treated by their friends and relatives as being entitled to that status. Mere cohabitation and repute do not constitute marriage and are only evidence tending to raise that presumption.

1923—*Stanley v. Rasnick,* 137 Va. 415, 119 S.E. 76.
Common law marriages are void in Virginia.

1923—*Heflinger v. Heflinger,* 136 Va. 289, 118 S.E. 316.
Common law marriages are not valid in State of Virginia.

§ 1-5. Miscellaneous.

See Va. Code § 8.01-19. Marriage of party shall not cause suit or action to abate.

§ 1-6. Promise to Marry.

See Va. Code § 8.01-220. No civil action shall lie or be maintained for breach of promise to marry.

1926—*Judd v. Commonwealth,* 146 Va. 267, 135 S.E. 710.
Seduction prosecution. Promise of marriage must be established. Corroboration is necessary. This may be established by proof of surrounding circumstances.

1915—*Ford v. Engleman,* 118 Va. 89, 86 S.E. 852.
Woman maintained that man had promised to marry her in return for spending night with him in motel. Woman released cause of action that she had against man. This cause of action was sufficient consideration for contract for transfer of negotiable notes. Man claimed duress as to that latter contract. Duress is type of fraud and therefore must be clearly proved.

1899—*Sanders v. Coleman,* 97 Va. 690, 34 S.E. 621.
Contract to marry is coupled with implied condition that both parties remain in enjoyment of life and health and, if condition of parties has so changed that marriage state would endanger life or health of either, breach of contract is excusable due to intervening act of God.

1895—*Burke v. Shaver,* 92 Va. 345, 23 S.E. 749.
Promise of marriage made in consideration of sexual intercourse is illegal and void.

§ 1-7. Restraint of Marriage.

See Va. Code § 20-118 as to prohibition of remarriage pending appeal from divorce decree.

1956—*Humphreys v. Baird,* 197 Va. 667, 90 S.E.2d 796.

> It is error to instruct jury in inclusive language that divorced persons may not again marry within four months. This restriction is applicable only to divorces granted on grounds arising subsequent to marriage and does not apply to void marriages.

1934—*Simpson v. Simpson,* 162 Va. 621, 175 S.E. 320.

> Prohibition against remarriage within six months of divorce does not apply where spouse has died.

1919—*Shelton v. Shelton,* 125 Va. 381, 99 S.E. 557.

> Divorce awarded to wife. Each party had been previously divorced in other proceedings. Divorce in this case was on grounds of desertion. Court in its order stated that neither party shall be allowed to remarry. Court exceeded its authority in that regard. Code authorizes such prohibition only as to guilty party in adultery action.

1894—*Smythe v. Smythe,* 90 Va. 638, 19 S.E. 175.

> Will devised property to testator's sisters provided they remain single and, in case of either marrying, property shall be enjoyed by one remaining single. That provision was held null and void as placing restraint upon marriage.

1888—*Phillips v. Ferguson,* 85 Va. 509, 8 S.E. 241.

> Condition as to marriage annexed to bequest is operative if it is not general and unreasonable restriction of marriage.

1854—*Maddox v. Maddox,* 52 Va. 804.

> Bequest which goes to woman during her single life, and forever, if her conduct should be orderly and she remains member of Society of Friends was found to contain condition that was unreasonable restraint upon marriage and therefore void, since it restricted her marriage to men within Society of Friends.

§ 1-8. Validity of Marriage.

See Annulment, § 2-1.

See Va. Code § 20-31 indicating that belief of parties in lawful marriage validates certain defects.

See Va. Code § 20-43 making void all bigamous marriages. See § 20-45.1 indicating that following marriages are void:

    (1) bigamous marriages;

    (2) marriages among certain relatives;

    (3) where either or both of parties, at time of marriage, are under age of 18 and have not complied with code sections 20-48 or 20-49.

    (4) marriages wherein either of parties lacked capacity to consent to marriage because of mental incapacity or infirmity shall be void from time they shall be so declared.

See Va. Code § 20-45.2 indicating that marriages between persons of same sex are prohibited.

See Va. Code § 20-90 as to suits to affirm marriage.

1975—*McConkey v. McConkey,* 216 Va. 106, 215 S.E.2d 640.

Voidable marriage is usually treated as valid marriage until it is decreed void.

1967—*George v. King,* 208 Va. 136, 156 S.E.2d 615.

Husband seeks order declaring present marriage void on grounds that wife's prior divorce was invalid. Since husband was stranger to prior divorce proceeding and had no pre-existing interest to be adversely affected by that proceeding, he had no legal right to attack that decree and as such this action was demurrable. In order that stranger to divorce action may attack decree collaterally, it must appear that he had legally protected interest which was adversely affected by decree.

1966—*Loving v. Commonwealth,* 206 Va. 924, 147 S.E.2d 78.

Miscegenation law forbidding interracial marriages was held to be constitutional. Decisions of U.S. Supreme Court invalidating separate but equal concept in areas other than marriage were held inapplicable.

1965—*DeRyder v. Metropolitan Life,* 206 Va. 602,145 S.E.2d 177.

Where both parties to first marriage are shown to be living at time of second marriage, it is presumed in favor of second marriage that first was dissolved by divorce. These presumptions arise because law presumes morality and legitimacy. And to overcome presumption is enough to introduce such evidence as in absence of counter testimony will afford reasonable grounds for presuming that allegation is true. When this is done, burden of proof is thrown on to adversary. In this case, husband deserted his first wife in 1930 in New York. In 1945, he remarried, having told second wife that he intended to get divorce. Prior to second marriage, he was domiciled at various places in Virginia where he might have obtained divorce by having process served on first wife. Wife's testimony did not negate possibility that she had been served with process in divorce action begun by husband nor did she produce evidence showing no divorce was obtained by him in all of places in Virginia where he was resident prior to second marriage. She therefore failed to overcome presumption that second marriage was valid.

1962—*Calma v. Calma,* 203 Va. 880, 128 S.E.2d 440.

Wife was white person; husband was Phillipino. Wife was denied divorce for alleged desertion on grounds that marriage, which was contracted in New Jersey, was not recognized as valid in Virginia.

1958—*Hargrow v. Watson,* 200 Va. 30, 104 S.E.2d 37.

In this personal injury action, defendant attempted to prove that he was married to decedent. Evidence however, was offered by opposing side that on date of alleged marriage he was already married to another woman. Contention that proof of marriage may be established by cohabitation and repute is qualified by principle that cohabitation and repute do not constitute marriage, they only constitute evidence tending to raise presumption of marriage. Any such presumption in this case was overcome by proof of fact that he was divorced from his first wife on date subsequent to alleged marriage to decedent.

1955—*Naim v. Naim,* 197 Va. 80, 87 S.E.2d 749.

Contract of marriage is traditionally subject to control of States. In this case, court held that miscegenation was properly matter of governmental control.

1951—*Alexander v. Kuykendall,* 192 Va. 8, 63 S.E.2d 746.

Innocent woman induced by fraud to contract void marriage with defendant, who subsequently lives with him, performing normal duties of wife, is entitled to recover damages in action for fraud.

1949—*Parker v. American Lumber Corp.,* 190 Va. 181, 56 S.E.2d 214.

Where two marriages of same person are shown, second marriage is presumed to be valid. Person who attacks validity of second marriage has burden of producing evidence of its invalidity. Where both parties to first marriage are shown to be living at time of second marriage, it is presumed in favor of second marriage that first was dissolved by divorce.

Presumption in favor of second marriage in this case was upheld, and second wife in this workmen's compensation case was therefore entitled to benefits, even though first wife maintained that she had never been divorced from her first husband.

1948—*Henderson v. Henderson,* 187 Va. 121, 46 S.E.2d 10.

Marriage void because by terms of previous divorce decree wife incapable of contracting valid marriage.

1946—*Ashby v. Red Jacket Coal Co.,* 185 Va. 202, 38 S.E.2d 436.

Workmen's compensation case. Judgment of acquittal in criminal prosecution for bigamy is not final determination of allegation that second marriage was lawful.

1945—*Needam v. Needam,* 183 Va. 681, 33 S.E.2d 288.

At time of marriage, husband was 18½ and wife 17½. Parties here were capable of entering into lawful contract of marriage. Minors over age of consent for marriage have capacity to enter into marriage relationship.

Public policy of Virginia has been to uphold validity of marriage status except where marriage is prohibited between certain persons. Provision for parental consent is directory and not prohibitive.

1943—*Kirby v. Gilliam,* 182 Va. 111, 28 S.E.2d 40.

Marriage by one under age fixed by statute is voidable not void.

1942—*McClaugherty v. McClaugherty,* 180 Va. 51, 21 S.E.2d 761.
In Virginia, marriage may be proved by reputation, declaration and conduct of parties. Although cohabitation and repute do not constitute marriage, they do constitute strong evidence to raise presumption of marriage.

1942—*McFarland v. McFarland,* 179 Va. 418, 19 S.E.2d 77.
Suit to affirm Virginia marriage in light of husband obtaining North Carolina divorce. Marriage affirmed. Award of costs and counsel fees within discretion of court.

1939—*Toler v. Oakwood Smokeless Coal Corp.,* 173 Va. 425, 4 S.E.2d 364.
General rule is that law of place of its celebration governs as to its validity with two exceptions: (1) marriages contrary to laws of nature as generally recognized in christian countries (2) marriages forbidden by statute because contrary to public policy. Void marriage confers no legal rights. Voidable marriage may be afterwards ratified and become valid. Rule of common law is that consanguinity, affinity and impotence render marriage voidable. Virginia follows this rule. Bigamous marriage is void ab initio.

1935—*Newsom v. Fleming,* 165 Va. 89, 181 S.E. 393.
While cohabitation and repute do not constitute marriage they do constitute strong evidence tending to raise presumption of marriage and burden is on him who denies marriage to offer countervailing evidence. Marriage may be proved in civil cases by reputation, declaration and conduct.

1933—*Cornwall v. Cornwall,* 160 Va. 183, 168 S.E. 439.
Code provides that all marriages solemnized when one party is insane shall be void when so declared by decree. No decree having been entered marriage remains valid.

1923—*Stanley v. Rasnick,* 137 Va. 415, 119 S.E. 76.
Validity of marriage is not affected by want of authority of person issuing marriage license or any defect, omission or imperfection in license. Accordingly, marriage of infant is valid, although license was issued by clerk without authority of parent or guardian as is required.

1923—*Heflinger v. Heflinger,* 136 Va. 289, 118 S.E. 316.
General rule is that marriage, valid where performed, is valid everywhere, but there are exceptions:
    (1) Marriage is deemed contrary to laws of nature as generally recognized in Christian countries, i.e., polygamy or incest;
    (2) Marriage is forbidden by statute because contrary to public policy of State.
In present case, complainant had been previously married and divorced. Within six months of prior divorce, he married defendant in State of Maryland, both being, at time, citizens and residents of Virginia and having no intention of changing their residence. Shortly after marriage, they returned to Virginia. Court held second mar-

riage to be void, in violation of six-month remarriage rule. Both parties being residents of State had actual or imputed knowledge of consequence of their act. This particular statute was held to have extra-territorial effect, i.e., it applied to second marriages performed outside State of Virginia. Under this code section, decree of divorce is not operative as to subsequent marriage until expiration of six months from date of decree.

1919—*Reynolds v. Adams,* 125 Va. 295, 99 S.E. 695.

This is suit for partition of real estate of decedent. Issue is whether or not there was valid marriage between decedent and his reputed wife under law of New Jersey. Factors to consider in determining whether or not valid marriage exists are following: (1) whether declarations as to marriage (which must have been deliberate and been part of res gestae) were made in good faith; (2) that cohabitation must have been matrimonial — that is, in relationship of husband and wife and not master or servant or some other relationship; (3) that family recognition must have been bona fide; (4) that general reputation in favor of marriage must have existed along with cohabitation as soon after beginning of cohabitation as it could be reasonably expected to arise. To prove existence of marriage, production of marriage license or certificate or of person present at its celebration is not absolutely necessary. Presumption of marriage from cohabitation apparently matrimonial is one of strongest presumptions known to law. This is especially true in case involving legitimacy. In this case, person challenging marriage presented testimony from clerk of city indicating that no such license had been issued for this marriage. His testimony, however, was not unequivocal, and therefore court held that it does not furnish them with cogent and satisfactory evidence which is requisite to repel presumption of marriage which arose in this case.

1899—*Eldred v. Eldred,* 97 Va. 606, 34 S.E. 477.

Marriage may be proved in civil cases by reputation, declaration and conduct of parties but to raise presumption of marriage reputation must be founded on general, not divided or singular, opinion. Law presumes marriage between man and woman when they live together and hold themselves out as being married, but cohabitation and reputation do not constitute marriage. Declarations of parties and cohabitation must be contemporaneous with intercourse and not subsequent. In this case, evidence was found insufficient as far as reputation and also due to absence of marriage certificate.

1885—*Greenhow v. Janes,* 80 Va. 636.

Law of place of celebration of marriage governs as to forms of ceremony which constitute marriage. Law of domicile governs as to capacity of parties. Rule which requires that marriage valid where celebrated is valid everywhere else has no application to marriage entered into that is in contravention of public policy and statutes of domicile of parties which pronounces marriage between them not only absolutely void but criminal. In this case, marriage was between white person and black person.

1883—*Womack v. Tankersley,* 78 Va. 242.

In this case, existence of marriage was established by proof of deliberate admissions and acts of parties, their cohabitation and recognition as husband and wife without production of registry or certificate or persons present at celebration of marriage.

1878—*Kinney v. Commonwealth,* 71 Va. 858.

While forms and ceremonies of marriage are governed by laws of place where marriage is celebrated, essentials of contract depend upon and are governed by laws of place where parties are domiciled at time of marriage and in which matrimonial residence is contemplated. This interracial marriage was deemed to be void even though it was performed in District of Columbia.

CHAPTER 2

TERMINATION OF THE MARRIAGE

§ 2-1. Annulment.

See Marriage — Validity.

See Va. Code § 20-89.1 as to grounds for annulment.

1972—*Sanderson v. Sanderson,* 212 Va. 537, 186 S.E.2d 84.

    Husband seeks annulment on grounds that wife had falsely represented before their marriage that she had been previously married and divorced only once when in fact she had been married and divorced five times. Court held that misrepresentation as to prior marital status is not ground for annulment.

11

1955—*Naim v. Naim,* 197 Va. 80, 87 S.E.2d 749.

White woman and Chinese man were married in North Carolina to avoid Virginia miscegenation statute. Marriage was declared void.

1952—*Ciarochi v. Ciarochi,* 194 Va. 313, 73 S.E.2d 402.

Wife sought annulment on grounds of fraud alleging that husband had preconceived intent to have no children and secondly that husband married her solely to obtain her money. First contention was rejected because it was not alleged in her bill. With regard to second contention, she contends that she spent large sum of money to establish him in restaurant business which failed, and then he shortly thereafter abandoned her. This was insufficient to prove alleged fraud.

1945—*Jacobs v. Jacobs,* 184 Va. 281, 35 S.E.2d 119.

Courts of equity have jurisdiction to annul marriage where assent thereto was induced by artifice or gross fraud. To justify annulment of marriage, there must be some clear evidence that one party did not intend before marriage or at time of marriage to become in truth spouse of other. In this case, 79-year-old man married 42-year-old woman. Evidence at trial was that man pursued woman and agreed to convey certain property to her with him retaining life estate. No fraud involved. In absence of fraud, duress or other improper elements affecting such transactions, annulment cannot be granted. Where it is proved that wife never intended that marriage should be consummated, then that may be basis for annulment.

1945—*Needam v. Needam,* 183 Va. 681, 33 S.E.2d 288.

Suit by infant for annulment of marriage wherein both parties were residents of Virginia, were married in Maryland without consent of their parents and then returned to Virginia to live. At time of marriage, male was 18$\frac{1}{2}$ and female 17$\frac{1}{2}$. Court found marriage was valid.

1941—*Pretlow v. Pretlow,* 177 Va. 524, 14 S.E.2d 381.

Unconsummated marriage is more readily annulled than one where parties have cohabited. Unconsummated marriage will be annulled for any kind of fraud which would render contract voidable. Divorce is creature of statute while annulment rests within inherent power of equity. Fraud which goes to fundamentals of marriage gives equity jurisdiction and property rights growing out of that fraud may also be adjusted.

1935—*Williamson v. Johnson,* 164 Va. 632, 180 S.E. 310.

Husband found to be insane at time of marriage. Annulment granted.

1935—*Kilbourne v. Kilbourne,* 165 Va. 87, 181 S.E. 351.

Infant filed suit to annul marriage. Decree vacated because suit was not prosecuted by next friend of infant.

1934—*Counts v. Counts,* 161 Va. 768, 172 S.E. 248.

> Marriage annulled on grounds husband insane at time of marriage. Suit for annulment affects both person and property of insane person.

1934—*Simpson v. Simpson,* 162 Va. 621, 175 S.E. 320.

> If answer is filed pleading good defense to suit for annulment then cross bill for divorce may be filed if there is grounds for it.

1923—*Heflinger v. Heflinger,* 136 Va. 289, 118 S.E. 316.

> Annulment of marriages that violate six-month remarriage rule is more effectual way of preventing such violations of statute and public policy of State than is affirmance of these marriages.

1949—*Kelly v. Scott,* 46 Va. 479.

> Marriage, having been declared null by order of court, husband has no interest in property which was wife's at time of marriage, and his creditors cannot subject it to payment of his debts.

§ 2-2. Corroboration Requirement.

See Va. Code § 20-99 indicating that bill of complaint shall not be taken for confessed nor shall divorce, annulment or affirmation of marriage be granted on uncorroborated testimony of parties or either of them. Whether defendant answers or not, cause shall be heard independently of admissions of either party in pleadings or otherwise.

1983—*Coe v. Coe,* 225 Va. 616, 303 S.E.2d 923.

> Wife alleged various incidents of cruelty by husband. Husband denied such. Only supporting evidence introduced by wife was that of neighbor, her physician and psychologist whom she consulted about her problem. These witnesses knew of her mental and physical condition in that she had marital trouble, but none had any personal knowledge of acts of cruelty, and as such, there was no corroboration.

1975—*McIlwain v. McIlwain,* 215 Va. 633, 212 S.E.2d 284.

> Statement made by wife to neighbor two hours after alleged act of cruelty was not admissible as res gestae. Even if it had been admissible it was not sufficient corroboration.

1972—*Johnson v. Johnson,* 213 Va. 204, 191 S.E.2d 206.

> Wife's evidence of acts of cruelty was not corroborated except by evidence or admissions of husband and, as such, were not sufficient.

1970—*Graham v. Graham,* 210 Va. 608, 172 S.E.2d 724.

> While divorce may not be granted on uncorroborated testimony of parties, such testimony is admissible and competent as evidence to defeat prayer for divorce.

1961—*Martin v. Martin,* 202 Va. 769, 120 S.E.2d 471.

> Main purpose of corroboration is to prevent collusion. Where it is apparent that there is no collusion, corroboration may be slight. Only essential facts need to be corroborated and corroborative testimony need not be sufficient, standing alone, to prove alleged ground for divorce.

1956—*DeMott v. DeMott,* 198 Va. 22, 92 S.E.2d 342.

Husband sought divorce on grounds of desertion but had no corroboration for his testimony. It was error to grant decree in his favor. Proof in divorce case must be by clear and adequate evidence.

1952—*Graves v. Graves,* 193 Va. 659, 70 S.E.2d 339.

It is not necessary that testimony of complaining spouse be corroborated on every element or essential charge. Corroboration need not be sufficient, standing alone, to prove alleged grounds for divorce. However, if it is apparent that there is no collusion, corroboration needs only to be slight.

1949—*Allen v. Allen,* 188 Va. 717, 51 S.E.2d 207.

Uncorroborated testimony of wife insufficient to justify divorce.

1945—*Griffin v. Griffin,* 183 Va. 443, 32 S.E.2d 700.

Divorce suits are different from other suits in equity in that (1) bill is never taken for confessed; (2) cause is heard independently of admissions of either party; (3) only authorized officers of this State are allowed to serve process within this State.

1944—*Forbes v. Forbes,* 182 Va. 636, 29 S.E.2d 829.

Purpose of this requirement is to prevent divorce by collusion. Only those facts necessary to judgment must be corroborated. It need not rest in testimony of witnesses but may be furnished by surrounding circumstances adequately established.

1939—*Hughes v. Hughes,* 173 Va. 293, 4 S.E.2d 402.

Uncorroborated testimony of party insufficient to establish grounds for divorce.

1936—*Martin v. Martin,* 166 Va. 109, 184 S.E. 220.

Corroboration rests in facts and circumstances of each case and only those facts necessary to judgment must be supported. Corroboration may be in form of surrounding circumstances adequately established.

1926—*Judd v. Commonwealth,* 146 Va. 267, 135 S.E. 710.

Seduction prosecution. Corroboration of promise of marriage may be established by proof of surrounding circumstances.

1922—*Black v. Black,* 134 Va. 246, 114 S.E. 592.

Policy of law is against divorce. Bill of complaint shall not be taken for confessed nor shall divorce be granted on uncorroborated testimony of parties or either of them.

1884—*Cralle v. Cralle,* 79 Va. 182.

In suit for divorce, admission of plaintiff is evidence to support allegations in answer.

1878—*Latham v. Latham,* 71 Va. 307.

Bill of complaint shall not be taken for confessed and cause must be heard independent of admissions of either party.

1871—*Bailey v. Bailey,* 62 Va. 43.
> Letters of parties were admissible in evidence to show intent of defendant to desert.

§ 2-3. Death.

1954—*Judd v. VanHorn,* 195 Va. 988, 81 S.E.2d 432.
> Where one party to divorce has died, then custody dispute between surviving parent and third party may be litigated during divorce proceeding.

1945—*Waters v. Harrell,* 183 Va. 764, 33 S.E.2d 194.
> In construing word widow, remarriage does not destroy status of woman as widow in construction of statutes relating to actions for wrongful death.

1920—*Cumming v. Cumming,* 127 Va. 16, 102 S.E. 572.
> Trial court granted husband divorce. Husband died pending appeal by wife. Husband's death would render inoperative decree granting wife divorce or allowing her alimony, and therefore no decree will be entered on those subjects by supreme court, except to reverse original decree granting husband divorce, which supreme court found to be in error.

§ 2-4. Divorce — Grounds.

(A) Adultery.

See Va. Code § 18.2-365 et seq.

1983—*Coe v. Coe,* 225 Va. 616, 303 S.E.2d 923.
> Evidence in this case, which was uncontradicted, was that detective had seen wife in apartment of her alleged paramour with lights out. Pictures of her exiting from apartment were offered into evidence. Testimony of detective in such case should be carefully scrutinized and acted on with great caution. In this case, testimony withstood such scrutiny. Adultery need not be proved beyond all doubt. Evidence must be clear and convincing as it was in this case.

1981—*Dooley v. Dooley,* 222 Va. 240, 278 S.E.2d 865.
> To establish charge of adultery evidence must be clear, positive and convincing. Raising considerable or even strong suspicion of guilt is not enough. In this case private investigator testified that wife's apartment was at times completely dark and then there were occasions when there was light on inside. At around 1:10 a.m. that evening wife and another man stood and embraced and kissed in open doorway of her apartment. Man then left and got into another vehicle. There was also testimony that attorney who previously had represented husband in divorce case spent night at wife's apartment although she testified that he slept on couch. Court held this evidence insufficient to find wife guilty of adultery.

1975—*Robertson v. Robertson,* 215 Va. 425, 211 S.E.2d 41.
No error to admit evidence of husband's adulterous conduct occurring after desertion, and to award divorce upon dual grounds of desertion and adultery.

1975—*Painter v. Painter,* 215 Va. 418, 211 S.E.2d 37.
Evidence in adultery action must be clear, positive and convincing. Strongly suspicious circumstances of guilt are inadequate. In this case, investigators testified that they observed husband's truck parked in Mrs. Henry's driveway. At that time, there was only one dim light on in living room. After midnight that evening, light came on in bathroom. That light went off shortly thereafter. At 1:05 a.m. light came on and stayed on for one minute. At 1:45 a.m., husband was seen leaving home. There were other instances of intimacy between husband and Mrs. Henry. Both husband and Mrs. Henry denied having sexual relations or being more than simply good friends. Court held that adultery had not been established.

1969—*Rosenberg v. Rosenberg,* 210 Va. 44, 168 S.E.2d 251.
Adultery allegedly occurred after filing of bill of complaint. Court held that amendment should be allowed so as to plead this additional grounds since it is highly relevant to issues of alimony, support and custody.

1964—*Higgins v. Higgins,* 205 Va. 324, 136 S.E.2d 793.
Wife was found in hotel room with lights out in state of undress with man other than her husband. This occasion plus other similar occasions were sufficient to allow Supreme Court to conclude that she was guilty of infidelity. Commissioner who actually heard evidence had concluded that there was no adultery. Supreme Court noted that credulity must not be stretched to breaking point.

1961—*Eubank v. Hayden,* 202 Va. 634, 119 S.E.2d 328.
Two sons testified that paramour was in their mother's bedroom at night and they heard him take his shoes off and heard him get into bed with their mother. Although there was some apparent conflicts in testimony of two sons, this was issue for jury to decide.

1957—*Daniels v. Morris,* 199 Va. 205, 98 S.E.2d 694.
Evidence in adultery case is frequently circumstantial. Adultery is wrong of darkness and secrecy wherein parties are rarely surprised. Rule for sufficiency of proven facts to infer adultery is that if they are not reasonably reconcilable with assumption of innocence, yet are so with that of guilt, conclusion of guilt will be authorized.

1952—*Fulton v. Fulton,* 193 Va. 255, 68 S.E.2d 485.
Evidence must be sufficient to leave guarded discretion of reasonable and just man to conclusion of guilt. In this case, adulterers were both drinking, were seen to leave her home and were later seen lying in field together. That combined with explanation offered by wife and other evidence of affection between two was sufficient to establish adultery.

1950—*Bowen v. Pernell,* 190 Va. 389, 57 S.E.2d 36.

Proof of adultery may be circumstantial as well as direct evidence. In this alienation of affection case, love letters and testimony were deemed to be sufficient proof.

1948—*Haskins v. Haskins,* 188 Va. 525, 50 S.E.2d 437.

Standard of proof is not guilt beyond reasonable doubt but is evidence that is at least clear and positive and convincing. In this case, husband was seen in apartment of another woman between 8 p.m. and midnight with lights out. This was insufficient to establish adultery.

1948—*Bennett v. Bennett,* 187 Va. 631, 47 S.E.2d 312.

Husband deserted wife three days after wedding. Wife found him in brothel. Adultery established.

1947—*Nix v. Nix,* 186 Va. 14, 41 S.E.2d 345.

Brother-in-law of appellee testified that he and appellant committed adultery; evidence also showed that he and appellant dined, drank and danced together late at night and that she went to his apartment late at night while his wife was not there; witness testified he saw them together in hotel room where they registered as man and wife. Evidence sufficient to establish adultery.

1946—*Russell v. Russell,* 185 Va. 64, 37 S.E.2d 753.

Witness testified that wife had lived night and day for 10 days in room with alleged lover. Another witness testified that everyone in vicinity knew of this and that wife even boasted of this. Evidence was held sufficient to justify divorce on grounds of adultery.

1943—*Gray v. Gray,* 181 Va. 262, 24 S.E.2d 444.

Testimony of private detective as to adultery on part of wife was rejected by trial court and verdict entered for wife. Adultery was alleged to have occurred on back porch, area where neighbors and others would have seen couple. These people all testified that nothing out of ordinary occurred on back porch.

1939—*Holt v. Holt,* 174 Va. 120, 5 S.E.2d 504.

Evidence of frequent contact between wife and paramour insufficient to establish adultery. If facts are not reasonably reconcilable with assumption of innocence yet are so with that of guilt then conclusion of guilt will be authorized.

1938—*Ingram v. Ingram,* 171 Va. 399, 199 S.E. 515.

Adultery may be proved by uncorroborated testimony of paramour if she is credible witness. Such testimony should be received with great caution. In this case court found testimony of paramour unworthy of belief.

1936—*Phipps v. Phipps,* 167 Va. 190, 188 S.E. 168.

Evidence showed only circumstances which cast shadow of suspicion. This was not sufficient to establish adultery. Facts were not set forth.

1936—*Martin v. Martin,* 166 Va. 109, 184 S.E. 220.

Uncorroborated evidence of private detective is seldom sufficient to sustain judgment. Private detective testified that husband was frequent visitor at woman's apartment, that name by which husband was known was on her door. Two other persons testified to seeing husband at woman's apartment frequently. Evidence sufficient. Evidence should be clear but it need not be beyond reasonable doubt.

1934—*Colbert v. Colbert,* 162 Va. 393, 174 S.E. 660.

Adultery will be found only on clearest and most convincing proof. Court is reluctant to find adultery where couple have lived together happily for many years and maintained good reputations in community. Testimony of detective should be acted on with great caution.

1933—*Cole v. Cole,* 161 Va. 116, 170 S.E. 621.

Divorce granted for adultery where circumstantial evidence indicated that husband had spent night in motel with another woman. Note signed by paramour as to whereabouts of husband at particular time was admissible.

1932—*Kirby v. Kirby,* 159 Va. 544, 166 S.E. 484.

Evidence of adultery is of necessity circumstantial. If facts are not reasonably reconcilable with assumption of innocence yet are so with that of guilt, then conclusion of guilt will be authorized. In this case husband rented apartment for divorced woman, frequently was with her alone for from 40 minutes to $2\frac{1}{2}$ hours and frequently lied to his wife about where he was. This was sufficient to establish adultery.

1930—*Johnson v. Johnson,* 154 Va. 788, 153 S.E. 670.

Wife presented evidence of three instances that evince adultery on part of husband. No one of them was sufficient. Occasions when husband was in family home with women when wife was away. Husband offered explanations that fact finder may find to be insufficient. Evidence must be such as to lead guarded discretion of reasonable man to conclusion of guilt. In another instance husband spent night in bungalow with woman. He was expecting additional friends to arrive that night. In light of circumstances this did not establish adultery even though he lied about who woman was.

1930—*Gloth v. Gloth,* 154 Va. 511, 153 S.E. 879.

Decree of divorce a mensa for desertion is bar to claim for adultery committed after first decree.

1929—*Johnson v. Commonwealth,* 152 Va. 965, 146 S.E. 289.

Simple adultery and fornication are not common law offenses in Virginia. This criminal prosecution was for common law misdemeanor of engaging in lewd behavior.

1919—*Lamb v. Lamb,* 126 Va. 256, 101 S.E. 223.

Bill alleged that there had been some adultery on part of wife but this was not relied upon as ground for divorce since these acts occurred more than five years prior to filing of suit.

1919—*Johnson v. Johnson,* 126 Va. 15, 100 S.E. 822.

Evidence of adultery was insufficient. Although there was some evidence of wife having some interest in another man and there being evidence of opportunity for adultery, there was insufficient evidence to establish adultery.

1917—*White v. White,* 121 Va. 244, 92 S.E. 811.

Pleadings in this case were held to be sufficient since they set forth, with reasonable certainty, time, place and circumstances of adultery. Witnesses who testified to alleged adultery were two small boys of parties. Although court expressed regret that these children would be involved in case like this, court noted that their testimony was substantially true and was sufficient to sustain charge. Evidence was that wife and paramour would go to her bedroom in family home and remain there for long periods of time.

1917—*Lewis v. Lewis,* 121 Va. 99, 92 S.E. 807.

Husband sued wife for adultery. Evidence in support of this consisted of statement of family servant and confession of alleged paramour. Servant was plainly under influence of husband, and her statements were improbable and inherently unreliable. Confession was supposedly coerced by threats. Wife presented evidence from several disinterested witnesses that in fact she and her husband were on good terms and that there were frequent instances when husband publicly displayed his affection for wife. Adultery must be proved by clear and convincing evidence. That was not done in this case.

1899—*Engleman v. Engleman,* 97 Va. 487, 34 S.E. 50.

Husband charged wife with adultery. Her alleged paramour testified against her as did supposed independent witness. Court found evidence to be inconsistent, incredible and wholly insufficient to sustain charge. Court further held that wife had established her own virtuous character.

1895—*Miller v. Miller,* 92 Va. 196, 23 S.E. 232.

Bill for divorce on grounds of adultery which simply charges that defendant has been guilty of adultery on many occasions is demurrable. Bill should state time, place and circumstances so as to enable defendant to disprove charge, although it need not state name of person with whom adultery was committed.

1891—*Musick v. Musick,* 88 Va. 12, 13 S.E. 302.

In suit for divorce, adultery may be proved by circumstantial evidence, such as visiting house of ill-fame, being shut up with unchaste woman, consorting with prostitutes. It is, generally speaking, necessary to prove that parties were in some place together where adultery might probably be committed.

1890—*Hampton v. Hampton,* 87 Va. 148, 12 S.E. 340.

Bill of complaint cannot be taken for confessed and shall be heard independent of admissions of either party. Evidence that defendant admitted charge and letter from her purporting to admit it are inadmissible. Bill of complaint in this case did not allege any specific acts of adultery, and there is nothing in testimony as to any act of adultery. Divorce was denied.

1890—*Throckmorton v. Throckmorton,* 86 Va. 768, 11 S.E. 289.

Fact that married man goes in to known brothel and there shuts himself up in room with woman of ill-repute and such is unexplained constitutes sufficient proof of adultery. These facts, however, were not established in this case. With regard to private dectectives, court stated that, when man sets himself up as private detective and when amount of his pay depends on extent of his employment and extent of his employment depends on discoveries he is able to make, then that man becomes most dangerous instrument. Proof in adultery case must be strict, satisfactory and conclusive.

1878—*Latham v. Latham,* 71 Va. 307.

Fact that married man is seen in house of ill-repute is strong evidence of adultery, yet it is not conclusive. In this case, his presence was satisfactorily explained.

(B) Constructive Desertion.

(1) ABUSE.

1983—*Vardell v. Vardell,* 225 Va. 351, 302 S.E.2d 40.

Absenting of one spouse from another after institution and during pendency of divorce suit is not desertion, indeed, one prosecuting suit for any form of divorce who cohabits with defendant usually condones offense. In this case wife sought injunction to have husband removed from home because she feared for her physical welfare. Court conducted adversary hearing and determined that there was reasonable likelihood that wife's health and safety would be endangered if parties remained together and therefore ordered husband out of house. This finding was supported by evidence. Such injunction requiring husband and wife to separate is not ipso facto basis for granting divorce to husband when wife is unsuccessful in proving her grounds for divorce.

1980—*Breschel v. Breschel,* 221 Va. 208, 269 S.E.2d 363.

Principle that spouse is unjustified in leaving other unless conduct of other is sufficient to establish foundation of divorce proceeding applies to claims of constructive desertion. Nevertheless, spouse may be free from legal fault in breaking off cohabitation and therefore entitled to support and maintenance even though she cannot establish conduct constituting foundation of divorce proceeding. In this case wife left marital home because she was physically unable to maintain home and because husband's son from prior marriage was adversely affecting her already poor health. Wife in this case was found to be free from legal fault. She had unsuccessfully taken whatever reasonable measures that could be taken to eliminate danger to her health. As such, there was no desertion on her part, nor any constructive desertion on part of husband.

1975—*McIlwain v. McIlwain,* 215 Va. 633, 212 S.E.2d 284.

Act of wife in obtaining injunction barring husband from family home, effective after institution of suit, does not make wife guilty of constructive desertion.

1974—*Rowland v. Rowland,* 215 Va. 344, 210 S.E.2d 149.

Husband's statements to wife to "get out" unaccompanied by sufficiently corroborated evidence of other acts contributing to her departure do not justify award of divorce on grounds of constructive desertion.

1959—*Ford v. Ford,* 200 Va. 674, 107 S.E.2d 397.

Husband sued wife. Evidence showed that over period of years she made false accusations of immoral acts, had tried to alienate him from his family and had otherwise been guilty of conduct detrimental to his health and happiness. Husband awarded divorce.

1959—*Brooks v. Brooks,* 200 Va. 530, 106 S.E.2d 611.

Wife sued for constructive desertion alleging that husband had her evicted from home by sheriff on false grounds. Court found this to be gross cruelty and humiliation which justified divorce on grounds of constructive desertion. It was also noted that husband later refused wife's offer of reconciliation.

1957—*Baytop v. Baytop,* 199 Va. 388, 100 S.E.2d 14.

Court awarded divorce on grounds of constructive desertion. Wife's evidence showed that she and husband had never had home together because she taught in Virginia and he in Delaware; that for some years he had been cruel to her, discouraged her weekend visits, had affair with another woman and on occasion cursed her publicly; that as result she had become nervous and ill and that after final unpleasant night spent at his family home she left him because she could not take any more abuse.

1948—*Williams v. Williams,* 188 Va. 543, 50 S.E.2d 277.

Constructive desertion is established when party is guilty of such ill-usage as endangers life and limb or is guilty of personal violence, although life or health of other spouse is not thus endangered. That is, one spouse has made home unreasonable and grossly unfit. It may also be established where one spouse is subjected to treatment which affects her mind to such degree as to destroy health or endanger life.

1947—*Defonis v. Clinchfield Coal Corp.,* 186 Va. 715, 43 S.E.2d 852.

Workmen's compensation claim. Evidence showed that few weeks before death of decedent, claimant assaulted him, causing him to leave home, and that he never lived with claimant again. Decedent had complained that claimant sometimes had run him out of house with knife and that he was afraid she would kill him. Conduct of claimant constituted desertion. When either spouse voluntarily so behaves that other can no longer remain with safety in marriage state and is forced to go elsewhere for protection, culpable spouse is guilty of desertion. One party may be forced to leave marital home due to conduct, even without violence, that renders marriage state impossible to be endured.

1945—*Edwards v. Cuthbert,* 184 Va. 502, 36 S.E.2d 1.

Spouse is not justified in leaving other unless conduct of wrongdoer could be made basis of divorce action. In this case, fact that husband's sister presided over family home did not constitute constructive desertion.

1944—*Fussell v. Fussell,* 182 Va. 720, 30 S.E.2d 555.

Husband beat wife, used vile language and caused her to become so upset and nervous as to leave him. Husband guilty of constructive desertion.

1942—*Cecil v. Cecil,* 179 Va. 274, 19 S.E.2d 64.

Evidence consisted of petty charges and counter charges which reflect fact that marital status had become irreconcilable. Not sufficient to establish desertion by wife.

1939—*Babcock v. Babcock,* 172 Va. 219, 1 S.E.2d 328.

Husband ordered wife to leave house on two occasions. On second occasion he became enraged and used rough and abusive language. Desertion established.

1936—*Phipps v. Phipps,* 167 Va. 190, 188 S.E. 168.

Only evidence presented was uncorroborated testimony of wife that husband in rude and violent manner drove her away from house in nighttime. Evidence insufficient. Decree for absolute divorce should not be granted unless evidence proves willful desertion without justification or excuse.

1924—*Elder v. Elder,* 139 Va. 19, 123 S.E. 369.

Cruelty, on part of spouse which results in other's enforced separation from family home, is tantamount to desertion on part of spouse inflicting cruelty.

1924—*Harman v. Harman,* 139 Va. 508, 124 S.E. 273.

Suit for assignment of dower interest in husband's estate. If leaving of home by wife is caused by such conduct on part of husband that he is guilty of constructive desertion, then this does not constitute leaving of husband "of her own free will" within meaning of statute. In this case, constructive desertion consisted of actual physical cruelty on part of husband in such degree as to cause wife to leave. In this case, acts of cruelty of husband were admissible, even though many of them occurred before wife's final departure. Fact that wife returned and cohabited with husband after some of these acts of cruelty does not render evidence of such repeated conduct any less cogent in establishing fact that such last departure of wife was not of her own free will.

1908—*Kaiser v. Kaiser,* 108 Va. 730, 62 S.E. 936.

Both parties sued on desertion grounds. Both parties indulged in unseemly conduct yet evidence was insufficient to support divorce as to either party.

1907—*Davenport v. Davenport,* 106 Va. 736, 56 S.E. 562.

Evidence in this case showed that husband used abusive language, seized wife with violence and threatened greater violence and further that as result of his treatment she could not live with him in safety and was compelled to move out. He was found guilty of desertion.

(2) MISCELLANEOUS.

1975—*Als v. Als,* 216 Va. 13, 216 S.E.2d 16.

One spouse is not guilty of desertion in separating from other after institution of suit for divorce or during its pendency.

1947—*Defonis v. Clinchfield Coal Corp.,* 186 Va. 715, 43 S.E.2d 852.

Who is guilty of voluntary desertion does not depend upon who leaves home, since desertion is not limited to desertion of home but has broader meaning of desertion of marriage relation.

1920—*Cumming v. Cumming,* 127 Va. 16, 102 S.E. 572.

In this case, husband deserted wife on night of marriage. If husband, however, had attempted to reconcile with wife and there was then conduct on her part amounting to cruelty that prevented him from cohabiting with her, then that would have justified his continuing to live apart from her so long as that situation continued. Wife, in that circumstance, would be considered guilty of desertion.

(3) SEX — DENIAL OF.

See Cruelty, § 2.4(c).

1981—*Goodwyn v. Goodwyn,* 222 Va. 53, 278 S.E.2d 813.

All evidence showed in this case was cessation of sexual intercourse for period of less than two months prior to wife's hospitalization. Unjustified withdrawal of sexual intercourse constitutes desertion when accompanied by willful breach and neglect of other marital duties. Evidence in this case failed to reveal that wife neglected her family duties.

1972—*Johnson v. Johnson,* 213 Va. 204, 191 S.E.2d 206.

Without clear evidence of permanent and unexcused refusal of sexual relations, showing of mere cessation of intercourse is not sufficient to prove cruelty or constructive desertion. Furthermore, in this case there is nothing to indicate that husband objected to parties occupying separate bedrooms.

1948—*Davis v. Davis,* 187 Va. 63, 45 S.E.2d 918.

Wife wrote letters to army officer containing expressions of endearment and affection. This correspondence was broken off before separation of parties and, in addition, had been condoned. This wholly fails to prove desertion.

Mere coolness at times and periodical refusal of sexual intercourse alone, with marital relationship otherwise unimpaired, does not constitute desertion.

1938—*Jones v. Jones,* 172 Va. 14, 199 S.E. 510.

Wife's refusal to consummate marriage throughout 10 years of its duration coupled with other conduct towards husband was sufficient to sustain divorce for constructive desertion.

1923—*Albert v. Albert,* 137 Va. 1, 119 S.E. 61.

Mere withdrawal of sexual intercourse, although based on no just cause or excuse, where marital duties are otherwise performed, does not constitute desertion. This however may constitute desertion when such withdrawal is accompanied with such willful breach and neglect of other marital duties as to practically destroy home life. If such conduct is willfully done without just cause or excuse, this constitutes willful desertion.

1922—*Chandler v. Chandler,* 132 Va. 418, 112 S.E. 856.

In this case, husband sued wife for constructive desertion based upon willful withdrawal without just cause of sexual intercourse and continuance of such up to time of suit accompanied by gross neglect of duties of wife in respect to keeping of husband's room, neglect and respect to meals, such desertion being preceded by repeated violent abuse of husband and repeated groundless charges of adultery. Decree granting divorce to husband was affirmed.

1890—*Throckmorton v. Throckmorton,* 86 Va. 768, 11 S.E. 289.

It seems not to be entirely clear whether withdrawal of one of parties from matrimonial bed, without any withdrawal from general cohabitation, is or is not legal desertion. That question was not answered in this case.

1878—*Latham v. Latham,* 71 Va. 307.

Desertion cannot be inferred against either from mere fact that they do not live together, though protracted absence, with other circumstances, may establish original intent. Court found in this case that cause of separation was wife's refusal to bear any more children and refusal to have any further relations with husband. Desertion is composed of breaking off of matrimonial cohabitation and secondly intent to desert. Mere separation by mutual consent is not desertion by either party.

(C) Cruelty.

(1) ALCOHOLISM.

1959—*Brooks v. Brooks,* 200 Va. 530, 106 S.E.2d 611.

Husband sued for cruelty tantamount to desertion, charging excessive use of alcohol by wife, neglect of their small son and threats against his life. Grounds alleged for divorce must be proved by full, clear and adequate evidence. Proof offered in this case was inadequate.

1958—*Hoffecker v. Hoffecker,* 200 Va. 119, 104 S.E.2d 771.

Uncontradicted evidence showed that wife became addicted to use of drugs and later to alcohol despite her husband's efforts to prevent this. This was frequent source of embarrassment to husband. Wife was abusive to husband, stated she did not love him and on various occasions ordered him out of house. There was evidence that effect on his health was serious. Cruelty established. Violence and apprehension of bodily hurt are not indispensable ingredients. Although addiction to drugs or alcohol is not generally regarded by itself as ground for divorce, such together with other misconduct may constitute cruelty.

1952—*Fulton v. Fulton*, 193 Va. 255, 68 S.E.2d 485.

Evidence in this case showed that alleged cruel conduct of husband was direct result of intolerable behavior of wife when under influence of alcohol. Evidence was insufficient to establish cruelty.

1943—*Hudgins v. Hudgins*, 181 Va. 81, 23 S.E.2d 774.

Repeated drunkenness at social affairs by wife and instance wherein she bit her husband justified decree of divorce for cruelty. Those facts plus wife's unproven charge of adultery established cruelty.

1911—*Haynor v. Haynor*, 112 Va. 123, 70 S.E. 531.

In suit on grounds of cruelty, facts constituting cruelty and not merely conclusions should be set forth with reasonable certainty. In suit for divorce on grounds of cruelty, opinions of witnesses based upon their knowledge of character or reputation of party that they not believe that other party could with safety cohabit is not admissible in evidence.

(2) MENTAL ABUSE.

1983—*Coe v. Coe*, 225 Va. 616, 303 S.E.2d 923.

Fault divorce should not be granted merely upon evidence of marital disharmony.

1967—*Hoback v. Hoback*, 208 Va. 432, 158 S.E.2d 113.

Spouse is not justified in leaving unless conduct of other spouse is sufficient to establish foundation for divorce. Mental anguish, repeated unrelenting neglect and humiliation may amount to cruelty and justify leaving. It must be so serious that it makes marital relationship intolerable or unendurable. In this case, although actions of husband's obviously were somewhat distant, it is apparent that wife did not regard conduct and attitude of husband toward her to be of such cruel nature that cohabitation with him was intolerable. In addition, there was no corroboration of wife's statement that he had excluded her from bedroom and had packed up some of her belongings. She was denied divorce on grounds of cruelty. Fact that she left him without justification, however, justified entry of divorce decree on his behalf on grounds of desertion.

1967—*Wimbrow v. Wimbrow*, 208 Va. 141, 156 S.E.2d 598.

Jealousy, accusations, threats to call IRS, did not amount to cruelty by wife for she had reason to suspect improper relations with other women and there was no actual proof of what she had said to IRS.

1966—*Lawyer v. Lawyer,* 207 Va. 260, 148 S.E.2d 816.
Wife's testimony as to abuse by her husband was vague and without corroboration. As such, she was not entitled to divorce on grounds of cruelty. Her departure from family home, however, did constitute desertion.

1960—*Todd v. Todd,* 202 Va. 133, 115 S.E.2d 905.
Both sides alleged cruelty and desertion. Evidence showed long period of worsening relations with difficulties over money, recurrent separations and various acts of unkindness on either side. Court concluded that neither party was entitled to divorce.

1957—*Baytop v. Baytop,* 199 Va. 388, 100 S.E.2d 14.
Evidence showed that husband and wife had never had home together because she taught in Virginia and he in Delaware; that for some years he had been cool to her, discouraged her weekend visits, had affair with another woman and on occasion cursed her publicly; that as result she had become nervous and ill and after final unpleasant night spent at his family home she left him because she could take no more abuse. There was no evidence of physical abuse. Court properly awarded divorce on grounds of cruelty. Authorities generally allow for exceptional cases in which there may be extreme cruelty without slightest violence.

1956—*Bisel v. Bisel,* 197 Va. 636, 90 S.E.2d 779.
Evidence showed that husband had at times physically mistreated wife, had left her and taken their children, and had repeatedly accused her of being crazy and had told her that she must get out and find work, for he intended to have children and home. This was sufficient to establish cruelty.

1947—*Davis v. Davis,* 187 Va. 63, 45 S.E.2d 918.
Wife wrote letters to army officer containing expressions of endearment and affection. Correspondence was broken off prior to separation of parties and, in addition, such conduct had been condoned. This fails to establish cruelty.

1944—*Montgomery v. Montgomery,* 183 Va. 96, 31 S.E.2d 284.
Cruelty must be very serious and be such as amounts to extreme cruelty entirely subversive of family relations, rendering association intolerable. In this case, wife alleged extreme interference on part of mother-in-law as constituting cruelty. Although such may constitute cruelty, in this particular case wife was not subservient to mother-in-law and was not subjected to abuse and unwarranted interference from her. As such, cruelty not established.

1944—*Fussell v. Fussell,* 182 Va. 720, 30 S.E.2d 555.
Husband beat wife, used vile and cruel language and caused her to become so nervous and upset as to leave him. Husband guilty of cruelty.

1944—*Forbes v. Forbes,* 182 Va. 636, 29 S.E.2d 829.

Wife's corroborated testimony was that husband choked her, struck her at times, cursed her and was frequently absent for extended periods. Cruelty established.

1943—*Hundley v. Hundley,* 182 Va. 14, 27 S.E.2d 902.

Cruelty on part of husband which results in wife's enforced separation is tantamount to desertion on his part.

1939—*Hughes v. Hughes,* 173 Va. 293, 4 S.E.2d 402.

Husband's uncorroborated testimony that wife was jealous, nagging and constantly bickering and that this impaired his health was insufficient.

1939—*Hendry v. Hendry,* 172 Va. 368, 1 S.E.2d 340.

Husband was cold, indifferent and sometimes unkind. So was wife. Wife denied divorce on cruelty grounds.

1938—*Rogers v. Rogers,* 170 Va. 417, 196 S.E. 586.

Allegedly cruelty was limited to two occasions. Subsequently wife resumed marital relations with husband. Alleged conduct was that husband cursed and threatened to kill wife. This was contradicted by other witnesses. Cruelty not established.

1930—*Johnson v. Johnson,* 154 Va. 788, 153 S.E. 670.

Use of profane and coarse language not sufficient. There must also be fair reason to apprehend injury to health, physical or mental. Husband in this case was very generous financially to his wife. That men may do this and at same time beat their wives is possible but not probable. Cruelty is anything that tends to bodily harm and thus renders cohabitation unsafe. Angry words and annoyances may also endanger health and be grounds for divorce. But what merely wounds feelings without being accompanied by bodily injury or actual menace does not amount to legal cruelty. In this case wife did as she pleased and husband said as he pleased. Cruelty not established.

1924—*Humphreys v. Strong,* 139 Va. 146, 123 S.E.2d 554.

Such cruelty, on part of husband, though unaccompanied by actual violence, that to live with him longer meant permanent impairment of wife's health, justifies change of domicile. Term "bodily hurt," when used in reference to cruelty, is not restricted to physical assault but includes conduct which leads to serious nervous or mental disease.

1921—*Twohy v. Twohy,* 130 Va. 557, 107 S.E. 642.

Violence and apprehension of bodily hurt, though nearly always appearing in suits for divorce on ground of cruelty, are not indispensable ingredients of that offense. In this case, wife presented corroborated evidence of husband's drunkenness, neglect, brutality, obscene language, vulgar behavior and cruelty on many occasions. There was no question from evidence that husband caused wife much mental anguish. Evidence was sufficient to support decree of divorce. Law does allow for exceptional cases in which there may be extreme cruelty without slightest violence.

1920—*Cumming v. Cumming,* 127 Va. 16, 102 S.E. 572.
Husband alleged cruelty on part of wife and contended that cruelty originally caused separation. In fact, husband deserted wife on night of marriage and, as such, any cruelty would have been subsequent to desertion and, as such, did not cause it.

1893—*Kinsey v. Kinsey,* 90 Va. 16, 17 S.E. 819.
It is proved that defendant habitually annoyed wife, was often drunk and struck her, came into her room at night with sword and pistol threatening her and finally drove her and her child from house at night. Cruelty established.

1878—*Latham v. Latham,* 71 Va. 307.
Cruelty that authorizes divorce is anything that tends to bodily harm and therefore renders cohabitation unsafe. There may be instances where spouse without violence, actual or threatened, may make marriage state impossible to be endured and these may effectively endanger life or health and therefore may be grounds for relief by court but what merely wounds feelings without being accompanied by bodily injury or actual menace does not amount to legal cruelty.

1872—*Carr v. Carr,* 63 Va. 168.
Fact that husband is rude and dictatorial in his speech to his wife, exacting in his demands, sometimes unkind and negligent in his treatment of her, even when she was sick and worn and weary, in watching and nursing their sick child, is no legal grounds for her leaving him.

(3) PHYSICAL ABUSE.

See Va. Code § 16.1-253.1 as to preliminary protective orders in cases of spouse abuse. See also Section 16.1-279.1 as to order of protection in cases of spouse abuse.

See Va. Code § 20-103 indicating that court has authority to impose certain restraining orders in situations where one spouse has reasonable apprehension of physical harm by other spouse.

1983—*Vardell v. Vardell,* 225 Va. 351, 302 S.E.2d 41.
Wife in this case sought injunction to have husband removed from house on grounds that she feared for her physical well-being. After adversary hearing, court decided there was reasonable likelihood that wife's health and safety would be endangered if parties remained together and ordered husband out of home. Such injunction requiring separation of parties is not ipso facto basis for granting divorce to husband when wife subsequently is unsuccessful in proving her grounds for divorce.

1980—*McCausey v. McCausey,* 221 Va. 500, 272 S.E.2d 36.
Husband sued on grounds of constructive desertion and wife cross-claimed alleging desertion and cruelty. Wife presented substantial

evidence of violent acts by husband. Court however, ruled that neither party was entitled to divorce on grounds of desertion or constructive desertion, but did indicate they had met criteria for no-fault divorce.

1975—*Capps v. Capps,* 216 Va. 382, 219 S.E.2d 898.

One instance of physical cruelty is insufficient to establish ground for divorce unless it is so severe as to endanger life or unless act indicates intention to do serious bodily harm or causes reasonable apprehension of serious danger in future or circumstances show that acts are likely to be repeated. In this case wife's testimony was sufficiently corroborated by her mother's observation of "big knot" on her forehead following alleged cruelty. Wife's testimony, however, did not indicate that she had reasonable apprehension of serious injury in future, and as such her suit on grounds of cruelty was denied.

1970—*Graham v. Graham,* 210 Va. 608, 172 S.E.2d 724.

Testimony of parties established physical assault on wife, vile and abusive language, temper tantrums and destruction of articles of furniture by husband. Wife testified that husband's excessive drinking, threats to her life, hatred and indifference which husband did not deny. While evidence shows that wife's conduct may have contributed to marital difficulties, actions on part of husband were totally out of proportion thereby justifying desertion by wife. Testimony as to cruelty, however, was uncorroborated and therefore she was not entitled to divorce on grounds of cruelty. He likewise was not entitled to divorce on grounds of desertion since her desertion was justified.

1961—*Sollie v. Sollie,* 202 Va. 855, 120 S.E.2d 281.

Wife's evidence indicated physical abuse on several occasions and continued course of unkindness and disrespect shown in private and in public. To this, she attributed partial facial paralysis and her decision to leave home. This evidence, corroborated by testimony of her mother, was held sufficient to justify finding of cruelty.

1958—*Green v. Green,* 199 Va. 927, 103 S.E.2d 202.

Wife testified, with corroboration, that over period of years her husband had been abusive, starting arguments and cursing her and that this conduct culminated in physical assault of serious nature and in his ordering her and her daughter from home. While single act of cruelty not serious enough to endanger life or cause reasonable apprehension of serious danger in future does not constitute ground for divorce, facts of this case removed it from that particular rule and divorce should have been granted.

1956—*DeMott v. DeMott,* 198 Va. 22, 92 S.E.2d 342.

No error in denying wife divorce for cruelty where cruelty was based on single incident of bodily assault which neither did her serious bodily harm nor caused her reasonable apprehension of serious danger in future.

1953—*Upchurch v. Upchurch,* 194 Va. 990, 76 S.E.2d 170.

Cruelty must be such that tends to bodily harm and thus renders cohabitation unsafe. There need not necessarily be violence, actual or threatened, but mere fact that couple live unhappily together is not sufficient. In this case, husband had certain physical disabilities and emotional instability. Wife had struck him on occasion and used defamatory language. Evidence failed to show, however, that husband had sufficient reason to apprehend danger to his life, limb or health.

1952—*Prindes v. Prindes,* 193 Va. 463, 69 S.E.2d 332.

To establish cruelty or reasonable apprehension of bodily harm, charges must be clearly proved. Because, in this case, testimony of husband was substantially uncorroborated and was directly controverted by wife, grounds for divorce were not established. Wife's corroborated evidence that husband had subjected her to coarse, vile and abusive language, including charges of prostitution and adultery and to actual violence to her person, established grounds for divorce due to cruelty.

1947—*Ward v. Ward,* 185 Va. 899, 41 S.E.2d 7.

If conduct is such as tends to endanger life, limb or health of other party, or such as to render cohabitation unsafe or improper, then this may be grounds for divorce for cruelty or reasonable apprehension of bodily harm. Conduct must be such as to be very serious and such as amounts to extreme cruelty, entirely subversive of family relations, rendering association intolerable. Merely because couple live unhappily together due to unruly tempers, lack of patience and uncongenial natures does not constitute basis for divorce. Wife alleged that husband choked her, knocked her against wall and tore her nightgown. These allegations were held insufficient to justify divorce on grounds of cruelty. Husband denied these allegations.

1942—*Bennett v. Bennett,* 179 Va. 239, 18 S.E.2d 911.

Evidence was that husband struck wife, treated her with indignity, directed profane language at her. Cruelty established. Violence and apprehension of body harm are not indispensable elements. Mental anguish and repeated and unrelenting neglect may be sufficient. Cruelty is cumulative. While acts of violence at earlier time, which have not prevented wife from going back to husband, cannot be sole basis for divorce they form basis for proof of whether she can live safely with him.

1940—*Owen v. Owen,* 175 Va. 245, 7 S.E.2d 890.

Desertion and cruelty claimed. Evidence showed that husband had left wife on prior occasions and had beaten and choked her. Court affirmed granting of a mensa divorce.

1939—*Wade v. Wade,* 172 Va. 282, 1 S.E.2d 331.

Wife used indecent names as to husband, was frequently away from home, neglected him when he was sick and struck and wounded him. Sufficient to establish cruelty and desertion.

1937—*Toler v. Toler,* 168 Va. 302, 191 S.E. 638.

Conduct must be very serious, entirely subversive of family relations rendering association intolerable. Mere fact that parties are unhappy due to their unruly tempers is insufficient. In this case wife alleged that husband struck her. No reasonable ground to believe he would do her serious body harm if she continued to live with him as wife.

1936—*Allen v. Allen,* 166 Va. 303, 186 S.E. 17.

Husband drank, stayed out late, quarreled with and nagged wife and on one occasion when son protested, engaged in scuffle with son, and ordered him to leave house. Wife testified she was afraid to stay in house without sons present. Wife required constant medical care. Evidence sufficient to establish cruelty for a mensa divorce.

1929—*Williams v. Williams,* 152 Va. 896, 148 S.E. 579.

Husband would drink to excess, publicly humiliate wife, slap wife in public. Sufficient to establish cruelty. Courts should be reluctant to grant divorce where people with high tempers quarrel and prove incompatible.

1927—*Cohn v. Cohn,* 148 Va. 467, 139 S.E. 251.

Evidence presented of physical violence and abusive language. Sufficient to establish cruelty.

1926—*Butler v. Butler,* 145 Va. 85, 133 S.E. 756.

Wife sued husband for cruelty. Husband sued for desertion. Evidence indicated wife was unreasonable and violent. At time of departure by wife, she kicked and scratched husband, and he slapped her on thigh. Husband not guilty of cruelty. Wife guilty of desertion. To constitute cruelty, conduct must be very serious, amount to extreme cruelty, entirely subversive of family relation.

1924—*Miller v. Miller,* 140 Va. 424, 125 S.E. 220.

Evidence of wife was that husband, without just cause, grabbed her, threw her down, choked her and beat her until she was insensible. There were additional threats of bodily harm. Weight of evidence supported her contentions. Test of whether or not there has been cruelty is whether spouse has so treated other spouse as to inflict bodily harm or cause reasonable apprehension of suffering or injury, physically or mentally.

1924—*Harman v. Harman,* 139 Va. 508, 124 S.E. 273.

In this case, court found admissible prior acts of cruelty of husband, even though many of them occurred long time before final departure of wife. Acts of cruelty consisted of drunken sprees of husband when he became quarrelsome, disorderly and dangerous and caused her to have reasonable apprehension of bodily harm. Fact that wife returned and cohabited with husband after some of these acts of cruelty does not make them inadmissible. Fact that wife cohabited with husband after these acts of cruelty, except those which were inflicted upon her at time of her final departure, does not render evidence of such repeated conduct any less cogent in establishing that departure was not of her own free will.

1924—*Elder v. Elder,* 139 Va. 19, 123 S.E. 369.

Preponderance of evidence was that husband had subjected wife to actual violence, threats of death or serious bodily injury, with pistol and knife, that he addressed her in abusive language and forced her to submit to most cruel insults, including charge of adultery, followed by command to leave house. Cruelty established. Violence and apprehension of bodily hurt are not indispensable elements of this offense. Mental anguish, repeated in unrelenting neglect and humiliation, may be as bad as physical wounds and bruises. Cruelty, on part of husband, which results in wife's enforced separation from home, is tantamount to desertion on his part.

1923—*Albert v. Albert,* 137 Va. 1, 119 S.E. 61.

There was conflicting evidence of abusive language and physical assault upon wife. Court found that evidence did not support allegation of cruelty.

1904—*House v. House,* 102 Va. 235, 46 S.E. 299.

In action for cruelty, opinions of witnesses based upon their knowledge of character or reputation of wife that they did not believe that husband could with safety cohabit with her are not admissible. Witnesses should state facts. Charge of cruelty should be clearly proved. Evidence in this case did not show satisfactorily that wife had attempted or really intended to do bodily harm to her husband or that he had reasonable ground to apprehend danger of life or limb.

1899—*Trimble v. Trimble,* 97 Va. 217, 33 S.E. 531.

Evidence in this case, although somewhat conflicting, was that husband did strike wife until there were bruises on her body, that he threatened to tie her and had rope bought for that purpose but afterwards abandoned that attempt, that he told her that he never expected to live with her another day and that either she had to leave or he would, that she asked to be reconciled with him and he refused, that wife and child were taken to her father's house in conveyance furnished by husband where she has since remained. Cruelty established.

1898—*Owens v. Owens,* 96 Va. 191, 31 S.E. 72.

Cruelty consists of successive acts of ill treatment, if not of personal injury; something of condonation of earlier ill treatment must, in such cases necessarily take place. It may be condoned and even forgiven for time and up to certain point without barring right to bring it all forward when continuance of it has rendered it no longer condonable. Malicious charge of adultery made by one spouse standing alone is not sufficient to justify divorce but when presented with other facts enhancing its significance it is act of gross cruelty. Evidence in this case established cruelty. Wife had been violently jerked from her bed by husband and compelled to sleep upon floor, had been accused in grossest terms of infidelity and her children denounced as illegitimate and finally had been ordered to leave and never return.

1896—*Hutchins v. Hutchins,* 93 Va. 68, 24 S.E. 903.
> Husband is head of family and as such is entitled to select place of residence. If he permits persons in home to treat wife with cruelty, cruelty is his and she may leave home without furnishing him cause for divorce. Long series of vexations, culminating in charge of larceny and serious assault by person of greatly superior physical force is cruelty. Husband's bill for divorce in this case was denied.

1893—*Heninger v. Heninger,* 90 Va. 271, 18 S.E. 193.
> Wife's proof established that husband did physically abuse her. She was awarded divorce on grounds of cruelty.

1887—*Myers v. Myers,* 83 Va. 806, 6 S.E. 630.
> Cruelty can be established by any conduct that renders cohabitation unsafe, that involves danger of life, limb or health. Angry words, coarse and abusive language, humiliating insults and annoyances may as well endanger life and health as personal violence and may therefore constitute grounds for cruelty. In this case, husband physically abused wife and threatened her with further physical harm. Cruelty was established.

(4) MISCELLANEOUS.

1963—*Beckner v. Beckner,* 204 Va. 580, 132 S.E.2d 715.
> Acts of cruelty which allegedly occurred while suit was pending could not be considered because not mentioned in pleadings and also because divorce can be granted only on proof of facts occurring before suit is brought.

(5) SEX — DENIAL OF.

See Constructive Desertion, § 2.4(B).

1975—*Aichner v. Aichner,* 215 Va. 624, 212 S.E.2d 278.
> Evidence failed to show clearly that wife permanently and excusably refused sexual intercourse and therefore does not support finding of cruelty or constructive desertion.

1970—*Carneal v. Carneal,* 211 Va. 162, 176 S.E.2d 305.
> Wife alleged cruelty on grounds that husband failed to support family adequately, and he refused sexual intercourse. Although evidence indicates that financial problems contributed primarily to marital discord, there was no cruelty or legal justification for separation by wife. Absent clear evidence of permanent and unexcused refusal of sexual intercourse, showing of mere cessation of intercourse is not sufficient to prove cruelty or constructive desertion.

1920—*Ringgold v. Ringgold,* 128 Va. 485, 104 S.E.2d 836.
> Husband, in this case, without justification, refused to permit his wife to occupy his room and bed. He stated that he would not take her back until such time as she had done penance for some prior act which he judged to be misdeed. He encouraged mistreatment of wife by his mother and sisters. She was entitled to divorce a mensa on

grounds of cruelty. Cruelty alone is not ground for divorce from bonds of matrimony. Violence and apprehension of bodily hurt are not indispensable ingredients of cruelty. Mental anguish, repeated and unrelenting neglect and humiliation may amount to cruelty. Virginia has not expressly decided whether or not cessation of marital intercourse alone constitutes cruelty.

1907—*Davenport v. Davenport,* 106 Va. 736, 56 S.E. 562.
Evidence showed that husband withheld from his wife affection that was due her, even though she was faithful, kind and considerate and further that he used abusive language, seized her person with violence and threatened her with greater violence. This was grounds for cruelty.

(D) Desertion.

(1) ELEMENTS.

1980—*Breschel v. Breschel,* 221 Va. 208, 269 S.E.2d 363.
Party is guilty of desertion when he breaks off cohabitation with intent to desert unless such conduct was justified. Once desertion is established, duty of going forward with evidence of justification rests upon defendant.

1970—*Graham v. Graham,* 210 Va. 608, 172 S.E.2d 724.
To prove desertion, it must be established that there was actual breaking off of matrimonial cohabitation combined with intent to desert in mind of offender. When such desertion is established, then duty of going forward with evidence of justification then rests on party deserting unless justification appears from testimony adduced by deserted party. There is no requirement that plaintiff negate every ground or reason which defendant might have for deserting.

1948—*Mullen v. Mullen,* 188 Va. 259, 49 S.E.2d 349.
Husband in this case did provide comfortable home for wife at residence of his parents. She was neither abused nor ill-treated there. His failure to provide separate home for wife did not justify her willful desertion nor amount to constructive desertion on his part. Actual breach and breaking off of marital cohabitation with intent to desert constitutes desertion.

1939—*Hughes v. Hughes,* 173 Va. 293, 4 S.E.2d 402.
Husband willfully and without just cause deserted wife.

1932—*Sussman v. Sussman,* 158 Va. 382, 163 S.E. 69.
Elements:
    (1) Has there been actual breaking off of cohabitation.
    (2) Was severance made with intent to desert.
    (3) Has injured party, before filing suit, sought in good faith reconciliation.

1926—*Markley v. Markley,* 145 Va. 596, 134 S.E. 536.
Elements:

    (1) Actual breaking off of matrimonial cohabitation.

    (2) Intent to desert in mind of offender.

    (3) Injured party must have, before institution of suit, sought in good faith reconciliation.

Evidence in this case indicated willful desertion.

1915—*Hairston v. Hairston*, 117 Va. 207, 84 S.E. 15.

Suit for divorce on grounds of desertion for three years was dismissed apparently due to fact that three-year period had not elapsed. Husband was not barred from subsequently bringing another suit for same cause if desertion continued. Desertion is breach of matrimonial duty and consists of actual breaking off of matrimonial cohabitation coupled with intent to desert in mind of offender. It can only be justified by showing such conduct on part of deserted party as would entitle other to divorce a mensa.

1910—*Washington v. Washington*, 111 Va. 524, 69 S.E. 322.

Uncontradicted evidence shows that husband abandoned wife for five or six years, did not live with her during that period of time, contributed nothing to her support even though she endeavored to induce him to return. Wherever there is actual breaking off of matrimonial cohabitation combined with intent to desert, desertion is established, as was case here. Long continued absence without detaining cause is most potent means of proof of intent to desert.

1872—*Carr v. Carr*, 63 Va. 168.

Fact that husband is rude and dictatorial, exacting in his demands, sometimes unkind and negligent, is no legal grounds for leaving him. To establish desertion, there must be actual breaking off of matrimonial cohabitation, combined with intent to desert in mind of offender.

1871—*Bailey v. Bailey*, 62 Va. 43.

Desertion consists of actual breaking off of marital cohabitation with intent to desert. In this case, husband left his home and family in November of 1865 and returned in November of 1866. He remained at home two weeks and then left and did not return until September of 1867, when wife filed her bill of complaint. Husband's intent to desert has been clearly proved, and she is entitled to divorce. Mere separation by mutual consent is not desertion nor can desertion be inferred from mere fact that parties do not live together, although protracted absence, with other circumstances, may establish original intent. Intent to desert may be established by statements from guilty party, absence for long time which is not necessary, making no provisions for wife although being able to do so and from prohibiting wife to live with husband.

(2) In General.

See Va. Code § 20-81 indicating that proof of desertion or neglect of spouse or children by any person shall be prima facie evidence that such desertion or neglect is willful and proof that person has left his or her spouse or child in necessitous circumstances or has contributed nothing to their support for period of 30 days and shall constitute prima facie evidence of intention to abandon such family.

1982—*Roberts v. Roberts,* 223 Va. 736, 292 S.E.2d 370.

One spouse is not guilty of legal desertion in separating from other after institution of suit for divorce or during its pendency. Although it's recognized that if this rule is applied inflexibly, it may result in certain inequities i.e., party may file frivolous suit simply to provide some justification for deserting. That was not so in this case. In fact, physical separation in such circumstances is justified and may even be commendable so as to separate parties.

1980—*McCausey v. McCausey,* 221 Va. 500, 272 S.E.2d 36.

Husband sued on grounds of constructive desertion and wife cross-claimed alleging desertion and cruelty. Wife presented substantial evidence of violent acts by husband. Court however, ruled that neither party was entitled to divorce on grounds of desertion or constructive desertion, but did indicate they had met criteria for no fault divorce.

1975—*Aichner v. Aichner,* 215 Va. 624, 212 S.E.2d 278.

Evidence, other than testimony or admissions of parties, showed only that husband moved out of family residence, not why he moved. As such, wife is not entitled to divorce on grounds of desertion.

1975—*Painter v. Painter,* 215 Va. 418, 211 S.E.2d 37.

One spouse is not guilty of legal desertion in separating from other after institution of suit for divorce. Spouse seeking divorce has burden of proving that desertion occurred prior to filing suit.

1974—*Rowland v. Rowland,* 215 Va. 344, 210 S.E.2d 149.

Wife forfeits her right to alimony only if her misconduct constitutes grounds for desertion. In this case, wife was free from legal fault when she left marital abode on husband's demand that she "get out" without justification and unprovoked by any legally recognized misconduct on her part.

1972—*Johnson v. Johnson,* 213 Va. 204, 191 S.E.2d 206.

Without clear evidence of permanent and unexcused refusal of sexual relations, showing of mere cessation of intercourse is not sufficient to prove constructive desertion. Wife in this case, in addition to moving into separate bedroom, was absent from house on day divorce proceedings were instituted and for about two weeks thereafter remained visiting members of her family. She thereafter returned to family home and remained there until court ordered husband to remove himself. These facts do not constitute desertion on her part. Mere fact that marriage had deteriorated does not mean that there is sufficient evidence to grant divorce on fault grounds. It is well settled that absenting of one spouse from family home after institution of suit is not desertion in law, indeed it may be highly proper to do so.

1965—*Huddle v. Huddle,* 206 Va. 535, 145 S.E.2d 167.

Wife committed adultery. Husband condoned adulterous action and took wife back to live with him. He thereafter left because of his suspicions that she was pregnant by another man. Resumption of cohabitation constituted condonation. His departure thereafter constituted desertion.

1963—*Beckner v. Beckner,* 204 Va. 580, 132 S.E.2d 715.

Husband sought divorce on grounds of desertion alleging that wife left him on June 1, 1961. She denied this. Evidence however showed that he actually left home on August 12, 1961, and as such there could not have been any desertion on June 1, 1961. Testimony offered by husband was not corroborated. As such, there was no basis for desertion claim. Misconduct, which is cause for legal separation must be such as to subvert family relations and render association intolerable.

1963—*Pollard v. Pollard,* 204 Va. 316, 130 S.E.2d 425.

Evidence showed desertion without cause by wife on January 28, 1947. She was adjudicated insane on February 26, 1947. She had given no indication of insanity prior to date of desertion. Insanity so occurring is no defense.

1962—*Stolfi v. Stolfi,* 203 Va. 696, 126 S.E.2d 923.

Evidence showed that disagreement arose among parties as to treatment and upbringing of wife's son by former marriage. She then sent child to live with her parents in California. She thereafter left family home without consulting her husband and took children to California with no intent to return. Her testimony as to mistreatment was not corroborated whereas his testimony was corroborated that he provided for his family and that their domestic situation seemed normal. On this evidence, it was held that wife had voluntarily, without justification, deserted. She was denied alimony.

1960—*Plattner v. Plattner,* 202 Va. 263, 117 S.E.2d 128.

Each party charged desertion as to other. Husband alleged desertion on part of wife which occurred after filing of her bill of complaint. No divorce for desertion could be awarded on that basis. Desertion must be alleged and proved to have occurred prior to bringing of suit.

1957—*Carter v. Carter,* 199 Va. 79, 97 S.E.2d 663.

After death of their only son, this couple stayed at home of wife's parents for some weeks until husband returned to his own home, at which time he alleged that wife refused to return with him. Her evidence showed that she was not physically well enough to move and that when week later she did go back he ordered her out and later refused her attempts at reconciliation. Court correctly concluded that desertion by wife had not been proved and that she was entitled to separate maintenance. Wife is not guilty of desertion when driven from home by her husband or if his behavior makes it impossible for her to live with him in safety and concord. Desertion is composed first of breaking off of matrimonial cohabitation and secondly of intent to desert in mind of offender. It does not necessarily depend upon who leaves home. It has broader meaning of desertion of marriage relation.

1957—*Beers v. Beers,* 198 Va. 682, 96 S.E.2d 139.

Record showed that husband had not been successful in business, that much of wife's separate estate had been used to support family, that she was emotionally disturbed and was under care of psychiatrist and that home atmosphere was one of hostility and argument so that husband moved to his private club and later determined to make separation permanent. These facts showed desertion on part of husband, not wife.

1956—*Hensley v. Hensley,* 198 Va. 414, 94 S.E.2d 211.

Wife sued for divorce on grounds of cruelty, desertion and non-support, all of which was amply confirmed by corroborating evidence as to lack of support, husband's drinking to excess, his cursing and physically mistreating her. Decree awarded.

1956—*Owens v. Owens,* 197 Va. 681, 90 S.E.2d 776.

Husband testified that he and wife lived together as man and wife for one day and that he then returned to Army and, upon his discharge year later, she wrote saying that she would not live with him. This letter was not offered as evidence, and his testimony was otherwise not properly corroborated. No basis for desertion. Plaintiff must prove willful desertion without justification or excuse. Full and satisfactory proof is required.

1955—*Miller v. Miller,* 196 Va. 698, 85 S.E.2d 221.

There was direct proof of wife's act of leaving and of her intention to desert. Fact that husband voiced no objection to her going was immaterial for it was her conduct and purpose and not his intent that determined whether or not there was desertion.

1952—*Prindes v. Prindes,* 193 Va. 463, 69 S.E.2d 332.

Evidence established that husband subjected wife to extensive cruelty and eventually deserted her without justification.

1952—*Raiford v. Raiford,* 193 Va. 221, 68 S.E.2d 888.

Testimony of parties indicated essentially differing accounts of three different quarrels. It reveals that neither party exercised control of temper, patience and forebearance which was their duty. Law does not permit courts to sever marriages merely because parties have unruly tempers, lack of patience and uncongenial natures and are living unhappily together. Grounds for separation must be very serious — that is, such as amount to extreme cruelty, entirely subversive of family relations rendering association intolerable. Wife in this case failed to prove her charge of willful desertion, without justification or excuse.

1949—*Allen v. Allen,* 188 Va. 717, 51 S.E.2d 207.
  Wife left marital home, drank to excess and constantly consorted with another man. Husband awarded divorce on grounds of desertion.

1948—*Bennett v. Bennett,* 187 Va. 631, 47 S.E.2d 312.
  Husband left wife three days after wedding. Wife found husband in brothel. Desertion established.

1947—*Ward v. Ward,* 185 Va. 899, 41 S.E.2d 7.
  Wife left family home and deliberately refused to perform marital duties. Trial court held this was not basis for divorce on grounds of desertion. That ruling was not appealed by husband.

1947—*Davis v. Davis,* 187 Va. 63, 45 S.E.2d 918.
  Husband left his wife and departed from home they occupied. He removed his furniture and sold it. This was not justified by anything wife had done and, as such, constituted grounds for desertion.

1944—*Moltz v. Moltz,* 182 Va. 737, 30 S.E.2d 561.
  Husband granted divorce apparently on grounds of desertion due to wife's unjustified refusal to live with him in Norfolk while he was in Navy.

1944—*Kerr v. Kerr,* 182 Va. 731, 30 S.E.2d 684.
  Wife left with intent to permanently abandon. Wife's evidence of justification was vague and indefinite.

1944—*Coxe v. Coxe,* 182 Va. 754, 30 S.E.2d 572.
  Evidence failed to establish that wife had abandoned family home.

1943—*Hundley v. Hundley,* 182 Va. 14, 27 S.E.2d 902.
  Wife left husband after severe beating. Wife did not leave voluntarily.

1943—*Hudgins v. Hudgins,* 181 Va. 81, 23 S.E.2d 774.
  Absenting of one spouse from other after institution of suit for divorce is not basis for desertion claim.

1942—*Bowman v. Bowman,* 180 Va. 200, 22 S.E.2d 29.
  Husband, without cause, willfully abandoned his wife for period of 20 months, failed to return to his wife and made no effort to resume marital relations and contributed nothing to her support. Proof of desertion established.

1942—*Cecil v. Cecil,* 179 Va. 274, 19 S.E.2d 64.
  Husband wrote letter to his father which proved his willful desertion of wife.

1942—*McFarland v. McFarland,* 179 Va. 418, 19 S.E.2d 77.
  North Carolina law permitting person guilty of desertion to secure divorce by persisting in his desertion for more than 2 years is repugnant to Virginia law.

1940—*McDaniel v. McDaniel,* 175 Va. 402, 9 S.E.2d 360.
> Wife's refusal to respond to husband's overtures of reconciliation did not constitute desertion under facts of this case.

1939—*Holt v. Holt,* 174 Va. 120, 5 S.E.2d 504.
> Husband received anonymous letter of wife's adultery. He refused to live with her and support her and did vilify her by publishing letter. Wife granted divorce on grounds of cruelty and desertion.

1939—*Wade v. Wade,* 172 Va. 282, 1 S.E.2d 331.
> Wife used indecent names to husband, was frequently away from home, neglected him when sick and struck and wounded him. Sufficient to establish cruelty and desertion.

1937—*Toler v. Toler,* 168 Va. 302, 191 S.E. 638.
> Husband sued wife for desertion. Wife remained in same apartment but occupied separate room and refused reconciliation. Evidence presented that wife struck husband; insufficient evidence of desertion.

1934—*Simpson v. Simpson,* 162 Va. 621, 175 S.E. 320.
> Where husband absent for more than seven years and therefore presumed dead wife may still file for divorce.

1934—*Gentry v. Gentry,* 161 Va. 786, 172 S.E. 157.
> Husband saw wife kissing another man. Such conduct did not justify husband leaving wife and did not excuse his failure to make offer of reconciliation. Wife made repeated attempts to reconcile. Husband refused. Wife entitled to divorce on grounds of desertion.

1926—*Butler v. Butler,* 145 Va. 85, 133 S.E. 756.
> Wife sued for cruelty. Husband sued for desertion. Evidence indicated wife was unreasonable and violent. At time of departure of wife, she kicked and scratched him. He slapped her on thigh. Cruelty claim overruled. Wife guilty of desertion.

1926—*Duff v. Duff,* 145 Va. 526, 134 S.E. 555.
> Desertion in question was second within two months by wife. After first desertion, she returned, due to earnest request of husband. She remained less than two weeks, leaving with statement that she never desired to return again. There was no further legal duty of husband to seek reconciliation.

1923—*Albert v. Albert,* 137 Va. 1, 119 S.E. 61.
> In this case, husband and wife lived together in same house, although wife had refused to cohabit with husband. She did, however, cook and wash for husband and they had their meals at same table. These facts did not warrant divorce on grounds of desertion.

1923—*Mowles v. Mowles,* 137 Va. 274, 119 S.E. 54.
> Husband sued wife on grounds of desertion. Supreme court found that it was not clear from whole evidence that wife had not been guilty of willful desertion. Certainly, she was not entirely free from fault. Since burden, however, was upon complainant, supreme court resolved its doubts in favor of wife and denied divorce.

1922—*Black v. Black,* 134 Va. 246, 114 S.E. 592.

In suit on grounds of desertion, burden is on complainant to show, with fair certainty and by full and satisfactory evidence, that other spouse has willfully deserted or abandoned. Evidence in such case should show all circumstances immediately preceding and succeeding separation. In this case, husband gave testimony, first by deposition and then later orally in open court. That testimony was inconsistent. The court denied desertion claim.

1920—*Ringgold v. Ringgold,* 128 Va. 485, 104 S.E. 836.

Where husband has withdrawn from marriage bed, has declined to allow his wife to keep house with him and has effectively separated her from him, this constitutes desertion, even though he did not decline to furnish his wife living in his home. In this case, husband indicated that he might take her back in 5-10 years. The desertion was permanent in this case in sense that it gave no promise of return within reasonable time. Desertion, which entitles party to divorce from bed and board differs from that which is cause for divorce from bonds of matrimony only in respect that for divorce of latter kind desertion must continue for 3 years. After lapse of that period, without any offer to return, right to divorce from bonds of matrimony becomes complete. Desertion is first actual breaking off of matrimonial cohabitation and secondly intent to desert. Mere separation by mutual consent is not desertion.

1920—*Dinsmore v. Dinsmore,* 128 Va. 403, 104 S.E. 785.

Uncontradicted evidence was that husband was drunken, worthless, without employment, that he failed to contribute to support of his wife and children and that, since date of abandonment, he had not returned or otherwise communicated with his wife. Abandonment had continued for 10 or 12 years. Wife was awarded divorce from bonds of matrimony.

1920—*Isgett v. Isgett,* 126 Va. 599, 101 S.E. 788.

Evidence in this case was held sufficient to establish desertion by husband. Evidence not set forth.

1919—*Lamb v. Lamb,* 126 Va. 256, 101 S.E. 223.

There were four disinterested witnesses who had known parties for many years who established that husband was hard-working, industrious man and kind and provident husband and father who also testified to wife's incontinency and her willful desertion. This uncontradicted evidence clearly sustained allegations. Quoting from prior case, court indicated that evidence in such case should show all of circumstances immediately preceding separation, i.e., whether departure was secret or open, whether it was accompanied by any threat to remain away or by promises to return and every other pertinent declaration or circumstance. It should also show events immediately succeeding separation, that is, efforts to ascertain new residence of consort as well as any efforts at reconciliation.

1919—*Johnson v. Johnson,* 126 Va. 15, 100 S.E. 822.

Evidence in this clearly showed that wife willfully abandoned husband. She refused to share same bed with him and did eventually leave home to live at her place of business.

1919—*Wright v. Wright,* 125 Va. 526, 99 S.E. 515.

Virginia law provides that divorce from bonds of matrimony may be decreed to party abandoned where either party willfully deserts or abandons other for three years. At any time during this three year period offending party has undoubted right to return to other and if that right is exercised there is no ground for divorce. Insane person, however, is incapable of forming intent either to continue desertion or to seek reconciliation and, as such, insanity during three year period is bar to action.

1919—*McCormick v. McCormick,* 123 Va. 778, 97 S.E. 305.

Wife sued husband on grounds of cruelty, desertion and incurable impotency. Husband filed answer denying such and asked that answer be treated as cross-bill on grounds of desertion. Husband's claim for desertion was granted and was upheld on appeal without any further comment on evidence.

1917—*Good v. Good,* 122 Va. 30, 94 S.E. 176.

Wife awarded divorce for desertion from bed and board where unimpeached evidence showed that defendant abandoned wife without sufficient cause, telling her that he was going away and did not want to have anything more to do with her and that only reason given for deserting wife was that she had contracted account in neighborhood for food and clothing. After desertion, husband lived in same county with wife but made no attempt to communicate with her.

1917—*Walker v. Walker,* 120 Va. 410, 91 S.E. 180.

Evidence in this case was that wife left of her own accord, that her husband gave her no cause to leave, that she just got tired and decided to leave. Desertion, in order to justify decree of absolute divorce, must be willful. Evidence should show all of circumstances immediately preceding separation, such as whether departure was secret or open, whether it was accompanied by any threat to remain away or by promises to return and every other pertinent declaration or circumstance to enable court to determine whether or not desertion was willful. It should also show events immediately succeeding separation, such as efforts to ascertain new place of residence of consort as well as efforts at reconciliation. Evidence in this case was equally consistent with separation by mutual consent or due to fault of either of parties as it was with willful desertion. Divorce was denied.

1916—*Tutwiler v. Tutwiler,* 118 Va. 724, 88 S.E. 86.

It was duty of husband when his wife left him, although she may not have been forced to leave as she claims, to thereafter seek reconciliation and to invite her return. When she asked permission to return and permission was not granted, he thereupon deserted her.

1916—*Kelly v. Kelly,* 118 Va. 376, 87 S.E. 567.

Wife filed petition in Massachusetts in court of competent jurisdiction for separate maintenance. Decree entered granting wife's petition. Husband thereafter files for divorce on grounds of desertion in Virginia. Under law of Massachusetts, decree, while it remains in force, is bar to proceedings by husband for divorce on ground of desertion. Benefit of that decree, when relied upon, is not waived by fact that wife defended on merits husband's suit for desertion. Where alleged desertion rests upon original separation, decree is necessarily conclusive. In this case, there were attempts at reconciliation by husband. Court, however, found that was not adequate evidence of subsequent desertion by wife.

1916—*Craig v. Craig,* 118 Va. 284, 87 S.E. 727.

Separation of husband from his wife during pendency of suit by him for divorce does not constitute desertion. If there was consummated act of desertion by him before he instituted suit, wife may prove this in her suit for desertion and her right to relief will not be suspended due to fact that after desertion he has filed his own suit for divorce.

1915—*Johnson v. Johnson,* 117 Va. 504, 85 S.E. 475.

Uncontradicted evidence showed that without adequate cause husband abandoned wife for more than three years with declared purpose of not returning to her and that during that period of time he did not cohabit with her, had no communication with her and made no effort to resume relations with her and contributed nothing to her support. Divorce awarded on those grounds.

1911—*Lee v. Lee,* 112 Va. 719, 72 S.E.2d 689.

Uncontradicted evidence showed that defendant abandoned husband and declared her purpose never to return. Husband entitled to divorce on grounds of desertion.

(3) Marital Home — Choice of.

1970—*Carneal v. Carneal,* 211 Va. 162, 176 S.E.2d 305.

Family home was sold so as to prevent foreclosure, and husband rented apartment for family. Wife instead rented single family residence and moved there with children. Since husband was not guilty of cruelty or constructive desertion, it was held that wife left without justification due to her refusal to move into apartment and therefore is guilty of desertion.

1966—*Lawyer v. Lawyer,* 207 Va. 260, 148 S.E.2d 816.

After retirement from military, husband and wife moved to Richmond where they stayed with his aunt and had free use of first floor of house but slept in room in basement. Both parties found work in Richmond. Wife demanded that they move, and they began looking for house. However, she would not agree to purchase of any house that he could afford and would not contribute to purchase type she wanted, even though she was working. She thereafter left home and took separate quarters, saying that she would not return. Her testimony as to abuse by husband was vague and was uncorroborated, although there was one instance of where he allegedly pushed her. It was held that she was not entitled to divorce on grounds of cruelty. He was entitled to divorce on grounds of desertion.

1961—*Martin v. Martin,* 202 Va. 769, 120 S.E.2d 471.

Wife wished to move to Florida while her husband preferred to remain at their home in Virginia. She left after argument without saying where she was going and took family car and drove to Florida with most of her personal belongings and established herself as resident and citizen of that State. Husband wrote to her affectionately but she never expressed any desire to return. This established adequate corroboration to support finding of desertion. Husband had right to select place of abode and it was duty of wife to acquiesce provided that decision of husband was not unreasonable, arbitrary or unjust and not used as means of provoking dissolution of marriage.

1959—*Canavos v. Canavos,* 200 Va. 861, 108 S.E.2d 359.

Parties were married in 1924 in Greece. Shortly after marriage, husband left for United States where he had business and from then until 1929 he lived alone in U.S., visiting his wife on occasion in Greece. For four years, entire family lived in Virginia but in 1933 husband built home in Greece and took his family there. He last returned from Greece in 1938. He claimed that wife deserted him in 1938 by refusing to return to U.S. with him. Corroborated testimony from wife was that husband would not let her live with him and would not support her or their children when she came to this country. Court incorrectly granted divorce to husband. Divorce should have been granted to wife on grounds of desertion. Although wife who refuses to accompany her husband upon his change of residence for business reasons is guilty of desertion, that rule was not applicable in this case.

1955—*Nash v. Nash,* 197 Va. 465, 89 S.E.2d 917.

Wife, with tacit consent of her husband, lived with her mother while husband lived at his place of work and visited her every other weekend and contributed to her support. Visits ceased in 1952, after disagreement, but he left her with unsigned checks. He continued to express his willingness to furnish home for her at his place of work. She refused. Husband has right to select place of marital abode. No desertion proved by wife. Husband did not press his crossbill on appeal although court did indicate that there was no evidence tending to indicate that wife was justified in refusing to live with husband.

1952—*Graves v. Graves,* 193 Va. 659, 70 S.E.2d 339.

If husband changes his place of abode and wife, without legal excuse, refuses to live there with him, such constitutes desertion. Husband has right to select place of abode and wife must acquiesce provided choice is not unreasonable, arbitrary and unjust and not used as means of procuring dissolution of marriage.

1929—*Robinette v. Robinette,* 153 Va. 342, 149 S.E. 493.

> Husband has right to select place of residence, provided wife not subjected to interference and indignities. Court erred in instructing husband to change residence.

1915—*Steckel v. Steckel,* 118 Va. 198, 86 S.E. 833.

> Domicile of husband is ordinarily that of wife also. Where husband abandons wife and rids himself of marital obligation, giving wife neither necessaries nor comforts suitable to their condition and relinquishes his marital control and protection, then he loses power and authority which alone makes his domicile hers. She may then select her own domicile.

1913—*Devers v. Devers,* 115 Va. 517, 79 S.E. 1048.

> Husband sues wife for desertion. He seems never to have made any provision for home for her nor to have taken care of her and when she left they parted as friends and she went with his consent. Since that time, he has made no effort to reconcile with her. It is his duty to provide home and his duty to invite her to return and share it with him. Husband was denied divorce.

(E) No Fault.

See Va. Code § 20-91 as to no fault grounds for divorce. Plea of res judicata or of recrimination shall not be bar to either party obtaining divorce on this ground, nor shall it be bar that either party has been adjudged insane. Decree of divorce on this ground shall in no way lessen any obligation any party may otherwise have to support spouse unless such party shall prove that there exists in favor of such party some other ground of divorce under this section or Section 20-95.

1983—*Thomasson v. Thomasson,* 225 Va. 394, 302 S.E.2d 63.

> No fault divorce decree is no bar to spousal support for either party unless there exist in favor of opposite party some other ground of divorce. Inability of wife to prove allegations of her cross-bill for desertion does not amount to marital fault and does not relieve husband's obligation to support wife.

1980—*McCausey v. McCausey,* 221 Va. 500, 272 S.E.2d 36.

> No alimony shall be awarded against either party if there exist in his or her favor, ground of divorce. In this case no fault divorce was granted with court having determined that neither party was entitled to divorce on fault grounds. As such, court should have considered issue of alimony.

1978—*Moore v. Moore,* 218 Va. 790, 240 S.E.2d 535.

> Under no fault statute husband has not applied for divorce when in fact he is not moving party asking for divorce either in original complaint or cross bill.

1975—*Robertson v. Robertson,* 215 Va. 425, 211 S.E.2d 41.

> Court is not required to grant no fault divorce to exclusion of all other proven grounds. It was not error to grant wife divorce on grounds of

desertion and adultery when husband had filed cross bill for divorce on grounds of two year separation.

1975—*Hooker v. Hooker,* 215 Va. 415, 211 S.E.2d 34.
In no fault case, there must be proof of intention on part of at least one party to permanently discontinue marital cohabitation, followed by physical separation for statutory period.

1972—*Young v. Young,* 212 Va. 761, 188 S.E.2d 200.
Husband sued wife alleging desertion. Court held that husband had not proved desertion. Husband thereafter amended his suit and obtained divorce on grounds of two-year separation. Trial court denied wife alimony. Since court held that wife's fault or misconduct was not sufficient to entitle husband to divorce and decree entered was not predicated on wife's fault or misconduct, it was error to deny wife alimony.

1965—*Davis v. Davis,* 206 Va. 381, 143 S.E.2d 835.
Husband's testimony in no-fault proceeding was supported by wife and also corroborated. Trial court erred in holding that this evidence was not sufficient.

1965—*Hagen v. Hagen,* 205 Va. 791, 139 S.E.2d 821.
Wife was granted separate maintenance by decree which dismissed her husband's cross-bill for divorce on grounds of desertion. After passage of no-fault statute, husband was awarded final decree of divorce on grounds of three-year separation. Supreme court indicated that judgment as to prior action was not res judicata as to no-fault action since second action was based on different claim or demand.

1965—*Canavos v. Canavos,* 205 Va. 744, 139 S.E.2d 825.
Party may be awarded divorce on no-fault grounds after statutory separation period regardless of fault.

§ 2-5. Divorce — Jurisdiction.

(A) Personal.

See Va. Code § 8.01-328.1 (longarm statute) as to court exercising personal jurisdiction over person as to cause of action arising from various contacts with this State in context of domestic matters. See also Va. Code § 8.01-329 as to service of process, once jurisdiction has been properly acquired.

1981—*Hosier v. Hosier,* 221 Va. 827, 273 S.E.2d 564.
Trial court found lack of jurisdiction in regards to this divorce action. That decree, however, was not adjudication on merits, and as such, action could be refiled later on when jurisdictional requirements were met.

1941—*McNeir v. McNeir,* 178 Va. 285, 16 S.E.2d 632.
Presumption favors finding of jurisdiction by foreign court until contrary is clearly shown.

Nevada divorce decree sustained since both parties were within jurisdiction of Nevada court.

1934—*Bray v. Landergren,* 161 Va. 699, 172 S.E. 252.

Decree for alimony is in personam. *Pennoyer v. Neff* held that personal judgment cannot be rendered against non-resident, present only by substituted service. However, where husband has property within State and that property is seized at commencement of proceeding and husband has opportunity to be heard, then court can properly enforce alimony decree.

1939—*Bailey v. Bailey,* 172 Va. 18, 200 S.E. 622.

Where original process in divorce action is served on defendant outside of State court is without jurisdiction to enter decree against defendant for payment of money, since such decree is in personam.

1927—*Dry v. Rice,* 147 Va. 331, 137 S.E. 473.

Determination by foreign court that it had jurisdiction to award divorce cannot be ignored except upon satisfactory evidence to contrary. Evidence must be of most satisfactory and convincing kind. In this case attack was barred by laches.

(B) Subject Matter.

See Va. Code § 20-96 indicating that circuit court on chancery side shall have jurisdiction for suits for annulment, affirmation of marriage or for divorce. Suit shall be brought in county in which parties last cohabited or at option of plaintiff in county in which defendant resides and in cases proceeding under order of publication then you may also be in county or city where plaintiff resides.

See Va. Code § 20-97 indicating that for purposes of this section only, upon separation of husband and wife, wife may establish her own and separate domicile though separation may have been caused under such circumstances as would not entitle wife to divorce or annulment.

See Va. Code § 20-97 indicating that no suit for annulment or divorce shall be maintainable unless one of parties is domiciled in and has been actual bona fide resident of this State for at least six months prior to commencement of suit. Military person who has been stationed in this State and has lived with his or her spouse for period of six months or more in this State preceding separation and such person or spouse continues to live in this State until and at time suit for divorce is commenced then such person and his or her spouse shall be presumed to be domiciled and to have been bona fide resident of this State during such period of time.

1954—*Westfall v. Westfall,* 196 Va. 97, 82 S.E.2d 487.

Circuit Court of Arlington, which first took jurisdiction of matter, had priority over Fairfax Circuit Court, and right to conclude that cause of action.

1952—*Evans v. Asphalt Road & Materials Co.,* 194 Va. 165, 72 S.E.2d 321.

Person may move from one State to another for purpose of procuring divorce provided removal is coupled with intention of acquiring bona fide residence in that State. Fact of domicile and not motive is controlling question. Domicile of one party to divorce creates adequate relationship with State to justify its exercise of power over marital relation. Each State has exclusive control over marital status of those domiciled within its borders. In divorce proceedings, each State may determine status of party domiciled therein and such determination is entitled to full faith and credit.

1943—*White v. White,* 181 Va. 162, 24 S.E.2d 448.
Power to grant divorces in Virginia is purely statutory. In this respect, courts have no power except such as is conferred upon them. Va. Code § 5105 provides that suit shall be brought in county in which parties last cohabited or at option of plaintiff in county in which defendant resides if resident of this State. If that jurisdictional requirement is not met, then decree for divorce is void.

1942—*McFarland v. McFarland,* 179 Va. 418, 19 S.E.2d 77.
Test for determining change of domicile does not include motive for change. Questions are: (1) Was there actual change (2) Is there absence of intention to move elsewhere. Every presumption will be recognized in favor of jurisdiction found by foreign court. In this case, Virginia court denied husband divorce. He moved to North Carolina. Evidence showed he became bona fide resident of North Carolina. That state had jurisdiction to award divorce, but Virginia decree was res judicata.

1942—*Howe v. Howe,* 179 Va. 111, 18 S.E.2d 294.
Residence or domicile contemplates intention to live there for indefinite period. Living there for definite time to accomplish particular purpose does not satisfy residence. In this case Arkansas court never acquired jurisdiction and therefore decree of divorce was void.

1939—*Hughes v. Hughes,* 173 Va. 293, 4 S.E.2d 402.
Va. Code § 5111 [now § 20-107.1] gives court discretion to enter decree for maintenance and custody where it has determined that neither party is entitled to divorce.

1939—*Bailey v. Bailey,* 172 Va. 18, 200 S.E. 622.
Suit for divorce is proceeding in rem.

1938—*Buchanan v. Buchanan,* 170 Va. 458, 197 S.E. 426.
Consent of parties cannot bestow subject matter jurisdiction on court.

1936—*Watson v. Mose,* 165 Va. 661, 183 S.E. 428.
Divorce court lacked jurisdiction to convey property of husband to wife. Judgment void and subject to attack at any time.

1935—*Hiles v. Hiles,* 164 Va. 131, 178 S.E. 913.
To be resident means to have actual bona fide permanent abode. This does not mean that he must be physically present in Virginia entire time. When person is absent for long period he must show that there was actuality of residence. Mere intent is not enough. Indications of continued residence while person's absent from State are:

    (1) He is supporting wife and child in state.

    (2) Keeps residence ready for his occupancy.

    (3) Preserves his identity as resident.

    (4) Maintains residence as mailing address.

In present case husband was in Navy and was sent to China for three years. He failed to maintain residence in Virginia.

1934—*Bray v. Landergren,* 161 Va. 699, 172 S.E. 252.

Divorce is in nature of in rem proceeding. Under certain circumstances court may render valid decree although it never acquired actual jurisdiction over defendant.

1927—*McCotter v. Carle,* 149 Va. 584, 140 S.E. 670.

In divorce case, court does not acquire jurisdiction upon any equitable grounds, but solely upon statutory grounds. Suit for divorce is proceeding in rem, and does not involve appeal to general jurisdiction of equity.

1925—*Barnes v. American Fertilizer Co.,* 144 Va. 692, 130 S.E. 902.

To extent that court exceeds its subject matter jurisdiction, its decree is null and void. Subject matter jurisdiction arises from State law or from Constitution. It cannot be conferred upon Court by agreement of parties.

1924—*Humphreys v. Strong,* 139 Va. 146, 123 S.E. 554.

Wife may establish separate domicile whenever it is necessary and proper that she should do so. In present case, wife went to Nevada, with intent to acquire bona fide residence in that State. Fact that she went there to obtain divorce does not necessarily mean that she did not acquire bona fide residence. Person may move to another State in order to avail himself of laws of that State, i.e., to obtain divorce. Only requirement being absolute good faith in taking up such residence and intent to make that residence their home.

1923—*Heflinger v. Heflinger,* 136 Va. 289, 118 S.E. 316.

Jurisdiction must always affirmatively appear and objection to jurisdiction of trial court may be made in supreme court for first time.

1922—*Chandler v. Chandler,* 132 Va. 418, 112 S.E. 856.

Domicile of origin, i.e., place of birth, of husband was in Virginia. That fact of itself was prima facie and sufficient evidence to establish fact that his domicile continued unchanged from his birth to time of suit unless abandonment of that domicile by acquisition of new domicile affirmatively appeared from evidence. Person's place of abode for business or pleasure is place of one's residence within meaning of divorce statute, as it is of statutes of limitation, attachment and like. One may be domiciled in one state and be resident of another within meaning of such statutes. Jurisdiction of Virginia courts to grant divorces is declared by statute. Fact that plaintiff has been domiciled in Virginia for at least one year preceding commencement of suit, that plaintiff was domiciled in Virginia at time suit was filed, that defendant was not resident of Virginia and that plaintiff was resident of city or county in which suit was instituted are jurisdictional.

1920—*Towson v. Towson,* 126 Va. 640, 102 S.E. 48.

Domicile and residence are not synonymous. Domicile has larger significance. While man can have but one domicile at time, he may have more than one residence at same time. Wife in this case challenged jurisdiction due to fact that she contended husband had not been domiciled in State for one year before suit was filed. Jury trial was demanded on this issue, and jury resolved issue in favor of husband.

1919—*Blankenship v. Blankenship,* 125 Va. 595, 100 S.E. 538.

In order for court to have jurisdiction in divorce action, one of parties must have been domiciled in State for at least one year preceding commencement of suit. Court, in divorce action, is acting in exercise of special statutory authority. As such, jurisdiction of court will not be presumed but must be made to affirmatively appear from record. Otherwise, any decree court may enter will be void for lack of jurisdiction to enter it.

1915—*Steckel v. Steckel,* 118 Va. 198, 86 S.E. 833.

Domicile is defined by Webster to be residence in particular place accompanied by intention to remain there for unlimited time. Where husband abandons wife and wife in good faith changes her domicile to another State, such as Virginia, and retains it for more than one year, then she may sue for divorce in this State.

1913—*Yates v. Yates,* 115 Va. 678, 79 S.E. 1040.

Husband sued wife for desertion. Court found lack of jurisdiction due to fact that matrimonial domicile was in D.C., wife lived in D.C., he proceeded against wife by order of publication even though he had her precise address, parties never cohabited in this State and evidence does not establish bona fide residence of plaintiff in county where suit was brought.

1891—*Brown v. Butler,* 87 Va. 621, 13 S.E. 71.

Party must reside in new place with intent to remain there in order to acquire new domicile.

1882—*Lindsay v. Murphy,* 76 Va. 428.

Domicile is residence with no present intention of removal. Mere absence, however long, affects no change of domicile. Burden of proof of change of domicile is on one who alleges it. In this case, party who had long resided in Virginia and had family here and homestead here left family here and took some personal property and went to South Carolina and commenced business there for purpose of raising money to pay his debts, with no intention of giving up his domicile in Virginia. Court held that he had in fact maintained his domicile here.

1878—*Long v. Ryan,* 71 Va. 718.

To constitute domicile, there must first be residence and second intent to remain there for unlimited time. Residence is to have permanent abode for time being as distinguished from mere temporary locality of existence.

§ 2-6. Divorce — Types.

(A) Bed and Board.

See Va. Code § 20-95 indicating that divorce from bed and board may be decreed for cruelty, reasonable apprehension of bodily harm or desertion.

See Va. Code § 20-116 indicating that in granting divorce from bed and board court may decree that parties be forever separated and protected in their persons and property. Such decree shall operate upon property thereafter acquired and upon personal rights and legal capacities of parties as decree for divorce from bonds of matrimony, except that neither party shall marry again during life of other.

1947—*Haskins v. Haskins,* 185 Va. 1001, 41 S.E.2d 25.

In reality, there are only two grounds for divorce a mensa — desertion and cruelty because cruelty and reasonable apprehension of bodily harm are so closely related. In suit based on either ground, bill must allege facts necessary to show cause of action with definiteness and certainty.

1940—*Eaton v. Davis,* 176 Va. 330, 10 S.E.2d 893.

Statute authorizing a mensa divorce is declaration of common law, but divorces a vinculo are wholly creatures of statute.

1937—*Casilear v. Casilear,* 168 Va. 46, 190 S.E. 314.

In divorce a vinculo marriage bond is completely broken. In divorce a mensa parties remain husband and wife although authorized to live separately. In a mensa divorce court is exercising its jurisdiction to regulate rights and duties of parties during continuation of marriage.

1930—*Gloth v. Gloth,* 154 Va. 511, 153 S.E. 879.

A mensa divorce does not sever marital bond; parties are allowed to live separate. Court retains jurisdiction to modify award of alimony.

1917—*Gum v. Gum,* 122 Va. 32, 94 S.E. 177.

Where divorce is from bed and board, decree has no effect on property rights of parties unless otherwise provided or unless separation is made perpetual, and, if latter is so, then it operates like divorce from bonds of matrimony in respect to after acquired property, barring claim of dower or curtesy as to such property.

1892—*Marshall v. Baynes,* 88 Va. 1040, 14 S.E. 978.

During pendency of suit for divorce from bed and board, husband and wife agreed to live separate, each to acquire and hold property free from claims of other and that decree be entered confirming agreement. Afterwards, decree was entered confirming agreement. Court held that decree was in substance divorce from bed and board and operated upon after acquired property and legal rights and capacities of parties as decree from bonds of matrimony, except that neither party could remarry.

(B) Bonds of Matrimony.

See Va. Code § 20-91 indicating that divorce from bonds of matrimony may be decreed for adultery, felony conviction in certain instances, cruelty, causing reasonable apprehension of bodily harm, desertion and on no fault grounds for having lived separate and apart.

See Va. Code § 20-117 indicating that granting of divorce from bed and board shall not be bar to either party obtaining divorce from bonds of matrimony unless cause for absolute divorce was existing and known to party applying for divorce from bonds of matrimony before decree of divorce from bed and board was entered.

See Va. Code § 20-121 as to merger of decree for divorce from bed and board with decree for divorce from bonds of matrimony.

1975—*Robertson v. Robertson,* 215 Va. 425, 211 S.E.2d 41.
> There is no error to award divorce upon dual grounds of desertion and adultery.

1932—*Craddock Administrator v. Craddock Administrator,* 158 Va. 58, 163 S.E. 387.
> Divorce a vinculo carries with it extinguishment of wife's marital rights in property of husband.

§ 2-7. Divorce — Defenses.

(A) Collusion.

1925—*Scott v. Scott,* 142 Va. 31, 128 S.E. 599.
> Decree will not be set aside at suit of party guilty of fraud in obtaining it or consenting thereto. Decree obtained by collusion cannot be attacked by either party.

1920—*Dinsmore v. Dinsmore,* 128 Va. 403, 104 S.E. 785.
> Court should consider testimony in uncontested divorce proceeding with most scrupulous care and, if collusion or consent appear, directly or indirectly, should deny relief sought.

(B) Condonation.

See Va. Code § 20-94 indicating that in actions for adultery, sodomy or buggery divorce shall not be granted if it appears that parties voluntarily cohabited after knowledge of such fact or that it occurred more than five years before institution of suit or that it was committed by procurement or connivance of party alleging such act.

1983—*Vardell v. Vardell,* 225 Va. 351, 302 S.E.2d 41.
> One prosecuting suit for any form of divorce who cohabits with defendant usually condones offense or affirms marriage sought to be terminated.

1975—*McIlwain v. McIlwain,* 215 Va. 633, 212 S.E.2d 284.
> Wife set forth proof of cruelty. Acts of cruelty were followed by reconciliation wherein wife forgave her husband and condoned act thereby

eliminating it as ground for divorce unless it was revived by subsequent cruel conduct. As there was no testimony corroborating any alleged continuation of cruel conduct this incident cannot be revived and relied on as basis for divorce.

1970—*Carneal v. Carneal,* 211 Va. 162, 176 S.E.2d 305.

Alleged acts of cruelty before reconciliation will not be considered as ground for subsequent separation unless those prior acts of cruelty are revived by subsequent acts of cruelty.

1967—*Wimbrow v. Wimbrow,* 208 Va. 141, 156 S.E.2d 598.

New incident of beating revived right to complain of previous beating which had been condoned. In this case, new incident of beating was corroborated.

1967—*Gibson v. Gibson,* 207 Va. 821, 153 S.E.2d 189.

Wherever it is attempted to prove that during pendency of divorce action there has been sexual relations, then proof of such cohabitation and condonation rests upon moving party, under principle that he who alleges fraud has burden of proving it by evidence which is clear and convincing.

1965—*Huddle v. Huddle,* 206 Va. 535, 145 S.E.2d 167.

Wife confessed to her husband that she had committed adultery whereupon he took her to her father's home and also had separation agreement prepared by attorney. Four days later, however, couple resumed marital relations but after two weeks he left her because of his suspicions that she was pregnant by another man. Under these facts, husband condoned wife's offense and therefore his claim for adultery was barred. Court also correctly held that he had deserted her thereafter.

1965—*McKee v. McKee,* 206 Va. 527, 145 S.E.2d 163.

Even where condonation is not raised as affirmative defense, court of its own motion should deny divorce where it appears that injured party has condoned acts complained of. Voluntary cohabitation after knowledge of spouse's misconduct bars divorce to condoning party. But where plaintiff, when he forgives defendant, knows of one marital offense but not of others, condonation does not bar action based on others. Repetition revives right to complain of known offense. Condoned adultery is revived where guilty party has resumed his association with his former paramour even without strict proof of actual repetition of offense.

1962—*Ware v. Ware,* 203 Va. 189, 123 S.E.2d 357.

Wife alleged that by husband resuming marital relations with her he condoned her offenses and thereby led her to believe that it was unnecessary for her to appear and make defense in this suit. Although there was some evidence of cohabitation between parties, court found that husband did not resume marital relations with wife and as such there was no condonation.

1959—*Brooks v. Brooks,* 200 Va. 530, 106 S.E.2d 611.

In this case, court noted that even if wife was guilty of certain fault these actions were condoned by husband by cohabiting with her thereafter.

1957—*Baytop v. Baytop,* 199 Va. 388, 100 S.E.2d 14.

Wife, in consenting to sexual relations with her husband to pacify him, did not condone his long continued course of mistreatment and cruelty. This conclusion is fortified by fact that next morning husband did nothing to indicate desire to have her remain or that he had any intention of treating her better in future than he had in past.

1948—*Williams v. Williams,* 188 Va. 543, 50 S.E.2d 277.

Condonation of matrimonial offenses may defeat suit based on such offenses. Right to separate maintenance ceases on resumption of cohabitation or other condonation of offense giving rise to allowance. Condonation is conditional and repetition of conduct complained of will revive condoned offense.

1945—*Tarr v. Tarr,* 184 Va. 443, 35 S.E.2d 401.

Voluntary cohabitation of parties after knowledge of adultery charged is conclusive defense. Term "cohabit" in this sense means to have sexual relations. Single voluntary act of sexual intercourse is sufficient to constitute condonation. This rule is applied more stringently against husband than it is against wife. Ordinarily, condonation is matter of affirmative defense which must be specially pleaded and proven. In this case, court held that there was duty upon complainant to reveal to court that parties have had sexual intercourse during course of this litigation. Failure to reveal such at time of entry of decree was basis for setting aside decree.

1938—*Rogers v. Rogers,* 170 Va. 417, 196 S.E. 586.

Subsequent to alleged acts of cruelty wife resumed marital relations with husband. Wife condoned acts by voluntarily resuming cohabitation.

1936—*Martin v. Martin,* 166 Va. 109, 184 S.E. 220.

Condonation must be specially pleaded. It is conditional forgiveness to which knowledge is necessary. Repetition of offense revives right to complain of injury forgiven.

1932—*Kirby v. Kirby,* 159 Va. 544, 166 S.E. 484.

Husband failed to establish condonation by wife.

1929—*Williams v. Williams,* 152 Va. 896, 148 S.E. 579.

Divorce action based on cruelty. Testimony of husband as to strained relations with wife showed no condonation. Burden to prove condonation is on party asserting it.

1924—*Harman v. Harman,* 139 Va. 508, 124 S.E. 273.

Cruelty, in this case, was cumulative. It may be condoned and even forgiven for time and up to certain point without any bar in sense or reason to bring it all forward when continuance of it has rendered it no longer condonable. While acts of violence committed in earlier period and which have not prevented wife from living with her husband, cannot be made sole foundation of action of separation, they form subject of investigation and proof with view to determine what is true issue in case, namely whether wife can safely live with husband.

1924—*Elder v. Elder,* 139 Va. 19, 123 S.E. 369.
 Essential elements of condonation are:
  (1) Freedom of consent.
  (2) Knowledge of offense.
  (3) Restoration of marital rights.
 Condonation is remission of offense of which party is aware on condition of being continually afterward treated by other with conjugal kindness. In this case, offer by wife to return upon promise of good treatment did not constitute condonation. After husband's response to that letter, wife wrote back indicating she had changed her mind and stated she was afraid that his treatment would be worse than ever.

1920—*West v. West,* 126 Va. 696, 101 S.E. 876.
 Husband had previous relations with his wife. At time of marriage, she was pregnant, and she alleged that he was father. He claimed that he learned immediately after marriage but that before it was consummated child was not his. Marriage was thereafter consummated by husband with this knowledge and therefore condoned wife's previous conduct. Husband was obliged to pay alimony to wife.

1917—*White v. White,* 121 Va. 244, 92 S.E. 811.
 This affirmative defense must be pleaded and burden of proof is on defendant. Court may, on its own motion, deny divorce on this basis if it appears from record that there has been condonation. Innocence and condonation are thoroughly inconsistent defenses, although they may both be raised in same suit. General rule is that where husband, after he learns of adultery on part of his wife, continues to reside with her, occupying same room and bed, he will be presumed to be continuing his marital cohabitation and such conclusively establishes defense of condonation.

1914—*Johnston v. Johnston,* 116 Va. 678, 82 S.E. 694.
 Supreme court noted that it appears that acts of infidelity, attributed to husband and sought to be proved by certain depositions that were suppressed, were known to wife and occurred long before marital relations between parties were broken off and therefore offenses had been condoned.

1898—*Owens v. Owens,* 96 Va. 191, 31 S.E. 72.
 Condonation is remission by one of married parties of offense known to have been committed by other against marriage, on condition of being continually afterwards treated by other with kindness. While condition remains unbroken, there can be no divorce, but breach of

condition revives original remedy. Prior acts of cruelty may be condoned and even forgiven for time up to certain point without barring right to bring it all forward when continuance of it has rendered it no longer condonable. While acts of violence on part of husband, which have been condoned, cannot be made sole foundation for divorce, they form subject of investigation and proof in order to determine whether wife can with safety continue to live with him.

(C) Connivance.

1942—*Upton v. Ames and Webb,* 179 Va. 219, 18 S.E.2d 290.
Law does not favor agreement in furtherance of divorce. But forebearance by one spouse to bring or prosecute meritorious suit for divorce is valid consideration for promise.

(D) Consent.

1960—*Smith v. Smith,* 202 Va. 104, 116 S.E.2d 110.
Husband was army officer stationed in Puerto Rico. Wife became ill and at his suggestion was taken by her parents to Norfolk. They never lived together again nor did he provide adequate support for her or children or come to see them. Wife filed suit for separate maintenance and he filed cross-bill alleging desertion as of date of their separation. He also filed supplemental bill alleging desertion on date of commissioner's hearing in light of her testimony on that date. Court held there was no desertion prior to institution of suit, only separation by mutual consent. Even if there was desertion by wife after filing of suit, it could not serve as grounds for divorce. When spouse assents to or acquiesces in other's separation from him, he cannot maintain suit for divorce on grounds of desertion. Separation by mutual consent will be presumed to continue by mutual consent until one of parties withdraws consent or offers to resume cohabitation in which case burden is on offering party to prove that offer was made in good faith and was refused without justification.

1959—*Nash v. Nash,* 200 Va. 890, 108 S.E.2d 350.
Wife moved from family home taking furniture and clothing. She said, however, she had no intent to desert husband and that if there was any idea of permanent separation it was by mutual consent. Evidence showed that relationship had deteriorated beyond repair, largely because of wife's difficulties with stepdaughter who lived in home and that she had prepared several separation agreements to which her husband did not consent. Court found that wife deserted. If separation was by mutual consent, there would not have been any willful desertion. Referring to another case, court noted that it is conduct and purpose of deserting spouse and not state of mind of other spouse that determines whether or not there was desertion. There is no requirement that other spouse make offer of reconciliation if in fact he has been deserted.

1954—*Arrington v. Arrington,* 195 Va. 86, 82 S.E.2d 548.

Wife left home by mutual consent and at husband's urging. He rejected her efforts to reconcile. Separation by mutual consent is not desertion.

1944—*Lowdon v. Lowdon,* 183 Va. 78, 31 S.E.2d 271.

Evidence in this case showed that parties had separated by mutual consent which does not constitute desertion.

1934—*Colbert v. Colbert,* 162 Va. 393, 174 S.E.2d 660.

After quarrel wife left husband. Husband agreed to pay wife support money. This agreement did not bar action for desertion.

1926—*Butler v. Butler,* 145 Va. 85, 133 S.E. 756.

Unrevoked agreement for separation, under which parties live apart, precludes divorce due to desertion. It makes no difference whether agreement was made before or after separation. Agreement, in this case, recognizes that parties had agreed to live separate and apart. Husband entered into agreement in order to avoid imprisonment as result of assault and battery prosecution that wife had brought against him. Agreement did adjust property rights of parties and custody. Husband made attempts thereafter to reconcile. This agreement did not preclude desertion claim by husband. One spouse may be guilty of desertion, even if there is separation agreement, if other spouse wants to reconcile and other refuses.

(E) Justification.

1975—*Capps v. Capps,* 216 Va. 382, 219 S.E.2d 898.

While wife was not entitled to divorce on grounds of cruelty husband is not entitled to divorce on grounds of desertion since evidence showed his wife left home without legal fault after husband physically abused her.

1975—*Jones v. Jones,* 216 Va. 161, 217 S.E.2d 800.

Neither wife's admissions nor husband's evidence showed justification for his leaving. Husband had duty of going forward with evidence to show justification unless wife's admissions established such. In this case testimony of many independent witnesses called by husband actually corroborated wife's position that he had left her with intention never to return. Therefore unless separation was with mutual consent, wife was entitled to divorce on grounds of desertion. Husband's claim of mutual consent was supported only by his equivocal testimony which was uncorroborated. Wife granted divorce on grounds of desertion.

1973—*Anthony v. Anthony,* 213 Va. 721, 196 S.E.2d 66.

Record does not support finding that wife did willfully, wrongfully and without just cause desert husband. Wife was only witness to testify as to events that led up to separation. Her testimony indicates that husband's conduct justified her in leaving.

1967—*Hoback v. Hoback,* 208 Va. 432, 158 S.E.2d 113.

Wife's claim of cruelty was not sufficiently proved. Her departure from family home under these circumstances, without proper justification, constituted desertion.

1967—*Wimbrow v. Wimbrow,* 208 Va. 141, 156 S.E.2d 598.

Leaving not justified unless conduct would constitute grounds for divorce. Brutal beating by husband in this case amounted to cruelty and justified wife leaving. General rule is that divorce will not be granted on grounds of cruelty when acts of cruelty complained of were provoked by misconduct of other spouse. In this case, wife knew or should have known that taking money from husband's wallet would provoke some violent reaction on his part, as indicated by his past behavior. Although this was act of provocation on her part, retaliation by him was totally out of proportion and as such he was guilty of cruelty.

1948—*Williams v. Williams,* 188 Va. 543, 50 S.E.2d 277.

Wife resumed cohabitation with husband thereby condoning his prior conduct. Thereafter she left home. Prior acts of husband did not justify wife's departure since she had condoned these acts.

1939—*Hendry v. Hendry,* 172 Va. 368, 1 S.E.2d 340.

One spouse not justified in leaving other unless conduct of wrongdoer is basis for divorce action. Husband was cold, indifferent and at times unkind. Wife was same. This did not justify wife leaving. Husband entitled to divorce a mensa due to desertion.

1936—*Martin v. Martin,* 166 Va. 109, 184 S.E. 220.

If husband was guilty of adultery, wife had right to leave him.

1927—*Byerly v. Byerly,* 149 Va. 53, 140 S.E. 121.

Wife was practically driven from house which was shared with parents of husband. She made repeated attempts to return and was repulsed. Desertion established.

1920—*Towson v. Towson,* 126 Va. 640, 102 S.E. 48.

Desertion by one party or other can only be justified by showing such conduct on part of deserted party as would entitle other to divorce a mensa, and nothing short of this will justify willful desertion or continuance of it.

1908—*Crounse v. Crounse,* 108 Va. 108, 60 S.E. 627.

Desertion is breach of matrimonial duty and consists of actual breaking off of matrimonial cohabitation coupled with intent to desert in mind of offender. Desertion by one consort or other can only be justified by showing such conduct on part of deserted party as would entitle other to divorce a mensa. Citing from another case, court stated that fact that husband is rude and dictatorial in his speech to his wife, exacting in his demands upon her and sometimes unkind and negligent in his treatment of her, even when she is sick is no legal grounds for leaving.

(F) Laches.

1976—*Richardson v. Moore,* 217 Va. 422, 229 S.E.2d 864.
Laches is equitable defense, but even court of equity cannot disregard provisions of lawful decree. In this case husband had been delinquent for 25 years in payment of court ordered alimony. Laches did not bar wife's claim for arrearage.

1963—*Bartsch v. Bartsch,* 204 Va. 462, 132 S.E.2d 416.
Husband obtained final decree of divorce in Reno. Wife was personally served but made no appearance. It was not until 11 years later that she took any action to attack Nevada decree, and that suit she dismissed voluntarily and continued to receive alimony payments. Twenty-one years after entry of that decree, when her ex-husband died, she filed present suit to be declared lawful widow since Nevada court lacked jurisdiction. Court held that she was barred by laches because of her unreasonable delay, death of her ex-husband who would have been material witness and injury which would result to second wife if relief should be granted.

1945—*Tarr v. Tarr,* 184 Va. 443, 35 S.E.2d 401.
Rule which requires defrauded party to act promptly for protection of his rights is peculiarly applicable to suits for divorce. In this case, three-month delay was held not to be excessive.

1942—*Howe v. Howe,* 179 Va. 111, 18 S.E.2d 294.
Divorce decree in this case was void. Laches defense does not apply.

1941—*McNeir v. McNeir,* 178 Va. 285, 16 S.E.2d 632.
Laches is neglect or omission to assert right for unreasonable and unexplained length of time under circumstances prejudicial to adverse party. Second marriage is evidence of prejudice.

1941—*Pretlow v. Pretlow,* 177 Va. 524, 14 S.E.2d 381.
He who discovers fraud imbedded in his contract must, upon its discovery and without delay, seek rescission if he is to prevail. Prejudicial delay must be shown before defense can be successfully maintained.

1936—*Watson v. Mose,* 165 Va. 661, 183 S.E. 428.
No laches where suit was brought promptly upon discovery of facts in case.

1934—*Counts v. Counts,* 161 Va. 768, 172 S.E. 248.
Laches implies knowledge or means of knowing one's rights and therefore cannot be imputed to one of unsound mind.

1934—*Hodnett v. Hodnett,* 163 Va. 644, 177 S.E. 106.
Wife alleged that husband procured divorce by fraud. Subsequent to divorce husband remarried. Wife's claim is barred by laches since she waited until after husband remarried before taking any action. Wife had known about divorce for almost three years.

1932—*Taylor v. Taylor,* 159 Va. 338, 165 S.E. 414.

> Laches may apply where application is made to set aside divorce decree if there is delay in face of knowledge of person's rights or negligence in acquiring such knowledge. This does not apply to insane.

1927—*Dry v. Rice,* 147 Va. 331, 137 S.E. 473.

> Divorce granted September 20, 1922. Two-and-one-half years later husband attacked decree on grounds of court lacking jurisdiction. Wife had remarried in interim. Claim barred by laches. Delay attended by loss of material evidence, death of witnesses, change of relation of parties which cannot be restored or by injury to innocent third person which cannot be compensated in damages, may constitute laches.

(G) Insanity.

See Va. Code § 20-93 indicating that insanity of guilty party after commencement of desertion is no defense.

1969—*Crittenden v. Crittenden,* 210 Va. 76, 168 S.E.2d 115.

> Husband seeks divorce on grounds of two-year separation from wife who had been adjudged mentally incompetent and was committed to institution. Court held that separation contemplated must be of parties sufficiently competent to be conscious of fact that separation has occurred. Wife in this case was held incapable as matter of law of being conscious that separation has occurred and as such divorce was denied.

1963—*Pollard v. Pollard,* 204 Va. 316, 130 S.E.2d 425.

> Evidence showed desertion without cause by wife on January 28, 1947. She was adjudicated insane on February 26, 1947. She had given no indication of insanity prior to date of desertion. Insanity so occurring is no defense.

1959—*Ford v. Ford,* 200 Va. 674, 107 S.E.2d 397.

> Husband sued wife for constructive desertion. Defense asserted by wife was insanity. If she was insane, she could not have been guilty of constructive, willful desertion. Burden of proof of insanity is upon wife. She is presumed sane until contrary is made to appear. In this case, her family physician testified that she was sane. Testimony of family physician is entitled to great weight because of his opportunity to make observations and to form opinions.

1932—*Taylor v. Taylor,* 159 Va. 338, 165 S.E. 414.

> Insanity of defendant at time of judgment is not sufficient cause to vacate judgment, although judgment in some instances may be voidable if there was fraud involved.

1929—*Fidelity & Deposit Co. v. Anderson,* 155 Va. 535, 150 S.E. 413.

> Statute under which committee was appointed did not require notice to insane person. Statute is not unconstitutional. Order of appointment made by court of general jurisdiction could not be collaterally assailed.

1919—*Wright v. Wright,* 125 Va. 526, 99 S.E. 515.

> Insanity of defendant is no bar to suit for desertion where cause of action accrued before insanity began. However, where insanity, as in this case, began within three months after alleged desertion, then insanity of defendant is bar to suit, since requisite intent has not existed for statutory period.

(H) Reconciliation.

See Cohabitation § 1-3.

See Va. Code § 20-102 indicating that it shall not be necessary in any suit for divorce on ground of desertion to allege or prove offer of reconciliation.

See Va. Code § 20-120 indicating that decree of divorce from bed and board may at any time thereafter, upon joint application of parties and production by them of satisfactory evidence of their reconciliation, be revoked by same court which made it and under such regulations and restrictions as court may impose.

1967—*Hoback v. Hoback,* 208 Va. 432, 158 S.E.2d 113.

> Case remanded with direction to enter divorce from bonds of matrimony if no reconciliation or probability of such.

1956—*Bundy v. Bundy,* 197 Va. 795, 91 S.E.2d 412.

> Wife denied divorce on grounds that she expressly stated she did not want divorce but wanted to resume living with her husband.

1954—*Anderson v. Anderson,* 196 Va. 26, 82 S.E.2d 562.

> Where husband and wife cohabited after entry of temporary decree, court held that there as no showing of no reconciliation and therefore merger into final decree was denied.

1952—*Prindes v. Prindes,* 193 Va. 463, 69 S.E.2d 332.

> Attitudes of husband towards reconciliation as compared with that of wife, who had borne him nine children, reflects little credit on his character and judgment.

1939—*Hendry v. Hendry,* 172 Va. 368, 1 S.E.2d 340.

> Supreme court talks of duty of husband to make good faith attempt to reconcile with wife who has left him.

1937—*Toler v. Toler,* 168 Va. 302, 191 S.E. 638.

> Not having established her charge of cruelty, wife was not justified in refusing to reconcile.

1934—*Gentry v. Gentry,* 161 Va. 786, 172 S.E. 157.

> Good faith attempt at reconciliation must be made prior to filing suit unless such is excused. Fact that husband had seen wife kissing and hugging another man did not excuse him from attempting reconciliation.

1934—*Colbert v. Colbert,* 162 Va. 393, 174 S.E. 660.

> Actions of wife excused husband for not having sought reconciliation prior to filing for divorce. Action of wife showed clearly that she was in love with another man. Good pleading requires that allegation of offer of reconciliation. Proof of such must be established.

1932—*Inman v. Inman,* 158 Va. 597, 164 S.E. 383.

Decree for divorce not justified without proof of offer of reconciliation or proof of facts excusing such offer. Where such facts exist they must be pled and proven. Offer of reconciliation must be made before suit is filed.

1932—*Sussman v. Sussman,* 158 Va. 382, 163 S.E. 69.

Good pleading requires allegation of offer of reconciliation. Such offer, made before filing suit, must be proved.

1926—*Markley v. Markley,* 145 Va. 596, 134 S.E. 536.

Before divorce will be granted on grounds of desertion, injured party must have, before institution of suit, sought good faith reconciliation.

1926—*Duff v. Duff,* 145 Va. 526, 134 S.E. 555.

This case involved second desertion by wife within two months. She returned after first desertion due to husband's request. She remained for approximately two weeks and then deserted second time, indicating that she would never return again. There is no further duty on part of husband to seek reconciliation. Letters to husband from wife's father and doctor did not constitute offer of reconciliation that would bar husband's right to divorce. If wife, after having deserted, makes sincere and good faith offer to return, free from any improper qualifications or conditions and husband refuses, then this constitutes desertion on his part. Offer of reconciliation after final decree is rendered comes too late.

1916—*Tutwiler v. Tutwiler,* 118 Va. 724, 88 S.E. 86.

It was duty of husband, when wife left him, although she may not have been forced to leave, to seek reconciliation and to invite her return. When she asked permission to return and permission was not granted, he thereupon deserted her. Overtures at reconciliation made after rendition of decree for divorce from bed and board come too late to have any effect upon correctness of decree but other relief may be provided.

1913—*Devers v. Devers,* 115 Va. 517, 79 S.E. 1048.

It is duty of husband to provide home for wife, however humble, and, in this instance, to invite her to return to that home and share it with her. Well-being of society demands that husbands and wives shall in good faith endeavor to reconcile. It is not province of court to grant relief to plaintiff whose misconduct has contributed to bringing about condition of which he complains in this case, i.e., desertion of wife. In this case, husband was denied divorce on grounds of desertion.

1911—*Haynor v. Haynor,* 112 Va. 123, 70 S.E. 531.

In this case, parties had lived together for over 20 years. It appears that their estrangement is not irreconcilable. It is therefore duty of both to attempt reconciliation.

(I) Recrimination.

1967—*Wimbrow v. Wimbrow,* 208 Va. 141, 156 S.E.2d 598.

Wife in this case was justified in leaving home due to cruelty of husband and was entitled to divorce unless her actions before that day constituted sufficient grounds for awarding divorce to husband. If her actions constituted sufficient grounds, rule of recrimination would bar granting of divorce to her.

1960—*Todd v. Todd,* 202 Va. 133, 115 S.E.2d 905.

Principle of recrimination is applicable in divorce cases.

1956—*Bundy v. Bundy,* 197 Va. 795, 91 S.E.2d 412.

Husband sued on grounds of cruelty. Divorce denied since he was found to have deserted.

1948—*Haskins v. Haskins,* 188 Va. 525, 50 S.E.2d 437.

Ground merely justifying divorce from bed and board does not constitute defense by way of recrimination to suit based upon ground justifying absolute divorce. State statute relied on. *Kirn v. Kirn* overruled.

1930—*Gloth v. Gloth,* 154 Va. 511, 153 S.E. 879.

Decree of divorce a mensa for desertion is bar to divorce action by other spouse for adultery committed after first decree.

1924—*Kirn v. Kirn,* 138 Va. 132, 120 S.E. 850.

Recrimination is defense that applicant has himself done what is grounds for divorce, either from bed and board or from bonds of matrimony. It bars suit founded on whatever cause, whether defendant is guilty or not. In present case, wife sued husband on grounds of desertion and cruelty and he filed cross-bill alleging desertion and adultery. Trial court found that charges in bill and cross-bill had been established and therefore divorce was denied as to both.

CHILDREN

§ 3-1. Adoption.

See Va. Code § 63.1-220 as to adoption procedures and effect of adoption.

1983—*Jolliff v. Crabtree,* 224 Va. 654, 299 S.E.2d 358.

> In this case parents were divorced in Indiana and thereafter wife had custody of child. Both parents lived rather migratory life and both remarried after divorce. Wife's new husband sought to adopt child. Burden of proof is on adoptive parent to establish by evidence that continuance of relationship between natural parent objecting to adoption and child would be detrimental to child's welfare. In this case, there was no evidence that continuation or broadening of legal affiliation between natural father and child would be detrimental to child. Evidence did indicate that prior to hearing on adoption, father had not seen his son for eight years and had not contributed financially to his support. He, however, was not solely responsible for this state of affairs since wife had abruptly terminated his visitation unilaterally when she took child from Indiana and concealed his whereabouts from father. Petition for adoption was dismissed.

1983—*Shortridge v. Deel,* 224 Va. 589, 299 S.E.2d 500.

> Findings made in adoption proceeding that natural parents withheld their consent to adoption contrary to best interest of child was not

appealable, since this was one of several determinations necessary to entry of order of adoption, and as such, was not final order.

1981—*Doe v. Doe,* 222 Va. 736, 284 S.E.2d 799.

Second wife and father attempted to adopt natural son. Natural mother opposed adoption. Natural mother was lesbian and admitted maintaining lesbian relationship with another woman. While welfare of child is of paramount concern in adoption cases, rights of natural parent will be maintained if at all consistent with child's best interest. Adopting parent must establish continuance of relationship would be detrimental to child's welfare. There was no evidence in this case introduced to establish unfitness of natural mother as parent. Evidence in this case did not support conclusion that lesbian relationship of mother would have detrimental affect on child, and as such, adoption was denied. Lifestyle of mother was proper factor to be considered in determining her fitness, but it does not determine present case since there was clear and convincing evidence that mother in every other respect was fit parent.

1981—*Cunningham v. Gray,* 221 Va. 792, 273 S.E.2d 562.

When step-father seeks to adopt child over objection of natural father, welfare of child is paramount consideration, but rights of natural parent will be maintained if at all consistent with child's best interest. Adoptive parent must show continuance of relationship between natural father and child would be detrimental to child's welfare. In this case, burden of proof was not met even though evidence was that father had not seen child in considerable period of time, that he had rather poor employment record, had been convicted of minor crime, and that his actions in general had been in derogation of his parental duties. Court held that this conduct has not amounted to permanent forfeiture of his parental rights.

1979—*Ward v. Faw,* 219 Va. 1120, 253 S.E.2d 658.

Step-father sought to adopt his wife's child and change child's name. Natural father objected and was allowed to intervene. Trial court approved adoption, holding that consent of natural father was withheld contrary to child's best interest. Case was reversed. When divorced natural parent objects to petition by step-parent for adoption, step-parent must show that continuance of child/parent relationship to natural parent would be detrimental to child's welfare, assuming there is no question of fitness of natural parent and natural parent has not, by conduct or previous legal action, lost his rights to child. Burden in this case is on step-parent to establish that continuance of relationship between father and child would be detrimental to child's welfare. There was no evidence that future visitation rights would be experiment with welfare of child which would have devastating effects upon him.

1976—*Watson v. Shepard,* 217 Va. 538, 229 S.E.2d 897.

In this case it was error to approve adoption by aunt and uncle while they were in process of getting divorce. Irrevocable step of terminating natural parents' rights should not be taken at time when adoptive parents are separated and their marital problems are unsettled.

1976—*Harry v. Fisher,* 216 Va. 530, 221 S.E.2d 118.
When execution of valid consent for adoption is proved, natural parent will be denied custody of child provided adoptive parents establish that child's best interest will be served if it remains in their custody. In this case natural mother claimed that consent was executed under duress. Trial court found to contrary. Supreme court ruled that child should stay with adoptive parents.

1974—*Szemler v. Clements,* 214 Va. 639, 202 S.E.2d 880.
After petition for adoption had been filed, natural mother revoked her consent to adoption. This was ineffective to divest court of jurisdiction. However, mother is not precluded from opposing adoption. Presumption in favor of parental custody is rebuttable by proof that code requirements for consent have been met as of date of filing petition. Those code requirements had been met in this case and as such presumption was rebutted. Burden of proof in this case then simply was to show that adoption was in child's best interest. There was no requirement to show that natural parents were unfit. Evidence in this case indicated that child's best interest would be served by awarding custody to adoptive parents. Presumption in favor of natural parents is rebuttable by clear, cogent and convincing proof of either voluntary relinquishment of right to custody or unfitness of parent.

1972—*Malpass v. Morgan,* 213 Va. 393, 192 S.E.2d 794.
In divorce proceeding, mother was awarded custody with father allowed visitation. Thereafter, mother remarried and stepfather sought to adopt child with consent of mother. Father withheld his consent. In this case, there is no question of fitness of father, and he has not by conduct or previous legal action lost his rights to child. As such, it must be shown that continuance of relationship between father and child would be detrimental to child's welfare. Rights of parents may not be lightly severed but are to be respected if at all consonant with best interest of child. That was case here. Mere fact that child's interest would be prompted by adoption by stepfather is not sufficient.

1971—*Dyer v. Howell,* 212 Va. 453, 184 S.E.2d 789.
Father killed mother. He was found not guilty by reason of insanity and confined in mental institution. He was thereafter released as being mentally competent. In interim, custody of his child had been awarded to child's aunt and uncle. They now seek adoption of child. Father's withholding of consent to adoption was held to be contrary to child's best interest and, as such, adoption was allowed.

1962—*Doulgeris v. Bambacus,* 203 Va. 670, 127 S.E.2d 145.
This was suit to determine next of kin and distributees of estate of James Odessett. Doulgeris claimed to be decedent's sister by adoption under Greek law. Court held that she had been adopted under Greek

law but that her status would not be recognized in Virginia, because Greek law was contrary in practice and concept to Virginia's public policy, which in adoption cases establishes welfare of child was controlling consideration whereas under Greek law primary consideration is interest of adoptive father. In this case, adoption was matter of convenience for adoptive parents who were elderly and who needed child for consolation and support. Adoption was held invalid.

1961—*Lowe v. Grasty,* 203 Va. 168, 122 S.E.2d 867.

By order of juvenile court, affirmed by circuit court, department of public welfare was given permanent custody with power to place child in question for adoption, which it did. Order was void because no guardian ad litem was appointed for infant as required by code, since its surviving parent was not present in court. Juvenile court had awarded custody of Mrs. Lowe's infant son to county department of public welfare because she was alcoholic. By later order, affirmed by circuit court, department was given permanent custody with power to place child for adoption, which it did. Mrs. Lowe now challenges this adoption by habeas corpus. Supreme court held that juvenile court lacked power, at date of its order, to empower department to place child for adoption. Therefore, order was void. Order also was void because no guardian ad litem had been appointed as required by code.

1959—*Newton v. Newton,* 201 Va. 1, 109 S.E.2d 105.

In this case, 15-year-old child was opposed to adoption by his sister and her husband. Natural parents also challenged adoption. In light of these factors, court set aside interlocutory order of adoption and returned child to natural parents.

1958—*Newton v. Wilson,* 199 Va. 864, 102 S.E.2d 299.

After entry of interlocutory order, petition was filed for revocation of order on grounds that natural parents had withdrawn their consent and that adoption would not be in child's best interest. Natural parents told investigator that adoptive parents were not morally fit and that child did not wish to be adopted. Court refused to hear this additional evidence from investigator. This was error.

1953—*Harmon v. D'Adamo,* 195 Va. 125, 77 S.E.2d 318.

Natural mother put child up for adoption without consent of natural father. After entry of interlocutory order, natural mother and father married, thereby legitimizing child. In this instance, father's lack of consent is legally sufficient ground for vacating order. Legal adoption exists only by statute there having been no such thing at common law.

1952—*Bidwell v. McSorley,* 194 Va. 135, 72 S.E.2d 245.

Interlocutory order was entered in April of 1951 granting adoption. In October of 1951, final order was entered vacating interlocutory order after hearing had been held. Supreme Court held that interlocutory order cannot be set aside simply because consenting mother has changed her mind. Interlocutory order can be vacated for "good cause shown." Where consent has been freely and knowingly given, and where it has been acted upon, it cannot be arbitrarily revoked. Purpose of interlocutory order is to give welfare department opportunity to see if child is being properly cared for.

1948—*Morris v. Children's Home Society,* 188 Va. 127, 49 S.E.2d 294.
Overwhelming weight of evidence in this case indicated that adoptive mother was suitable person to have care and custody of child. Change in marital status of adoptive mother merited remand to trial court for reconsideration of petition for adoption.

1946—*Fletcher v. Flanary,* 185 Va. 409, 38 S.E.2d 433.
Right to adopt children was unknown in common law and as such it is not in derogation of common law. Therefore, adoption statutes are to be liberally construed, particularly in contest between adopted son and estate of his intestate foster parents.

1946—*Clarkson v. Bliley,* 185 Va. 82, 38 S.E.2d 22.
Right to inherit as adopted child cannot be created by private contract, statutory steps being absolutely essential to creation of artificial relationship of parent and child. Equity cannot consummate or treat as consummated, adoption which has stopped short of decree by which alone status of parent and child is created.

1936—*Shepherd v. Soverign Camp,* 166 Va. 488, 186 S.E. 113.
Legal adoption exists only by statute. There is no such thing as common law legal adoption. Simple adoption extends only to treatment of child as member of household. Legal adoption may confer on him all rights of actual relationship. In this case terms of insurance policy covered "adopted child" even though she had not been legally adopted.

§ 3-2. Custody.

(A) Criteria.

(1) IN GENERAL.

1983—*Keel v. Keel,* 225 Va. 606, 303 S.E.2d 917.
Welfare of child is primary consideration. Court must analyze circumstances of both parents and children. Positive as well as negative changes should be considered. Here trial court focused only upon issue of whether there had been negative change in circumstances surrounding custodial parent rather than also upon positive changes in circumstances of noncustodial parent. Although stability in custody matters is desirable, settled environment is only one factor to be considered in determining best interest of child and should not preclude examination of other factors. Court should consider broadest range of evidence sufficient to allow it to make rational comparison between circumstances of both parents. In determining what is in best interest of children, court should engage in comparative analysis

to determine which home will provide children with greatest opportunity to fulfill their potentials as individuals and as members of society. Trial court in this case incorrectly referred to code sections within Title 16.1 dealing with emergency removal orders. That was not case here. Trial court incorrectly found irrelevant such evidence as whether wife had had criminal charges filed against her, whether she had engaged in adulterous relationships with married men, whether her relatives had negative and antagonistic attitude towards her, whether she had abortion, whether child in custody of father had opinion on which parent should be awarded custody, and whether children themselves had opinion on which parent should be awarded custody. Some of this evidence may have been relevant.

1982—*Leisge v. Leisge,* 223 Va. 688, 292 S.E.2d 352.

In evaluating respective homes court considered child's age and sex, social worker's statement that child was flourishing in her mother's care and also considered emotional problems of mother which although bizarre, court found they would not reoccur. Custody was awarded to mother.

1982—*Durrette v. Durrette,* 223 Va. 328, 288 S.E.2d 432.

Suitability of respective homes is one factor to be considered in determining custody. Suitability depends largely on warmth, stability and general nature of home life. Evidence is undisputed that home environment of father's abode is more conducive to well-being of children, and that stability provided by father is greater than can be furnished by mother given their respective work schedules, home environments and arrangements for care of children during parents absence. Custody awarded to father.

1977—*McCreery v. McCreery,* 218 Va. 352, 237 S.E.2d 167.

Court considered adequacy of living facilities and convenience of location of home to church, school and other such institutions. Trial court also commented on fact that wife after separation from husband had given key to her apartment to her male supervisor and that he stored some of his clothes and other personal effects in apartment. In this case court found that other things were not equal and that tender years presumption did not apply. Custody was awarded to father.

1977—*Brown v. Brown,* 218 Va. 196, 237 S.E.2d 89.

Mother awarded temporary custody of children upon separation from husband. After oral hearing trial court transferred custody of children to father on grounds that mother was not fit and proper person because of her adulterous relationship with man who is living in same household with her and children. Moral climate in which children are to be raised is important consideration and illicit relationship to which minor children have been exposed cannot be condoned.

1977—*Clark v. Clark,* 217 Va. 924, 234 S.E.2d 266.

For approximately three years infant boys, ages five and three, have resided with their father in family home where they have spent most of their lives. They were doing well in that environment. There was no error for trial court on basis of evidence heard orally before commissioner to confirm commissioner's report that while both parents were fit, other things between them were not equal because father's home was more suitable than present or proposed home of mother. Custody was awarded to father.

1976—*Harper v. Harper*, 217 Va. 477, 229 S.E.2d 875.

Father obtained juvenile court order awarding him custody of son. Mother appealed. Instead of prosecuting her appeal mother elected to seek custody of child in same trial court in which she sought divorce. Under these circumstances, only burden on wife as moving party was to show that she was fit parent. Even though there was prior adjudication, there was no burden upon her in this instance to prove material change in circumstance.

1976—*McEntire v. Redfearn*, 217 Va. 313, 227 S.E.2d 741.

Supreme court noted that children in this case were residing with father and his new wife pending appeal. Supreme court indicated that until there is rehearing in circuit court children will remain temporarily in father's custody pending further proceedings.

1976—*Burnside v. Burnside*, 216 Va. 691, 222 S.E.2d 529.

Both parties remarried after divorce. Father was granted custody of child. Father remained in Virginia with child. Mother moved to Arizona. Neither parent is unfit. Statute provides for primary consideration to be given to welfare of child and as between parents there shall be no presumption of law in favor of either. Finding of trial court indicating that custody should remain with father, where child has been for last two-and-one-half years, should be sustained.

1975—*Als v. Als*, 216 Va. 13, 216 S.E.2d 16.

Since record showed that wife's failure to establish home with child may well have been due to husband's failure to provide for her support and for support of child, award of custody to father should be reconsidered.

1975—*White v. White*, 215 Va. 765, 213 S.E.2d 766.

Husband was granted divorce on grounds of desertion by wife. Custody awarded to father. Both parents loved child and neither was unfit to care for child. Suitability is not determined simply by comparing physical property or material advantages. Suitability in this case depends to great extent on warmth of home environment and kind of home life child can be expected to experience. In usual course welfare of young child will be best promoted by awarding custody to mother. This is applied even where father has obtained divorce. Evidence in this case, however, was that wife's home was not as suitable for child as was father's home.

1971—*Moore v. Moore*, 212 Va. 153, 183 S.E.2d 172.

Mother left husband, taking daughters with her and went to live with her mother because she was in love with another man whom she planned on marrying when she was free to do so. Daughters are well-adjusted in their new home. Trial court found that father was good parent but that was not sufficient to justify award of custody to him. Father did not submit definite plan as to how he would take care of children. Trial court found atmosphere of mother's home to be immoral, because she had left her husband with plan of marrying another man. Supreme court said that before finding wife unfit to have custody of her children evidence must be clear and convincing. That was not case here and as such she was awarded custody.

1971—*Rowlee v. Rowlee,* 211 Va. 689, 179 S.E.2d 461.

Controlling consideration is welfare of children, and custody is never to be given to one parent to punish other. Although trial court order appears to award custody to father in order to punish mother and makes no findings that mother is not fit and proper person, nevertheless record fully demonstrated that mother is not fit, and therefore custody was properly awarded to father.

1970—*Hall v. Hall,* 210 Va. 668, 173 S.E.2d 865.

Statute provides that as between parents there is no presumption of law in favor of either parent in terms of custody. Where mother did not see children or seek custody for extended period of time after separation, where children live with father and stepmother, are well-adjusted and happy, expressed desire to remain with their father where they will have numerous advantages and when transfer to mother would be painful disruption of their lives, it was error to award custody to mother.

1969—*Lundeen v. Struminger,* 209 Va. 548, 165 S.E.2d 285.

It was improper for decree of trial court to provide that children be reared in father's Jewish faith and that they attend Jewish Sunday school and services in synagogue each week. This violated State constitution. Trial court awarded divorce to husband on grounds of desertion. Alternate custody was awarded to husband for six months and to wife for six months. Both parties have remarried. When older child became of school age, husband petitioned for sole custody. Court held that welfare of young children is promoted by awarding custody to mother if she is fit and proper person and if other things are equal as is case here. Case was remanded for determination as to whether or not father should have custody during summer months.

1966—*Moyer v. Moyer,* 206 Va. 899, 147 S.E.2d 148.

Husband awarded divorce on grounds that wife deserted him. Custody given to mother by agreement. Child was to be brought to father once month. When child was six, husband petitioned for change of custody on grounds that this latter provision was not being complied with and also because mother had not put child in public school. She testified that he was kept out of school, under private instruction, thinking this was best for his health. Her disregard of prior decree was not contemptuous. Mother is not to be punished for this through loss of custody. Controlling interest is what is in best welfare of child.

Even though wife was found to be at fault, her fault was not based on any moral delinquency. Custody is not to be ordered with view of heaping punishment upon one party.

1964—*Higgins v. Higgins,* 205 Va. 324, 136 S.E.2d 793.

It is held on appeal that wife had in fact been guilty of infidelity, was away from home on business activities much of time in company of men and was unfit person to have custody of child due to her lack of attention to children and due to her repeated acts of infidelity. Custody was awarded to husband. Factors to be considered are qualifications and fitness of parents, their adaptability to task of caring for child, their ability to control and direct it, age, sex and health of child, its temporal and moral well-being as well as its proposed home and influences likely to be exerted upon it.

1961—*Campbell v. Campbell,* 203 Va. 61, 122 S.E.2d 658.

Welfare of child is controlling issue. Where contest is between parents, their respective fitness to care for and direct child, its age, sex and health and environment of proposed home are matters to be considered. In this case, if father had custody, children would be staying with father's sister who also had children from previous marriage. Court noted that such situations of mixing children of different families should be avoided where possible since in such homes jealousy and other problems often develop.

1958—*Andrews v. Geyer,* 200 Va. 107, 104 S.E.2d 747.

Husband awarded custody by divorce court. Wife thereafter instituted proceedings to obtain exclusive custody alleging that husband's remarriage had created situation to which child should not be subjected. Trial court awarded exclusive custody to husband, whereas formerly wife had custody during summer months. This was granted on grounds that wife had shown herself to be unusually vindictive by calling husband's second wife to witness stand. Court also based its determination on fact that child seemed to be upset when returning from visits with mother. Those were improper considerations and custody should have remained as is.

1956—*Lawson v. Lawson,* 198 Va. 403, 94 S.E.2d 215.

Although paramount consideration is welfare of child, rights of parent are also to be considered. Father in this case had tuberculosis and was apparently permanent invalid and as such not physically fit person capable of having custody and care of his infant children.

1956—*DeMott v. DeMott,* 198 Va. 22, 92 S.E.2d 342.

Paramount consideration is welfare of children. In this case, since evidence was insufficient to base decree of custody case was remanded.

1956—*Bisel v. Bisel,* 197 Va. 636, 90 S.E.2d 779.

Divorce awarded to wife on grounds of cruelty. Custody of two children was awarded to husband since mother had no suitable home and was of nervous temperament. Children had been happily reared in father's home by his mother since parties had separated.

1955—*Florance v. Florance,* 197 Va. 432, 90 S.E.2d 111.

Controlling consideration is welfare of child. This takes precedence over rights of parents.

1954—*Hepler v. Hepler,* 195 Va. 611, 79 S.E.2d 652.

Governing principle in determining custody is best interest and welfare of children. This is superior to claim of either parent.

1952—*Oliver v. Oliver,* 193 Va. 571, 69 S.E.2d 350.

Primary consideration is welfare of child. In considering qualifications and fitness of parents, court must look to their adaptability to task of caring for child, their adaptability to control and direct it, age, sex and health of child, its temporal and moral well being as well as environment and circumstances of its proposed home and influences likely to be exerted upon child. In this case, wife had been somewhat nomadic whereas home offered by husband was more stable. Custody awarded to husband.

1951—*Williams v. Williams,* 192 Va. 787, 66 S.E.2d 500.

Character and habits of person seeking custody must be shown to be such that provision for child's comfort and moral development can be reasonably expected.

1950—*Burton v. Russell,* 190 Va. 339, 57 S.E.2d 95.

Guiding principle in determining custody is welfare of child. As between parents, there shall be no presumption of law in favor of either parent in terms of custody. Father sought custody in this case. Court considered fact that both father and new wife worked full time. Father's petition denied.

1949—*Allen v. Allen,* 188 Va. 717, 51 S.E.2d 207.

Husband awarded divorce on grounds of desertion. Although record reflects no credit on fitness of wife to have custody, record is bare of any evidence as to fitness of husband. Case remanded for further evidence on that issue.

1948—*Williams v. Woolfolk,* 188 Va. 312, 49 S.E.2d 270.

Custody and welfare of children are not subject of barter.

1948—*Mullen v. Mullen,* 188 Va. 259, 49 S.E.2d 349.

In considering qualifications and fitness of parents, court must look to their adaptability to task of caring for child, their adaptability to control and direct it, age, sex and health of child, its temporal and moral well being as well as environment and circumstances of proposed home, and influences likely to be exerted upon child. Welfare of infant is primary concern of court. This rule is to be administered with as much consideration for tender ties of affection of parents as possible, especially when each is shown to be fit and proper parent. Virginia has abandoned common law rule that favored father.

1948—*Davis v. Davis,* 187 Va. 63, 45 S.E.2d 918.

Father sought custody. If such had been awarded, then actual control would have been with grandparents. Custody awarded to mother.

Court considered fact that father had previously absconded with child in violation of court order, his lack of stability as to employment, his failure to make clear where his future home would be.

1947—*Sutton v. Menges,* 186 Va. 805, 44 S.E.2d 414.
Several witnesses testified as to reputation of father.

1946—*Taylor v. Taylor,* 185 Va. 126, 37 S.E.2d 886.
In dealing with custody of infant, conditions in existence when petition was tendered is major concern of court.

1944—*Elam v. Elam,* 182 Va. 469, 29 S.E.2d 222.
False statement by wife as to her marital status followed by bigamous marriage and cohabitation ordinarily would be sufficient to deny her right to custody. However uncontradicted evidence shows in this case that husband is not fit and proper parent. Husband refused to comply with support and visitation orders of court and physically abused wife.

1942—*Darnell v. Barker,* 179 Va. 86, 18 S.E.2d 271.
If visitation conditions are burdensome to spouse at fault, then he is to blame since he broke up family. Ties of affection between child and parent and rights of latter must be respected.

1940—*Rogers v. Commonwealth,* 176 Va. 355, 11 S.E.2d 584.
Determining factor is welfare of child. Custody of twins was awarded to children's bureau. Children were found residing in house of ill-repute.

1939—*Hughes v. Hughes,* 173 Va. 293, 4 S.E.2d 402.
Husband sued for divorce for cruelty. Divorce denied. Trial court should have granted custody of child to mother. Wife was fit and suitable parent.

1938—*Buchanan v. Buchanan,* 170 Va. 458, 197 S.E. 426.
Natural rights of parents are entitled to due consideration. Contract between parents as to custody of children is not binding on court. Nor will court allow parent to transfer under any and all circumstances his common law obligation to his children.

1934—*Colbert v. Colbert,* 162 Va. 393, 174 S.E. 660.
Custody to father. Wife had allowed her affection for another man to dominate her life, had insufficient income to take care of herself, and her future course of action was uncertain. Husband was established in business, owned home and was devoted to child.

1932—*Surber v. Bridges,* 159 Va. 329, 165 S.E. 508.
Although often said that welfare of child is of paramount concern this is not without qualification. Parents also have rights that must be safeguarded. Father who has done nothing to forfeit his rights, who is of good character, possessed of decent home should not be deprived of his children. In this case children have no affection for their father and wish to stay with their grandparents, who are excellent people.

Father recently married woman almost same age as one of his sons. Mother had recently married and divorced man and remarried. Considering all of these factors court felt it best to award custody to grandparents with father having visitation.

1929—*Robinette v. Robinette,* 153 Va. 342, 149 S.E. 493.
Parties sued each other for desertion. Divorce denied. Custody of children should have been given to husband since he could keep them in home of grandparents where they had attention of husband, grandfather and grandmother. Wife had no fixed place of abode.

1926—*Markley v. Markley,* 145 Va. 596, 134 S.E. 536.
Husband granted divorce on grounds of desertion. Custody of four-and-one-half year old girl was awarded to mother. While Virginia law recognizes primary right of father to custody of children, it is also well-established that, where he does not have custody but is seeking that custody be given to him, court will exercise its discretion according to facts, consulting wishes of child, if of age of discretion. Both parents in this case were suitable. If custody had been awarded to father, child would have stayed with his parents in city of Roanoke. Although his father had expressed willingness to have child, there is nothing in record to indicate willingness of paternal grandmother to have child. Grandmother is semi-invalid. Also living in grandparents' home is invalid sister. Father's business is in Salem and, as such he often would not be in position to devote requisite care to child. Maternal grandparents, on other hand, both indicated their willingness to have child. Custody awarded to mother.

1926—*Butler v. Butler,* 145 Va. 85, 133 S.E. 756.
Separation agreement gave custody to wife. Husband sued wife for desertion and prevailed. Evidence indicated father more stable person to raise children. Custody given to husband.

1925—*Fleshood v. Fleshood,* 144 Va. 767, 130 S.E. 648.
Best interest of child is primary criteria. Court noted that child's welfare will be best promoted by having him cared for by one who loves him best.

1922—*Butler v. Commonwealth,* 132 Va. 609, 110 S.E. 868.
Wife, in this case, without reasonable excuse, kept children away from father. During this period of time, father had very little income. Court noted that upon these facts husband is entitled to custody of children. His failure to resort to legal process to bring them back from state of North Carolina to his home in Virginia affords no ground upon which to hold him liable for their maintenance and support. Father has right at common law to maintain his children in his own home and he cannot be compelled against his will to do so elsewhere unless he has refused or failed to provide for them where he lives.

1922—*Barnard v. Barnard,* 132 Va. 155, 111 S.E. 227.
Primary criteria is welfare of child. In this case, divorce was awarded to wife on grounds of desertion. Custody was split between parents, with each having custody on alternate weeks.

1916—*Burton v. Burton,* 118 Va. 519, 88 S.E. 51.
Custody of eight-year-old girl was awarded to mother. There was no discussion of facts of case.

1915—*Wyatt v. Gleason,* 117 Va. 196, 83 S.E. 1069.
Ordinarily, father is entitled to custody of his infant child. However, court will exercise its discretion according to facts and continue what will be best calculated to promote child's welfare, especially where father has voluntarily relinquished custody of child to suitable female relative in whose care child has grown and expanded.

1914—*Parrish v. Parrish,* 116 Va. 476, 82 S.E. 119.
Virginia law fully recognizes primary right of father to custody of child. When father is claiming to recover custody of child, court, however, will exercise its discretion according to fact as would appear as best calculated to promote child's welfare, having due regard to legal rights of party claiming custody. In this case, custody was split between mother and father.

1905—*Taylor v. Taylor,* 103 Va. 750, 50 S.E. 273.
Primary consideration is welfare of child. Father is natural guardian of his children and has paramount right to their custody. This right is not absolute. In this case, evidence fully established ability of father, morally, financially and in every way to tenderly care for and raise children and his paramount right to their custody and welfare of those children, both demand that they should be in his custody. In this case, wife abandoned husband and took children with her.

1902—*Meyer v. Meyer,* 100 Va. 228, 40 S.E. 1038.
Ordinarily, father is entitled to custody of infant child, but, when father is claiming custody of child, court will exercise its discretion according to facts of case and what appears to be in best interest of child. In this case, father was granted divorce on grounds of desertion. Custody, however, was awarded to mother.

1894—*Slater v. Slater,* 90 Va. 845, 20 S.E. 780.
Where father, though not very affectionate, is thoughtful and solicitous for personal and spiritual welfare of his family and successful in business and able to provide for them, while mother, though affectionate, is dependent on her parents for support, then children must be put into custody of father.

1887—*Myers v. Myers,* 83 Va. 806, 6 S.E. 630.
Wife awarded divorce on grounds of cruelty. Court gave her custody of minor child. By common law father is legal guardian of infant. However, in this case, court held that, due to behavior of husband, child was best left in custody of mother.

1886—*Coffee v. Black,* 82 Va. 567.

Father transferred his daughter, then three years old, to her mother's sister who reared child and desired to keep child. Child likewise wanted to stay with her aunt. Father's writ of habeas corpus was denied, since it appeared that change was calculated not to promote child's welfare.

1878—*Latham v. Latham,* 71 Va. 307.

If application by wife for divorce is refused, if court is satisfied that she is chief obstacle to reconciliation and if husband, under all circumstances, is entitled to custody of child, it is impossible to impose terms upon him to say that he shall have child at particular places and times so as to gratify wishes of mother. Father is legal custodian of minor children and they will not be taken from him without strongest reasons.

(2) FAULT.

1981—*Dooley v. Dooley,* 222 Va. 240, 278 S.E.2d 865.

In this case court placed great weight on finding of adultery on part of wife in terms of awarding custody. Since conclusion of adultery was overturned on appeal, award of custody to husband likewise was reversed for reconsideration.

1969—*Rosenberg v. Rosenberg,* 210 Va. 44, 168 S.E.2d 251.

Husband filed suit seeking divorce on grounds of desertion. After commissioner's hearing and before hearing on exceptions to commissioner's report, husband sought leave to file amended and supplemental bill on grounds of adultery that occurred after commissioner's report was filed. Since adultery is highly relevant to issues of alimony, support and custody, court found that this does not state completely new case and was proper subject of amended bill. Had alleged adultery occurred at time prior to filing of original bill and been discovered afterwards, husband would clearly have been entitled to amend his suit. Such amendment should also be allowed here. Generally, amended bill states fact which was in existence at time original bill was filed, whereas supplemental bill states fact which came into existence after original bill was filed.

1968—*Clark v. Clark,* 209 Va. 390, 164 S.E.2d 685.

It was error to award custody to mother of child, age 4 at time of award, when mother had committed four separate acts of adultery, producing illegitimate child who resides with mother. Custody should have been awarded to father who is person of good, moral character, highly educated and devoted to child. Trial court had noted that aside from acts of adultery mother was fit person.

1965—*McKee v. McKee,* 206 Va. 527, 145 S.E.2d 163.

Husband was granted divorce on grounds of adultery on part of wife. Trial court concluded, and supreme court affirmed, that wife was unfit person to have custody.

1964—*Higgins v. Higgins,* 205 Va. 324, 136 S.E.2d 793.

Mother is natural guardian of her children of tender years if proper person. In this case, father was shown to be suitable person and mother was shown unfit. Under certain circumstances, tender years principle is not applicable where mother is not innocent one and divorce has been granted to father.

1948—*Mullen v. Mullen,* 188 Va. 259, 49 S.E.2d 349.

Mother given custody, even though she was found to be at fault in deserting her husband. Her fault, however, was not based on any moral delinquency and no fault was committed against child. Custody of child is not to be ordered with view of punishing parent at fault, where substantial evidence shows that that parent is fit person for custody.

1947—*Nix v. Nix,* 186 Va. 14, 41 S.E.2d 345.

In suits for divorce, general rule is that innocent parent is entitled to custody of children. Adultery established in this case.

1945—*Collins v. Collins,* 183 Va. 408, 32 S.E.2d 657.

In course of custody dispute, wife offered marital agreement signed by husband in which he admitted he had been guilty of infidelity during marriage. This was dated prior to divorce action being filed. Inadmissible on grounds that it had no bearing on present status of husband. Wife had condoned infidelity. Welfare of child is paramount consideration although it is not unqualified. Parents, too, have rights which must be safeguarded.

1936—*Martin v. Martin,* 166 Va. 109, 184 S.E. 220.

Welfare of child is of paramount importance. Innocent parent usually will be granted custody.

1898—*Owens v. Owens,* 96 Va. 191, 31 S.E. 72.

In this case, wife was awarded custody of minor children. Innocent parent on whose prayer divorce is granted will usually have custody of children. Woman compelled by her husband to resort to divorce ought not to obtain it at expense of leaving her children.

(3) LEGITIMACY.

1983—*Brown v. Kittle,* 225 Va. 451, 303 S.E.2d 864.

In this case father of illegitimate child sought custody. Court determined that both mother and father are fit parents, but that because of wife's family situation, other things were not equal, and that father's home was more suitable for child. Such finding justifies awarding custody to father.

1974—*Commonwealth v. Hayes,* 215 Va. 49, 205 S.E.2d 644.

Unwed mother consented to adoption of child by adoptive parents, whose fitness is unquestioned, and with whom child has lived almost since birth. It was error to award custody to putative father who court found to be unfit and who had offered no financial or other assistance to child or to mother. Upon birth of child, rights of natural mother to custody were superior to that of father. In this case, mother, having that superior right, did relinquish child for adoption. Issue then became what is in best interest of child.

1948—*Henderson v. Henderson,* 187 Va. 121, 46 S.E.2d 10.
Issue of void marriage is legitimate. Statute on legitimacy is liberally construed. Husband has right to their custody to same extent as if they were legitimate.

1928—*Hayes v. Strauss,* 151 Va. 136, 144 S.E. 432.
Father of illegitimate child cannot be assumed to be wanting in affection. Father has same rights to custody as between himself and maternal grandmother as if child legitimate. On death of mother, father has right to custody provided he can care for child.

(4) TENDER YEARS.

See Va. Code § 20-107.2 indicating that, as between parents, there shall be no presumption or inference of law in favor of either.
See Va. Code § 31-15 indicating that when any husband and wife live in state of separation, without being divorced and having minor child of marriage, any court of record having equity jurisdiction or juvenile and domestic relations court of that jurisdiction may, upon petition of mother or father, award to petitioner custody and control of child for such time and with such provisions and directions as case requires and as will best promote welfare of child. As between parents, there shall be no presumption or inference of law in favor of either.

1982—*Leisge v. Leisge,* 223 Va. 688, 292 S.E.2d 352.
When child is of tender years court first determines whether both parents are fit. If not, child is awarded to fit parent. If so, court considers whether all other things are equal. If court finds each home environment equal, then inference arises that mother should have custody.

1982—*Durrette v. Durrette,* 223 Va. 328, 288 S.E.2d 432.
Primary consideration is child's welfare in child custody matter. It is permissible and rebuttable inference, not rule of law, that if mother is fit and proper person, and if other factors are equal, mother should be awarded custody of child of tender years. Supreme court held that as matter of law, children three years, nine months old are of tender years.

1977—*McCreery v. McCreery,* 218 Va. 352, 237 S.E.2d 167.
Tender year presumption still applies in Virginia. By definition, inference controls only when evidence shows that mother is fit and other things affecting child's welfare are equal.

1977—*Clark v. Clark,* 217 Va. 924, 234 S.E.2d 266.
Even though there was no presumption that favors one parent or other, when all things are equal custody should be given to mother. That is simply permissible inference.

1976—*Harper v. Harper,* 217 Va. 477, 229 S.E.2d 875.

So-called tender years rule is not rule of law. § 31-15 of Virginia Code provides that in child custody case court shall give primary consideration to welfare of child and that there shall be no presumption of law in favor of either parent. So-called tender years rule is no more than permissible inference that when mother is fit and other things are equal she, as natural custodian, should have custody of child of tender years. In this case, custody was awarded to mother.

1976—*Burnside v. Burnside,* 216 Va. 691, 222 S.E.2d 529.

Court applied statute indicating that as between parents there shall be no presumption of law in favor of either. Custody was awarded to father.

1971—*Monahan v. Monahan,* 212 Va. 406, 184 S.E.2d 812.

Law favors awarding custody of young girls to their mother. In absence of evidence that mother is not fit person, it was error not to award custody to her.

1971—*Moore v. Moore,* 212 Va. 153, 183 S.E.2d 172.

Mother is natural guardian and custodian of children of tender years, especially girls. This principle is followed even though father is without fault and divorce is awarded to him.

1971—*Rowlee v. Rowlee,* 211 Va. 689, 179 S.E.2d 461.

Mother is generally recognized as custodian of minor children of tender years. Custody in this case was given to father.

1961—*Campbell v. Campbell,* 203 Va. 61, 122 S.E.2d 658.

Mother is natural custodian of her children of tender years assuming she is proper person. This is especially so when children are girls. This rule applies even though divorce has been awarded to father.

1959—*Semmes v. Semmes,* 201 Va. 117, 109 S.E.2d 545.

Court noted that generally children of tender years, especially girls, should be awarded to mother where they will be equally well cared for. This, however, was not done in this case because wife had been proven to be unsuitable custodian previously and because mother had not borne burden of proof to show that her character and demeanor in that regard had sufficiently changed.

1959—*Brooks v. Brooks,* 200 Va. 530, 106 S.E.2d 611.

Generally, where child is of tender years and will be equally well cared for by either parent, preference should be shown to mother.

1956—*DeMott v. DeMott,* 198 Va. 22, 92 S.E.2d 342.

As respects custody of young daughter, other things being equal, law favors mother if she is fit person. In this case, while weight of evidence favored wife for custody, evidence offered at trial tended to show her lack of emotional stability. Case was remanded for additional evidence on fitness of parents.

1948—*Mullen v. Mullen,* 188 Va. 259, 49 S.E.2d 349.

If mother is fit and proper person for custody, other things being equal, she should be given custody of child of tender years. This is especially so with girls.

1899—*Trimble v. Trimble,* 97 Va. 217, 33 S.E. 531.

Custody of seven-month-old child was given to mother. Court stated that no argument is required to show that mother is proper custodian of child of that age.

1872—*Carr v. Carr,* 63 Va. 168.

Wife, having left her husband without good legal grounds and having taken child with her, and wife having been found guilty of desertion, child was returned to husband. Child in this case was three-year-old female. Tender nursing period had passed and time for moral training and impressions had arrived, and court considered that in awarding custody to father.

(5) WISHES OF THE CHILD.

1983—*Deahl v. Winchester Dep't of Social Servs.,* 224 Va. 664, 299 S.E.2d 863.

In this action to terminate residual parental rights, if child is 14 or over or has attained age of discretion, then child is to be afforded opportunity to object before residual parental rights are terminated. Objection of child will bar further proceedings. In this case, child was nearly 14. Trial court failed to make determination as to whether or not child was of age of discretion and further failed to consult child as to what his preference was. As such, case was remanded for hearing as to those issues. Phrase "age of discretion" in Va. Code § 16.1-283(E) although not defined, has same meaning as used in child custody cases. Test is whether child is sufficiently mature to have intelligent views and wisdom on subject of termination of residual parental rights.

1970—*Hall v. Hall,* 210 Va. 668, 173 S.E.2d 865.

Wishes of children, if they are of age of discretion, should be considered and given weight, although their wishes are not conclusive.

1969—*Addison v. Addison,* 210 Va. 104, 168 S.E.2d 281.

Children were 13 and 16 years of age. Court noted that their wishes and attitudes are entitled to weight.

1961—*Jones v. Henson,* 202 Va. 738, 120 S.E.2d 286.

Child in this case was 12 years of age. Though child's wishes should be considered, they are not controlling.

1956—*Lawson v. Lawson,* 198 Va. 403, 94 S.E.2d 215.

Such should be considered if child is of age of discretion, and matter to be determined by court on facts of each case. In this case, since child did not testify, his wishes were properly excluded.

1954—*Hepler v. Hepler,* 195 Va. 611, 79 S.E.2d 652.

On petition for modification in custody order, court abused its discretion in refusing to hear testimony of 12-year-old child. Where child has reached age of discretion, his wishes should be considered, although they are not conclusive.

1951—*Williams v. Williams,* 192 Va. 787, 66 S.E.2d 500.

Wish of infant is entitled to be considered but it is not conclusive, especially in case of child of five years of age.

1947—*Sutton v. Menges,* 186 Va. 805, 44 S.E.2d 414.

Wishes of children are to be considered but they are not conclusive.

1944—*Taylor v. Taylor,* 182 Va. 602, 29 S.E.2d 833.

In considering violent temper of husband, fact that he had no home but only rented room and fact that 14-year-old child wanted to stay with mother, wishes of child should prevail.

1921—*Mihalcoe v. Holub,* 130 Va. 425, 107 S.E. 704.

Primary consideration is interest of child. If child be of age of discretion, it should be consulted, and due weight given to its decision. Law prescribes no age at which child shall be presumed to have discretion adequate for this purpose. Decision shall be made based upon competency of child. Custody battle, in this case, was between natural parents and grandparents. Teenage child expressed her preference to stay with grandparents. Child had been with grandparents intermittently since birth. At time of this proceeding, child was with grandparents. Court noted that it would be disruptive to move her back to her natural parents, since she was well-settled with grandparents. Court held that child may elect, at any time, whether she will go to her parents. If she elects to stay with her grandparents, then natural parents shall have full and free opportunity to visit and confer with her. Additional factor that court considered was that health of child seemed to be much better when she was with grandparents than with parents.

1886—*Merritt v. Swimley,* 82 Va. 433.

As general rule, father is entitled to custody and control of his infant child. That rule does not apply, however, where father is unfit and unsuitable. In this case, father had abandoned and transferred motherless infant to its aunts who reared it in happy contentment until age 12. At that age, father was not allowed to resume custody and control against wishes of child. Court noted in this case that rights of child are first to be considered and those rights are clearly to be protected in enjoyment of its personal liberty, according to its own choice if arrived at age of discretion.

1852—*Armstrong v. Stone,* 50 Va. 102.

Child in this case being seven years of age was too young to judge for herself as to what was proper custodial arrangement.

(B) Divided Custody.

1982—*Leisge v. Leisge,* 292 Va. 688, 292 S.E.2d 352.

In this case juvenile court granted joint custody, but ordered that mother have child majority of time and that husband pay support.

1966—*Crounse v. Crounse,* 207 Va. 524, 151 S.E.2d 412.

By agreement, mother had custody during school year and father during summer months. Father later on challenged that custody arrangement, but it was essentially affirmed by court.

1961—*Campbell v. Campbell,* 203 Va. 61, 122 S.E.2d 658.

Custody in this case was awarded to mother, with father having custody for three summer months.

1958—*Andrews v. Geyer,* 200 Va. 107, 104 S.E.2d 747.

Mother awarded custody during summer months and on some holidays. Remainder of year husband had custody. While there are certain disadvantages in joint custody, there are also important advantages and benefits. It gives child experience of two separate homes.

1948—*Mullen v. Mullen,* 188 Va. 259, 49 S.E.2d 349.

In this case, court awarded custody to mother for 10 months out of year and to father for two months out of year with reasonable visitation rights.

1927—*Cohn v. Cohn,* 148 Va. 467, 139 S.E. 251.

Custody awarded to wife for nine months and to husband for three months.

1926—*Duff v. Duff,* 145 Va. 526, 134 S.E. 555.

Husband obtained divorce from wife on grounds of desertion. Custody of preschool children was awarded to father for six months and to mother for six months.

1923—*Wilson v. Wilson,* 136 Va. 643, 118 S.E. 270.

Trial court granted wife charge of children from June 20th to September 10th of each year. Husband had custody for remainder of year.

1922—*Barnard v. Barnard,* 132 Va. 155, 111 S.E. 227.

If record discloses that custody of father is as suitable and proper as that of mother, there is no error in assigning to father custody of child each alternate week.

1919—*Cover v. Widener,* 125 Va. 643, 100 S.E. 459.

Custody in this case was awarded to maternal grandmother during school year and to father during remainder of year.

1914—*Parrish v. Parrish,* 116 Va. 476, 82 S.E. 119.

Custody in this case was awarded to mother who lived in Virginia during school year and to father who lived in Chicago during summer months.

(C) Grandparents.

1963—*Forbes v. Haney,* 204 Va. 712, 133 S.E.2d 533.

Court awarded custody of 10-year-old child to grandparents. They were shown to be proper persons and child testified she wishes to live with them where her half sister was also living. Alleged father was shown to be man of immoral character due to his prior relationships. If in fact child was awarded to him, then child would in essence be living with his mother and maiden sister with whom he lived. Though legal rights of natural parent are to be regarded, controlling factor is welfare of child.

1954—*Judd v. VanHorn,* 195 Va. 988, 81 S.E.2d 432.

Upon death of natural mother, maternal grandmother was given temporary custody. Natural father, upon remarriage, petitioned for custody. Custody was awarded to him since he was neither morally unfit nor financially unable to provide suitable home.

1952—*Oliver v. Oliver,* 193 Va. 571, 69 S.E.2d 350.

In this case, custody awarded to husband even though child was essentially living with paternal grandparents.

1951—*Williams v. Williams,* 192 Va. 787, 66 S.E.2d 500.

Burden of proof in this case was on grandparents to show that child had been voluntarily given to them.

1948—*Mullen v. Mullen,* 188 Va. 259, 49 S.E.2d 349.

Experience teaches that children grow up more normally when reared by young people rather than older people. In this case, custody was awarded to wife because, if custody had been awarded to father, then grandparents would have been actual custodian of child during working day.

1947—*Davis v. Davis,* 187 Va. 63, 45 S.E.2d 918.

Rights of parents, as to custody, are greater than those of grandparents. In this case, where father sought custody, if such had been awarded then child actually would have been within control of paternal grandparents. Court rejected that in favor of custody and control by mother.

1947—*Sutton v. Menges,* 186 Va. 805, 44 S.E.2d 414.

Where wife is dead but husband is still alive, grandparents in such situation do not stand in loco parentis. Custody awarded to father.

1932—*Surber v. Bridges,* 159 Va. 329, 165 S.E. 508.

Husband awarded divorce due to misconduct of wife. Custody awarded to grandparents. Children wanted to stay with grandparents and had no affection towards father.

1925—*Fleshood v. Fleshood,* 144 Va. 767, 130 S.E. 648.

Child had been under care of paternal grandfather for almost two years. Custody given to natural father, primarily in light of health and medical history of grandfather. If health and medical history had not been factor, then custody most likely would have remained with grandfather.

1921—*Mihalcoe v. Holub,* 130 Va. 425, 107 S.E. 704.
Teenage child had been in custody of grandparents for some time at time of this habeas corpus proceeding. Throughout her life, she had intermittently been with grandparents. Her health seemed to be much better when she was with grandparents than with natural parents. Court held that child may elect at any time whether she will go to her parents or remain with her grandparents. If she decides to remain with her grandparents, then natural parents shall be afforded full and free opportunity to visit and confer with her.

1919—*Cover v. Widener,* 125 Va. 643, 100 S.E. 459.
Custody awarded to maternal grandmother where father had abandoned mother and child when child was infant and had had no communication with child for nearly 10 years. Mother had since passed away.

1852—*Armstrong v. Stone,* 50 Va. 102.
Grandparents in this case were in decline of life, in doubtful circumstances as to solvency and somewhat dependent on their own children for home. Mother was shown to be of excellent moral character. Father was deceased. Mother, after death of husband, supported herself by teaching school and during that period of time child was left in custody of grandparents. Custody was awarded to mother. Conduct of mother, in permitting child to remain with grandparents while she was working to provide for herself, does not impair her right to custody.

(D) Habeas Corpus.

1962—*Walker v. Brooks,* 203 Va. 417, 124 S.E.2d 195.
Grandmother brought habeas corpus proceeding to recover custody of her two grandchildren from their mother. Mother moved to quash on grounds that writ that was issued in one county could not be served in another county where she and children resided. This contention was rejected.

1950—*Burton v. Russell,* 190 Va. 339, 57 S.E.2d 95.
In this case, father filed habeas corpus petition to obtain custody of child who was then in possession of another couple.

1948—*Williams v. Woolfolk,* 188 Va. 312, 49 S.E.2d 270.
Jurisdiction acquired by court in divorce proceedings over subject of custody is continuing and is exclusive and cannot be altered by filing of habeas corpus petition in another court within State.

1947—*Sutton v. Menges,* 186 Va. 805, 44 S.E.2d 414.
Father in this case filed petition for habeas corpus on grounds that grandparents had custody of children. Custody awarded to father.

1938—*Buchanan v. Buchanan,* 170 Va. 458, 197 S.E. 426.

> Primary purpose of habeas corpus is to determine legality of restraint under which person is held. In case of infants purpose is to determine in whose custody best interests of child will be served. Aim of habeas corpus is swift and summary justice. Contest for guardianship cannot be properly determined upon writ of habeas corpus. Only those matters having necessary connection to issue of validity of detention will be considered in habeas corpus. Order entered by agreement as part of habeas corpus proceeding modifying monthly support was void. However, it was evidence of binding contractual obligation.

1928—*Hayes v. Strauss,* 151 Va. 136, 144 S.E. 432.

> Bastard child subject of habeas corpus proceeding as to father and maternal grandmother. Custody to father. On appeal burden is on appellant in habeas corpus to show error as is true in all other cases. Court in this case did not have authority to change guardianship but simply to award custody.

1852—*Armstrong v. Stone,* 50 Va. 102.

> Where custody issue is to be resolved through petition of habeas corpus, court will exercise its discretion as to what is in best interest of child.

(E) Jurisdiction.

See Va. Code § 16.1-241 as to jurisdiction of Juvenile and Domestic Relations Court.

See Va. Code § 20-125 et seq., Uniform Child Custody Jurisdiction Act.

1984—*Middleton v. Middleton,* 227 Va. 82, 314 S.E.2d 362.

> Purposes of UCCJA are (a) to avoid jurisdictional competition, (b) to assure that custody litigation occurs in state most closely connected with child, (c) to assure that Virginia courts decline jurisdiction where another state is more closely connected with matter, (d) to discourage continuing controversies over custody, (e) to deter abductions, (f) to facilitate enforcement of foreign custody orders, (g) to promote exchange of information among states. General policies of act extend to international area. Home state under UCCJA is defined in part as state in which child immediately preceding time involved lived with his parents, parent or person acting as parent for at least six consecutive months. Evidence in regards to Middleton case indicated that England was child's home state. Substantial evidence concerning care, protection and training and personal relationships of Middleton children was more readily available in England than in Virginia. In this case, father retained custody of children in violation of visitation order and court noted that to approve retention by Virginia courts would tend to encourage similar conduct. Under act, physical presence of child as jurisdictional basis has been eliminated in all but most extreme cases. Virginia court has jurisdiction to make initial custody decree under act if (a) Virginia has been child's home state within six months before commencement of proceeding (b) child

is absent from Virginia because of removal by person claiming custody (c) parent continues to live in Virginia. In this case, child has been spirited away to England and as such, comity should not have been accorded to order of English court even though father made appearance in that case and litigated custody issue there. Father in essence was forced to litigate in England since failure to do so would increase likelihood of unfavorable foreign ruling.

1983—*Rochelle v. Rochelle,* 225 Va. 387, 302 S.E.2d 59.

Circuit court has original jurisdiction over petition for custody, support and visitation only where such matters are incidental to cause properly before court. In this case wife filed petition for separate maintenance which is in inherent jurisdiction of court of equity and therefore circuit court had jurisdiction over issue and issues of child custody, support and visitation. Court's custody, once properly invoked is not lost because of part of claim, in this case claim for separate maintenance, is later found to be without merit. Jurisdiction is retained until matter is fully adjudicated. Once circuit court acquires jurisdiction, then domestic relations court is divested of such.

1981—*Hosier v. Hosier,* 221 Va. 827, 273 S.E.2d 564.

Once child reaches age of majority, jurisdiction of divorce court to provide for his support and maintenance terminates unless otherwise provided by agreement incorporated into divorce decree.

1980—*Oehl v. Oehl,* 221 Va. 618, 272 S.E.2d 441.

Court which has personal jurisdiction over both parents may enter child custody order even in absence of child. Under necessitous circumstances, custody jurisdiction may attach when child is present even though both parents are absent. In determining whether comity should be granted to child custody order entered by foreign nation, Virginia courts should conduct threefold inquiry: (1) Did foreign court have jurisdiction over parties and subject matter, (2) was procedural and substantive law applied by foreign court reasonably comparable to that of Virginia, (3) was foreign order based upon determination of best interest of child. In this case all three of these questions were answered affirmatively, and as such, principle of comity should have been applied. Virginia court should grant comity to order of foreign court of competent jurisdiction when in terms of moral standards, values, personal rights and public policy foreign procedural and substantive law is reasonably comparable to that of Virginia. In this case, English rules of procedure and substantive law are comparable to that of Virginia.

1969—*Addison v. Addison,* 210 Va. 104, 168 S.E.2d 281.

In this case, husband sought custody of child which had been awarded to mother by Texas court incident to divorce decree there. Supreme court said it was error for corporation court to entertain jurisdiction since juvenile court had exclusive, original jurisdiction of question of custody. In this case, plaintiff did not seek change in custody upon writ of habeas corpus nor was question of custody incidental to cause pending in that court.

1969—*Branham v. Raines,* 209 Va. 702, 167 S.E.2d 355.

Parties were divorced in Ohio. Custody was awarded to mother, with child to be surrendered to father for off-premises visitation during months of July and August each year, with child to be returned to mother at conclusion of visitation periods. Father had failed to return child to mother in September of 1966. In December of 1966, mother regained possession of child for overnight stay and refused to return child to Ohio, even though Ohio court had given father temporary custody. Virginia court, upon petition of mother, restricted father's visitation to keeping child in county of her residence in Virginia. Virginia court had jurisdiction since child lived in Virginia and was justified in changing visitation because of change in circumstances in light of father's prior wrongful retention of child.

1968—*Falco v. Grills,* 209 Va. 115, 161 S.E.2d 713.

While passing through Virginia en route to Tennessee, parents, who were domiciled in New York, were killed in auto accident. Their nine-year-old child was seriously injured. While child was in hospital in Virginia, dispute arose between uncle in Tennessee and uncle in New York as to who should have custody. Tennessee uncle prevailed. By statute and inherent power of court, jurisdiction and venue properly rested with juvenile and domestic relations court of Staunton, Virginia, to determine custody. Statute in question requires physical presence of child within State. In passing this statute, General Assembly was concerned with welfare of children within borders of State. Majority of courts have not been too concerned with questions of technical domicile or legal residence but primarily concerned with welfare of infant if physically present within jurisdiction of court.

1964—*Gramelspacher v. Gramelspacher,* 204 Va. 839, 134 S.E.2d 285.

Husband deserted wife and moved to Mississippi and then later returned to Virginia where he was personally served by her in divorce action. Wife lived with children at their family home in Indiana. At time of trial, she brought three of children with her to Virginia while fourth child was in school in Tennessee. Court held that proceeding was in personam insofar as it involved custody and that court acted within its power since it had jurisdiction of proceeding and in personam jurisdiction of both parents.

1948—*Williams v. Woolfolk,* 188 Va. 312, 49 S.E.2d 270.

Jurisdiction acquired by court in divorce cases over subject of custody is continuing and exclusive and precludes any other court in this State from thereafter acquiring or exercising jurisdiction over same subject.

1944—*Kern v. Lindsey,* 182 Va. 775, 30 S.E.2d 707.

Divorce and custody order entered in Virginia. Removal of child from Virginia does not deprive court of jurisdiction.

1940—*Rogers v. Commonwealth,* 176 Va. 355, 11 S.E.2d 584.

Juvenile and domestic relations court has jurisdiction to determine custody of any neglected child within its territory. Bastard child takes domicile of its mother from birth and such continues until new one is acquired. Local court of infant's legal domicile has jurisdiction to determine its custody.

1923—*Wilson v. Wilson,* 136 Va. 643, 118 S.E. 270.

Custody in this case was awarded to father in habeas corpus proceeding. Mother thereafter filed suit for divorce in Maryland and was awarded divorce and awarded custody. That Maryland decree was not entitled to full faith and credit in Virginia in light of prior adjudication of custody. Question of residence arose in this matter. Court determined that children were residents of State of Virginia in part based upon prior habeas corpus petition that had been filed.

(F) Leaving Jurisdiction.

1979—*Carpenter v. Carpenter,* 220 Va. 299, 257 S.E.2d 845.

There was no abuse of discretion by court in enjoining removal of children to New York. Evidence showed close relationship with father who lived in Virginia, whose visits would be curtailed by move, many friends locally, and that mother had no job or home for children in New York.

1952—*Oliver v. Oliver,* 193 Va. 571, 69 S.E.2d 350.

Court considered fact that mother was non-resident and had no permanent home in awarding custody to father.

1950—*Burton v. Russell,* 190 Va. 339, 57 S.E.2d 95.

Father filed petition for habeas corpus seeking custody of his child from couple that presently had custody. Court stated that father's intent to move child to Florida, to live with strangers, beyond jurisdiction of Virginia courts would be dangerous experiment.

1946—*Taylor v. Taylor,* 185 Va. 126, 37 S.E.2d 886.

Mother stated that she intended to take child out of Virginia to another jurisdiction. Husband filed motion asking for change of custody, with him having sole custody. Trial court should have allowed petition to be filed and heard matter.

1942—*Darnell v. Barker,* 179 Va. 86, 18 S.E.2d 271.

Mother remarried and sought to move child to Kansas. Father asked for custody. Father found to be of intemperate habits. Custody continued with mother; father having reasonable visitation rights in Kansas.

(G) Modification of Custody.

See Va. Code § 20-108 indicating that court may from time to time after entering decree revise and alter such decree as circumstances of parents and benefit of children may require.

1983—*Keel v. Keel,* 225 Va. 606, 303 S.E.2d 917.

Except in extreme circumstances there should be no reluctance by court to change custody once awarded. Although stability in custody matters is desirable, it is only one factor to be considered. Test that should be applied is (a) has there been change in circumstances since most recent custody award, and (b) would change be in best interest of child. This consideration should include changes involving children such as their maturity, their special educational needs and other changes that may have occurred affecting them. It should include positive changes in circumstances of non-custodial parent and negative changes in home of custodial parent.

1969—*Addison v. Addison,* 210 Va. 104, 168 S.E.2d 281.

Husband was awarded permanent custody of children at time of divorce. Several years later, mother moved to Virginia with children. Children had been with mother for approximately three years when trial court heard this matter. Children testified that they preferred to stay with their mother. All of these circumstances constituted change in circumstance justifying change in custody award.

1969—*Branham v. Raines,* 209 Va. 702, 167 S.E.2d 355.

Parties awarded divorce in Ohio, with mother to have custody and father to have off-premises visitation privileges during months of July and August. Father failed to return child in September of 1966, and in fact did not return child to mother until December, 1966. Court found change in circumstance in light of these conditions, and thereafter restricted visitation to county of child's residence. Change in circumstance was found to exist due to father's wrongful retention of child and his threat to remove child from country.

1968—*Portewig v. Ryder,* 208 Va. 791, 160 S.E.2d 789.

Although mother is natural custodian of children of tender years, this rule is flexible and is not to be applied without regard to surrounding circumstances. In this case, in 1961, wife was awarded custody of children on her divorce on grounds of desertion. In 1962, husband assumed custody of children when wife was committed to mental institution. Husband remarried and is providing good home for children. Three years after her commitment to institution, wife now seeks change of custody. She, too, is remarried and can also supply good home. Court concluded that custody should remain with husband. There was evidence of potential recurrence of wife's mental illness and also wrenching experience that children suffered initially when there was change of custody.

1966—*Crounse v. Crounse,* 207 Va. 524, 151 S.E.2d 412.

When parents were divorced, they agreed that child would stay with mother during school year and with father during summer months. Mother moved to Connecticut and remarried. Father stayed in Virginia and remarried. Thereafter, child developed severe emotional problems and in 1964 father decided to keep child and enrolled him in private school in Virginia where he improved. He now requests full custody of child. At hearing, he produced medical testimony that mother was emotionally unstable and immature and that her husband had feelings of hostility towards child. Chancellor, however, concluded that mother was fit and proper and left custody arrangement essentially as is. Since these findings were supported by evidence, they were binding.

1959—*Semmes v. Semmes,* 201 Va. 117, 109 S.E.2d 545.

Father awarded custody under original divorce decree. Wife thereafter remarried and sought full custody of child. Court found that although mother's prior bad habits had changed there had not been sufficient lapse of time definitely to establish this fact. Custody was left with father. Mother thereafter filed another petition for change of custody. Court found that both homes were suitable but found mother had not borne burden of proof that custody should be modified.

1955—*Florance v. Florance,* 197 Va. 432, 90 S.E.2d 111.

Under terms of property settlement agreement, wife was given custody of one child and father custody of other. Father moved for custody for both children and was granted such. He had remarried and his new wife was fond of both boys and wanted them. Elder boy who had been living with him was happy, normal and bright. Mother ran boarding house and was somewhat unstable and child that had been living with her had had several problems. Court made reference to her subsequent marriage and divorce and her questionable judgment in regards to relationship with another man during second marriage.

1954—*Wallihan v. Hughes,* 196 Va. 117, 82 S.E.2d 553.

Property settlement agreement made part of Nevada divorce decree. Wife contended agreement facilitated divorce and was void. Court held that with regard to custody, agreement was subject to modification by Virginia court.

1954—*Hepler v. Hepler,* 195 Va. 611, 79 S.E.2d 652.

Husband was entitled to have children during summer months. In August of 1952, he applied to court for modification of custody order. He refused to return children to mother in September of 1952. He was not in contempt of court in doing so since he was exercising right given to him under State code to seek change in custody. There was no willful disobedience of prior order. Court in this case changed custody because it was deemed to be in best interest of children so as to award custody of two of children to husband and one of children to mother.

1946—*Taylor v. Taylor,* 185 Va. 126, 37 S.E.2d 886.

In this case, decree of divorce awarded custody to each of parents for six months of year. Subsequent decree vested custody in mother for three months and father for remainder of year. Thereafter, father moved court to reinstate case on docket asking for sole custody of children. Trial court should have reinstated case on docket to allow petition for change of custody to be heard. Unless there is rehearing on evidence already adduced, no change in decree of custody should be made, except upon showing of competent evidence that such change is for child's best interest. Such evidence should be based upon or proceed by filing of formal pleading alleging necessity of such change.

1945—*Collins v. Collins,* 183 Va. 408, 32 S.E.2d 657.
Ordinarily change in custody of child of tender years should be based on some change of condition which is for better interest of child. In this case husband was in military when custody was initially awarded. His release from military was change of condition. Court modified custody arrangement.

1944—*Kern v. Lindsey,* 182 Va. 775, 30 S.E.2d 707.
Evidence showed sufficient change of condition and circumstance for better as to justify change in decree so as to allow father more contact with child.

1942—*Darnell v. Barker,* 179 Va. 86, 18 S.E.2d 271.
Ordinarily change of custody of child of tender years should be based on change of condition which is for better interest of child. Evidence indicated that father was man of intemperate habits. There was no indication that he had changed and therefore change of custody was denied.

1928—*Hayes v. Strauss,* 151 Va. 136, 144 S.E. 432.
Issuance of letter of guardianship on ex parte application is not adjudication of right to custody so as to preclude changing custody in interest of child.

(H) Natural Parents.

See Va. Code § 31-1 indicating that father and mother of every legitimate unmarried minor child, if living together and being themselves respectively competent to transact their own business and not otherwise unsuitable, shall be joint natural guardians of person of such child with equal legal powers and equal legal rights with regard to such child. Upon death of either parent, survivor shall be natural guardian. If either parent has abandoned his or her family, other shall be natural guardian.

1983—*Todaro v. Alexandria Dep't of Social Servs.,* 226 Va. 307, 309 S.E.2d 303.
Without reciting evidence, court indicated that termination of residual parental rights was supported by clear and convincing evidence. Prior to termination of such rights, agency must file with court foster care plan.

1983—*Deahl v. Winchester Dep't of Social Servs.,* 224 Va. 664, 299 S.E.2d 863.
In this case evidence was sufficient to satisfy requirements for termination of residual parental rights. Record showed countless incidents of parental abuse of child, that there was little likelihood that conditions which resulted in abuse would improve so as to allow child to

return to home within reasonable time, and finally evidence indicated that termination would be in child's best interest.

1983—*Shortridge v. Deel,* 224 Va. 589, 299 S.E.2d 500.

Voluntary relinquishment by parent of custody of child must be shown by clear, cogent and convincing evidence. Evidence in this case was clear, cogent and convincing that natural mother voluntarily gave up custody of her child, and that man now claiming to be natural father relinquished whatever custodial and parental rights he had. Once relinquishment of custody is established, natural parents who seek to regain custody had burden of proving that regaining custody is in child's best interest. In this case, court determined that child should not be returned to natural parents. Evidence, including psychiatric testimony, amply supports conclusion that child should not be returned.

1982—*Richardson v. Henry County Dep't of Social Servs.,* 223 Va. 670, 292 S.E.2d 342.

Department in this case having established that mother without good cause failed to respond to their rehabilitation efforts, this is prima facie evidence of conditions set forth in Va. Code § 16.1-283(B)(2). Because mother did not go forward with sufficient evidence to contrary, requirements of this code section, that it is not reasonably likely that conditions which resulted in neglect can be substantially corrected or eliminated, have been proven, and mother's residual parental rights have been correctly terminated.

1982—*Walker v. Dep't of Pub. Welfare,* 223 Va. 557, 290 S.E.2d 887.

When parents appealed to circuit court from final order of juvenile court terminating residual parental rights under Va. Code § 16.1-283 burden of proof is on department to prove by clear and convincing evidence that termination of residual parental relationship is in best interest of child and that: (a) neglect or abuse suffered by such child presented serious and substantial threat to his life, health or development; and (b) that it was not reasonably likely that condition which resulted in such neglect or abuse could be substantially corrected or eliminated so as to allow child safe return to his parents. This type of case is to be distinguished from any case involving termination of parental custodial rights. Final order terminating parental custodial rights does not sever residual parental rights.

1982—*Harris v. Lynchburg Div. of Social Servs.,* 223 Va. 235, 288 S.E.2d 410.

Trial court terminated parental rights of natural parents. Under Va.Code § 16.1-283, court is required to find that termination of parental rights will support best interest of child and that certain factors listed in statute are present. Finding of these factors existing is tantamount to finding of parental unfitness. Court made such determination in this case as to mother and such finding was supported by clear and convincing evidence that mother was unwilling or unable without good cause, and despite assistance of social agencies, to remedy conditions that led to her loss of custody, and they further found that her incarceration in jail is no excuse for her prior neglect. As to natural father, undisputed evidence is that he was not provided services by social services agency, and this places burden upon division of social services to prove factors listed in Va. Code § 16.1-283(C)(2). In absence of such proof, reversal of termination order was required as in this case.

1982—*Toombs v. Lynchburg Div. of Social Servs.*, 223 Va. 225, 288 S.E.2d 405.

After children had been placed in foster home, natural parents sought visitation. Va. Code § 16.1-283 does require parental visitation in every case where social service agency assumes responsibility for foster care of child. Instead, question must be resolved in light of facts of each case. Action of circuit court in denying visitation is presumed correct. There was nothing in record to indicate motion was denied without hearing or that parents were denied opportunity to present evidence and therefore presumption controls. Clear and convincing evidence supports trial court's decision that termination of parental rights is in child's best interest and that parents, without good cause and not withstanding reasonable efforts of social agencies, failed to remedy substantially conditions that led to children's foster care placement.

1982—*Knox v. Lynchburg Div. of Social Servs.*, 223 Va. 213, 288 S.E.2d 399.

Under Va. Code § 16.1-283, court is required to find both that termination of parental rights will promote best interest of child and that certain factors listed in statute are present. Finding of these factors is tantamount to finding of parental unfitness. Record in this case clearly showed that mother was either unwilling or unable within reasonable time to remedy substantially conditions which led to her children's foster care placement despite reasonable and appropriate efforts by division. Standard of proof in case such as this is clear and convincing evidence, and statute in question is not unconstitutional.

1982—*Grigg v. Commonwealth*, 224 Va. 356, 297 S.E.2d 779.

This is civil action brought by state to compel parents to enroll their children in school or to otherwise properly provide for their education as required by state law. Proper standard of proof in this case is clear and convincing evidence since children in need of services may suffer deprivations of liberty. Although this standard is more stringent than that used in ordinary civil matters, it is lesser burden than reasonable doubt standard applied in criminal cases. In this case, commonwealth proved that children were in need of services.

1980—*Weaver v. Roanoke Dep't of Human Resources*, 220 Va. 921, 265 S.E.2d 692.

Husband had custody of children after separation. In 1976 he petitioned court to be relieved of custody because of financial problems. Custody was granted to Department of Human Resources which placed children in foster care. During next three years, neither parent paid support. Both changed residences frequently and visited children sporadically. From mid 1978 however, father made progress towards financial independence, trial court terminated residual parental rights of both parents, finding that they had been unable to remedy conditions leading to foster care placement. This order was overturned since record does not indicate what measures, if any, were taken by agencies to provide parents with assistance in remedying their financial problems. Final order which terminates parental custodial rights does not sever residual parental rights and does not place upon parents burden of demonstrating that their residual parental rights should not be terminated.

1976—*Watson v. Shepard,* 217 Va. 538, 229 S.E.2d 897.

Juvenile court entered order, based upon voluntary relinquishment of custody, investigation, hearing, that relieved mother of child custody and awarded custody to aunt and uncle. For mother to be entitled to later change in custody, burden was on her to show change in circumstances in child's best interest. Record in this case showed that child's best interest would be served by remaining in present environment with her aunt and uncle.

1976—*Shank v. Dep't of Social Servs.,* 217 Va. 506, 230 S.E.2d 454.

Common law rule on custodial status of child has been modified by statute pursuant to which court's may permanently sever parental rights of child. That is what trial court did in this case, and as such, natural parents lost whatever interest they had in child.

1976—*McEntire v. Redfearn,* 217 Va. 313, 227 S.E.2d 741.

In this case juvenile court determined custody on merits at hearing at which father was present and made no appeal. Father, couple of years later at custody proceeding, is not entitled to parental presumption generally accorded to natural parents. At subsequent hearing welfare of children is paramount consideration and burden is on father to prove that circumstances have so changed that it would be in child's best interest to transfer custody to him.

1975—*Berrien v. Greene County,* 216 Va. 241, 217 S.E.2d 854.

In custody case natural parent prevails unless non-parent bears burden of proving by clear and convincing evidence both that parent is unfit and that best interest of child will be promoted by granting custody to non-parent. Record does not show unfitness and therefore custody is awarded to mother. Supreme court held that no useful purpose would be served by another evidentiary hearing and therefore entered final judgment. Proof of unfitness must be clear and convincing evidence.

1975—*Rocka v. Roanoke County Dep't of Welfare,* 215 Va. 515, 211 S.E.2d 76.

Parent is entitled to custody of child unless non-parent proves by clear and convincing evidence that parent is unfit and that best interest of child will be promoted by granting custody to non-parent. In this case record was insufficient to divest parent of custody, and trial court reversed and held that mother should be given trial period of six months to show that she can care for child in suitable home. Rule of comparative best interest applied in child custody cases between parents is not applicable to contest between parent and non-parent.

1973—*Wilkerson v. Wilkerson,* 214 Va. 395, 200 S.E.2d 581.
Law presumes child's best interest will be served when in custody of its parents. Burden is on party opposing right of natural parent to establish parent's unfitness by clear and convincing evidence. In absence of showing of unfitness of parent, special facts and circumstances must be shown constituting extraordinary reason for taking child from its parent. In this case, husband entered into agreed temporary custody order of juvenile court giving custody to relative of child during pendency of wife's divorce action against him. Wife had been committed to mental institution. After divorce action was over, father sought to have child returned to him. Custody awarded to father.

1971—*Dyer v. Howell,* 212 Va. 453, 184 S.E.2d 789.
Husband killed wife, was found not guilty by reason of insanity and was confined to mental institution. He was thereafter released as being mentally competent. In interim, his daughter had been put in custody of her aunt and uncle by juvenile court. Father now seeks change of custody. Criteria to be applied is what is in best interest of child. Presumption in favor of natural parent does not apply in this circumstance. Father had burden of showing that circumstances had so changed that it would be in child's best interest to transfer custody to him. He was unable to show that in this case. Under circumstances proposed transfer of custody was problematical experiment in light of father's past experience and his recent remarriage.

1962—*Walker v. Brooks,* 203 Va. 417, 124 S.E.2d 195.
Grandmother filed petition for habeas corpus seeking custody of grandchildren. Children had lived with her for some years after their father's death. Grandmother failed to carry burden to show by clear and convincing evidence that mother had voluntarily relinquished her natural right to custody of children or that mother was unfit. Grandmother was separated from her husband and had monthly income of only $66.00 and some small savings. Mother's new husband earned between $6,000-$7,000 year and testified that he was willing to support children. Even though trial court found that mother had relinquished custody of children to grandmother, supreme court reversed and awarded custody to mother.

1961—*Jones v. Henson,* 202 Va. 738, 120 S.E.2d 286.
Parents of child are its natural guardians, and there is strong presumption that child's best interest will be served by placing it in their custody. Evidence justifying separation of child from its parents must be cogent and convincing. In this case, father had been awarded custody of child after divorce. Father died. Thereafter, mother, stepmother and grandmother sought custody. All three were found to be fit persons to have custody. Mother at no time voluntarily relin-

quished her claim to child. Stepmother did not stand in loco parentis and did not carry burden of proving facts which would deprive mother of her right to child.

1958—*Phillips v. Kiraly,* 200 Va. 345, 105 S.E.2d 855.

Mother died when one child was three years of age and recovering from polio. At that time, other child was even younger. Father, unable to care for children and in financial distress, placed daughter in home of his wife's sister. Two years later he had remarried, had paid or arranged to settle his indebtedness and had moved to Cleveland where he secured adequate employment. He filed this habeas corpus action to obtain custody of child. There is strong presumption that child's best interest will be served by placing it in custody of its natural parents. Evidence justifying separation from natural parents must be cogent and convincing. Father awarded custody.

1956—*Lawson v. Lawson,* 198 Va. 403, 94 S.E.2d 215.

One seeking custody against parent must show by convincing evidence circumstances sufficient to deprive parent of his normal rights. In this case, mother, during period of illness, sent her two children to home of her husband's brother. When mother recovered, she sought and was granted order awarding her custody. This was proper, since she was person of good character and was able to furnish suitable home. There was no clear showing that separation from her would be in best interest of children. There is strong presumption that best interest and welfare of child will be best served by placing it in custody of its natural parents and showing of such relationship in absence of anything more makes out prima facie case for parents. To separate child from its parents, evidence must be cogent and convincing.

1954—*Judd v. Van Horn,* 195 Va. 988, 81 S.E.2d 432.

Burden of showing that natural father should be deprived of custody is on parties opposing custody. Parents of unmarried minor children are their natural guardians and upon death of either parent survivor shall be natural guardian. To separate child from his parents, evidence of their unfitness must be cogent and convincing.

1951—*Williams v. Williams,* 192 Va. 787, 66 S.E.2d 500.

Rights of parents are to be respected unless they have been abandoned or relinquished. Ordinarily, rights of parents to custody are greater than that of grandparents. To separate child from its parents, evidence must be cogent and convincing. In this case husband and wife left their children with grandparents. Grandfather ordered wife away from home. Wife's failure to return to home alone does not show unfitness on her part to rear children. Fit parents with suitable home, who have not forfeited their rights should be allowed to keep child.

1950—*Burton v. Russell,* 190 Va. 339, 57 S.E.2d 95.

In this case, custody was given to couple who were no blood relation to child. Mother had agreed to adoption by this couple, and father, in divorce decree, had been adjudged to have deserted wife and child. His petition now for custody was denied.

1947—*Sutton v. Menges,* 186 Va. 805, 44 S.E.2d 414.

Wife deceased. Grandparents claiming custody. Even if it be conceded that at sometimes some dignity was wanting in demeanor of father, that is not enough to deprive him of custody. To separate child from its parents evidence of their unfitness must be cogent and convincing. Common law right of father to keep with him his legitimate children, when mother is dead, is not questioned.

1925—*Fleshood v. Fleshood,* 144 Va. 767, 130 S.E. 648.

Mother died when child was 18 months old. Child was originally cared for by paternal grandparents and then later by maternal grandfather. Approximately two years after maternal grandfather taking child in, natural father sought custody of child, after remarrying. Father had done nothing for his son, since mother's death and appears to have manifested relatively little interest in his welfare. If those were only relevant facts, then custody would most likely remain with paternal grandfather. He, however, is not particularly robust, and there is significant family history of tuberculosis. In light of that, custody goes to father, with right of visitation to paternal grandfather.

1919—*Cover v. Widener,* 125 Va. 643, 100 S.E.2d 459.

Father of 13-year-old girl had abandoned her and her mother when girl was infant. Girl was placed with maternal grandmother, with full consent and knowledge of father when she was few months old. Evidence from father was that he himself had been man of bad character up to about two years ago when he reformed. He stated that, if awarded custody, he would place his daughter in home of his sister whose husband was wealthy individual. While grandmother was not woman of substantial means, she was of highest character and had provided loving environment for child. Custody was awarded to grandmother.

1915—*Wyatt v. Gleason,* 117 Va. 196, 83 S.E. 1069.

Father voluntarily relinquished custody of his infant child to suitable female relative in whose care child has grown and expanded and who has warm ties of affection and love for child. Foster parents are people of highest moral character and of sufficient means to provide for child. They had been in highest sense father and mother to child. Child is happy and contented in her present environment. To change custody to father would at best be experimental. Child had been in possession of foster parents since shortly after birth. This action was filed when child was approximately two years old. Custody awarded to foster parents.

1911—*Moon v. Children's Home Society,* 112 Va. 737, 72 S.E. 707.

Society has no authority to deprive mother of custody simply because she has remarried into family of lower social standing even though her new husband has some Negro blood in him unless he has such amount as would make marriage void.

1898—*Stringfellow v. Somerville,* 95 Va. 701, 29 S.E. 685.

Mother, in her will, designated that custody of minor child was to be in her sister. Father acquiesced in this for years. In these intervening years, child became very attached to mother's sister and was well cared for. Ordinarily, father is entitled to care and custody of child. But when father is claiming to recover custody of his child, court will exercise its discretion according to what is in best interest of child. Parent in such circumstance will not be permitted to reclaim child unless he can show that change of custody will materially promote child's welfare.

1852—*Armstrong v. Stone,* 50 Va. 102.

Father in this case being dead, mother is entitled to custody as of right. In this case, since wife was seeking custody from grandparent through petition for habeas corpus, court said that this is case where it can use its discretion as to whether it is best for infant to be assigned to custody of mother. If child is of age of discretion, then court will consult his wishes. Custody in this case was awarded to mother.

(I) Visitation.

See Va. Code § 20-107.2 dealing with custody and support. Court has authority to enter order concerning visitation rights of parents and visitation privileges for grandparents, stepparents and other family members.

See Va. Code § 31-16 as to access by certain persons to child in custody of another. Court, upon petition of parent when any minor child is in sole custody of other parent or if anyone by his or her authority, or any guardian of child, father or mother being dead, may make order for access of petitioner to minor child.

1980—*Oehl v. Oehl,* 221 Va. 618, 272 S.E.2d 441.

Visitation rights of noncustodial parent are subordinate to welfare of infant.

1980—*West v. King,* 220 Va. 754, 263 S.E.2d 386.

Va. Code § 16.1-241 does not grant juvenile court authority to award visitation privileges to grandparent over objection of custodial parent.

1968—*Portewig v. Ryder,* 208 Va. 791, 160 S.E.2d 789.

Supreme court indicated that in this case visitation rights should be specific so as to provide for days and times of visitation and noted that wife's rights should not be restricted to seeing children in husband's home.

1961—*Taylor v. Taylor,* 203 Va. 1, 121 S.E.2d 753.

> Husband did not object to visitation provision in court below and as such any error is waived. However, upon showing of changed conditions, he could apply for relief to trial court.

1960—*Brooks v. Brooks,* 201 Va. 731, 113 S.E.2d 872.

> Wife was awarded divorce, alimony and custody of her son. Trial court stated that visitation should be allowed every weekend from Friday to Monday morning. Supreme court found that was not visitation but instead was joint custody and as such set that order aside. Father was then allowed visitation one weekend month and one month during summer. Court noted that this previous arrangement of joint custody was not in best interest of child, for it would result in his having no real home and no permanent associations.

1948—*Davis v. Davis,* 187 Va. 63, 45 S.E.2d 918.

> Father had previously absconded with child in violation of court order. Before he is granted any visitation after final decree he should be required to execute bond.

1942—*Darnell v. Barker,* 179 Va. 86, 18 S.E.2d 271.

> If visitation conditions are burdensome to spouse at fault then he is to blame since he broke up family. In spite of that, in present case, reasonable provision should be made for visitation.

1935—*Bausell v. Commonwealth,* 165 Va. 693, 181 S.E. 462.

> Father has no right to forcibly take custody of child where child is in possession of mother and is in no serious danger.

1924—*Elder v. Elder,* 139 Va. 19, 123 S.E. 369.

> Supreme court, in this case, awarded custody to mother, with husband having right to visit children once every two weeks if he so desires.

1898—*Stringfellow v. Somerville,* 95 Va. 701, 29 S.E. 685.

> In this case, custody was awarded to mother's sister. That custody arrangement had been originally acquiesced in by father but later on was challenged by him. In order refusing custody, it is error to provide for such interaction between father and child as would be subversive of discipline of those who have custody.

§ 3-3. Legitimacy.

See Va. Code § 20-31.1. If person having had child shall afterwards intermarry with mother or father, such child, if recognized by both of them as their own child, jointly or separately, before or after marriage, shall be deemed legitimate. Children of marriages prohibited by law, deemed null or void or dissolved by court, shall nevertheless be legitimate.

See Va. Code § 64.1-7.1 indicating that child conceived by artificial insemination is presumed legitimate.

1983—*Brown v. Kittle,* 225 Va. 451, 303 S.E.2d 864.

Father of illegitimate child awarded custody. Foremost concern is welfare of child. Father of illegitimate child seeking custody cannot be denied relief as punishment for violating court orders of foreign jurisdictions if granting custody to father would be in best interest of child.

1980—*Cassady v. Martin,* 220 Va. 1093, 266 S.E.2d 104.

Trial court erred in ruling on paternity issue as matter of law in this wrongful death action. Person who claims to be decedent's child has burden of proving this. Presumption of law exists in favor of legitimacy of child born in wedlock. To rebut presumption evidence must be clear and positive. Nonaccess of husband to wife must be proved beyond all reasonable doubt. It was for jury to determine whether or not presumption had been overcome.

1980—*All State Messenger Serv. v. James,* 220 Va. 910, 266 S.E.2d 86.

In this workmen's compensation case decedents' supposed son filed claim for benefits. Under compensation act only test for determining paternity is acknowledgement. That is question of fact. Here testimony supporting acknowledgement was uncontradicted and was credible.

1977—*Brown v. Commonwealth,* 218 Va. 40, 235 S.E.2d 325.

Children of marriages deemed to be null or dissolved by court are nevertheless legitimate.

1967—*Gibson v. Gibson,* 207 Va. 821, 153 S.E.2d 189.

Both parties sought divorce. Both alleged May 6, 1964, as date of last cohabitation. In its decree, court awarded husband divorce stating that separation of parties had continued without interruption since that date. Husband was ordered to pay support for child born to Mrs. Gibson on March 16, 1965. This was held error. Not only had court found no cohabitation during time when child was conceived but many witnesses testified to wife's promiscuous associations during this period. As late as January, 1965, wife had testified under oath that she was not pregnant. On this record, presumption of legitimacy was rebutted. Improbability of known access by husband merely of itself is not sufficient to rebut presumption. When evidence forces conclusion of non-access beyond all reasonable doubt, it is sufficient to rebut presumption. Several cases cited dealing with legitimacy.

1959—*Parker v. Harcum,* 201 Va. 441, 111 S.E.2d 449.

To establish legitimacy, it is necessary to identify father, prove his marriage with mother and show that before or after marriage he recognized child. Term recognize means to acknowledge, accept, admit or own. In this case, mother positively identified Parker as father and testified that he promised to marry her, that he did marry her to end prosecution for seduction and acknowledge in presence of jury that he was father, failed to deny charge in mother's subsequent divorce action and when confronted by child years later inferentially admitted paternity. This evidence was held sufficient even though parents never lived together and Parker never contributed to support of child and consistently denied paternity to his relatives and others.

1957—*Hyson v. Dodge,* 198 Va. 792, 96 S.E.2d 792.
Dispute as to ownership of property. Recitation in deed stating that John Kelley died intestate and that Ida Ball was his sole heir created prima facie presumption. Opposing side introduced evidence at trial to show that Ida Ball was illegitimate. Since no evidence was offered to prove Ida Ball's legitimacy, other than deed, court's finding that she was not legitimate child was proper.

1943—*Withrow v. Edwards,* 181 Va. 344, 25 S.E.2d 343.
Virginia Code removed stigma of bastardy from innocent issue of void marriages, as well as issue born of out wedlock whose parents afterwards intermarried, provided such issue was recognized by father as his child before or after marriage.

1942—*McClaugherty v. McClaugherty,* 180 Va. 51, 21 S.E.2d 761.
Issue of marriages deemed null in law shall nevertheless be legitimate. Even where marriage is common law marriage which is not recognized by Virginia courts as valid, statute still makes these children legitimate.

1933—*Cornwall v. Cornwall,* 160 Va. 183, 168 S.E. 439.
Child born after marriage is legitimate even though marriage is void.

1932—*Harper v. Harper,* 159 Va. 210, 165 S.E. 490.
For child to be legitimated it is necessary that:
    (1) Man should have had child by woman.
    (2) They married after birth.
    (3) Child was recognized by man before and after marriage.

1928—*Denny v. Searles,* 150 Va. 701, 143 S.E. 484.
Whether legatee of testator, resident of Virginia, was legitimate was matter of Virginia law.

1928—*Hayes v. Strauss,* 151 Va. 136, 144 S.E. 432.
Habeas corpus proceeding to determine proper custody of bastard child as between maternal grandmother and father. Mother, prior to death, requested that custody be in child's father. Father was employed, of good habits; child would be living with paternal grandparents and father. Maternal grandmother would leave child with her 15-year-old daughter during work day. Custody properly given to father.

1928—*Goodman v. Goodman,* 150 Va. 42, 142 S.E. 412.
Wife was never divorced from first husband when she remarried and gave birth. Both parties believe they had right to marry. If marriage is entered into in accord with terms and ceremonies of law and child is recognized by father either before or after marriage, then child is legitimate. Legitimacy statutes are remedial and should be liberally construed.

1923—*Vanderpool v. Ryan,* 137 Va. 445, 119 S.E. 65.

In order to legitimize, there must be marriage of some kind. Statute does not legitimize children which are result of illicit intercourse. There must be marriage, although it may be one which is null and void for any of several reasons. In this case, evidence did not establish any marriage and, as such, child was not legitimate and therefore not entitled to inherit from alleged father.

1920—*Cumming v. Cumming,* 127 Va. 16, 102 S.E. 572.

Child born out of wedlock may be made legitimate by father marrying mother of child.

1920—*Hoover v. Hoover,* 131 Va. 522, 105 S.E. 91.

Under common law subsequent marriage of parents did not render bastard legitimate. Under statute it is necessary that:
(1) man should have had child by woman
(2) they intermarried
(3) child was recognized by man

1917—*Francis v. Tazewell,* 120 Va. 319, 91 S.E. 202.

Children of marriages deemed null in law or dissolved by court shall nevertheless be legitimate. This particular case involved offspring of slave marriage. Children were held to be legitimate.

1914—*Lemons v. Harris,* 115 Va. 809, 80 S.E. 740.

By statute, children of Negroes who had cohabited together as man and wife and were then so cohabiting were legitimate regardless of whether rites of marriage had been celebrated.

1903—*Patterson v. Bingham,* 101 Va. 372, 43 S.E. 609.

Under statute in existence at time, child of two former slaves was deemed to be illegitimate since parents never intermarried.

1894—*Herkert v. Hile,* 90 Va. 390, 18 S.E. 841.

Wife leaves her husband and goes to another state. He marries again and has children born of second marriage before first is dissolved. Those children are legitimate.

1892—*Scott v. Raub,* 88 Va. 721, 14 S.E. 178.

Plaintiff was born in 1862 of parents living together as husband and wife, he being colored man and she slave. Plaintiff was held to be legitimate.

1888—*Scott v. Hillenberg,* 85 Va. 245, 4 S.E. 379.

Law presumes legitimacy where husband recognizes child as his and impossibility is not established. Such presumption is not repelled by proof of circumstances, which only create doubts and suspicion. Evidence of non-access must be clear and positive.

1885—*Greenhow v. James' Ex'r,* 80 Va. 636.

Children in this case were born prior to marriage. Parents were of different races. Even though parents intermarried and recognized children, they were still deemed to be illegitimate since marriage itself was absolutely void and criminal.

1885—*Smith v. Perry,* 80 Va. 563.

Law presumes legitimacy where husband recognizes child is his and impossibility of procreation is not established. Illegitimate child in Virginia is person born out of wedlock, lawful or unlawful, or not within competent time after termination of coverture; or, if born out of wedlock, whose parents do not afterwards intermarry, and father acknowledges child; or who are born in wedlock when procreation by husband is impossible.

1884—*Fitchett v. Smith,* 78 Va. 524.

Offspring of two Negroes who never married but did cohabit was deemed to be legitimate.

1811—*Bowles v. Bingham,* 16 Va. 442.

Husband's statement that child born in wedlock is not his is not sufficient evidence to prove child to be illegitimate in spite of fact that it was born three months after marriage, and separation between his wife and him soon thereafter took place by mutual consent.

1805—*Sleigh v. Strider,* 9 Va. 439.

Child born out of wedlock was legitimated by subsequent marriage and acknowledgment of parents.

1804—*Stones v. Keeling,* 9 Va. 143.

Child of woman by second marriage, which took place during lifetime of her first husband, is legitimate.

1797—*Fall v. Overseers,* 17 Va. 495.

If woman accuses man of being father of her child, then he may present testimony at about nine months before birth of child that she was guilty of intercourse with other men. If defendant admits, however, that he had intercourse with her about same time, such proof may be rejected, and he may be confined to proof of general character of woman.

§ 3-4. Parent — Child.

(A) Discipline.

1972—*Lovisi v. Commonwealth,* 212 Va. 848, 188 S.E.2d 206.

Stepfather was charged with abuse of children. He had never adopted children, but he did provide support for them. Under this statute, custody of child is not limited to legal custody. Question of whether or not he had custody in this context was jury issue.

1947—*Carpenter v. Commonwealth,* 186 Va. 851, 44 S.E.2d 419.

Parent has right to punish child within bounds of moderation and reason, so long as he does it for welfare of child. If he exceeds due moderation, he becomes criminally liable.

1918—*Flippo v. Commonwealth,* 122 Va. 854, 94 S.E. 771.

Custody of 13-year-old boy placed by State with plaintiff to bring him up. If boy's conduct was such as to require reasonable and moderate correction for his welfare, it was right and duty of plaintiff to administer it. Conviction in this criminal prosecution for cruelty was reversed. Although there was some evidence of physical contact, this was properly explained.

(B) In Loco Parentis.

1976—*Lyles v. Jackson,* 216 Va. 797, 223 S.E.2d 873.
Step-father and children's mother purchased house trailer and established their home where they lived with her four children. Although husband did not adopt children, neighbors testified he held children out as members of his family and appeared to discharge parental functions. There is no error to hold husband in loco parentis as to children.

1947—*Carpenter v. Commonwealth,* 186 Va. 851, 44 S.E.2d 419.
Generally, it is held that persons standing in loco parentis have same right as natural parents as to punishment of child.

1928—*Doughty v. Thornton,* 151 Va. 785, 145 S.E. 249.
Where step-father receives step-child into his family, treats him as member, then he stands in place of natural parent with reciprocal rights and duties so long as relationship continues. Where step-child is induced by step-father to care for him in later years there may be implied promise to pay. There is no legal duty to do so on step-child where parties stand in loco parentis at time service provided, then there can be no recovery on implied promise to pay.

(C) Miscellaneous.

See Va. Code §§ 8.01-43, 8.01-44. Parents may be liable for willful or malicious destruction of property by minor children.

1938—*Buchanan v. Buchanan,* 170 Va. 458, 197 S.E. 426.
Action by minor children and divorced wife to compel husband to pay monthly sum for future maintenance and education of children. Suits by child against parent are not encouraged.

1928—*Harlow v. Harlow,* 152 Va. 910, 143 S.E. 720.
Although parents have right to interfere that is superior to strangers, they may not influence their child to separate from spouse with impunity.

1923—*Stanley v. Rasnick,* 137 Va. 415, 119 S.E. 76.
Action by parent for loss of his child's services and society will not, unless allowed by statute, against anyone for loss of infant child's service after marriage, although marriage has been brought about by wrongful and illegal enticing of child, where child is of age of consent and did in fact consent thereto, and marriage is either at common law or by statute, valid marriage.

1885—*Bell v. Moon,* 79 Va. 341.
Where child marries and leaves parental home and then returns to reside there while having adequate means of support, law presumes promise to pay from acceptance of that benefit.

1884—*Valley Mut. Life Ass'n v. Teewalt,* 79 Va. 421.

It is well-settled that father has insurable interest in child's life, and child in father's.

(D) Paternity.

See Va. Code § 20-61.2 as to admission of blood test results in divorce or support proceedings where question of paternity arises.

1982—*Smith v. Givens,* 223 Va. 455, 290 S.E.2d 844.

Absent presumption of legitimacy which attaches to child born in wedlock, standard of proof of paternity in wrongful death case is proved by preponderance of evidence. In this case, only evidence of paternity were hearsay statements made by putative father. This hearsay evidence however, did not come in under pedigree exception since there was better evidence that could have been obtained of relationship. As such, there was no evidence that was admissible to establish paternity.

1980—*Cassady v. Martin,* 220 Va. 1093, 266 S.E.2d 104.

Statement of paternity signed under oath by decedent is admissible under Va. Code § 20-61.1, but other paternity statements of deceased putative father are inadmissible as hearsay.

1977—*Brown v. Commonwealth,* 218 Va. 40, 235 S.E.2d 325.

Brown denied paternity of child of bigamous marriage. Parties had lived together as husband and wife for five weeks. He contended that absent express admission by him, his paternity could be established only by evidence of type outlined in Va. Code § 20-61.1. Trial court found child to be issue of void marriage and legitimate under former Va. Code § 64.1-7. Court found that he was father of child, cohabiting with mother during period when child was conceived, and therefore child is entitled to support by father.

1967—*Gibson v. Gibson,* 207 Va. 821, 153 S.E.2d 189.

Paternity of husband was not established, and legitimacy was rebutted in light of finding of court that last cohabitation between couple occurred on May 6, 1964, child was born on March 16, 1965, 314 days later. Wife had alleged that last date of cohabitation was May 6, 1964, and testified under oath on January, 1965, that she was not pregnant. Presumption of legitimacy was rebutted, and father was not obliged to pay child support.

1959—*Distefano v. Commonwealth,* 201 Va. 23, 109 S.E.2d 497.

Commonwealth offered evidence of defendant having claimed two children in question as his dependents on IRS returns. Court concluded that these returns are not acts voluntarily admitting paternity in writing under oath as is contemplated by statute. As such, although he may have been father of children, he could not be found guilty of non-support.

(E) Support of Parents.

See Va. Code § 20-88 as to support of parents by children.

1938—*Mitchell — Powers Hdwe. v. Eaton,* 171 Va. 255, 198 S.E. 496.
> Child is liable for support of parent if parent is in necessitous circumstances. He must furnish such support as comport with health, comfort and welfare of normal individuals according to their standard of living considering child's means.

1928—*Wheatley v. Stapleton,* 151 Va. 295, 144 S.E. 471.
> Suit by daughter against estate of parents on alleged contract to pay daughter for supporting parents. Suit is in nature of creditor's bill. Daughter awarded $720.

1902—*Nicholas v. Nicholas,* 100 Va. 660, 42 S.E. 669.
> Claim of son for board of and attention to his father in his lifetime must be established by satisfactory evidence of contract for payment. Law will not imply contract to pay.

1901—*Davis v. Anderson,* 99 Va. 620, 39 S.E. 588.
> Son is under no legal obligation to support his mother and his contract to pay for her support, furnished without his request, is without consideration. Moral obligation to be sufficient to sustain promise or contract must be one which has been once valuable consideration but was not binding on account of some rule of law or has ceased to be binding for some supervening cause.

1898—*Jackson v. Jackson,* 96 Va. 165, 31 S.E. 78.
> Whenever compensation is claimed for services rendered near relatives, such as father, brother or grandfather and like, law will not imply promise of payment and no recovery can be had unless express contract or its equivalent is shown. Moral obligation to pay is not sufficient. This is especially so when party sought to be charged is dead. Generally services of child, grandchild or other near relative are presumed to have been rendered in obedience to promptings of affection and not with view to compensation.

CHAPTER 4

SUPPORT—CHILD AND SPOUSAL

§ 4-1. In General.

(A) Criteria.

1984—*Lapidus v. Lapidus,* 226 Va. 575, 311 S.E.2d 786.

Husband in this case had gross annual income of approximately $50,000 and received $8,000 per year tax exempt interest on bonds. His total assets were approximately $204,000. Wife was unemployed although she worked periodically and she was college graduate. She had savings accounts of approximately $41,000 which produced interest of around $3,000 per year. Court set permanent alimony at $1,875 per month. Supreme court noted that although that amount was large, it was not excessive, and therefore was upheld. Such awards will not be disturbed on appeal absent clear injustice. Wife has right to be maintained in manner to which she was accustomed during marriage.

1983—*Thomasson v. Thomasson,* 225 Va. 394, 302 S.E.2d 63.

Trial court in determining whether alimony should be awarded must first determine whether or not alimony is barred by existence of marital fault. If claim is not barred, then court shall consider relative needs and obligations of parties being guided by six specific factors stated in code. Where court gives due consideration to these factors as shown by evidence in this case determination as to spousal support will not be disturbed except for clear abuse of discretion. In this case, alimony was denied.

1980—*McCausey v. McCausey,* 221 Va. 500, 272 S.E.2d 36.

Husband's net income was $833 per month. Wife's monthly income was approximately $400. If she was required to make mortgage payments on family home, her expenses would total $838. Trial court incorrectly ruled that there was no need on part of wife for alimony.

1980—*Bristow v. Bristow,* 221 Va. 1, 267 S.E.2d 89.

No fault divorce decree does not relieve husband of any obligation he may otherwise have to support wife. Court has discretion to award alimony, but in exercising this discretion, it must consider all factors set forth in Va. Code § 20-107. Failure to do so is reversible error. Neither party has absolute obligation to support other. Husband and wife are on equal footing in that either spouse now may be awarded support and maintenance from other.

1979—*Featherstone v. Brooks,* 220 Va. 443, 258 S.E.2d 513.

Both parents owe their child duty of support during minority. In allocating this burden, court considers among other things, earning capacity, obligations, needs, and financial resources of parties. Decree of court in resolving questions of facts regarding these issues will stand unless plainly wrong. Wife alleged in this case that her necessary living expenses exceeded her disposable income and therefore she should not be obliged to pay child support. Court found there was no merit in this contention, especially since court found that her necessary living expenses did not actually exceed her disposable income.

1979—*Jacobs v. Jacobs,* 219 Va. 993, 254 S.E.2d 56.

Courts are empowered to assess spousal support awards, not to penalize or reward either party to marriage contract, but rather to do equity between two and to protect societies' interest. Award must be made based on circumstances disclosed by evidence at time of award and not speculative future changes in circumstance.

1977—*Brooker v. Brooker,* 218 Va. 12, 235 S.E.2d 309.

Alimony should not be denied by court in no fault divorce without finding by court as to various factors required to be considered under former Va. Code § 20-107 [now § 20-107.2]. This case was reversed for that reason and remanded for determination as to those factors.

1976—*Thomas v. Thomas,* 217 Va. 502, 229 S.E.2d 887.

Evidence established wife's need for support and husband's ability to pay, and since there was no showing of her being guilty of misconduct entitling husband to divorce, court had no choice but to award wife alimony. In this case award of alimony was $200 per month and husband's income was approximately $28,000 per year. Although that amount was modest, supreme court indicated that it was not without evidence to support it.

1976—*Butler v. Butler,* 217 Va. 195, 227 S.E.2d 688.

Husband within his limits of his financial ability is required to maintain his former wife in manner to which she was accustomed during marriage. Husband's voluntary decision to remain in low-salaried, career-oriented staff position as neurosurgeon, sacrificing immediate income for future expectations will not be permitted to penalize wife. Even with his present income there are certain things he could do to increase his monthly take home by changing his exemptions and by withdrawing from retirement plan. Wife was awarded $500 per month. $300 of this was for child support and $200 for alimony. There were two children. Husband's annual salary was $26,500. Husband was also ordered to pay monthly mortgage and taxes on family home occupied by family. Mortgage payment was $440 per month. Order of trial court was affirmed.

1976—*Ingram v. Ingram,* 217 Va. 27, 225 S.E.2d 362.

Wife awarded alimony of $800 per month and child support of $400 per month for one child. Husband's annual income was approximately $100,000 and his net worth was $1.6 million. Award was not excessive.

1975—*Russell v. Russell,* 216 Va. 432, 219 S.E.2d 689.

Wife claimed her monthly expenditures were $1,000 month so as to maintain her former lifestyle. Husband and his new wife had combined income of approximately $70,000 per year which was derived primarily from successor corporation that formerly had been family business. Parties also owned substantial real estate. Alimony award of $200 week was affirmed.

1975—*Jones v. Jones,* 216 Va. 161, 217 S.E.2d 800.

Record failed to sustain husband's contention that wife is financially able to support herself without assistance from husband. Award of alimony was affirmed.

1975—*Wickham v. Wickham,* 215 Va. 694, 213 S.E.2d 750.

Property settlement provided that husband was to pay $930 per month for support and maintenance of wife and three minor children. Payments were to be reduced by $150 per month upon death or emancipation of each child. This agreement provided basis from which to calculate and determine whether change had occurred in children's financial needs. Court in this case unnecessarily apportioned award upon petition of wife. That had adverse affect upon tax advantage secured to husband.

1975—*Gagliano v. Gagliano,* 215 Va. 447, 211 S.E.2d 62.

Husband's income was $10,900. Wife's take home monthly income was $441. Husband had substantial debts due to education. Court properly denied wife's claim for alimony, but should have included reservation of power to reinstate case and award alimony upon proper showing of change in circumstance and conditions.

1975—*Robertson v. Robertson,* 215 Va. 425, 211 S.E.2d 41.

Wife awarded alimony of approximately $20,000 per year. Husband's gross earnings were approximately $70,000 per year of which he paid approximately $40,000 per year in alimony and child support for previous marriage. Award in this case was set aside because it was not supported by evidence on record. Wife argued that award was justified because husband should have received greater return on certain investments. Evidence, however, indicated that rate of return was established with advice of competent counsel, and as such, should not have been considered. Likewise, potential receipt of substantial money from trust fund should not have been considered since it was too speculative. Case remanded with both parties given opportunity to submit additional evidence.

1974—*Brauer v. Brauer,* 215 Va. 62, 205 S.E.2d 665.

Wife awarded $500 per month alimony. Husband's income was approximately $10,000. Wife's monthly expenses were $541 and husband's monthly expenses were $535. Court found that $500 per month was too high and remanded. Wife, who is physically able to work and has capacity to earn, has no right to remain idle at expense of her former husband. In this case, there was considerable question as to whether or not wife would be able to become gainfully employed. Husband had life estate in property assessed at over $200,000. Judgment that wife had obtained for alimony arrearages might very well absorb amount equivalent to husband's life estate in property that was valued at excess of $200,000.

1972—*Turner v. Turner,* 213 Va. 42, 189 S.E.2d 361.

Husband has duty to support wife and family according to station in life to which he has accustomed them. Needs of wife and children and financial ability of husband are to be considered. In this case, husband was making more than $50,000 per year and, by his own admission, had net worth in excess of one million dollars. Wife was awarded $800 per month alimony and $400 per month child support for two children.

1970—*Moon v. Moon,* 210 Va. 575, 172 S.E.2d 778.

Wife was awarded $125 per month separate maintenance when husband deserted her. After two years, wife was granted divorce and alimony was then fixed at $25 per month. As of that date, her income had increased by approximately $15 per week. Her estimated needs had increased almost as much. Husband's income had remained same. Case was reversed and remanded with trial court instructed to take further evidence to fix award of alimony related to reasonable needs of wife and ability of husband to pay.

1967—*Wimbrow v. Wimbrow,* 208 Va. 141, 156 S.E.2d 598.

Husband had previously given financial statement to bank reflecting net worth of over $200,000. At trial, he testified his net worth was approximately $20,000. Trial court improperly refused admission of this financial statement. Admission of statement will not imply that it reflects husband's present worth, but counsel should be permitted to ask him what disposition he has made of assets listed in financial statement.

1965—*Davis v. Davis,* 206 Va. 381, 143 S.E.2d 835.

Wife served notice on husband's counsel of claim for support for child, attorney's fees and costs. There was no requirement that such request be made in form of cross-bill.

1964—*Gramelspacher v. Gramelspacher,* 204 Va. 839, 134 S.E.2d 285.

Wife was awarded support of $350 per month for herself and four children. Husband's monthly income was $750, and he received dividends of more than $2,000 per year. His father made substantial contributions to his former wife and children. Such payments, however, would not relieve husband of his obligation to his wife and children. Terms of decree showed that lower court had given husband credit for certain payments made by his father for support of wife.

1962—*Klotz v. Klotz,* 203 Va. 677, 127 S.E.2d 104.

Wife who has been awarded divorce and held blameless for marital breach is entitled to be supported by her former husband within limits of his ability, according to station in life to which she was accustomed. Factors to be considered are wife's age, ability to earn and needs, balanced against husband's ability to pay. Wife is not required to invade her separate estate to relieve obligation of husband. In this case, parties had been married for long time. Wife's separate estate was over $100,000 and husband's net worth was over $200,000. Her income was approximately $90 per month, and she had unsuccessfully sought employment. Husband's annual income was $12,500. Trial court had awarded $290 per month alimony. Supreme court increased this to $400 per month. Wife had claimed monthly expenses of $750. Court noted that several of these items were for expenses incurred in connection with her separate estate which were not chargeable to husband. Certain other items she had failed to show were necessary to maintain her proper station in life.

1961—*Taylor v. Taylor,* 203 Va. 1, 121 S.E.2d 753.

Criteria in determining alimony are financial ability of husband, needs of wife and style of life to which they have become accustomed. Husband had been making approximately $14,000 per year. He left that job to take another job at lesser income. Evidence showed that he could go back to his former job at approximately $13,000 per year. Court found that income they would consider was approximately $13,000 per year and awarded $150 per month alimony, $300 per month child support for three children and ordered that he pay mortgage payments of $100 per month. This left husband, after payment of taxes and other expenses, with approximately $275 per month which he testified was minimum amount of his living expenses.

1960—*Oliver v. Oliver,* 202 Va. 268, 117 S.E.2d 59.

In fixing amount of support money, court has wide discretion and will not be interfered with unless it is clear that some injustice has been done. Factors to be considered are needs of wife and children, their ages and physical condition, financial ability of husband. It is duty of husband to support his wife and family consistent with his financial ability according to station in life to which he has accustomed them to live. Husband in this case made approximately $21,000 per year. He was ordered to pay $850 per month for support of wife and six children, whose ages ranged from 8 to 19; to furnish them family dwelling rent free and automobile; to pay taxes and insurance premiums on dwelling; major medical expenses and tuition of oldest child at college. There was no showing of abuse of discretion by chancellor and decree was affirmed.

1960—*Todd v. Todd,* 202 Va. 133, 115 S.E.2d 905.
Wife had net worth of $62,000 and husband of $100,000. He was employed at annual salary of $7,000. Both parties were in their fifties. It was not abuse of discretion to award wife alimony.

1960—*Brooks v. Brooks,* 201 Va. 731, 113 S.E.2d 872.
Husband in this case owned his own residence worth approximately $10,000 and also service station with equity of approximately $7,000. His annual net income was approximately $1,800. He was in his early 50s and in good health. Based on those factors, award of alimony and child support of $15 per week was inadequate. Supreme court held that alimony should be set at $12.50 per week and $10 per week for child support. In determining support, court should consider needs of wife and ability of husband to pay, not necessarily what his actual earnings are.

1960—*Hinshaw v. Hinshaw,* 201 Va. 668, 112 S.E.2d 902.
In this case, parties lived together for approximately 90 days and thereafter separated. Wife developed nervous condition which prevented her from working. Husband's net worth was approximately $124,000 and his annual income was $9,600. Court allowed separate maintenance as to wife because of cruelty and desertion on part of husband but allowed only $15 per month alimony. Court noted that wife materially changed her condition when she married. She gave up apartment and job and she cannot reestablish her home without considerable expense. She is physically unable to work. For these reasons, court found that trial court abused its discretion as to amount of alimony awarded and set alimony at $50 per week.

1957—*Beers v. Beers,* 198 Va. 682, 96 S.E.2d 139.
It was error to deny wife's request for alimony where evidence indicated that husband was one who deserted. In determining sum of alimony to be awarded, court should consider earnings of parties, their monthly expenses, necessary expenditures for support of their children, and needs of wife.

1957—*Baytop v. Baytop,* 199 Va. 388, 100 S.E.2d 14.
Award of $150 month alimony was not justified, wife being able to earn salary ample to maintain her in her station in life. Wife was making approximately $3,100 per year and husband approximately $4,200 per year. Court should not award alimony as punishment to transgressor husband or as reward to wronged wife.

1956—*Bundy v. Bundy,* 197 Va. 795, 91 S.E.2d 412.

Husband deserted wife. She was denied divorce because she stated that she wished to continue to live with him. It was error, however, to deny her alimony. Alimony may be awarded without divorce. Husband has legal duty to support his wife. However, her needs and his ability to pay must be considered in determining amount. Husband earns approximately $200 per month. Wife worked but no evidence as to her income. Child support awarded of $50 per month for one child. Husband agreed to pay rent of $55 per month. Case remanded for award of alimony since trial court had not awarded any.

1954—*Hepler v. Hepler,* 195 Va. 611, 79 S.E.2d 652.

Mother earned $220 per month. Father earned $175 to $225 per month. Trial court modified agreement of parties so as to order husband to pay $20 per month for one child in custody of mother. Considering earning capacity, mode of life and agreement of parties this was error. No child support allowed.

1954—*Wilson v. Wilson,* 195 Va. 1060, 81 S.E.2d 605.

Husband's suit for divorce was denied. Wife prevailed as to separate maintenance, alimony and custody. Although she was not entitled to have family home designated for her use, wife was entitled to select and occupy, subject to approval of court, comparable home, rental of which should be paid by husband. Record showed calculated effort by husband to minimize income and conceal assets. In such case, court should appoint accountant to make complete inventory and appraisal.

1948—*Davis v. Davis,* 187 Va. 63, 45 S.E.2d 918.

Evidence meager as to husband's earning capacity. He testified he could properly provide for child. $40 per month awarded.

1948—*Hawkins v. Hawkins,* 187 Va. 595, 47 S.E.2d 436.

Allotment of alimony is within discretion of trial court. In fixing amount, court must consider needs of wife and husband's ability to earn. Duty of husband to provide adequate support according to station in life in which he has placed them consistent with his financial ability. While alimony is not to be used as method of punishment where husband at fault, court will not seek to find how light burden may possibly be made. Husband making $70 per week. Court ordered $110 per month alimony and support for two children. Amount reasonable. Wife making approximately $112 per month. Supreme court indicated that such amount leaving husband with nearly one half of net earnings in many circles would not be considered unfavorable ratio. Appellate court will not interfere with determination of amount of alimony unless it is clear that some injustice has been done.

1946—*Ring v. Ring,* 185 Va. 269, 38 S.E.2d 471.

There is no rule of law that requires wife of substantial means to expend her estate to ameliorate condition of husband brought about by his faithlessness to marriage vows. It is duty of husband to provide adequate support for wife and children according to station in life in which he has placed them, consistent with his financial ability. Trial court has very broad discretion in fixing amount of alimony and will not be overturned on appeal unless it is clear that some injustice has been done. Husband's net worth was $112,000. Annual income was approximately $20,000. Wife's income was approximately same and her estate was approximately $150,000. Alimony fixed at $300 per month and child support at $100 per month for each of three children.

1942—*Cecil v. Cecil,* 179 Va. 274, 19 S.E.2d 64.

Not intended as penalty or reward. Amount rests in sole discretion of court. Factors to consider: (1) financial condition of husband (2) needs of wife (3) all other circumstances of case.

1941—*Hulcher v. Hulcher,* 177 Va. 12, 12 S.E.2d 767.

Alimony is not intended as penalty or reward. Factors to consider: (1) needs of wife (2) ability of husband to pay in light of earning capacity (3) all other circumstances of case. Husband not relieved of obligation due to ability of children to take care of mother.

1939—*Hughes v. Hughes,* 173 Va. 293, 4 S.E.2d 402.

Prior to institution of suit husband may in large measure decide for himself what he will contribute to support wife. After suit filed this will be decided by court.

1939—*Wade v. Wade,* 172 Va. 282, 1 S.E.2d 331.

Wife at fault. Husband 75 years old, heavily in debt and in poor health. Wife comparatively young and in good health. No alimony allowed.

1939—*Babcock v. Babcock,* 172 Va. 219, 1 S.E.2d 328.

There is open to wife practically every avenue for making money as is open to husband. Wife has no right to remain idle at expense of former husband although he is at fault. In this case, marriage lasted 82 days; he was 70 years old and she was comparatively young; he had afflicted son; he had been liberal in providing for their joint comforts. No alimony awarded.

1936—*Allen v. Allen,* 166 Va. 303, 186 S.E. 17.

Husband made $2,100 per year. Wife under continual care of physician. Alimony of $75 per month not excessive.

1932—*Lindsey v. Lindsey,* 158 Va. 647, 164 S.E. 551.

Inability to pay alimony because of poverty or insolvency is adequate excuse, but unwillingness is not substitute for inability. Husband in this case claimed insolvency. Evidence showed he was running business of some magnitude with five employees, one of whom was paid $100 per month. This, coupled with prior conduct, was basis for contempt finding. Court noted that in spite of his insolvency he has been able to retain distinguished counsel and does not proceed in forma pauperis.

1926—*Branch v. Branch,* 144 Va. 244, 132 S.E.2d 303.

Supreme court cannot take judicial notice of price per day of farm labor, but everyone knows that young, healthy man could have made more than twice amount of alimony he was paying per day. Husband claimed that his duty to his aged mother was excuse for his failure to pay. While duty to his aged mother is not to be minimized, his first duty in this instance is to those for whose existence he is responsible. Order awarding alimony is presumed to be correct.

1922—*Barnard v. Barnard,* 132 Va. 155, 111 S.E. 227.

Husband was young lawyer who, in year 1919, made $3,500 and for six months prior to date of testifying his income did not exceed $100 per month. His debts were between $1,000 and $1,500. Court awarded alimony in amount of $100 per month. That was held to be sufficient. In fixing alimony, it must be born in mind that, under modern conditions, there is open to wife practically every avenue for making money that is open to her husband. By decree of Court, she is released from her household duties and has no right to remain idle, even though it was through fault of husband that contract of marriage was rescinded.

1921—*Twohy v. Twohy,* 130 Va. 557, 107 S.E. 642.

Wife awarded divorce on grounds of cruelty. Husband's annual income was something over $11,500. His estate was estimated at something like $300,000. Alimony was set at $3,600 per year and child support for three minor children was set at $3,600 per year. Quoting from *Minor,* court stated that ordinarily wife ought to be allowed for permanent alimony from $1/3$ to $1/2$ of joint income, $2/5$ being no uncommon proportion. Quoting from another text, court stated that where he is possessed of estate, it would be improper, under any circumstances, to give her less that what her dower interest therein would be since he should not be allowed to profit by his own wrong.

1920—*Lovegrove v. Lovegrove,* 128 Va. 449, 104 S.E. 804.

Wife awarded divorce on grounds of cruelty. General rule is that wife is not entitled to have any specific parcel of real estate assigned to her. Alimony is usually allowance in money out of husband's estate but not estate itself. Husband's property, in this case, was not estimated to exceed $5,000 and his earning capacity was $2.50 per day. Court awarded alimony in amount of $30 per month. Court noted that, while not deciding that there could be no case in Virginia in which trial court, in exercise of its discretion, could permit wife with her infant children to occupy specific house owned by husband, there was no reason under circumstances of this case for departing from general rule. Appellate court will not interfere with trial court's decision as to alimony unless it is clear that some injustice has been done.

1920—*West v. West,* 126 Va. 696, 101 S.E. 876.

Husband in this case was strong man, 33 years old, employed, owner of real estate worth $800 and of boat which he used in connection with his business as oyster man. Alimony awarded was $15 per month pending litigation. Decree for alimony is essentially different from ordinary judgment. It is allowance in nature of partition of husband's property, of which wife is entitled to reasonable share for her maintenance.

1899—*Trimble v. Trimble,* 97 Va. 217, 33 S.E. 531.

Before fixing amount of alimony to be paid for support of wife and infant child, court should ascertain value of his property and extent of his income. Although that was not done in this case, amount awarded by trial court was found to be minimum allowable. If necessary, motion could be filed to increase or decrease amount.

1895—*Miller v. Miller,* 92 Va. 196, 23 S.E. 232.

Amount of alimony to be decreed is within sound discretion of trial court and is to be fixed according to established principles and upon equitable view of all of circumstances of case.

1893—*Heninger v. Heninger,* 90 Va. 271, 18 S.E. 193.

General rule is that husband's income is fund from which allowance for support is made. Court shall take into consideration past conduct of parties, source of husband's property, what persons, if any, each is under legal obligation to court, earnings and earning capacity of each, wife's pecuniary means equally with husband's, health of each, their age and especially, but not exclusively, what sum, chargeable upon erring husband, will leave financial condition of innocent wife not inferior to what it would be if his conduct had been correct.

1887—*Cralle v. Cralle,* 84 Va. 198, 6 S.E. 12.

In fixing amount of alimony, evidence of decree in favor of husband for legacy is admissible as consideration. General rule with respect to alimony is that wife is entitled to support corresponding to her condition in life and fortune of husband. When delinquency of husband has been established and wife is injured party, then she should be supported liberally. Factor to be considered is husband's ability to earn money.

1887—*Myers v. Myers,* 83 Va. 806, 6 S.E. 630.

Wife awarded divorce on grounds of cruelty. Evidence was that she owns and possesses estate ample for purpose of providing for herself and child. Court therefore refused to decree that husband should contribute to their support.

1871—*Bailey v. Bailey,* 62 Va. 43.

Where wife obtains divorce from husband due to his misconduct, court will not seek to find how light burden may possibly be but what, under all of circumstances, would be fair allotment. When fault of husband has been established, wife should be liberally supported.

(B) Enforcement.

See Procedure —Contempt, § 8-9.

See Va. Code § 8.01-427. Persons entitled to benefit of any decree or order requiring payment of money shall be deemed judgment creditors, although money be required to be paid into court or bank or other place of deposit.

See Va. Code § 8.01-460 deals with decrees for support constituting lien on real estate of obligor.

See Va. Code § 20-61 for criminal penalty as to desertion or non-support of wife, husband or child in necessitous circumstances.

See Va. Code § 20-64 et. seq. as to support enforcement.

See Va. Code § 20-78.2 indicating that entry of order or decree of support for spouse or child shall constitute final judgment for any sum or sums in arrears. This order shall also include amount for interest on arrearage if person to whom amount is payable requests that legal interest be charged.

See Va. Code § 20-79.1 authorizing court to order payroll deductions as to support payments.

See Va. Code § 20-88.12 for Revised Uniform Reciprocal Enforcement of Support Act.

See Va. Code § 20-113 as to procedure when spouse fails to perform order for support and maintenance of child or spouse.

See Va. Code § 63.1-275 as to alternative methods of enforcing support of children and caretakers.

1983—*Scott v. Sylvester*, 225 Va. 304, 302 S.E.2d 30.

> Registration privilege of RURESA extends to any judgment decree or order of support whether temporary or final or subject to modification. When statutory requirements for registration are met, foreign support order shall be treated in same manner as support order issued by Virginia court. Parties in such instance are to be accorded all substantive rights regarding modification granted them in issuing state. Under Virginia law court lacks authority to relieve spouse of arrearage obligation to pay child support because right to each installment vests on its due date. This case however, involved interpretation of Maryland law wherein obligation to pay child support whether in arrears or not yet due, may be modified.

1982—*Carswell v. Masterson*, 224 Va. 329, 295 S.E.2d 899.

> Court of equity has power to award attorney's fees incurred incident to contempt proceedings instituted to obtain enforcement of support order of court. In this case, husband had failed to pay child support and wife was awarded attorney's fees for enforcement of that order.

1981—*Pace v. Pace*, 222 Va. 524, 281 S.E.2d 891.

> Proper forum for challenging errors in Virginia RURESA proceedings is appeal from trial court's order which wife did not pursue in this case, and as such, she is precluded from collaterally attacking 1977 Virginia order on non-jurisdictional grounds. Alleged errors she raises do not render '77 order void for lack of jurisdiction. Entry of subsequent orders in another state do not render Virginia order void. Judgment for accrued support payments is entitled to full faith and credit if obligee had vested right to payments after they became due.

1981—*Butler v. Butler,* 221 Va. 1035, 277 S.E.2d 180.

Congressional intent in 42 U.S.C. § 662(C) was to make federal incomes subject to garnishment for delinquent spousal support payments whether payments are court ordered or required only by private agreement. In this case husband's Marine Corps retirement pay is subject to garnishment under 42 U.S.C. § 659 for arrearages for support arising under contract for which judgment has been awarded. Judgment decree upon which garnishment was based in this case, was not court order for support and therefore is subject to 25% limitation contained in Virginia Code § 34-29.

1979—*Scott v. Sylvester,* 200 Va. 182, 257 S.E.2d 774.

RURESA mandates enforcement of foreign support decrees in Virginia even though decree is retroactively modifiable. Since statute is remedial, it is to be liberally construed. Conflict of laws rule contained within act applies only when request for support is based upon Virginia order, duty of support being that imposed by law of state where obligor was present during period for which support is sought. When request for support is based upon foreign court order, then order upon registration, will be treated in same manner as support order issued by court of this state and collection may be had as to entire arrearage.

1979—*Alig v. Alig,* 220 Va. 80, 255 S.E.2d 494.

Maryland alimony decree, since it is subject to modification in Maryland, is not subject to full faith and credit, yet under RURESA, it is entitled to comity, and therefore to be enforced. In enforcing foreign decree for alimony arrearages under comity doctrine, due process requires that court consider any questions of modification raised by either party which could have been presented to courts of state where decree was originally entered. There was no equitable estoppel of wife from recovering arrearages for alimony simply because she told husband she did not want his money any more. Husband was under clear duty to comply with terms of alimony decree until modified by further court order.

1977—*Shoosmith v. Scott,* 217 Va. 789, 232 S.E.2d 787.

Divorce decree approved property settlement agreement, but did not expressly incorporate agreement or order husband to perform its obligations. Decree was not, therefore, award of alimony, but rather approval of private contract for payments in lieu of alimony. Like other contracts, this one may not be impaired by legislative enactments. In this instance, failure to perform obligations under agreement does not constitute sufficient basis to hold husband in contempt.

1976—*Richardson v. Moore,* 217 Va. 422, 229 S.E.2d 864.

Wife's passive acquiescence for 25 years does not excuse husband's noncompliance with divorce court's alimony decree. Wife awarded judgment against husband's estate for arrearages with interest from date of order. Court of equity in effort to do equity, cannot disregard provisions of lawful court decree. Payments ordered by original decree become vested as they accrue and court is without authority to make any change as to past due installments.

1976—*T. . . v. T. . .*, 216 Va. 867, 224 S.E.2d 148.

Before marriage, husband had promised to treat pregnant wife's child by another man as if it were his own, thereby agreeing to assume child support obligation of biological father. Marriage ensued, and husband carried out this obligation for more than four years of marriage. Court held that express oral contract for support had been established. Wife maintained that husband is liable for child support in this case because of express oral contract, estoppel, common law adoption and husband's standing in loco parentis as to child. Supreme court found existence of express oral contract. It also noted that if any one of these theories is applicable, then order of trial court would have to be reversed.

1975—*Carter v. Carter*, 215 Va. 475, 211 S.E.2d 253.

In this case trial court erred to extent that it altered or canceled accrued installments of support payments.

1975—*Gagliano v. Gagliano*, 215 Va. 447, 211 S.E.2d 62.

There was no error to credit husband with pendente lite support and alimony payments for wife and child which were received and which were used for purposes prescribed although checks were drawn to four-year-old child rather than to mother as provided in order. In addition, it was noted by court that wife, having entered into agreement for these payments in lieu of those fixed in decree and having accepted these payments and used funds for purposes specified in decree she is estopped to deny that such payments are proper credit against payments fixed in decree.

1971—*Jenkins v. Jenkins*, 211 Va. 797, 180 S.E.2d 516.

Husband must pay support according to terms of decree, not influenced by any prior proceedings. His only alternative is to seek modification of decree.

1970—*McLoughlin v. McLoughlin*, 211 Va. 365, 177 S.E.2d 781.

Divorce decree contained directive to pay alimony pursuant to terms of agreement. That meant that court could use its contempt power to enforce agreement.

1967—*Fearon v. Fearon*, 207 Va. 927, 154 S.E.2d 165.

Wife was awarded custody of three children, and husband was to pay support of $400 per month. Wife thereafter sought to recover certain arrearages. It was agreed that husband had made equivalent payments to children or to alternative persons on their behalf. Supreme court held that husband must make payments in accord with terms of decree and cannot vary these to suit his convenience. Other payments that were made by him must be regarded as gifts and they cannot be credited to his obligation to pay wife. Court is without authority to modify its decree retroactively and relieve husband of obligation to pay past due installments.

1966—*Sheffield v. Sheffield,* 207 Va. 288, 148 S.E.2d 771.

Husband was personally served and appeared in action in which his wife obtained divorce and order of alimony and support for children. Court thereby obtained continuing jurisdiction over him as to these payments. Several years later, wife filed petition for judgment for arrearages, and husband was personally served in another State. This court had jurisdiction to enter judgment.

1965—*Davis v. Davis,* 206 Va. 381, 143 S.E.2d 835.

Husband failed to comply with court order for support. Trial court should not have dismissed his bill of complaint for that reason. Court, however, may have properly refused to proceed with his case until such time as he was in compliance.

1965—*Cofer v. Cofer,* 205 Va. 834, 140 S.E.2d 663.

Court is without authority to relieve husband of duty to pay past due amounts of support money for right to these payments had become vested.

1965—*Canavos v. Canavos,* 205 Va. 744, 139 S.E.2d 825.

Trial court properly ruled that alimony payments should not be lien on husband's real estate, which was already encumbered, where any further encumbrance might delay or prevent possible advantageous sale or result in forced sale eliminating property as potential source of income. Wife, however, was afforded security by requiring bond of husband in amount of $3,000.00 with surety approved by court.

1964—*Martin v. Martin,* 205 Va. 181, 135 S.E.2d 815.

Divorce decree awarded wife confirmed and incorporated by reference prior separation agreement under which husband promised to pay certain sum to his wife weekly so long as he should live. This was not decree for alimony, and court therefore erred in holding husband in contempt for failing to obey order to pay up arrears in sums for which he was obligated under agreement. Settlement was in lieu of alimony and was accepted as such by court since there was no provision in decree ordering husband to make any payments. Contract between parties for payments in lieu of alimony and for sum of property rights is not decree for alimony, and court has no jurisdiction in divorce suit to enforce compliance with contract. Decree approving property settlement agreement, unlike decree for alimony, is not lien upon real estate of husband nor can it, like alimony, be enforced in divorce suit.

1963—*Durrett v. Durrett,* 204 Va. 59, 129 S.E.2d 50.

Divorce decree ratified agreement between parties under which husband was to make alimony payments. Decree for alimony during life of beneficiary or until her remarriage constitutes lien upon all of her husband's real estate from time such decree is recorded on judgment lien docket where such land is situated. Lien may be enforced as other liens are enforced and for failure to make payments divorce court may punish by contempt. Husband is not relieved from any future payments by discharge in bankruptcy.

1961—*Newton v. Newton,* 202 Va. 515, 118 S.E.2d 656.

Separation agreement which was incorporated into final decree ordered husband to pay $75 per month for each child in custody of wife and additional $200 per month for her support on condition that she use this sum to maintain private household. This latter sum was actually additional support money for children. When wife sued for arrears, husband could not defend on grounds that she had forfeited such payment by alleged violation of agreement in not allowing daughter to visit him. It was husband's duty to comply with original order until such time as it was modified. Agreement provided that additional payment was to be reduced to $150 per month if wife had custody of only one child. In 1957, she surrendered custody of one child to husband but he continued to pay full $200. He was not entitled to setoff as to this overpayment against wife's claim for arrears.

1960—*Barnes v. Craig,* 202 Va. 229, 117 S.E.2d 63.

Wife obtained divorce in Florida. Property settlement agreement containing provision for child support was incorporated into decree. Judgment in Virginia was properly entered against husband for arrears in support money. Although decree provided for reduction of support money for such time as children spent with father, evidence showed that they spent very little time with him.

1952—*Morris v. Henry,* 193 Va. 631, 70 S.E.2d 417.

Decree for alimony payable in monthly installments during lifetime of beneficiary constitutes lien in her favor upon husband's real estate from date of such decree, not only for installments presently due but for those that shall fall due under such decree in future. Decree in this case enjoined husband from disposing of his real estate.

1951—*Hall v. Hall,* 192 Va. 721, 66 S.E.2d 595.

Divorce decree ordered husband to pay alimony. Nearly two years after decree wife secured issuance of writ of fieri facias. Husband moved to quash execution on grounds that decree was void. Trial court refused to hear motion until husband paid arrearage.

1948—*Eddens v. Eddens,* 188 Va. 511, 50 S.E.2d 397.

Proceeding to enforce payment of alimony is civil and not criminal contempt proceeding.

1946—*Ring v. Ring,* 185 Va. 269, 38 S.E.2d 471.

Court in this case impounded stock belonging to husband to ensure payment of alimony. Court had no power to do so. To enforce its decrees, court may rely upon its contempt power and may require of husband recognizance to abide by its decree and, upon failure to do so, he is subject to incarceration.

1946—*McKeel v. McKeel,* 185 Va. 108, 37 S.E.2d 746.

Florida order for alimony, even though subject to future amendment, is entitled to full faith and credit in Virginia and may be enforced with all of equitable remedies available to court.

1944—*Kern v. Lindsey,* 182 Va. 775, 30 S.E.2d 707.

Arrearage of husband in support payment is not alone automatic grounds for abatement of his motion to modify custody but is only circumstance to be considered.

1943—*Diggs v. Commonwealth,* 181 Va. 49, 23 S.E.2d 788.

Wife may not proceed against her husband by criminal warrant of arrest for support but instead must do so by petition verified by oath. If there is reasonable cause to believe that husband or father is about to leave jurisdiction, then warrant may be issued.

1942—*McClaugherty v. McClaugherty,* 180 Va. 51, 21 S.E.2d 761.

Under criminal code, deserted wives may prosecute their husbands and if he is found guilty wife is entitled to receive his wages if he is physically able to work on roads. These statutes do not wipe out other remedies of deserted wife.

1940—*Eaton v. Davis,* 176 Va. 330, 10 S.E.2d 893.

Alimony is not to be considered property settlement upon dissolution of marriage. Accrued alimony is lien on husband's real estate. Alimony is not discharged in bankruptcy.

1940—*Buchanan v. Buchanan,* 174 Va. 255, 6 S.E.2d 612.

Court has jurisdiction to compel specific performance of property settlement agreement even though it only called for payment of money. Power of court to see that money dedicated to support of children is forthcoming and properly applied is sufficient to confer jurisdiction.

1938—*Golderos v. Golderos,* 169 Va. 496, 194 S.E.2d 706.

Agreement to reduction of alimony did not constitute consent to reopening of case wherein order was final. Agreement could be offered to show release of defendant for failure to pay alimony in subsequent enforcement proceedings.

1936—*Boaze v. Commonwealth,* 165 Va. 786, 183 S.E. 263.

Wife obtained divorce. Decree provided for child support. Husband failed to pay. Criminal prosecution initiated. Wife having elected to proceed under decree of divorce is bound by that election.

1936—*Watson v. Mose,* 165 Va. 661, 183 S.E. 428.

Specific property of husband cannot be assigned or transferred to wife as alimony without agreement between parties. Real estate of non-resident defendant may be subjected to decree for alimony, i.e., through enforcement.

1935—*Eaton v. Davis,* 165 Va. 313, 182 S.E. 229.

While extract of decree of alimony had not been recorded in judgment lien book, beneficiaries of deeds of trust had accepted their respective securities with knowledge that wife had obtained decree of alimony and that husband had paid alimony in obedience to decree. Decree of alimony constituted lien on all real estate of husband and such was superior to judgment liens and deeds of trust.

1935—*Wright v. Wright,* 164 Va. 245, 178 S.E. 884.

Wife has two remedies: criminal and contempt. Wife must elect as to which to pursue. In this case wife elected to pursue criminal prosecution and lost. She cannot then pursue same remedy through divorce action.

1931—*Searles' Adm'r v. Gordon's Adm'r,* 156 Va. 289, 157 S.E. 759.

Judgment for alimony is obligation which must be deducted before estate of decedent can be distributed.

1930—*Gloth v. Gloth,* 154 Va. 511, 153 S.E. 879.

Duty is to comply with support order until such has been modified. Failure to do so may result in contempt finding. Dismissal of husband's suit is not appropriate punishment in this case; staying suit may be appropriate pending payment of support.

1926—*Branch v. Branch,* 144 Va. 244, 132 S.E. 303.

Proceeding for contempt is quasi-criminal and guilt of defendant must be shown beyond reasonable doubt. In this case, husband had failed to pay alimony. Prior to contempt proceeding, husband had opportunity to challenge wife's claim for alimony but he had failed to do so. Decree awarding alimony is presumed to be correct.

1924—*Painter v. Commonwealth,* 140 Va. 459, 124 S.E. 431.

Criminal prosecution for desertion and non-support. It was not error to instruct jury that burden was on accused to establish mental or physical disability relied upon as defense to prosecution. If, however, jury should have reasonable doubt as to disability, then they should find him not guilty. In this case, due to defendant's addiction of drugs and his physical condition, evidence did not support conviction of willful desertion and non-support.

1920—*West v. West,* 126 Va. 696, 101 S.E. 876.

In spite of prohibition of imprisonment for debt, court of equity can commit to jail for failure to pay alimony. Imprisonment should be ordered only where conduct of defendant is contumacious. In this case, husband was imprisoned for failure to pay $30 in alimony.

1917—*Gum v. Gum,* 122 Va. 32, 94 S.E. 177.

Nothing is more common with regard to awards for support, suit money, alimony than to charge these sums of money as liens on property of husband.

1915—*Isaacs v. Isaacs,* 117 Va. 730, 86 S.E. 105.

Decree for alimony payable in monthly installments constitutes lien upon all of husband's real estate from date of that decree for installments presently due and for those due in future. Where temporary decree is subsequently made permanent, lien for whole amount dates from time of temporary decree and takes priority over subsequent judgments against husband or liens created by him.

1911—*Newman v. McComb,* 112 Va. 408, 71 S.E. 624.

Parties had agreed that husband would make certain monthly payments to wife in lieu of alimony, pending suit by her for divorce. Action in question was not one to recover alimony but was action of assumpsit to recover monthly installments not paid.

1899—*Trimble v. Trimble,* 97 Va. 217, 33 S.E. 531.

Money to be paid as alimony should be charged upon land of husband, but it is error to enjoin him from disposing of or encumbering his real estate unless facts of particular case show it to be necessary or proper.

(C) Jurisdiction.

See Va. Code § 16.1-241 as to jurisdiction of Juvenile and Domestic Relations Court.

1981—*Ceyte v. Ceyte,* 222 Va. 11, 278 S.E.2d 791.

Question of personal jurisdiction requires examination of foreign state's law. In this case wife entered general appearance in Illinois. This constituted personal jurisdiction over her. Full faith and credit therefore would be accorded divorce decree from this court barring spousal support.

1978—*Newport v. Newport,* 219 Va. 48, 245 S.E.2d 134.

Wife's right to alimony survives absolute divorce decree obtained by husband in ex parte proceeding in another state. Full faith and credit will be accorded to foreign divorce decree as to property and support rights, as well as marital status, where divorce court had personal jurisdiction over parties.

1974—*Osborne v. Osborne,* 215 Va. 205, 207 S.E.2d 875.

Husband filed for divorce in Texas and wife entered general appearance. Wife filed in Virginia, and husband was personally served. Texas judgment in 1972 was res judicata and must be given full faith and credit in Virginia as to divorce and alimony. Virginia court had entered decree pendente lite awarding custody of children and child support to wife before divorce decree was entered in Texas. Children resided in Virginia, and Virginia courts retained jurisdiction over them. As such, Virginia court may make proper child support award under Virginia law. Virginia is not required to give full faith and credit to child custody decrees of another state and declines to give full faith and credit to child support order entered in another state in uncontested proceeding. No proof of change of circumstances required before Virginia court may make child support award that differs from award of another state. Welfare of child is always primary consideration.

1972—*Werner v. Commonwealth,* 212 Va. 623, 186 S.E.2d 76.

Juvenile court entered support order. Subsequently, circuit court granted divorce decree which was silent on alimony. Either party could have asked that divorce decree include provision on alimony, and this would have ousted juvenile court of jurisdiction. Neither party did so, and wife may have preferred to use machinery of juvenile court to enforce her right to support. Jurisdiction of juvenile court continued after divorce.

1966—*Sheffield v. Sheffield,* 207 Va. 288, 148 S.E.2d 771.

In this action on part of wife to enforce court order for alimony and child support, it was determined that court did have jurisdiction to enter judgment against husband even though he was now out of State. To force wife to begin new action in jurisdiction where husband was located would be far more inequitable than requiring husband to return to this State.

1965—*Minton v. First Nat'l Exch. Bank,* 206 Va. 589, 145 S.E.2d 139.

Wife filed action to recover accrued alimony payments. Action was defended by executor of ex-husband's estate. Executor alleged that record in divorce suit showed on its face no personal jurisdiction existed over husband in that there was no service of process or appearance but simply order of publication. Summary judgment was entered for executor since record showed on its face that decree was void due to absence of in personam jurisdiction over husband. Introduction of extrinsic evidence should not have been allowed since record showed on its face lack of jurisdiction. It is true that presumption is liberally indulged in favor of court of competent jurisdiction that proper party is before court. There is, however, no place for presumption where want of jurisdiction appears affirmatively on face of proceedings.

1964—*Martin v. Martin,* 205 Va. 181, 135 S.E.2d 815.

Final decree did not expressly order husband to make alimony payments. As such, court lacked jurisdiction to hold husband in contempt for failure to make payments. Fact that husband had previously proceeded against wife by contempt proceedings alleging violation of agreement did not work as estoppel against him since court simply had no jurisdiction in this instance.

1948—*Henderson v. Henderson,* 187 Va. 121, 46 S.E.2d 10.

Four situations in which court may decree concerning estate and maintenance of parties and care and custody of children: (1) decree dissolving marriage; (2) divorce from bond of matrimony; (3) divorce from bed and board; and (4) decree that neither party entitled to divorce.

1943—*White v. White,* 181 Va. 162, 24 S.E.2d 448.

Since equity courts have power to grant alimony independently of suit for divorce, they have jurisdiction over subject matter. It is transitory right, and defendant in such case, living in Virginia, upon whom process is served is bound by judgment rendered against him.

1943—*White v. White,* 181 Va. 162, 24 S.E.2d 448.

Right to child support also is transitory and shifts with abode of children. Court where they chance to be living has jurisdiction.

1942—*McClaugherty v. McClaugherty,* 180 Va. 51, 21 S.E.2d 761.

In this action brought by child against her father for determination of legitimacy and child support, circuit court was found to have jurisdiction.

1941—*Heflin v. Heflin,* 177 Va. 385, 14 S.E.2d 317.

Court may entertain suit for alimony even though no divorce is sought. Jurisdiction rests on inadequacy of legal remedy. This suit for alimony was properly maintained in circuit court.

1934—*Bray v. Landergren,* 161 Va. 699, 172 S.E. 252.

Alimony is usually allowance in money out of husband's estate but not estate itself. Decree should not set aside specific property for its satisfaction. Alimony is lien on husband's real estate for sums due or to be due. Alimony may be awarded in independent suit therefor. Power to decree alimony is power inherent in courts of equity. Where marriage is void ab initio, there is no right to alimony.

1925—*Barnes v. American Fertilizer Co.,* 144 Va. 692, 130 S.E. 902.

Alimony is usually allowance in money out of husband's estate but not estate itself. Court possesses no power to vest in wife title to specific portion of husband's real estate.

1924—*Humphreys v. Strong,* 139 Va. 146, 123 Va. 554.

Where in divorce proceedings in Nevada, court failed to get actual service of process in territorial limits of that court's jurisdiction upon defendant, resident of Virginia, and he declined to voluntarily appear, no valid personal judgment for alimony could be entered against him and that portion of judgment will not be recognized in Virginia.

1913—*Isaacs v. Isaacs,* 115 Va. 562, 79 S.E. 1072.

Decree for alimony rendered by court of this state having jurisdiction over persons and subject matter, insofar as it affects rights of property established by that decree, cannot in any way be affected by decree rendered by court of another state in suit between same parties.

1826—*Almond v. Almond,* 25 Va. 662.

Court of chancery has power to grant alimony to wife, even without contract for separation where misconduct of husband is such as to render it unsafe for wife to live with him or he turns her out of doors without support. Such claim does not give wife right to any specific property of husband.

1810—*Purcell v. Purcell,* 14 Va. 507.

Court of chancery has jurisdiction in cases of alimony. This case dealt with what evidence of marriage is deemed sufficient to entitle wife to alimony. It also dealt with enforcement of decree for alimony.

(D) Survival.

See Va. Code § 20-107.2 indicating that court has no authority to decree child support payable by estate of deceased party.

1952—*Morris v. Henry*, 193 Va. 631, 70 S.E.2d 417.
> Nothing in Virginia Code prohibits court in divorce suit from decreeing that liability for child support shall survive death of parent against whom it is decreed. In this case, part of decree that applied to child support was held to survive death of father.

1923—*Moore v. Crutchfield*, 136 Va. 20, 116 S.E. 482.
> General rule is that death of party does not terminate contract if it is not of personal nature. In present case, husband and wife entered into agreement under which husband was to pay wife $25 per month in lieu of alimony and upon final adjudication to pay her $5,000 in full settlement of all property rights by reason of marriage. Decree was entered granting complainant divorce from bed and board, and decree contained clause approving agreement. Thereafter, wife died. Court held that promise to pay $5,000 was absolute promise and that death of wife was not to be given effect of default on her part. Payment of $5,000 became fixed after lapse of reasonable time after her death, defendant having received entire consideration for promise of payment.

§ 4-2. Child Support.

(A) Education.

1960—*Barnes v. Craig*, 202 Va. 229, 117 S.E.2d 63.
> Within property settlement agreement which was incorporated into Florida divorce decree, husband agreed to attempt to provide for college education of children. Allowance of $300 per month for support and education of eldest child, girl now of college age, was proper. Father stated he wished to provide college training for her and amount required for this purpose was matter of discretion for court. Father complained that he had been precluded from decision as to which college she would be sent to. Evidence was to contrary.

1938—*Buchanan v. Buchanan*, 170 Va. 458, 197 S.E. 426.
> If father has forfeited right to supervise education of his children, mother may defray such expenses and recover all money so expended.

1893—*Heninger v. Heninger*, 90 Va. 271, 18 S.E. 193.
> Jurisdiction of court to provide for education of children is unquestionable. Parent who sends his son into world uneducated does great injury to mankind, for he defrauds community of useful citizen.

(B) Emancipation.

1953—*Brumfield v. Brumfield*, 194 Va. 577, 74 S.E.2d 170.
> Father, after death of his wife, had turned child over to his mother to rear as she saw fit and did not contribute to her maintenance, yet he

did claim her as dependent for income tax purposes and did not intend to be completely relieved of her support. Complete emancipation means freeing of child for all period of its minority and for all purposes. Child in this case had not been completely emancipated.

1946—*Buxton v. Bishop,* 185 Va. 1, 37 S.E.2d 755.
Twenty year old son in this case worked away from home, drew his own wages and spent them as he desired. Under these circumstances, he was emancipated and was liable for his own medical bills incurred.

1943—*Kirby v. Gilliam,* 182 Va. 111, 28 S.E.2d 40.
Marriage of infant emancipates child from custody of parents.

1898—*Jackson v. Jackson,* 96 Va. 165, 31 S.E. 78.
Father may emancipate his minor child and permit him to contract for and receive his wages and in case of such contract father is not allowed to recover child's wages.

(C) Modification.

See Va. Code § 20-108 indicating that court may from time to time alter such decree as circumstances of parents and benefit of children may require.

1979—*Cutshaw v. Cutshaw,* 220 Va. 638, 261 S.E.2d 52.
Husband petitioned trial court to amend decree to require wife to contribute to support of children who were in his custody. Evidence showed husband's net salary had increased less than $300 per month while his expenses had increased $600 per month. Wife's salary had increased more than 45 percent, and she had established monthly savings plan. Court ordered wife to pay $100 per month as child support. Father's salary increase in amount less than his expenses establishes material change supporting court's modification.

1979—*Featherstone v. Brooks,* 220 Va. 443, 258 S.E.2d 513.
Court increased child support in March of 1974 from $25 to $50, and then in September 1974 decreased it to $35. While parent is legally obligated to support child only during minority, parent can contract to support child thereafter, and when such contracts are incorporated into final decree, these contracts can be modified only to extent of jurisdiction of court. In this case court did not have jurisdiction to order support payments over $25 after child turned 18, since $25 was figure agreed to in contract.

1976—*Thomas v. Thomas,* 217 Va. 502, 229 S.E.2d 887.
Court has continuing jurisdiction, when changed circumstances are demonstrated, to increase/decrease or terminate alimony upon petition of either spouse.

1975—*Morris v. Morris,* 216 Va. 457, 219 S.E.2d 864.
Evidence in this case was insufficient to show father had met his burden to prove justification for modification of child support. Many of his estimated expenses were directly related to care of his new

family. Burden is on father to show material change in his financial condition. Husband offered no proof to substantiate his contention that he could not fulfill child support obligations which he had agreed to assume. Although his debts had increased his income also had increased.

1975—*Hammers v. Hammers,* 216 Va. 30, 216 S.E.2d 20.

Court has continuing jurisdiction to modify custody and support of minor child. Burden is on father to prove by greater weight of evidence that there has been material change in condition and circumstances that has rendered him unable to keep up payments and he must make full and clear disclosure relating to his ability to pay. He must also show that his lack of ability is not due to his own voluntary action or his neglect. His remarriage and existence of another family dependent upon him for support is entitled to little, if any, consideration. In this case husband's debts had increased, but his income had also increased. Modification denied.

1974—*Paul v. Paul,* 214 Va. 651, 203 S.E.2d 123.

Property settlement agreement provided that payments were to be made until child turned 21 or was otherwise emancipated. Term "otherwise emancipated" did not result in child support payments being terminated when age of majority was reduced to 18. Intent of parties from agreement was that payments would continue until children reached majority as it was defined at time of agreement.

1953—*Foster v. Foster,* 195 Va. 102, 77 S.E.2d 471.

Although Virginia chancery court, in entering decree for divorce, has no power, in absence of stipulation or contract between parties, to extend alimony beyond death of husband, this rule does not apply to child support payments since basic reason for two allowances spring from different sources.

1952—*Morris v. Henry,* 193 Va. 631, 70 S.E.2d 417.

Court has continuing jurisdiction to change or modify child support and child custody orders.

1944—*Crosby v. Crosby,* 182 Va. 461, 29 S.E.2d 241.

Husband's income decreased to almost one-half of what it had been, although it was still substantial. Mere fact that he has been unable to pay his income taxes does not necessarily mean that he lacks financial ability to pay. Burden is on husband to show that his lack of ability to pay is not due to his own voluntary act or neglect. Modification denied in this case.

1939—*Bailey v. Bailey,* 172 Va. 18, 200 S.E. 622.

Provision for custody placed in original decree of divorce. Once court properly acquired jurisdiction over husband then decree could be modified to allow for child support.

1936—*Martin v. Martin,* 166 Va. 109, 184 S.E. 220.

Trial court properly reserved right to make such changes in support provisions as changing conditions might demand.

1936—*Boaze v. Commonwealth,* 165 Va. 786, 183 S.E. 263.

Court has power to modify support decree to meet changing conditions.

1930—*Gloth v. Gloth,* 154 Va. 511, 153 S.E. 879.

Court has continuing jurisdiction to modify decree as to support and custody. This cannot be contracted away.

1920—*Lovegrove v. Lovegrove,* 128 Va. 449, 104 S.E. 804.

Award of child support is subject to revision where it can be shown that other party's circumstances justify increase in allowance.

(D) Parental Duty to Support.

See Va. Code § 20-61.1 as to support of children of unwed parents by father.
See Va. Code § 63.1-248.1 as to child abuse and neglect.
See Va. Code § 63.1-249 as to support of dependent children and their caretakers.

1979—*Gazale v. Gazale,* 219 Va. 775, 250 S.E.2d 365.

In this case husband agreed to make child support payments until such time as each child shall attain age of 21, become married, self-supporting or otherwise emancipated. Reduction in age of majority did not affect this contract, and husband was obligated to pay child support until children turned 21.

1976—*Meredith v. Meredith,* 216 Va. 636, 222 S.E.2d 511.

Agreement which was incorporated into divorce decree required father to make child support payments until child reached majority. Majority is status rather than vested right and is subject to change by legislature. It was error for trial court to rule that father was required to make child support payments after child became 18 and after legislature lowered age of majority to 18.

1976—*Mack v. Mack,* 217 Va. 534, 229 S.E.2d 895.

Property settlement agreement indicated father agreed to pay $300 per month for support of two minor children. When age of majority was reduced father filed petition for termination of child support. Supreme court indicated termination should be granted based on language of agreement.

1975—*Eaton v. Eaton,* 215 Va. 824, 213 S.E.2d 789.

On July 1, 1972 General Assembly changed age of majority from 21 to 18. In November 1972 court entered order requiring payment by father to mother of $125 each month for support and maintenance of minor child until further order of court. Prior to divorce parties had entered into property settlement agreement providing for support to child until he reaches age of 21. That agreement between parties filed with court was only incidentally involved herein since it had been supplanted by court order. Decree entered after effective date of change in law is to be construed under that new law. As such, support obligations ceased when child turned 18.

1973—*Anthony v. Anthony,* 213 Va. 721, 196 S.E.2d 66.

Trial court abused its discretion in refusing child support for child who was sophomore at VPI. Child had voluntarily moved to domitory at VPI with consent of mother but contrary to wishes of her father. This did not in any way relieve husband of his obligation to support child.

1972—*Department of Mental Hygiene v. Shepard,* 212 Va. 843, 188 S.E.2d 99.

Mother, herself incompetent, had duty, after death of father, to support incompetent adult son under statute which provided for recovery by state hospital for charges for maintaining son. Duty of support rests not only with father but also with mother after death of father.

1959—*Distefano v. Commonwealth,* 201 Va. 23, 109 S.E.2d 497.

Commonwealth offered evidence of defendant having claimed two children in question as his dependents on IRS returns. Court concluded that these returns are not acts voluntarily admitting paternity in writing under oath as is contemplated by statute. As such, although he may have been father of children, he could not be found guilty of non-support.

1946—*Harris v. Diamond Constr. Co.,* 184 Va. 711, 36 S.E.2d 573.

Legal obligation to support infant was upon father and not upon deceased brother, and in absence of showing to contrary, presumption is that father discharged this duty.

1946—*McKeel v. McKeel,* 185 Va. 108, 37 S.E.2d 746.

It is elementary that husband's duty to support his wife and children is not merely contractual but is one in which public has vital intcrest.

1946—*Buxton v. Bishop,* 185 Va. 1, 37 S.E.2d 755.

Health care provider stated to parent that he would send him bill for medical services provided to son. Father replied, "to do so". Court held that evidence tending to support any contract obligation on part of father is so slight that it amounts to no proof at all. In this case, son was emancipated and, as such, responsible for his own medical bills.

1944—*Brown v. Brown,* 183 Va. 353, 32 S.E.2d 79.

Without legislation, father of illegitimate child cannot be required to provide for its support. Under laws of Virginia, there is no legal duty to provide such support.

1942—*McClaugherty v. McClaugherty,* 180 Va. 51, 21 S.E.2d 761.

It is common law duty of father to support his infant child. This is principle of natural law.

1938—*Buchanan v. Buchanan,* 170 Va. 458, 197 S.E. 426.
Action at law by divorced wife and minor children to compel husband to pay monthly sum for future maintenance and education of children. Judgment on law side awarding such relief was void. Action should have been initiated as bill in equity. Actions by child against parent should not be encouraged. Duty of father to support minor children is similar to obligation to support blameless wife.

1936—*Boaze v. Commonwealth,* 165 Va. 786, 183 S.E. 263.
Father has legal and moral duty to support his dependent infant children.

1933—*Indemnity Ins. Co. v. Nalls,* 160 Va. 246, 168 S.E. 346.
Father has duty to support mentally incapacitated adult child.

1927—*Bruce v. Dean,* 149 Va. 39, 140 S.E. 277.
Father confined to penitentiary for life is still liable for support of minor child. Father contracted with industrial school to maintain his children and in consideration of such he conveyed to school all of his equity in real estate. This was not fraudulent conveyance.

1926—*Branch v. Branch,* 144 Va. 244, 132 S.E. 303.
Husband in contempt proceeding claimed that he was not paying alimony because of condition of his aged mother. While duty of son to his mother cannot be minimized, his first duty is to support those for whose existence he was responsible.

1922—*Butler v. Commonwealth,* 132 Va. 609, 110 S.E. 868.
Man is under legal obligation to support his children, and he may often be required to do so when they are not living with him, but he cannot be said to willfully neglect and refuse to support them where his wife, without reasonable excuse, and without consent and aid of father, keeps them away from him. Father, in this case, had been out of work for some time and thereafter mother removed children to her father's home. Conviction of husband, under non-support statute, cannot be sustained. Court held that in this case wife cannot charge husband in civil suit for support and maintenance of children where she has kept children away from father. Where child is living away from father, question of father's liability for support will depend on circumstances. If he abandons child or drives him from home, he is liable to any person who furnishes necessary support. But person furnishing it must bear burden of proving that there was unjustified abandonment, that support was necessary and that credit of father was in contemplation of law, basis of advances.

1921—*Mihalcoe v. Holub,* 130 Va. 425, 107 S.E. 704.
Father owes his infant children duty of maintenance. This is legal duty. In this case, instruction stating that husband is not bound by law to support his wife or even to furnish her with necessaries while she is living separate and apart from him if she so lives without his consent and without any good and sufficient reason or cause therefor was correct statement of law since there was evidence to support it.

Liability of father for necessary support supplied his abandoned child does not attach where support has been assumed by others as purely voluntary undertaking without any regard to obligation on father's part.

1910—*Atkinson v. Solenberger,* 112 Va. 667, 72 S.E. 727.

Money spent by wife for support of family is proper setoff to demand of husband against her for services, and his creditors can occupy no higher ground than he does. Where husband renders services for his wife, whether under expressed or implied agreement, his creditors have right to subject value of such services to payment of their debts less amount necessary for reasonable support of husband and his family.

1909—*Burton v. Commonwealth,* 109 Va. 800, 63 S.E. 464.

Criminal prosecution for non-support. Quarrel or series of quarrels for which wife is responsible, in whole or in part, do not constitute just cause for desertion on part of husband or for his willful neglect to provide for her support and that of their minor child. Under this statute, what shall constitute destitute or necessitous circumstances shall depend upon circumstances of particular case and is question for jury. Evidence in this case did not show that wife was at any time in destitute circumstances and as such conviction is set aside.

1905—*Watts v. Watts,* 104 Va. 269, 51 S.E. 359.

It is common law duty of father to support his infant child if able to do so. Where child has property of its own, court will look to position and wealth of parties in determining amount. Stepmother who is chargeable as guardian de facto of her infant stepson, whose father is insolvent, should be allowed credit for support and maintenance of stepson where support of family has fallen upon her.

1898—*Owens v. Owens,* 96 Va. 191, 31 S.E. 72.

Husband and father is bound to support his wife and children and, if by his misconduct he renders it impossible for them to remain under his roof, he cannot, by his misconduct, escape performance of this duty.

1860—*Evans v. Pearce,* 56 Va. 513.

Father had property of his infant children in his possession and during his life does not apply to Court to have any of profits of that property applied to their support nor does he make any charges against them during his life. His estate will not be allowed anything for their support without clearest proof that justice requires it.

§ 4-3. Spousal Support.

(A) Fault of Wife.

1983—*Coe v. Coe,* 225 Va. 616, 303 S.E.2d 923.

Trial court properly denied alimony to wife since she was found guilty of adultery.

1983—*Blevins v. Blevins,* 225 Va. 18, 300 S.E.2d 743.

Absent finding by trial court that spousal separation was caused by fault or misconduct of wife, husband is not relieved of his obligation of support.

1977—*Brooker v. Brooker,* 218 Va. 12, 235 S.E.2d 309.

When no fault divorce is granted, husband is not relieved of alimony obligation unless it is shown that separation was caused by fault or misconduct on wife's part so as to constitute grounds for divorce. Fact that wife was not entitled to divorce on fault grounds is not finding of fault or misconduct on her part.

1974—*Rowland v. Rowland,* 215 Va. 344, 210 S.E.2d 149.

Wife forfeits her right to alimony only if her misconduct constitutes grounds for desertion. In this case, wife was free from legal fault when she left marital abode on husband's demand that she "get out" without justification and unprovoked by any legally recognized misconduct on her part.

1972—*Young v. Young,* 212 Va. 761, 188 S.E.2d 200.

Husband sued wife alleging desertion. Court held that husband had not proved desertion. Husband thereafter amended his suit and obtained divorce on grounds of two-year separation. Trial court denied wife alimony. Since court held that wife's fault or misconduct was not sufficient to entitle husband to divorce and decree entered was not predicated on wife's fault or misconduct, it was error to deny wife alimony.

1970—*Carneal v. Carneal,* 211 Va. 162, 176 S.E.2d 305.

Wife found guilty of desertion. Therefore, it was error to award alimony to wife.

1970—*Guy v. Guy,* 210 Va. 536, 172 S.E.2d 735.

Divorce was granted on no-fault grounds. Husband is not relieved of his obligation to support his wife unless it is shown that separation was caused by her fault or misconduct. There was no error to grant wife alimony when it cannot be said as matter of law that she deserted her husband.

1969—*Mason v. Mason,* 209 Va. 528, 165 S.E.2d 392.

Alimony will not be awarded to wife when husband is granted divorce because of her fault or misconduct. In this case, husband was granted divorce under no-fault statute. There was no evidence presented of fault. Where husband sues for divorce under no-fault statute, he is not relieved of his obligation to support his wife and in absence of showing of cause of separation, it was not error to award alimony and counsel fees.

1966—*McClung v. McClung,* 206 Va. 782, 146 S.E.2d 195.

Divorced wife has no right to alimony if divorce was granted to husband because of her misconduct.

1948—*Mullen v. Mullen,* 188 Va. 259, 49 S.E.2d 349.

Wife at fault for divorce. Court declined to award either permanent alimony or temporary alimony pending appeal. Award of such alimony is highly discretionary.

1944—*Elam v. Elam,* 182 Va. 469, 29 S.E.2d 222.

Wife made false statement as to marital status and then entered into bigamous marriage. Wife denied alimony.

1939—*Hendry v. Hendry,* 172 Va. 368, 1 S.E.2d 340.

Trial court denied divorce but awarded wife alimony. Supreme court reversed and granted husband divorce.

1938—*Ingram v. Ingram,* 171 Va. 399, 199 S.E. 515.

Action by husband to terminate alimony due to adulterous acts of wife. Petition to terminate was filed after divorce decreed. Petition denied. Evidence not sufficient to establish adultery.

1934—*Hodnett v. Hodnett,* 163 Va. 644, 177 S.E. 106.

While alimony may be granted without divorce, alimony cannot be allowed to wife who has been divorced on adultery grounds.

1930—*Gloth v. Gloth,* 154 Va. 511, 153 S.E. 879.

Adultery or other misconduct of wife may be grounds for revoking decree of alimony.

1926—*Duff v. Duff,* 145 Va. 526, 134 S.E. 555.

Wife, who voluntarily abandons husband, should not be allowed alimony unless abandonment was without her fault, rendered necessary for her safety and happiness and was consistent with social order and public policy.

1923—*Mowles v. Mowles,* 137 Va. 274, 119 S.E. 54.

In this case, husband sued wife for desertion. Husband was dependent upon his own labor for his support. He offered to take wife back; however, she refused. Wife, having temporarily relieved herself of all of her wifely duties, she was denied alimony. Wife had vowed that she would never return to home so long as her mother-in-law still lived there.

1920—*West v. West,* 126 Va. 696, 101 S.E. 876.

Husband had previous relations with his wife. At time of marriage, she was pregnant, and she alleged that he was father. He claimed that he learned immediately after marriage but that before it was consummated child was not his. Marriage was thereafter consummated by husband with this knowledge and therefore condoned wife's previous conduct. Husband was obliged to pay alimony to wife.

1911—*Haynor v. Haynor,* 112 Va. 123, 70 S.E. 531.

Wife who has voluntarily abandoned her husband should not have decree for her separate maintenance unless her abandonment was without fault, rendered necessary for her safety and happiness and it was consistent with social order and public policy. In this case, both parties were at fault, and decree for divorce and alimony should be refused.

1904—*House v. House,* 102 Va. 235, 46 S.E. 299.
Husband sued wife on grounds of cruelty and wife filed cross-bill on grounds of desertion and cruelty. All claims were denied. Wife, however, is more to blame than her husband for unhappy manner in which they had lived and she had, by her misconduct, provoked mistreatment of which she complained and therefore was not entitled to alimony.

1878—*Latham v. Latham,* 71 Va. 307.
There may be cases in which court might refuse divorce and yet allow alimony wife. If husband, however, is willing to be reconciled to wife upon terms she can properly accept, if he has not abandoned her and if his conduct has not been such as to justify her separating from him, then she is not entitled to alimony.

1872—*Carr v. Carr,* 63 Va. 168.
Wife, having left her husband without good legal grounds, is not entitled to alimony.

(B) Miscellaneous.

1983—*Blevins v. Blevins,* 225 Va. 18, 300 S.E.2d 743.
Benefits which wife receives in her own right, and which remain unaffected by provisions of divorce decree, such as Social Security, are not considered as spousal support. In addition, in this particular case, wife was not entitled to share of her husband's black lung benefits, and as such, these benefits should not be considered as spousal support. Case was remanded to trial court for determination of what amount of alimony wife was entitled to.

1981—*Butler v. Butler,* 221 Va. 1035, 277 S.E.2d 180.
This case dealt with definition of term alimony as was expansively defined in 42 U.S.C. § 659. Court noted that term alimony may be subject to varying interpretations in different jurisdictions and indeed, term has been eliminated in Virginia.

1979—*Alig v. Alig,* 220 Va. 80, 255 S.E.2d 494.
Absent factors making it inequitable, interest should be assessed on unpaid installments of alimony from date they mature or become due until date they are paid.

1974—*Young v. Young,* 215 Va. 125, 207 S.E.2d 825.
It is matter of discretion for trial court as to when alimony shall become effective. On April 24, 1972, supreme court had previously remanded this case to trial court for award of alimony. Supreme court in this case held that alimony was effective as of that date and wife was entitled to interest running from that date.

1971—*Lawrence v. Lawrence,* 212 Va. 44, 181 S.E.2d 640.

Time when permanent alimony shall commence is within sound discretion of court and may be made effective as of date of commencement of suit. In this case, court made alimony effective as of date of order.

1963—*Durrett v. Durrett,* 204 Va. 59, 129 S.E.2d 50.

Decree entered in divorce suit approving contract between parties in lieu of alimony and for settlement of property rights is not decree for alimony, and court has no jurisdiction in divorce suit to enforce compliance with contract.

1946—*Henebry v. Henebry,* 185 Va. 320, 38 S.E.2d 320.

Parties entered into property settlement agreement and stipulated for payment of monthly allowance in lieu of alimony. Decree of court approving contract between parties providing for payments in lieu of alimony is not decree for alimony, and court has no jurisdiction in divorce suit to enforce compliance with contract nor to alter its terms.

1940—*Eaton v. Davis,* 176 Va. 330, 10 S.E.2d 893.

Alimony is not considered income for income tax purposes.

1935—*De Hart v. De Hart,* 164 Va. 455, 178 S.E. 884.

Husband agreed to pay wife monthly sum in lieu of alimony should divorce action be filed. Suit made no request for alimony and decree did not provide for alimony. Agreed monthly payment was not alimony even though agreement was approved by court.

1930—*Gloth v. Gloth,* 154 Va. 511, 153 S.E. 879.

Prior to institution of suit a mensa husband may in large measure determine amount of alimony. After suit is filed this is for court to determine. Contract to pay wife monthly amount until remarriage or her death is alimony and not annuity.

1926—*Eschner v. Eschner,* 146 Va. 417, 131 S.E. 800.

Contract to pay money in lieu of alimony is not contract to pay alimony. There being valuable consideration contract is valid. Annuity agreed to is not lien on husband's property.

1923—*Moore v. Crutchfield,* 136 Va. 20, 116 S.E. 482.

Validity of contracts for payment of alimony made by parties during pendency of suit has been questioned, yet contract for payment of money in lieu of alimony will be sustained. Decree of court approving agreement for payments in lieu of alimony is not decree for alimony, and court has no jurisdiction in divorce suit to enforce compliance nor to alter its terms.

(C) Modification.

See Va. Code § 20-109 indicating that court may increase, decrease or cause to cease any support and maintenance for spouse that may thereafter accrue. However, if stipulation or contract signed by party is filed with pleadings or depositions, then no decree or order directing payment of support and maintenance for spouse, suit money or counsel fee or establishing or imposing any other condition or consideration, monetary or non-monetary, shall be entered except in accordance with that stipulation or contract. If former spouse for whom provisions for support and maintenance have been made in such stipulation or contract shall thereafter marry, court shall upon such remarriage order that such support and maintenance shall cease, and upon death of any such former spouse court shall order that no payment shall be made to estate of such decedent unless such stipulation or contract otherwise specifically provides in event of remarriage or death.

1979—*Alig v. Alig,* 220 Va. 80, 255 S.E.2d 494.

Alimony decree in Maryland may be modified both in respect to installments accrued and those not yet due, and as such, does not possess degree of finality to be entitled to full faith and credit. It is, however, entitled to comity under RURESA. Evidence in this case was insufficient to show material change in circumstance in financial position of parties as to justify modification of monthly alimony payments.

1979—*Jacobs v. Jacobs,* 219 Va. 993, 254 S.E.2d 56.

Spousal support award with escalator clause premising future increase on uncertain future circumstance, ignores design and defeats purpose of statutory scheme. Insertion of escalator clause within court order was error.

1977—*Lindsay v. Lindsay,* 218 Va. 599, 238 S.E.2d 817.

In 1971 parties entered into property settlement agreement. In 1975 they entered into consent order. Court held order was binding on parties, its terms being made subject to further order of court as to support. Parties having agreed that court should retain jurisdiction over allowance of support payments, counsel fees and cost, court did not purport to approve and incorporate 1971 agreement and then modify it in violation of Va. Code § 20-109, but acted instead pursuant to consent order.

1977—*Harris v. Harris,* 217 Va. 680, 232 S.E.2d 739.

When agreement between parties providing for alimony has been approved and made enforceable by decree in divorce proceedings, usual power of court to modify alimony is restricted. Court's jurisdiction over awarding alimony is restricted to terms of agreement. In this case court did not have authority to decrease alimony.

1976—*Thomas v. Thomas,* 217 Va. 502, 229 S.E.2d 887.

Trial court put two-year time limit on alimony in this case. Record was devoid of any evidence that wife's need or husband's ability to pay would have substantially changed within immediate or reasonably foreseeable future and, as such, it was error to limit award to two years.

1976—*Shoosmith v. Scott,* 217 Va. 290, 227 S.E.2d 729.

Provision in property settlement agreement, confirmed by court, creates vested property rights in parties that cannot be impaired by subsequent retroactive legislation.

1976—*Thomas v. Thomas,* 216 Va. 741, 222 S.E.2d 557.

Parties filed agreement which was incorporated into a mensa decree which provided for alimony. That decree was merged into a vinculo decree which provided that agreement was incorporated into decree only insofar as it relates to real property rights. Husband contended that a vinculo decree therefore cut off wife's right to alimony since that decree did not incorporate agreement insofar as it included alimony. Supreme court held that a vinculo decree completely subsumed a mensa decree and that all of provisions of prior decree not lawfully modified by trial court assumed identity of a vinculo decree. Under Va. Code § 20-109 court's jurisdiction is restricted to awarding alimony consistent with terms of contract. In this case trial court had no authority to alter alimony terms that were incorporated in a mensa decree. Therefore husband was still obliged to pay alimony.

1975—*Russell v. Russell,* 216 Va. 432, 219 S.E.2d 689.

In support of his petition for reduction in alimony husband was given full opportunity to introduce evidence as to his ability to pay and to needs of his former wife. Supreme court said that it will not interfere with trial court's discretion in awarding alimony unless it was arbitrarily used or some injustice has been done.

1975—*McConkey v. McConkey,* 216 Va. 106, 215 S.E.2d 640.

When divorced wife enters into subsequent voidable marriage she thereby forfeits her right to alimony from her former husband. Alimony is not reinstated when voidable second marriage is annulled.

1972—*Treger v. Treger,* 212 Va. 538, 186 S.E.2d 82.

Wife awarded divorce which included $200 per month alimony and $600 per month child support for two children. His income at time was approximately $28,000. Thereafter, his income decreased to $12,480, and he asked court for reduction in support payments. Court reduced child support to $300 per month and terminated alimony. It was error to terminate alimony. Reduction or temporary suspension may have been justified by husband's reduced income. Husband's remarriage was entitled to little, if any, consideration. Absent material and permanent change in circumstances, husband could not be forever relieved of his obligation to support wife.

1971—*Losyk v. Losyk,* 212 Va. 220, 183 S.E.2d 135.

Authority to modify alimony provisions of final divorce decree must be found either in language of decree or in applicable statute. In this case, order indicated that temporary alimony was to cease as of certain date. After alimony ceased wife returned to court asking for award of permanent alimony. Supreme court held that alimony had ceased as of date stated in order, and there was nothing within order that gave court continuing jurisdiction to modify alimony.

1970—*McLoughlin v. McLoughlin,* 211 Va. 365, 177 S.E.2d 781.

While divorce suit was pending, husband agreed to pay $100 per month for support of wife, and this agreement was incorporated into divorce decree. On wife's remarriage, husband petitioned for termination of alimony. Trial court correctly dismissed petition since, under statute, court cannot make order in conflict with property settlement agreement. This, however, did not bar husband from filing suit for construction of agreement.

1969—*Dienhart v. Dienhart,* 210 Va. 101, 168 S.E.2d 279.

Under statute where parties had agreed on alimony and settlement contract was filed with wife's depositions and husband made no objection to decree incorporating settlement agreement, it was error for trial court to thereafter eliminate alimony on basis of change of circumstance.

1965—*Canavos v. Canavos,* 205 Va. 744, 139 S.E.2d 825.

Award of alimony in this case was substantially increased on showing by wife that she was unable to work and that her husband, though not working, had property from which he could derive income. Evidence threw doubt on his assertion that he was without funds and failed to show that he was unable to work. Even accepting his statement as true that he is without funds, there was nothing to prevent him from renting his property and obtaining employment in order to have some visible means of income. Trial court had initially awarded alimony of $17.50 per week. Supreme court increased that to $35 per week.

1963—*Durrett v. Durrett,* 204 Va. 59, 129 S.E.2d 50.

Alimony ceases entirely upon death of either husband or wife.

1961—*Perry v. Perry,* 202 Va. 849, 120 S.E.2d 385.

Divorce decree made no reference to alimony. Case was stricken from docket "with leave to either party to have same reinstated for good cause shown." Later, at wife's request, case was reinstated, and she petitioned for alimony and was awarded such. Supreme court held that trial court had lost jurisdiction to enter such order. Only to extent allowed by statute or provided by reservation in decree may final divorce decree be modified to affect alimony. Since decree made no award, statutory power was inapplicable. Nor was decree sufficiently specific to allow subsequent award.

1960—*Barnes v. Craig,* 202 Va. 229, 117 S.E.2d 63.

Florida divorce decree incorporated separation agreement wherein husband agreed to pay $50 per month for support of each of their three children. Wife petitioned Virginia court for increase in child support. This was proper in light of increased age of children and greater expense of supporting them, father's financial ability and proof by mother that more than sum fixed was actually being spent for their maintenance and education.

1953—*Foster v. Foster,* 195 Va. 102, 77 S.E.2d 471.
Decree of divorce did not expressly provide for alimony after death of husband. Such payment could not be implied from language in decree that alimony be paid until wife's death or remarriage. Virginia court, in entering decree for absolute divorce, has no power, in absence of stipulation or contract between parties, to extend alimony beyond death of husband.

1946—*Henebry v. Henebry,* 185 Va. 320, 38 S.E.2d 320.
Intent of parties in property settlement agreement was to conclude question of alimony by providing for payments in lieu of alimony. Therefore no alimony was decreed and therefore it could not be modified.

1942—*Cecil v. Cecil,* 179 Va. 274, 19 S.E.2d 64.
Husband sought reduction in alimony due to his entry into Army and ability of wife to support herself. Court found that he joined Army to avoid alimony and that condition of wife justified alimony.

1941—*Hulcher v. Hulcher,* 177 Va. 12, 12 S.E.2d 767.
Husband's default in failure to pay alimony is only one factor to be considered in hearing husband's request for reduction. Husband's income averaged out to be about $130 per month. Reduction of alimony from $60 to $35 in light of his poor health.

1940—*Eaton v. Davis,* 176 Va. 330, 10 S.E.2d 893.
Decree of alimony in a mensa divorce may always be altered even though there is no reservation of such power in decree.

1938—*Golderos v. Golderos,* 169 Va. 496, 194 S.E. 706.
Decree of divorce, which contained award of alimony, became final upon adjournment of court for that term as to all matters litigated or that should have been litigated as incidental thereto. Court had no authority to modify.

1937—*Casilear v. Casilear,* 168 Va. 46, 190 S.E. 314.
Divorce a mensa granted. Wife sought increase in alimony. Husband claimed that contract by which he conveyed property to wife released him of further alimony obligations. It was duty of court to exercise continuing supervision over amount of alimony, taking into consideration changed condition. i.e., with reference to property acquired, income received, and amount necessary for reasonable support of wife. Trial court has inherent power to award alimony. Its jurisdiction cannot be ousted by agreement which court does not approve. In final decree of divorce, court has power to retain jurisdiction to enter orders dealing with alimony. Even in vinculo decrees court has power to retain jurisdiction to enter orders dealing with alimony and to supervise agreements made by parties.

1936—*Allen v. Allen,* 166 Va. 303, 186 S.E. 17.
Court may make proper adjustment for alimony as changing conditions and circumstances may require.

1935—*Capell v. Capell,* 164 Va. 45, 178 S.E. 894.

> Agreement of parties to modify alimony decree does not supersede decree. Decree for alimony is something more than order for payment of money. This involves public as well as marital duty. After final decree court has power to retain jurisdiction to enter such further orders as are necessary.

1930—*Gloth v. Gloth,* 154 Va. 511, 153 S.E. 879.

> Alimony awarded in decree a mensa may be modified due to changed conditions. In decree a vinculo alimony may not be modified unless such right is reserved in decree. Provision for support and maintenance in contract incorporated into decree may be modified. Reason for continuation of jurisdiction in divorce cases is same as applies in custody cases, i.e., continuation of relationship out of which duty arises.

1927—*Brinn v. Brinn,* 147 Va. 277, 137 S.E. 503.

> Upon entry of final decree from bonds of matrimony which provides for monthly payments of alimony, decree cannot be modified after passage of appeal time. Result may be different if there are minor children to be provided for or if decree allows reopening where decree simply indicates that parties reserved right "to apply to court for such orders as are authorized by law." This did not authorize court to modify alimony.

(D) Pendente Lite.

1886—*Cralle v. Cralle,* 81 Va. 773.

> Virginia Code authorizes trial court, pending suit, to compel husband to pay money to wife to maintain her and enable her to carry on suit yet it does not justify it to make any order for such purpose pending appeal here from decree rendered in same suit for alimony.

(E) Remarriage — Effect of.

See Va. Code § 20-110 indicating that if any former spouse to whom support and maintenance has been awarded shall thereafter marry, such support and maintenance shall cease as of date of such marriage.

(F) Right to.

See Va. Code § 20-107.1 as to maintenance and support of spouses. Court has no authority to decree maintenance and support payable by estate of deceased spouse. No permanent maintenance and support shall be awarded from spouse if there exists in such spouse's favor ground of divorce on fault. Court may order support payments in periodic payments or in lump sum or both.

1983—*Thomasson v. Thomasson,* 225 Va. 394, 302 S.E.2d 63.

> Neither party to divorce has automatic obligation to support other.

1980—*Bristow v. Bristow,* 221 Va. 1, 267 S.E.2d 89.

> Neither party to divorce has automatic obligation to support other. Husband and wife are on equal footing in that either spouse now may be awarded support and maintenance from other.

1978—*Newport v. Newport,* 219 Va. 48, 245 S.E.2d 134.

Right of wife to support is inherent right which may be asserted divorce suit or in independent suit.

1971—*Monahan v. Monahan,* 212 Va. 406, 184 S.E.2d 812.

Having found wife was entitled to divorce on grounds of constructive desertion, trial court erred in denying her alimony.

1971—*Lancaster v. Lancaster,* 212 Va. 127, 183 S.E.2d 158.

In this no-fault action, court, not having determined that separation was caused by wife's fault or misconduct, husband was not relieved of his obligation to support her.

1956—*Bundy v. Bundy,* 197 Va. 795, 91 S.E.2d 412.

Husband has legal duty to support wife, although her needs and his ability to pay must be considered in determining amount, i.e., his ability to earn.

1946—*McKeel v. McKeel,* 185 Va. 108, 37 S.E.2d 746.

It is elementary that husband's duty to support his wife and children is not merely contractual but is one in which public has vital interest.

1944—*Montgomery v. Montgomery,* 183 Va. 96, 31 S.E.2d 284.

As general rule where husband has committed no breach of marital duty, he is under no obligation to provide alimony for his wife. Equity has jurisdiction to entertain suits for alimony on behalf of wronged wife even though no divorce is sought.

1941—*Heflin v. Heflin,* 177 Va. 385, 14 S.E.2d 317.

Duty to support wife exists regardless of whether she is destitute.

1941—*Wilson v. Wilson,* 178 Va. 427, 17 S.E.2d 397.

Court has power to allow alimony in suit for divorce or in suit for alimony alone. Trial court denied wife alimony although evidence indicated need. This was reversed on appeal.

1940—*Eaton v. Davis,* 176 Va. 330, 10 S.E.2d 893.

Right to alimony continues to exist even after parties cease to live together. Final decree for future alimony is not vested property right. Alimony ceases upon death of either party.

Right of wife to support during coverture is not property right. Likewise right to alimony is not property right.

1939—*Hughes v. Hughes,* 173 Va. 293, 4 S.E.2d 402.

Where no divorce is awarded court must exercise its discretion as to whether decree will be entered providing for maintenance. Husband has legal obligation to support wife and child and if he, without fault on their part renders it impossible for them to remain under his roof, then he will not be allowed to escape.

1929—*Robinette v. Robinette,* 153 Va. 342, 149 S.E. 493.

Parties sued each other for desertion. Claims denied. Wife also sought and was awarded alimony. Held: alimony should not have been awarded.

1927—*Byerly v. Byerly,* 149 Va. 53, 140 S.E. 121.

Without explaining basis for conclusion, supreme court ruled that wife had waived right to alimony.

1921—*Mihalcoe v. Holub,* 130 Va. 425, 107 S.E. 704.

Husband has legal duty to support his wife, independent of any separate estate which she may possess. Law prescribes character of support in that it must be in keeping with his circumstances and his wife's needs. When parties live apart through no fault of wife, then husband's duty to support her is not affected by separation, and he is liable to third persons who furnish her with necessary means of support on his credit.

1908—*Kaiser v. Kaiser,* 108 Va. 730, 62 S.E. 936.

Both parties had sued on grounds of desertion. Divorce was denied to both parties. Without deciding whether permanent alimony may be granted to wife where divorce is refused, decree for $350 for permanent alimony will not be disturbed where this amount also included compensation for contingent right of dower of wife. Wife is old and no longer capable of working and without means of support. Uniform practice is under such circumstances to make allowance for alimony.

1878—*Latham v. Latham,* 71 Va. 307.

If husband is willing to be reconciled to wife upon terms she can properly accept and if he has not abandoned her and if his conduct has not been such as to justify her separating from him, then she is not entitled to alimony.

§ 4-4. Separate Maintenance.

1960—*Plattner v. Plattner,* 202 Va. 263, 117 S.E.2d 128.

Although wife was denied divorce, court did not err in awarding her separate maintenance. It was matter of discretion for trial court.

1960—*Smith v. Smith,* 202 Va. 104, 116 S.E.2d 110.

Separation in this case was with husband's consent and as such wife did not forfeit her right to reasonable support and maintenance. This right exists until wife refuses without just cause to live with husband.

1953—*Upchurch v. Upchurch,* 194 Va. 990, 76 S.E.2d 170.

Wife, who did not ask for divorce and was not at fault was entitled to separate maintenance where husband refused to reconcile and was able to support her.

1948—*Williams v. Williams,* 188 Va. 543, 50 S.E.2d 277.

If husband's conduct amounts to cruelty or constructive desertion, then wife may depart and maintain action for separate maintenance and support. Wife is not entitled to separate maintenance and support if she has permanently left her husband for cause legally insufficient to be made basis for divorce.

PROPERTY DISTRIBUTION

§ 5-1. Dower and Curtesy.

See Va. Code § 8.01-70.

Court-authorized sales of lands belonging to persons under disability shall operate to bar contingent right of dower of wife and contingent right of curtesy of husband. See also Va. Code § 8.01-71 as to how dower or curtesy passes when spouse is person under disability.

See Va. Code § 55-35 indicating that husband shall be entitled to curtesy in wife's real estate other than her equitable separate estate when requisites therefor exist, and he shall not be deprived thereof by her sole act but neither husband's right to curtesy nor his marital rights shall entitle him to possession or use or to rents, issues and profits of such real estate during marriage; nor shall property of wife be subject to debts or liabilities of husband.

See Va. Code § 64.1-19 as to dower and curtesy.

See Va. Code § 64.1-23 indicating that if husband or wife willfully desert or abandon his or her spouse and such desertion or abandonment continues until death of spouse, party who deserted deceased spouse shall be barred of all interest in estate of other as tenant by dower, tenant by curtesy, distributee or heir.

1954—*Wilson v. Wilson,* 195 Va. 1060, 81 S.E.2d 605.

    Under circumstances of case and particularly in view of husband's attitude and actions towards his family and their support, it was error to decree that wife's contingent dower interest in husband's realty was extinguished. It was error to order special commissioner to sign wife's name to deed conveying lots owned by husband to corporation controlled by him, at price of questionable fairness.

1937—*Tusing v. Tusing,* 169 Va. 769, 194 S.E. 676.

    Wife's inchoate right of dower existed when conveyance was made and jointure came into being. Husband could not of his own volition abrogate it nor could subsequent divorce proceedings nullify it.

1933—*Powell v. Tilson,* 161 Va. 318, 170 S.E. 750.

    Under Va. Code § 5135 [now § 55-40] wife could not convey her contingent right of dower to any person, including husband, while husband owns real estate in question.

1931—*Puckett v. Draper,* 156 Va. 238, 158 S.E. 68.
> Wife of partner has no dower rights in partnership properties.

1926—*Eschner v. Eschner,* 146 Va. 417, 131 S.E. 800.
> Relinquishment by wife of inchoate right of dower is valuable consideration for settlement.

1926—*Jones v. Kirby,* 146 Va. 109, 135 S.E. 676.
> Husband who obtains divorce a vinculo is not entitled to curtesy as tenant by curtesy in land owned by wife at time of divorce where decree says nothing as to property rights.

1924—*Harman v. Harman,* 139 Va. 508, 124 S.E. 273.
> This was suit for assignment of dower. Before widow can be barred of her dower in her husband's estate, it must be proven that wife, of her own free will, deserted her husband and that afterwards, when requested by him to return, she refused without just cause. In present case, acts of cruelty justified wife's departure and, as such, departure was not of her own free will pursuant to statute.

1917—*Gum v. Gum,* 122 Va. 32, 94 S.E. 177.
> Divorce decree in favor of husband for desertion stated that marital rights of each party to any property owned by other is hereby extinguished. Court held that this extinguished dower interests of wife in husband's property. In absence of such special provision in decree, dower and curtesy, having already attached to existing property, are not impaired as to that property by divorce.

1911—*Fraser v. Stokes,* 112 Va. 335, 71 S.E. 545.
> Agreement by wife to support and maintain her infant children and not to claim dower in her husband's other lands adequate consideration for settlement made upon her by husband.

1901—*Banker's Loan & Inv. Co. v. Blair,* 99 Va. 606, 39 S.E. 231.
> Husband has no interest, during coverture, in wife's statutory separate estate upon which judgments can attach as liens; alienation by husband and wife, during coverture, defeats his curtesy.

1884—*Cralle v. Cralle,* 79 Va. 182.
> Curtesy and dower are barred by decree of divorce from bonds of matrimony and same principle applies to maintenance in absence of any provisions in decree as to party's property rights.

§ 5-2. Equitable Distribution.

See Va. Code § 20-107.3.
See Va. Code § 8.01-81 et seq. as to partition of property.

§ 5-3. In General.

See Va. Code § 6.1-125.3. Joint account belongs, during lifetime of all of parties, to parties in proportion to net contributions by each to sums on deposit, except that joint account between married persons shall belong to them equally unless there is clear and convincing evidence of different intent.

See Va. Code § 6.1-125.4. Upon entry of decree of divorce, all rights of either party in any multiple party account, including right of survivorship, shall be extinguished and any joint account shall then be converted into tenancy in common in proportions provided for in Va. Code § 6.1-125.3(A) unless otherwise ordered by court.

See Va. Code § 20-111 indicating that decree of divorce from bonds of matrimony extinguishes contingent property rights. Upon entry of such decree, estates by entirety shall be converted to tenancy in common.

See Va. Code § 55-47.1 indicating that no presumption of ownership of tangible personal property shall arise by operation of law to prefer one spouse of marriage over other if such presumption is based solely on sex of spouse.

1981—*Pleasants v. Pleasants,* 221 Va. 1017, 277 S.E.2d 170.

Evidence in this case was conclusive that parties understood they took conveyance as tenants by entirety, secured loans upon land, and otherwise dealt with it as joint owners and even described it as tenancy by entirety in property settlement agreement preceding their divorce action. In fact, property had been conveyed exclusively to husband. Deed would have been subject to reform to reflect this intent, and parties are now entitled to equal ownership of proceeds of sale of property.

1971—*Jenkins v. Jenkins,* 211 Va. 797, 180 S.E.2d 516.

Co-tenant in common who discharges encumbrances upon common property is entitled to ratable contribution. In this case, wife paid mortgage payments and taxes after divorce decree was entered. She lived in family home. Former husband never asserted claim for wife's use and occupancy of home. As such, he was liable to her for one-half of payment she had made as to mortgage and taxes.

1962—*Klotz v. Klotz,* 203 Va. 677, 127 S.E.2d 104.

Wife claimed that court erred in division of personal property. Evidence was in almost hopeless conflict as to purchase, payment and ownership of items. Wife failed to point out any error in rulings of trial court and as such supreme court could not say that division was unreasonable.

1956—*Commonwealth v. Terjen,* 197 Va. 596, 90 S.E.2d 801.

Community character of property already acquired will not be changed by owner's change of domicile to common law state. In this case, husband and wife moved from California to Virginia, bringing with them personalty held in California as community property. $19,000 of this was used to buy home, title of which was taken in wife's name. Entire $19,000 was deemed to be subject to gift tax because value of wife's separate estate acquired by transaction in Virginia was $19,000.

1951—*Vasilion v. Vasilion,* 192 Va. 735, 66 S.E.2d 599.

Virginia Code § 55-20 provides that if any estate, real or personal, be conveyed to husband and wife, then they shall take and hold same by moieties in like manner as if distinct moiety had been given to each by separate conveyance unless it manifestly appears from instrument that part of one dying shall belong to other. When estate by entireties is set up, neither spouse can sever it by his or her sole act. Property held in this manner is completely immune from claims of creditors against either husband or wife alone.

1947—*Vellines v. Ely,* 185 Va. 889, 41 S.E.2d 21.

Not only is right to collect cash surrender value of life insurance policies property right, but right to change beneficiary is also property right. Extinction of rights of one spouse to property of another also extinguishes any rights to complain about change of beneficiaries.

1938—*Rogers v. Rogers,* 170 Va. 417, 196 S.E. 586.

Wife's understanding was that she had one-half interest in house purchased by husband. She admitted husband never told her this. Wife used property as boarding house, paid for some additions and retained all profits. Subsequently property was rented with income going to wife. No resulting trust.

1935—*Eaton v. Davis,* 165 Va. 313, 182 S.E. 229.

Where husband spends his own money in permanent improvements on real property owned by husband and wife, such moneys are presumed to be gifts or expenditures for her benefit.

1924—*Edmonds v. Edmonds,* 139 Va. 652, 124 S.E.2d 415.

In this case, husband built house upon wife's property as home for himself and for her. Wife deserted and filed suit for unlawful detainer against him to recover possession of room in house which he occupied. Where husband purchases real estate and pays for it but puts title in his wife's name, then wife holds real estate as gift and not in trust. Under Married Women's Act, husband has no right to occupy wife's property without her consent. In this case, wife was entitled to possession of property that was in her name.

1916—*DeBaun's Ex'r v. DeBaun,* 119 Va. 85, 89 S.E.2d 239.

Where husband buys land and takes deed for it and subsequently borrows money from his wife and uses it for purpose of retiring some of notes given for deferring payments on land, no trust in land results in favor of wife.

1876—*Porter v. Porter,* 68 Va. 599.

Husband was awarded divorce on grounds of adultery. Decree did not contain any directives as to property of parties. Upon dissolution of marriage, all of husband's claims to wife's lands which depended on marriage were extinguished, and she is entitled to possession of land.

§ 5-4. Jurisdiction.

1984—*Lapidus v. Lapidus,* 226 Va. 575, 311 S.E.2d 786.

Jurisdiction in divorce suits is purely statutory. Divorce court lacks authority to compel husband to contract for life insurance or to adopt punitive measures to support its ruling. Such decree is void.

1983—*Johnson v. Johnson,* 224 Va. 641, 299 S.E.2d 351.

Jurisdiction in divorce suits is purely statutory. In this case, trial court did not have jurisdiction to order husband to pay his wife one half of savings deposit held in joint names of parties. Va. Code § 6.1-73 dealing with joint accounts did not confer jurisdiction upon divorce court to divide money formerly held by spouses in joint account.

1982—*Ernsberger v. Ernsberger,* 224 Va. 1, 294 S.E.2d 794.

Trial court directed husband to transfer stock certificates to wife which he was wrongfully withholding. Supreme court found that trial court did not have jurisdiction to decree disposition of personal property of parties and that portion of court order was declared void.

1980—*Watkins v. Watkins,* 220 Va. 1051, 265 S.E.2d 750.

Trial court had no power to enjoin disposition of stock held by husband because it had effect of impounding husband's personal property. Jurisdiction in divorce suits is purely statutory. Such jurisdiction does not inherently extend to disposal of personal property of husband.

1975—*Robertson v. Robertson,* 215 Va. 425, 211 S.E.2d 41.

Husband was ordered to replace with suitable substitute, any furniture or furnishings which he or anyone other than wife might remove from wife's apartment. In doing so, court did not award use in possession or ownership of property. Court merely provided that apartment occupied by wife would be furnished according to standard to which she was accustomed.

1972—*McCotter v. Carle,* 149 Va. 584, 140 S.E. 670.

There can be no decree as to property rights where divorce is denied. Such issues must be resolved by separate suit.

1972—*Turner v. Turner,* 213 Va. 42, 189 S.E.2d 361.

Husband seized possession of household furnishings and equipment and changed locks on house while wife was temporarily absent. Husband's net worth was in excess of one million dollars. Trial court properly exercised its discretion to award wife $6,000 for purpose of providing furnishings and equipment in addition to other sums awarded for alimony and child support. Court noted that where special equities exist and there is impelling reason for its necessity or desirability, court may award lump sum in addition to periodic payments of alimony and child support.

1971—*Lawrence v. Lawrence,* 212 Va. 44, 181 S.E.2d 640.

Divorce court's jurisdiction is purely statutory and does not include authority to determine and settle rights of party's daughter to certain securities held by father.

1971—*Jackson v. Jackson,* 211 Va. 718, 180 S.E.2d 500.

Upon entry of divorce decree, family home was converted to tenancy in common. Since property rights of wife and husband were not created by marriage court was without jurisdiction to enter decree awarding use of jointly owned property to wife as part of award of alimony and joint support.

1970—*Guy v. Guy,* 210 Va. 536, 172 S.E.2d 735.

Jurisdiction in divorce suits is purely statutory. It was error for trial court to decide issues of ownership of furniture and furnishings since court lacked jurisdiction to do so.

1958—*Smith v. Smith,* 200 Va. 77, 104 S.E.2d 17.

Wife contributed major part of payments towards family home which was owned as tenants by entirety. Since divorce decree had been entered, state law converted tenancy by entirety into tenancy in common. Trial court had no authority to order that wife be allotted greater share in property because of her larger contribution. Resulting trust did not arise in this instance. One who asserts resulting trust in real property, which is clearly effort to convert duly executed and recorded deed, must establish it by clear and convincing evidence.

1958—*Smith v. Smith,* 200 Va. 77, 104 S.E.2d 17.

Subject matter jurisdiction may be raised at any point in proceedings. Trial court in this case properly decreed that jointly owned property be equally divided between husband and wife pursuant to Va. Code § 20-111. Trial court had jurisdiction to adjudicate that property was jointly and equally owned and to order its partition. It had authority to make decrees concerning estate of parties as well as to settle their status.

1954—*Wilson v. Wilson,* 195 Va. 1060, 81 S.E.2d 605.

In this action for separate maintenance, it was held that, although wife was not entitled to have family home designated for her use since specific property should not be allotted for wife as alimony, wife was entitled to select and occupy comparable home, rental of which husband should pay.

1946—*Ring v. Ring,* 185 Va. 269, 38 S.E.2d 471.

Divorce court does not inherently have jurisdiction to dispose of husband's property, either real or personal.

1936—*Watson v. Mose,* 165 Va. 661, 183 S.E. 428.

So much of divorce decree that conveyed property of husband to wife was void and was subject to attack at any time in any court. Court has authority to fix rights of each party in property of other, but no right to transfer.

1925—*Humphreys v. Strong,* 141 Va. 146, 126 S.E. 194.

Husband is not entitled to possession or use of rents and profits of his wife's real estate during marriage. As to wife's property rights during marriage, husband and wife are as strangers. In this case, husband conveyed piece of property to wife upon consideration of natural love and affection of wife. He later sought to rescind deed on ground that wife had abandoned and deserted him without cause. Wife had previously obtained Nevada divorce. Nevada court concluded that there was no willful desertion on her part. That decision was recognized by Virginia Supreme Court in prior case and as such is res judicata as to this matter.

1925—*Barnes v. American Fertilizer Co.,* 144 Va. 692, 130 S.E. 902.

Court possesses no power to vest in wife title to specific portion of husband's real estate. Court is empowered to settle in cases of divorce contingent rights of dower and curtesy. Court, however, does have authority to approve valid agreements between parties for settlement of property rights. This, however, is not decree for alimony. Agreement of parties, in this case, was approved and adopted by Court and incorporated into final decree. Decree, in this case is contract between parties and is binding unless secured by fraud or mistake.

1917—*Gum v. Gum,* 122 Va. 32, 94 S.E. 177.

Court has right to make decrees extinguishing marital rights of wife in her husband's property.

§ 5-5. Property Settlement Agreement.

(A) Ante-Nuptial.

1957—*Batleman v. Rubin,* 199 Va. 156, 98 S.E.2d 519.

Wife made out prima facie case that ante-nuptial agreement was invalid when she proved, without aid of her own testimony, that (1) while she was engaged couple executed ante-nuptial contract; (2) thereafter they were married; (3) consideration stated in contract was unreasonably small in proportion to value of property then owned by husband. Proof of these facts raised presumption that wife did not know and was not fully and frankly informed by husband of value of property then owned by him and cast upon husband burden of meeting or overcoming presumption. For agreement to be valid, there must be full disclosure of husband's worth and intelligent and voluntary agreement by wife. In this case, agreement stated that husband would leave wife $20,000 at his death and relinquish all rights in her property and that she should have dower in all real estate thereafter acquired by him. She in turn released all marital rights in his estate. Evidence showed that husband was worth $250,000 at time and had substantial income. This evidence that wife agreed to accept, at her husband's death, sum less than 1/3 of her rights in his property, if married, on day contract was signed, raised presumption that husband did not make full and frank disclosure.

1932—*Garrett v. Andis,* 159 Va. 150, 165 S.E. 657.

> Oral ante-nuptial settlement agreement which gave wife all of personal estate and life estate in realty was not effective. No writing as is required by statute of frauds.

1920—*Cumming v. Cumming,* 127 Va. 16, 102 S.E. 572.

> Ante-nuptial contracts designed to encourage or facilitate separation after marriage are void. Such contract cannot fix in advance husband's liability for alimony in case either shall obtain divorce. Contract which invites hope of financial profit from separation of married people should not be enforced. Same principle is true of post-nuptial contracts. What makes these contracts void are:
>
> 1. They are made for purpose of providing contract limitation of legal obligation with view to controlling action of parties;
> 2. Grounds relied on for divorce arise from action of husband and wife after contract is executed. Post-nuptial contracts which precede separation may be valid where they contemplate immediate separation for some ground existing prior to contract having been executed. Weight of authority is that even valid contracts cannot bind court on subject of alimony.
>
> Parol evidence is admissible to show illegality of contract in contemplation of marriage, as tending to encourage or facilitate separation after marriage.

1907—*Smith v. Smith,* 107 Va. 112, 57 S.E. 577.

> If female infant, upon eve of her marriage, unites with her intended husband in settling her real estate upon herself and contemplated issue of such marriage, act is voidable and can be disaffirmed by her when disabilities of infancy and coverture have been removed, where she has in meantime done no act to ratify or affirm such settlement.

1907—*Jenkins v. Rhodes,* 106 Va. 564, 56 S.E. 332.

> Man about to be married may dispose of his estate as he pleases provided it is done with proper motives and without intention to defraud intended wife. Such conveyance becomes bad only upon imputation of fraud. In this case, there was no secrecy about execution of deed and evidence failed to disclose any fraudulent purpose on part of grantor.

(B) Post-Nuptial.

See Va. Code § 20-109.1 dealing with affirmation, ratification and incorporation by reference in decree.

1980—*Cooley v. Cooley,* 220 Va. 749, 263 S.E.2d 49.

> Agreement between husband and wife is void if its purpose is to facilitate separation or divorce. Marital property settlements based on valid consideration are favored. Since agreement was entered into after long period of marital discord, and contract modifying this agreement was executed when wife had no defense to husband's suit for divorce due to one year separation, neither agreement nor contract facilitated divorce and both should be enforced.

1977—*Lindsay v. Lindsay,* 218 Va. 599, 238 S.E.2d 817.

In 1971 parties entered into property settlement agreement. In 1975 they entered into consent order. Court held order was binding on parties, its terms being made subject to further order of court as to support. Parties having agreed that court should retain jurisdiction over allowance of support payments, counsel fees and cost. Court did not purport to approve and incorporate 1971 agreement and then modify it in violation of Va. Code § 20-109, but acted instead pursuant to consent order.

1977—*Winn v. Winn,* 218 Va. 8, 235 S.E.2d 307.

Property settlement agreement incorporated into final decree. To have party held guilty of contempt for violation of property settlement agreement, duties imposed upon party must be expressed rather than implied. In this case there was no contempt because language of agreement was somewhat ambiguous.

1977—*Shoosmith v. Scott,* 217 Va. 789, 232 S.E.2d 787.

Divorce decree approved property settlement agreement, but did not expressly incorporate agreement or order husband to perform its obligations. Decree was not, therefore, award of alimony, but rather approval of private contract for payments in lieu of alimony. Like other contracts, this one may not be impaired by legislative enactments. In this instance, failure to perform obligations under agreement does not constitute sufficient basis to hold husband in contempt.

1976—*T. . . v. T. . .,* 216 Va. 867, 224 S.E.2d 148.

Contract governed by statute of frauds is not void ab initio, but cannot be enforced. Statute is not enforced when to do so would cause fraud and wrong to be perpetrated. Under certain conditions, equity will avoid statute and enforce oral agreement. Ordinarily marriage is not such part performance as will take case outside statute. In this case, however, wife abandoned her plans for employment and for disposition by adoption of her expected baby in light of husband's promise to support child who is not his. In addition, there was substantial performance by both husband and wife under agreement for more than four years, i.e., to support child. Husband obliged to pay support.

1976—*Mack v. Mack,* 217 Va. 534, 229 S.E.2d 895.

Question of interpretation of settlement agreement. Supreme court assumed, but did not decide that extrinsic evidence was admissible. Court noted however, that even if it was admissible, it obviously is in direct conflict, and as such, it was cast aside as having no value in search for intent of parties.

1975—*Capps v. Capps,* 216 Va. 378, 219 S.E.2d 901.

Agreement that if either party to marriage institutes proceedings for divorce or separate maintenance then wife must surrender her interest in home, tends to support marriage and does not violate public policy. Agreements which tend to encourage or facilitate separation or divorce are void. However court has held that property settlements when entered into by competent parties upon valid consideration for lawful purposes are favored in law and therefore are enforceable unless their illegality is clear and certain. Therefore such agreements even though in contemplation of divorce are not violative of established public policy unless collusive or made to facilitate separation or to aid in procuring divorce. Where consideration for promise of one party is promise of other there must be absolute mutuality of engagement so that each party has right to hold other to positive agreement. Both parties must be bound or neither is bound. Marital agreement in this case was held to be valid and enforceable.

1975—*Wickham v. Wickham,* 215 Va. 694, 213 S.E.2d 750.

Property settlement provided that husband was to pay $930 per month for support and maintenance of wife and three minor children. Payments were to be reduced by $150 per month upon death or emancipation of each child. This agreement provided basis from which to calculate and determine whether change had occurred in children's financial needs. Court in this case unnecessarily apportioned award upon petition of wife. That had adverse affect upon tax advantage secured to husband. Error to apportion award unnecessarily.

1975—*Morris v. Morris,* 216 Va. 457, 219 S.E.2d 864.

Statute facilitates enforcement, by use of contempt power of court, of terms of agreement incorporated in decree. Resolution, by court approved agreements, of problems concerning minor children and property rights should be encouraged. All provisions having at least indirect bearing on maintenance of children should be held to be incorporated into decree. Court retains continuous jurisdiction to modify maintenance of children in spite of existence of contract.

1975—*Carter v. Carter,* 215 Va. 475, 211 S.E.2d 253.

Wording of agreement approved by court, as well as other evidence, supported court's ruling that agreement covered both alimony and child support for three children. Initially wife had custody. Due to her being institutionalized husband assumed custody. Total support award had been $600 per month pursuant to agreement. After change in custody this was reduced by two thirds since one of children had been emancipated and two other children were now in custody of father. Court may apportion unitary award of alimony and support pursuant to settlement agreement.

1970—*McLoughlin v. McLoughlin,* 211 Va. 365, 177 S.E.2d 781.

While divorce suit was pending, husband agreed to pay $100 per month for support of wife, and this agreement was incorporated into divorce decree. On wife's remarriage, husband petitioned for termination of alimony. Trial court correctly dismissed petition since, under statute, court cannot make order in conflict with property settlement agreement. This, however, did not bar husband from filing suit for construction of agreement.

1958—*Ryan v. Griffin,* 199 Va. 891, 103 S.E.2d 240.

If agreement in fact or in effect facilitated or promoted separation or divorce, then it is void. Contract that is entered into before separation and which facilitates or promotes separation or divorce is void. Agreements which contemplated immediate separation for some ground existing prior to contract, sufficient of itself to bring about separation, are upheld in most jurisdictions on principle that parties have already irrevocably determined upon separation for pre-existing cause. If court determines that agreement was part of scheme to effect separation or obtain divorce by agreement or legal grounds therefore did not already exist, agreement will be declared nullity.

1955—*Higgins v. McFarland,* 196 Va. 889, 86 S.E.2d 168.

Suit by ex-wife against estate of husband to enforce contract wherein husband agreed to pay off deed of trust on her home. Under agreement, wife agreed to obtain divorce to which she was entitled. Agreement, under circumstances, was not invalid because it contravened public policy. No public good would have been advanced by denying its approval. Divorce decree granted to husband in North Carolina approved and adopted agreement. Since husband did not contest it and complied with agreement up until his death, his administrator could not contest its validity in present case. Public policy is sometimes defined as that principle of law under which freedom of contract or private dealings is restricted by law for public good.

1954—*Wallihan v. Hughes,* 196 Va. 117, 82 S.E.2d 553.

Agreement made part of Nevada divorce decree. Wife contended agreement facilitated divorce and was void. With regard to property rights, agreement was binding on parties, even though it might, for reasons of public policy, have been unenforceable between parties in Virginia. It may not be given recognition with regards to custody issues.

1954—*Arrington v. Arrington,* 196 Va. 86, 82 S.E.2d 548.

Agreement signed at husband's insistence was contrary to public policy and void because its object was to facilitate separation and promote divorce. Such agreements are held valid in most states only where they contemplate immediate separation for some ground existing prior to contract which is sufficient of itself to bring about separation.

1951—*Shelton v. Stewart,* 193 Va. 162, 67 S.E.2d 841.

Ante-nuptial or post-nuptial agreements, object and result of which is to facilitate and promote separation, are illegal and void. Objectionable paragraph within such agreement is not divisible or severable from other parts of agreement. In this case, agreement was one to sell land wherein intent was that wife should sue for divorce.

1947—*Vellines v. Ely,* 185 Va. 889, 41 S.E.2d 21.

Agreement between spouses settling property rights will be upheld in divorce cases if it is fair, free from fraud and not promotive of divorce.

In construing such agreement, courts look to intention of parties and to written word, but intention must be gathered from attendant circumstances.

1946—*Henebry v. Henebry,* 185 Va. 320, 38 S.E.2d 320.
Contract between parties affirmed and adopted by court at request of party to whom relief might otherwise be awarded should not be accorded less validity than contract merely executed by parties and filed with pleadings.

1943—*Lewis v. Stroebel,* 181 Va. 882, 27 S.E.2d 218.
Action by wife against estate of her divorced husband for alleged failure of husband to comply with written property settlement agreement. Supreme court reversed finding of trial court and entered final judgment.

1940—*Buchanan v. Buchanan,* 174 Va. 255, 6 S.E.2d 612.
There must be mutuality before there can be decree for specific performance. In this property settlement agreement there clearly was mutuality. To determine whether contract is entire or severable intention of parties must be looked at, i.e., situation of parties, subject matter of agreement and object which parties intended to accomplish.

1939—*Hughes v. Hughes,* 173 Va. 293, 4 S.E.2d 402.
Even if husband entered into voluntary binding agreement to support wife and child, if court finds it insufficient, court may modify it.

1938—*Buchanan v. Buchanan,* 170 Va. 458, 197 S.E. 426.
Contract between mother and father as to custody of children is not binding on court. Nor will court permit parent under any and all circumstances to transfer his common law obligations due his children.

1937—*Casilear v. Casilear,* 168 Va. 46, 190 S.E. 314.
Contract between parties will not supersede provisions for support in court decree.

1931—*Puckett v. Draper,* 156 Va. 238, 158 S.E. 68.
Post-nuptial settlement is good against subsequent creditors, even where there is no consideration, provided settler is not indebted when he makes it and transaction is free from circumstances of fraud. Good faith of transaction must be proved by clear and satisfactory evidence.

1930—*Gloth v. Gloth,* 154 Va. 511, 153 S.E. 879.
Court has authority to approve and confirm in final decree contracts as to property settlement, support and maintenance. Whether property rights are fixed by decree mensa or terms of contract incorporated, court has no power to divest these property rights due to changed conditions or subsequent misconduct. Provision for support of wife and child may be modified. Husband claims contract procured by fraud and duress. His failure to promptly repudiate resulted in estoppel.

1926—*Eschner v. Eschner,* 146 Va. 417, 131 S.E. 800.

Husband contended that agreement was severable and consideration only applied to part of agreement and not to entire agreement. To determine whether it is entire or severable must consider: situation of parties, subject matter, object that parties had in view. In this case agreement was held entire.

1926—*Barnes v. American Fertilizer Co.,* 144 Va. 692, 130 S.E. 902.

Where creditor seeks to set aside post-nuptial settlement, which is shown to have been founded upon valuable consideration, burden is on creditor to show that settlement was excessive, so excessive as to raise presumption of fraud. In this case, consideration of agreement was settlement of property rights, claims for alimony and suit money and release of wife's contingent right of dower. This constituted valuable consideration. Agreement was approved and adopted by court and incorporated into decree. It became contract and is binding unless secured by fraud or mistake. In this case, creditor sought to attach property that had been conveyed to wife pursuant to property settlement agreement. Judgment lien in this case is subject to every possible description of equity held by third party against debtor at time judgment attached. So long as equitable interest is prior in time to judgment, it will be preferred to judgment lien. Fact that parties later on reconciled does not abrogate prior agreement between parties.

1926—*Butler v. Butler,* 145 Va. 85, 133 S.E. 756.

Wife prosecuted husband for assault and battery. Husband found guilty. To avoid penalty of criminal case, husband entered into separation agreement. Court later declared this agreement was simply to adjust property rights and did not bar claim by husband for desertion. Agreement gave custody to wife, but court gave custody to husband.

1908—*Moreland v. Moreland,* 108 Va. 93, 60 S.E. 730.

Deed of separation between husband and wife who have already separated is not contrary to public policy and is enforceable but, even if provision to live separate and apart were contrary to public policy and not enforceable, that does not destroy other provisions of contract adjusting property rights and providing maintenance for wife. That is, remainder is valid and enforceable. In construing contract made in another State, if there is no proof as to what law of other State is, it will be presumed to be same as law of this State.

1875—*Switzer v. Switzer,* 67 Va. 574.

Wife, under apprehension that her husband will sue her for divorce on grounds of adultery and anxious to avoid scandal, enters into deed of separation with husband, whereby she relinquishes all interests she has in her real estate in return for some minimal support payments. Agreement was held invalid on grounds of disability of coverture, want of freedom of will on part of wife executing it and also due to inadequacy of consideration. Such contract cannot be sustained where wife was not in position where she could act with perfect freedom, nor with full knowledge and appreciation of all of circumstances of her situation.

MISCELLANEOUS

§ 6-1. Alienation of Affections.

See Va. Code § 8.01-220. No civil action shall lie or be maintained for alienation of affection or criminal conversation.

1957—*Daniels v. Morris,* 199 Va. 205, 98 S.E.2d 694.
Husband filed suit for alienation of affection and criminal conversation and recovered verdict in amount of $17,000.

1950—*Bowen v. Pernell,* 190 Va. 389, 57 S.E.2d 36.
Punitive damages are awarded only where wrongful act is done with bad motive or is characterized by circumstances of aggravation or in manner so wanton or reckless as to manifest willful disregard of rights of others. In this alienation of affections case, jury issue was presented as to punitive damages.
Jury verdict in amount of $15,000 upheld.

1935—*Newsom v. Fleming,* 165 Va. 89, 181 S.E. 393.
Married woman may sue third person for alienation of affection.

1928—*Harlow v. Harlow,* 152 Va. 910, 143 S.E. 720.
Wife sued husband's family for alienation of affection. Defendants being Roman Catholics felt that second marriage of husband was unlawful and attempted to convince husband of this. Verdict for $20,000 reduced to $13,500.

1915—*Ratcliffe v. Walker,* 117 Va. 569, 85 S.E. 575.
Parents may advise their children about domestic affairs without incurring liability if advice be given in good faith and prompted by worthy motives, even though such advice results in separation of husband and wife. Improper motives as to parents must be clearly proved. Mere fact that defendant manifested ill will towards plaintiff would not be sufficient to overcome legal presumption in their favor.

§ 6-2. Bond.

See Va. Code § 20-114 indicating that court in its discretion may require giving of recognizance for compliance with its order.

1971—*Lawrence v. Lawrence,* 212 Va. 44, 181 S.E.2d 640.
> There was no abuse of discretion in not requiring husband to give security for alimony payments that had been ordered.

1971—*Jenkins v. Jenkins,* 211 Va. 797, 180 S.E.2d 516.
> Requiring security for alimony and child support payments out of proceeds of sale of home is matter within sound discretion of trial court.

1948—*Davis v. Davis,* 187 Va. 63, 45 S.E.2d 918.
> Father previously absconded with child in violation of court order. Bond should be required before additional visitation allowed.

1914—*Parrish v. Parrish,* 116 Va. 476, 82 S.E. 119.
> Trial court imposed bond upon father who was to have custody of child for three months out of year. Supreme court found that bond to be unnecessary given status and reputation of father.

§ 6-3. Change of Name.

See Va. Code § 8.01-19. If party changes his name, suit shall proceed in new name but, if change of name be not suggested before judgment, judgment shall be as valid and may be enforced in like manner as if no such change of name had taken place.

See Va. Code § 8.01-20. If at any time after verdict or judgment in trial court during pendency of appeal marriage or change of name of party be suggested or relied on in abatement in court of appeals or supreme court, court may in its discretion take or retain jurisdiction and enter judgment in case as if such event had not occurred.

See Va. Code § 8.01-217 as to how name may be changed.

See Va. Code § 18.2-504.1 as to unlawful change of name.

See Va. Code § 20-121.4 as to restoration of former name upon entry of decree of divorce.

1978—*In re: Change of Name of Miller,* 218 Va. 939, 243 S.E.2d 464.
> Under common law person may adopt any name he or she wishes provided it is not done for fraudulent purpose or it does not infringe upon rights of others. Although married woman customarily assumes her husband's surname there is no statute requiring her to do so. In this case court abused its discretion in forbidding married woman from resuming her maiden name. It is speculation to reason that name change of mother would have embarrassing effect on children. In this case wife agreed that if there were any children born to marriage they would bear father's last name.

1977—*Flowers v. Cain,* 218 Va. 234, 237 S.E.2d 111.
> Application by mother to have names of children born of previous marriage changed to name of present husband. Father objected to

this. Name change not allowed. Father has interest in having his children continue to use his name, and this parental interest is relevant in determining child's best interest. Generally, name change of child will not be ordered over father's objection unless: (a) father has abandoned natural ties, (b) he has engaged in misconduct sufficient to embarrass child, (c) child will suffer substantial detriment in continued use of father's name or (d) child is of sufficient age and discretion to make intelligent choice and desires to change name. In this case children were six and seven, and as such, neither was capable of making intelligent choice. Burden of proof was on mother to prove that change of name would be in best interest of children. And she failed to meet that burden.

1975—*In re: Strikwerda and Antell,* 216 Va. 470, 220 S.E.2d 245.
Statute authorizing change of name after divorce proceeding is not exclusive statutory authority for such change of name. Under common law person is free to adopt any name if it is not done for fraudulent purpose or infringement of rights of others. In this case married woman was authorized to resume her maiden name during course of marriage. Court noted that there were no children of marriage and any children to be born of marriage, it was agreed, would take father's name.

§ 6-4. Duress.

1977—*Jacobs v. Jacobs,* 218 Va. 264, 237 S.E.2d 124.
Suit to rescind deed by which wife conveyed land to husband. Couple had history of disharmony with evidence of threat to wife and physical abuse by husband. This was corroborated by two adopted daughters. Wife testified that she signed deed because she feared her husband would kill her. No testimony was offered by husband. Uncontradicted testimony offered by wife with surrounding circumstances clearly and convincingly established duress and therefore deeds should be set aside. Evidence of duress must be clear and convincing.

1915—*Ford v. Engleman,* 118 Va. 89, 86 S.E. 852.
Duress is form of fraud and therefore it must be clearly proved.

§ 6-5. Fraud.

1962—*Ware v. Ware,* 203 Va. 189, 123 S.E.2d 357.
Wife in present case sought to have uncontested divorce decree set aside on grounds that it was procured by fraud. She alleged that suit papers and notice of taking depositions were served on her and that her husband told her to disregard them and that without reading them she destroyed them. Husband testified to contrary and was substantiated by independent witness. Fraud must be proved by evidence that is clear and convincing. Wife failed to meet burden in this case.

1956—*Humphreys v. Baird,* 197 Va. 667, 90 S.E.2d 796.

> Plaintiff married defendant in reliance on his statements that he had obtained final divorce. In fact, he had not. Jury awarded verdict to Plaintiff for humiliation and mental anguish. These statements were mixed questions of law and fact. When party occupies relationship of trust his misrepresentations of law may be actionable.

1952—*Ciarochi v. Ciarochi,* 194 Va. 313, 73 S.E.2d 402.

> Wife sought annulment on grounds of fraud alleging that husband had preconceived intent to have no children and secondly that husband married her solely to obtain her money. First contention was rejected because it was not alleged in her bill. With regard to second contention, she contends that she spent large sum of money to establish him in restaurant business which failed, and then he shortly thereafter abandoned her. This was insufficient to prove alleged fraud.

1951—*Alexander v. Kuykendall,* 192 Va. 8, 63 S.E.2d 746.

> Innocent woman induced by fraud to contract void marriage with defendant, who subsequently lives with him, performing normal duties of wife, is entitled to recover damages in action for fraud.

1950—*Ballard v. Cox,* 191 Va. 654, 62 S.E.2d 1.

> Fraud is not to be presumed but must be proved by clear and convincing evidence.

1945—*Jacobs v. Jacobs,* 184 Va. 281, 35 S.E.2d 119.

> Where fraud is relied upon, burden of proof is strict and clear proof.

1941—*Pretlow v. Pretlow,* 177 Va. 524, 14 S.E.2d 381.

> Fraud which goes to fundamental of marriage relation gives equity jurisdiction and property rights growing out of that fraud may also be adjusted. Equity is alert to search out fraud.

1932—*Taylor v. Taylor,* 159 Va. 338, 165 S.E. 414.

> Equity has jurisdiction to inquire and give relief where there is fraud in obtaining divorce. To set aside judgment fraud must be extrinsic or collateral to matter tried by first court.

1927—*Bruce v. Dean,* 149 Va. 39, 140 S.E. 277.

> Fraud must be proved by clear and convincing evidence.

1925—*Scott v. Scott,* 142 Va. 31, 128 S.E. 599.

> One who alleges fraud must prove allegation by clear and convincing evidence.

§ 6-6. Husband — Wife.

(A) Liability.

See Va. Code § 55-37 indicating that spouse shall not be responsible for other spouse's contract or tort liability to third party whether such liability arose before or after marriage. Doctrine of necessaries as it existed at common law shall apply equally to both spouses except where they are permanently living separate and apart. No lien arising out of judgment under this section shall attach to judgment debtor's principal residence held by them as tenants by entireties.

1984—*Wright v. Bryan,* 226 Va. 557, 311 S.E.2d 776.

Contract to convey land held by husband and wife as tenants by entirety was not void for lack of wife's signature. In this case, buyers had signed contract to purchase home and had made deposit. They later on wished to get out of contract and argued that because wife (co-owner) had not signed contract, that it was therefore void. Court disagreed and held contract was binding.

1983—*McComb v. McComb,* 226 Va. 271, 307 S.E.2d 877.

Wife's parents lent couple $4,000 to be used as down-payment on house. Husband gave them note with no time for repayment which was signed solely by him. Parol evidence was admitted at trial to show that wife was co-obligor on note. Both parties were liable and since husband paid entire amount, he was entitled to contribution from wife.

1983—*Schilling v. Bedford County Hosp.,* 225 Va. 539, 303 S.E.2d 905.

Wife obtained services at hospital and thereafter, hospital sued husband to recover cost of these services. Trial court held that husband was liable under agency theory in that his wife pledged his credit with apparent authority to do so. This holding was not supported by evidence and therefore was overturned.

1982—*Dere v. Montgomery Ward,* 224 Va. 277, 295 S.E.2d 794.

Wife purchased furniture and paid by check. Checking account was in joint name of herself and her husband. Check was dishonored for insufficient funds. Wife thereafter arranged with department store to pay part of bill in cash and to transfer balance to credit account in her husband's name. Husband, however, had already closed this account, and as such, wife and furniture store were both on notice of wife's lack of authority. Judgment properly entered against wife.

1962—*Littreal v. Howell,* 203 Va. 394, 124 S.E.2d 16.

Husband built house on wife's land in which plaintiff installed heating equipment. Wife was present when estimate was given, acquiesced in contract and indicated during installation where she wanted units placed. Bills were submitted to her and her husband, and she promised to pay bill even after her husband and she were separated. These facts conclusively show that her husband was her agent and judgment was entered against her.

1956—*Cooper v. Knox,* 197 Va. 602, 90 S.E.2d 844.

Plaintiff extended credit to Mr. Knox, contractor. Plaintiff sued Mr. and Mrs. Knox alleging that she was partner in business. Plaintiff showed that greater part of receipts of business were deposited in her account and that she drew on this account to pay business expenses and personal expenses. Husband and wife denied that she had any voice in business or any financial stake in it. Plaintiff failed to establish community of interest as common owners and, as such, she was not partner.

1952—*Painter v. Lingon,* 193 Va. 840, 71 S.E.2d 355.

Husband is under legal and moral obligation not only to support and maintain his wife but to provide reasonable means for her recreation and pleasure. When performing any of these obligations he acts for himself and not as agent of his wife.

1939—*Fruit Grower's Express v. Hulfish,* 173 Va. 27, 3 S.E.2d 160.

Negligence of husband not imputable to wife where she is simply passenger in auto and had no control over its operation.

1923—*Brown v. Commonwealth,* 135 Va. 480, 115 S.E. 542.

It was common law rule that there is rebuttable presumption that, when wife commits crime, except for certain felonies, in presence of and by direction of her husband, she acts under his coercion and is immune from punishment. This presumption could be overcome by slight evidence that she was acting independently and without any coercion from her husband.

1922—*Wampler v. Norton,* 134 Va. 606, 113 S.E. 733.

Prosecution for possession of intoxicating liquors. Husband is responsible and authoritative head of family and director of conditions in home. In absence of proof to contrary, he is to be regarded as person in charge of home within contemplation of statute in question in this prosecution. Wife cannot excuse herself from criminal charge merely by showing marriage and pleading consequent technical coercion by husband.

1916—*DeBaun's Ex'r v. DeBaun,* 119 Va. 85, 89 S.E. 81.

Wife, having legal title to money, loaned it to her husband. Relationship of parties to that transaction is that of creditor and debtor and not that of trustee. Where husband buys land and takes deed for it and subsequently borrows money from his wife and uses it for purpose of retiring some of notes given for deferred payments on land, no trust in land results in favor of wife.

1908—*Chilton v. Hannah,* 107 Va. 661, 60 S.E. 87.

Statute declaring that all property of married women theretofore or thereafter acquired should be free from debts and liabilities of their husband is, so far as it affects debts and liabilities of husband created after date of act, valid statute.

1903—*Young v. Hart,* 101 Va. 480, 44 S.E. 703.

Contract of married woman valid where made and to be performed is generally held to be valid everywhere, except when sought to be enforced in jurisdiction where there is total incapacity on part of married woman to contract. In this case, there being evidence tending to show that contract was binding on her, both in jurisdiction where made and to be performed, personal judgment of trial court rendered against her was affirmed.

1902—*Stewart v. Conrad,* 100 Va. 128, 40 S.E. 624.

Under common law, contracts of married women are void.

1881—*Coles v. Hurt,* 75 Va. 380.

Liability of husband for his wife's debts is legal liability and must be prosecuted by action at law. In this case, husband and wife agreed before marriage that property of husband would be solely liable for his debts and that of wife solely liable for her debts. After marriage, creditor of wife sued to collect on debt incurred before marriage. Husband and his property shall be exempt from all liability.

1849—*Uhl v. Commonwealth,* 47 Va. 706.

Where wife acts in furtherance of combination to commit felony in presence of her husband, she will be presumed to have acted under his coercion, but if circumstances show that she was not acting under such coercion but of her own free will, then she is accountable for her acts.

(B) Miscellaneous.

1952—*Graves v. Graves,* 193 Va. 659, 70 S.E.2d 339.

Husband has right to select place of abode and wife must acquiesce in such selection, provided decision of husband is not unreasonable, arbitrary and unjust and not used as means of procuring dissolution of marriage.

1944—*Kerr v. Kerr,* 182 Va. 731, 30 S.E.2d 684.

While trend is to extend equal rights to male and female husband is still regarded as head of family and ordinarily is entitled to select family home provided wife is not thereby subjected to interference and indignities.

1948—*Mullen v. Mullen,* 188 Va. 259, 49 S.E.2d 349.

Husband, consistent with his financial ability, should provide his wife home free from interference from his family members. This rule is dependent upon facts of particular case.

1941—*Fairfax v. Commonwealth,* 177 Va. 824, 13 S.E.2d 315.

Presumption exists that husband is head of house. This may be rebutted by evidence of uncontradicted witness when it is not inherently improbable.

1926—*Levine v. Levine,* 144 Va. 330, 132 S.E. 320.

Wife sues husband claiming that gift of $1,000 from her father was her property. Husband claimed that gift was given directly to him by her father. Gift was wedding present and was made payable to both parties. Wife claimed that she had given check to husband based upon his promise of speedy repayment. Fact that husband claimed sole ownership of proceeds did not preclude him from claiming lesser sum if evidence showed he was entitled to it. Jury issue was presented as to that question.

1924—*Fowlkes v. White,* 138 Va. 438, 121 S.E. 888.

It is matter of common knowledge that it was habit of many women in past to rely implicitly upon their husbands for attention to all of their business affairs.

1923—*Brown v. Commonwealth,* 135 Va. 480, 115 S.E. 542.

New independence of women in political, social and economic matters import increased responsibilities, and if Courts, whose function is not to enact but to declare law, are so hampered by ancient precedents as to be unable to apply new and logical rules to changed, modern conditions, then it should be done by statute.

1917—*Va. Ry. & Power Co. v. Gorsuch,* 120 Va. 655, 91 S.E. 632.

In spite of advances made by modern women towards political and economic independence, it still remains true that normal woman married to normal man recognizes obligation of obedience contained in marriage vow and observes Pauline injunction to remain subject to her husband.

(C) Rights.

See Va. Code § 55-35 as to how married women may acquire and dispose of property.

1984—*Weishaupt v. Commonwealth,* 227 Va. 389, 315 S.E.2d 847.

Wife can unilaterally revoke her implied consent to sexual intercourse whereas here, she has manifested her intent to terminate marital relationship by living separate and apart from husband, has refrained from voluntary intercourse with her husband and has conducted herself in manner that establishes de facto end to marriage. Where implied consent has been revoked, then husband may be convicted of attempted rape even though parties are not yet divorced.

1983—*Knox v. Commonwealth,* 225 Va. 504, 304 S.E.2d 4.

Under married women's act, once joint occupancy of marital abode owned by wife is terminated by separation, husband's common law marital rights in his wife's property no longer prevail over her right to exclusive possession and control of premises. Husband may be prosecuted for criminal acts against his wife's property. If he breaks and enters her dwelling with intent to commit assault, he is guilty of statutory burglary.

1950—*Ballard v. Cox,* 191 Va. 654, 62 S.E.2d 1.

It is duty of husband and wife to live together. Each has right to society, comfort and affection of other. Promise made after marriage to fulfill this duty is not valid consideration.

1939—*Daniels v. Commonwealth,* 172 Va. 583, 1 S.E.2d 333.

Husband is head of house. He is charged with support of wife. Husband has right to go upon wife's premises if jointly occupied by them because he has right of access to her. Husband who assaults his wife is not liable in damages.

1935—*Newsom v. Fleming,* 165 Va. 89, 181 S.E. 393.

> Married woman may sue in her own name without joinder of husband. Citing from earlier decision court stated that wife is on equality with husband in all matters pertaining to their civil and political rights unless otherwise indicated by statute.

1924—*Edmonds v. Edmonds,* 139 Va. 652, 124 S.E. 415.

> Effect of Virginia Married Women's Act is to give wife as full control over her property during marriage as husband has over his. She may sue her husband as if he were stranger. His right to curtesy and his marital rights give him no more power or authority over his wife's property than if he were stranger. She has right to acquire, hold, use, control and dispose of her property as if she were unmarried.

1907—*Lewis v. Palmer,* 106 Va. 522, 56 S.E. 341.

> Wife has insurable interest in life of her husband and may purchase and take assignment of insurance policy on his life and, upon his death, may collect full amount of policy regardless of what she paid for assignment.

(D) Necessaries.

See Va. Code § 8.01-220.2. On and after July 1, 1984, each spouse shall be jointly and severally liable for all emergency medical care furnished to other spouse by physician licensed to practice medicine in Virginia or by hospital located in Virginia, including all follow-up inpatient care provided during initial emergency admission which is furnished while spouses are living together.

1983—*Schilling v. Bedford County Hosp.,* 225 Va. 539, 303 S.E.2d 905.

> By necessaries doctrine, husband is responsible for necessary goods and services furnished his wife by third party. In this case wife was hospitalized and husband refused to guarantee payment of bill. Neither hospital nor wife intended to make wife solely liable for hospital bills. Therefore, necessaries doctrine applies. For sex-based classification to pass constitutional scrutiny, it must serve important governmental objective and be substantially related to achievement of that objective. Necessaries doctrine is not substantially related to promoting important state objective of prompt and efficient provision of medical service because it does nothing to encourage treatment of male patients. Doctrine therefore is sexually discriminatory and denies equal protection of laws.

1950—*Floyd v. Miller,* 190 Va. 303, 57 S.E.2d 114.

> Hospital and medical services for one's wife are necessities for which husband is liable. Married Woman Act expressly gives to wife right to recover every item of damage incident to her personal injury.

1945—*Edwards v. Cuthbert,* 184 Va. 502, 36 S.E.2d 1.

> At common law, husband was charged with funeral expenses of his wife. Now property rights of women, for most part, are fixed by statute. Estate was entirely personal. Husband not obliged to pay funeral expenses.

1923—*Hall v. Stewart,* 135 Va. 384, 116 S.E. 469.

> At common law, husband was liable for funeral expenses of his wife as for necessaries. Since enactment of Married Women's Statute, husband is still entitled to services of wife and is bound for her support. Expenses of last illness are necessaries for which husband is still bound and for which wife is not bound in absence of any contract or agreement on her part. As to funeral expenses of wife, there was common law liability on husband for these expenses, credit was extended to him and he paid debt and court is of opinion that he cannot recover amount from his wife's estate.

1921—*Mihalcoe v. Holub,* 130 Va. 425, 107 S.E. 704.

> When husband and wife live apart through no fault of wife, husband's duty to support her is not affected by separation, and he is liable to third persons who furnish her with necessary means of support on his credit. She has authority to pledge his credit for this purpose. If separation is due to her fault, then she forfeits her right of support and third persons cannot hold husband liable for necessaries absent express contract. Burden of proving that husband was at fault and that articles furnished are in fact necessaries and were in legal sense furnished on his credit, rests upon parties seeking to hold husband liable.

1889—*Geiger v. Blackley,* 86 Va. 328, 10 S.E. 43.

> Where wife contracts for such domestic matters as husband is held by law responsible for, presumption is that contract is on behalf of husband.

(E) Privilege.

See Va. Code § 8.01-398. Husband/wife privilege does not apply in cases where Commonwealth confers upon spouse right of action against other spouse. In cases other than above, neither husband nor wife, without consent of other, shall be examined in any action as to any communication privately made by one to other while married, nor shall either be permitted without such consent to reveal in testimony after marriage relation ceases any such communication made while marriage subsisted.

See Va. Code § 19.2-271.2. In criminal cases, husband and wife shall be allowed and may be compelled to testify on behalf of each other but neither shall be compelled nor, without consent of other, allowed to be called as witness against other except in cases of prosecution for offense committed by one against other or against minor child of either and except in cases of forgery or uttering of signature of other.

See Va. Code § 63.1-248.11 indicating that in any legal proceeding dealing with child abuse or neglect, husband-wife privileges shall not apply.

1982—*Brown v. Commonwealth,* 223 Va. 601, 292 S.E.2d 319.

> See Va. Code § 19.2-271.1 providing that husbands and wives are competent witnesses to testify for or against each other in criminal cases except as otherwise provided, exceptions being contained in § 19.2-271.2. Competency is general rule and disqualification exception.

1982—*Hudson v. Commonwealth,* 223 Va. 596, 292 S.E.2d 317.

Va. Code § 19.2-271.2 permitting husband and wife to testify against each other for property offenses as well as personal offenses committed by one against other.

1966—*Stevens v. Commonwealth,* 207 Va. 371, 150 S.E.2d 229.

Husband committed assault against wife prior to marriage. It was error to require wife to testify against husband at time of trial, since they were married at time of trial. Law at that time was that husband and wife could not be compelled to testify against each other except as to offenses committed by one against other. Since this offense was committed prior to marriage, it was not "one committed by one against other."

1957—*Daniels v. Morris,* 199 Va. 205, 98 S.E.2d 694.

In this case for criminal conversation and alienation of affection, examination of plaintiff's wife did not violate privilege relative to spouse testifying as to private communications during marriage.

1949—*Menefee v. Commonwealth,* 189 Va. 900, 55 S.E.2d 9.

Privilege against disclosure of confidential communications survives termination of marriage and extends to conduct, acts, signs and words. This is not to be confused with rule which disqualified husband or wife to testify for or against other.

1947—*Meade v. Commonwealth,* 186 Va. 775, 43 S.E.2d 858.

In criminal cases, neither husband nor wife shall be compelled nor, without consent of other, be allowed to be called as witness against other except in case of prosecution for offense committed by one against other.

1936—*Thomas v. First Nat'l Bank,* 166 Va. 497, 186 S.E. 77.

Confidential communications between husband and wife during marriage are privileged. Statement does not lose its confidentiality simply because made in presence of third person. Important criteria is whether statement was intended to be confidential.

1932—*Wilson v. Commonwealth,* 157 Va. 962, 162 S.E. 15.

In no case, except for offense by husband against wife, shall she be allowed to testify against him without his consent.

1927—*Byerly v. Byerly,* 149 Va. 53, 140 S.E. 121.

Suit for desertion. Error to exclude all communications between parties. Communications were oral and for most part in presence of third parties.

1915—*Pilcher v. Pilcher,* 117 Va. 356, 84 S.E. 667.

Communications between husband and wife in presence of third person are not confidential or privileged.

1910—*Atkinson v. Solenberger,* 112 Va. 667, 72 S.E. 727.

In this suit by creditor to set aside deed from husband to his wife, neither husband nor wife is competent witness to testify for or against other.

1901—*Davis v. Commonwealth*, 99 Va. 838, 38 S.E. 191.

At common law, wife was competent witness to testify against her husband in relation to offenses alleged to have been committed by him upon her and this rule of common law was not changed by statute of 1898.

1899—*Hoge v. Turner*, 96 Va. 624, 32 S.E. 291.

Common law disqualification of husband and wife to testify for or against each other has been retained in proceedings by creditors to avoid or impeach conveyances, gifts or sales from one to other on ground of fraud or want of consideration.

1873—*Murphy v. Commonwealth*, 64 Va. 960.

Victim of crime in this criminal case was asked whether or not he had made certain statements to his wife. Those statements are confidential and therefore not subject to disclosure. Likewise, wife was incompetent to testify as to statements.

§ 6-7. Miscellaneous.

1961—*Newton v. Newton*, 202 Va. 515, 118 S.E.2d 656.

It is well-settled that where one under mistake of law but with full knowledge of all of facts or with means of such knowledge, and in absence of fraud or improper conduct on part of other party, voluntarily and without compulsion pays money on demand not legally enforceable against him, he cannot recover it.

§ 6-8. Release.

1950—*Ballard v. Cox*, 191 Va. 654, 62 S.E.2d 1.

Husband agreed to release rights given to him by law in wife's property if wife would return to live with him. Release is invalid because it lacks consideration, since wife's promise was mandated by terms of marriage contract.

§ 7-1. Competency.

1951—*Williams v. Williams,* 192 Va. 787, 66 S.E.2d 500.

> Minor child, in this case, was not allowed to testify. Question of competency is left to discretion of court, and its judgment will not be reversed except for manifest error.

1947—*Carpenter v. Commonwealth,* 186 Va. 851, 44 S.E.2d 419.

> Examination of competency of child witness was waived because of failure of defendant to request preliminary examination of her or to object to her testimony at proper time. Test of competency is normally made by subjecting child to preliminary examination concerning its mental capacity, intelligence and sense of moral responsibility.

1908—*Smith v. Lutry,* 108 Va. 799, 62 S.E. 789.

> Widow is incompetent witness to prove loss of deed alleged to have been executed and delivered to her by her husband during his lifetime.

§ 7-2. Hearsay.

1982—*Smith v. Givens,* 223 Va. 455, 290 S.E.2d 844.

> Pedigree exception to hearsay rule allows consideration of hearsay evidence regarding person's family relationship as proof of existence of that relationship. That testimony is admissible provided no better evidence can be obtained and that declarant or source of witness' information was member of family or related to family and was deceased or out of state. In this case pedigree exception was not applicable because there was better evidence of identity of who actual father was.

1980—*Cassady v. Martin,* 220 Va. 1093, 266 S.E.2d 104.

> Pedigree exception to hearsay rule does not apply when testimony can be obtained from another witness, in this case child's mother.

1975—*McIlwain v. McIlwain,* 215 Va. 633, 212 S.E.2d 284.

Wife sought to corroborate allegation of cruelty by self-serving statements she made to neighbor. Interval of time between alleged cruelty and statements was at least two hours, and circumstances therefore compel conclusion that it was not part of res gestae and was inadmissible. Even if it had been admissible it was not sufficient corroboration.

1961—*Sollie v. Sollie,* 202 Va. 855, 120 S.E.2d 281.

Husband was allowed to testify fully from notes as to telephone conversations with his wife after their separation. It was not error to refuse to hear tape recordings of these same conversations.

1939—*Holt v. Holt,* 174 Va. 120, 5 S.E.2d 504.

Letters of parties in suit for divorce (except where it is shown they were written by collusion) may be admissible as in any other case.

§ 7-3. Impeachment.

1957—*Daniels v. Morris,* 199 Va. 205, 98 S.E.2d 694.

Plaintiff's wife, during her cross-examination by plaintiff's attorney in this case of criminal conversation was repeatedly contradicted by use of previously written statement made by her in attorney's office. While this procedure is not to be condoned, defendant at no time made objection. As such, objection was waived.

1943—*Lewis v. Stroebel,* 181 Va. 882, 27 S.E.2d 218.

Witness testified who had alleged interest in outcome of litigation. Court should have required witness to disclose his interest.

§ 7-4. Judicial Notice.

1981—*Doe v. Doe,* 222 Va. 736, 284 S.E.2d 799.

Judicial notice is taken only of generally known or easily ascertainable facts and will not be taken of effect of mother's lifestyle on her child's welfare.

1942—*Darnell v. Barker,* 179 Va. 86, 18 S.E.2d 271.

Consideration of facts not set forth in record is improper. Facts not judicially cognizable must be proved, even though known to judge personally.

1926—*Branch v. Branch,* 144 Va. 244, 132 S.E. 303.

Court cannot take judicial notice of wages for farm labor. Court indicated that, what everybody knows, court also knows. Everybody knows that active healthy, young man could make more than double amount of alimony he was to be paying per day.

1924—*Fowlkes v. White,* 138 Va. 438, 121 S.E. 888.

It is matter of common knowledge that it was habit of many women in past to rely implicitly on their husbands for attention to all of their business affairs.

1923—*Wilson v. Wilson,* 136 Va. 643, 118 S.E. 270.

Courts are not held to have judicial knowledge of other proceedings, even in their own courts.

§ 7-5. Opinion.

1904—*House v. House,* 102 Va. 235, 46 S.E. 299.

Opinions of witnesses, based upon their knowledge of character or reputation of wife that they did not believe that husband could with safety cohabit with her, are not admissible in evidence. Witnesses should state facts and not their opinions.

§ 7-6. Prior Acts.

1959—*Canavos v. Canavos,* 200 Va. 861, 108 S.E.2d 359.

Acts done by one of parties prior to institution of suit, which are entirely inconsistent with testimony given by that party at trial, will be given great weight in determining what credence should be given to his testimony in conflict with testimony of his adversary.

§ 7-7. Presumptions.

See Validity of Marriage § 1-8.

1949—*Parker v. American Lumber Corp.,* 190 Va. 181, 56 S.E.2d 214.

Where two marriages of same person are shown, second marriage is presumed to be valid. Law presumes morality and legitimacy, not immorality or bastardy.

1942—*McClaugherty v. McClaugherty,* 180 Va. 51, 21 S.E.2d 761.

Although it is true that cohabitation and repute do not constitute marriage, they do constitute strong evidence tending to raise presumption of marriage.

1934—*Simpson v. Simpson,* 162 Va. 621, 175 S.E. 320.

Rebuttable presumption of death after seven years absence.

1923—*Vanderpool v. Ryan,* 137 Va. 445, 119 S.E. 65.

In this case, wife claimed that there was ceremonial marriage in Kentucky. She was unable to present any supporting evidence of that. Defendant, however, did present evidence to indicate there had been no ceremonial marriage. To raise presumption of marriage, reputation must be founded on general opinion and not on divided or singular opinion. Evidence, in this case, was insufficient to prove even common law marriage.

1923—*Brown v. Commonwealth,* 135 Va. 480, 115 S.E. 542.

There is common law presumption that, when wife commits crime, except for certain felonies, in presence of and by direction of her husband, then she acts under his coercion and is immune from punishment.

§ 7-8. Witnesses.

1977—*Jacobs v. Jacobs,* 218 Va. 264, 237 S.E.2d 124.

Husband offered no evidence on his behalf. When defendant can by his own testimony, throw light upon matters at issue necessary for his defense and peculiarly within his own knowledge, if fact exist, and he fails to go on witness stand, presumption is raised that fact does not exist.

1961—*Sollie v. Sollie,* 202 Va. 855, 120 S.E.2d 281.

There was no error in refusing to examine child of parties where there was no avowal of what child would say that would constitute pertinent evidence.

1957—*Daniels v. Morris,* 199 Va. 205, 98 S.E.2d 694.

In this suit for criminal conversation and alienation of affection, there was no error in permitting plaintiff's wife to be called as adverse witness. Test is whether or not witness has adverse interest. Here, wife's interest was plainly adverse, since her reputation was attacked and her right to support money and custody of her children might be later affected.

1933—*Cole v. Cole,* 161 Va. 116, 170 S.E. 621.

Where party has power to elicit evidence from witness, who is competent to speak and he does not avail himself of such testimony, then presumption is that it would be against him.

1931—*Puckett v. Draper,* 156 Va. 238, 158 S.E. 68.

Where defendant has information peculiarly within his knowledge and he fails to testify, presumption is raised that facts do not exist.

1895—*Burke v. Shaver,* 92 Va. 345, 23 S.E. 749.

Examination of witnesses lies chiefly in discretion of trial court and its exercise is rarely, if ever, to be controlled by appellate court. Much latitude should be given to trial court in matter of recalling witnesses and its action will not be reversed by appellate court except for palpable error.

CHAPTER 8

PROCEDURE

§ 8-1. Appearance.

1971—*Lawrence v. Lawrence*, 212 Va. 44, 181 S.E.2d 640.

> Husband in this divorce action had previously made special appearance. He thereafter filed petition for rehearing as to decree of divorce. Trial court denied petition but held that it amounted to general appearance by husband.

1965—*Minton v. First Nat'l Exch. Bank,* 206 Va. 589, 145 S.E.2d 139.

Attorney for husband simply appeared at taking of depositions but did not participate. That did not constitute appearance. Appearance by party requires some act on his part evidencing intention to submit himself to jurisdiction of court.

1952—*Baker v. Baker,* 194 Va. 284, 72 S.E.2d 632.

Defendant in suit may employ counsel to follow proceeding and advise him with respect thereto without entering appearance. Unless that attorney makes appearance of record on behalf of Defendant in usual way, he is in no position to waive required notice.

§ 8-2. Appeal and Error.

See Commissioner in Chancery, § 8-6.

1984—*Lapidus v. Lapidus,* 226 Va. 575, 311 S.E.2d 786.

Where trial court hears evidence orally, its findings will not be disturbed unless they are plainly wrong or without evidentiary support.

1983—*Rochelle v. Rochelle,* 225 Va. 387, 302 S.E.2d 59.

Trial court's finding on conflicting evidence heard orally which is not plainly wrong or without support in evidence will not be disturbed on appeal.

1983—*Shortridge v. Deel,* 224 Va. 589, 299 S.E.2d 500.

Findings of trial court based upon judge's evaluation of testimony of witnesses heard orally are entitled to great weight. In this custody proceeding evidence was to be reviewed on appeal in light most favorable to party prevailing below.

1982—*Leisge v. Leisge,* 223 Va. 688, 292 S.E.2d 352.

Trial court's factual determinations have weight of jury verdict and will be upheld unless plainly wrong or without evidence to support them. On appeal from juvenile court, appeal is governed by Va. Code §§ 16.1-296 and 16.1-136, latter section requiring hearing de novo.

1982—*Walker v. Department of Pub. Welfare,* 223 Va. 557, 290 S.E.2d 887.

Only final orders or judgments of juvenile and domestic relations district court are appealable. Interlocutory order is not appealable. Such case in circuit court is heard de novo.

1982—*Durrette v. Durrette,* 223 Va. 328, 288 S.E.2d 432.

Trial court's finding of fact on conflicting evidence heard orally has weight of jury verdict and will stand unless plainly wrong or without evidence to support it. But trial court's conclusion, which is opinion based on evidence not in material conflict, does not have same binding weight on appeal.

1982—*Greene v. Greene,* 223 Va. 210, 288 S.E.2d 447.

Once appellate court acquires jurisdiction over parties involved in litigation and subject matter of their controversy, jurisdiction of trial court must cease.

1981—*Dooley v. Dooley,* 222 Va. 240, 278 S.E.2d 865.

In this case trial court disapproved report of commissioner and therefore supreme court must review evidence and ascertain whether under correct application of law evidence supports findings of commissioner or conclusions of trial court.

1978—*In re: Change of Name of Miller,* 218 Va. 939, 243 S.E.2d 464.

In this change of name case trial court abused its discretion in denying applicant's petition to resume her maiden name. Exercise of discretion must be based on evidence and not on speculation. In this instance, trial court speculated that change of name would infringe upon rights of others.

1975—*Capps v. Capps,* 216 Va. 382, 219 S.E.2d 898.

Divorce decree based solely on depositions is not as conclusive as one heard orally. Such decree, however, is presumed correct and will not be overturned if supported by substantial, competent and credible evidence.

1975—*Als v. Als,* 216 Va. 13, 216 S.E.2d 16.

Evidence was heard orally by court. Court's findings have weight of jury verdict and will not be disturbed unless plainly wrong or without evidence to support them.

1971—*Dyer v. Howell,* 212 Va. 453, 184 S.E.2d 789.

In determining what is in child's best interest, trial court is vested with wide discretion, and its judgment, which is presumed correct, cannot be disturbed unless it is plainly wrong or without evidence to support it.

1971—*Moore v. Moore,* 212 Va. 153, 183 S.E.2d 172.

Decree based on testimony in deposition form, while presumed to be correct, is not given same weight as one where evidence is heard orally by trial court.

1970—*Carneal v. Carneal,* 211 Va. 162, 176 S.E.2d 305.

Divorce decree was entered on April 29th, but execution was suspended on May 17th for period of 21 days. By subsequent order of June 7th, decree was made final as of June 8th. Appeal was filed as of July 29th which is within 60-day period allowed.

1968—*Clark v. Clark,* 209 Va. 390, 164 S.E.2d 685.

Trial court's finding, based upon hearing of oral evidence, should be accorded great weight and ought not to be disturbed unless plainly wrong. However, when finding is not based on conflicting evidence, trial court's conclusions on questions of custody of children become matter of opinion.

1967—*Hoback v. Hoback,* 208 Va. 432, 158 S.E.2d 113.

Decree of trial court, based upon depositions, is not as strong as one based upon evidence heard orally but it is presumed to be correct and will not be overturned by Supreme Court if it is reasonably supported by substantial competent and credible evidence.

1966—*Crounse v. Crounse,* 207 Va. 524, 151 S.E.2d 412.

Conclusion reached by trial court upon ore tenus hearing cannot be disturbed unless it is plainly wrong or without evidence to support it.

1966—*McClung v. McClung,* 206 Va. 782, 146 S.E.2d 195.

Pending appeal, wife moved this court to compel trial judge to file opinion to clarify basis upon which he granted divorce, evidently hoping that it would be shown that divorce was not granted on grounds of desertion but simply on grounds of voluntary separation. Motion was denied as being outside court's authority and because in any event judge's underlying reasons could not be used to controvert plain findings made in decree.

1965—*Cofer v. Cofer,* 205 Va. 834, 140 S.E.2d 663.

Order that was entered on September 4th decreasing child support was void. On November 6th, court refused to vacate prior order. Appeal was taken from that latter order. Appeal was timely filed since it was within 30 days of second order.

1964—*Gramelspacher v. Gramelspacher,* 204 Va. 839, 134 S.E.2d 285.

Husband, at time of trial, testified that Order had been entered by Mississippi court compelling support payments by him. No copy of Order was produced at trial and, as such, there was no record upon which court could rule as to that issue.

1962—*Ware v. Ware,* 203 Va. 189, 123 S.E.2d 357.

Finding of trial court having passed upon credibility of witnesses and weight to be given their testimony stands on same footing as jury verdict and should not be overturned on appeal unless plainly wrong or without evidence to support it.

1961—*Martin v. Martin,* 202 Va. 769, 120 S.E.2d 471.

Decree of trial court based upon depositions, while not as strong and conclusive as one based on evidence heard ore tenus, it is presumed to be correct, and burden is on moving party to show that it is manifestly wrong. Decree will not be reversed if it is reasonably supported by substantial competent and credible evidence.

1961—*Eubank v. Hayden,* 202 Va. 634, 119 S.E.2d 328.

Where two trials of same case have been held, errors will be considered in order in which they were committed.

1960—*Todd v. Todd,* 202 Va. 133, 117 S.E.2d 679.

Evidence in this divorce action was taken ore tenus. Decree was entitled to same weight as jury verdict and could be reversed only if plainly wrong. In this case, since verdict was supported by substantial credible evidence, it was affirmed.

1959—*Canavos v. Canavos,* 200 Va. 861, 108 S.E.2d 359.

Decree based on depositions is not as conclusive as one based on evidence heard orally. However, it is presumed to be correct and one who attacks it on appeal must show that it is manifestly wrong.

1959—*Ford v. Ford,* 200 Va. 674, 107 S.E.2d 397.
> Decision of trial court supported by substantial credible evidence is presumed correct. Burden is upon party challenging that decision to show that it is manifestly wrong.

1958—*Phillips v. Kiraly,* 200 Va. 345, 105 S.E.2d 855.
> Finding of trial judge who heard evidence orally had effect of jury verdict, settling all conflicts in evidence in favor of prevailing party and it was presumed to be correct.

1956—*DeMott v. DeMott,* 198 Va. 22, 92 S.E.2d 342.
> Appellant has primary responsibility of designating all of evidence necessary for determination of issue on appeal. Appellant's failure to observe rules in this respect is plain invitation to dismissal of appeal.

1955—*Florance v. Florance,* 197 Va. 432, 90 S.E.2d 111.
> Decree of trial court, based upon ore tenus hearing, will be disturbed only if plainly wrong or without evidence to support it.

1954—*Arrington v. Arrington,* 196 Va. 86, 82 S.E.2d 548.
> Finding of chancellor after ore tenus hearing had effect of jury verdict and settled all disputed fact questions.

1953—*Brumfield v. Brumfield,* 194 Va. 577, 74 S.E.2d 170.
> Where evidence is taken ore tenus, conclusion of trial judge supported by that evidence is controlling on appeal.

1952—*Prindes v. Prindes,* 193 Va. 463, 69 S.E.2d 332.
> When trial court has nothing but written record before it, it has little if any advantage over supreme court in determining case.

1952—*Oliver v. Oliver,* 193 Va. 571, 69 S.E.2d 350.
> Once trial court and ore tenus hearing makes findings, this is equivalent to findings of jury.

1951—*Hall v. Hall,* 192 Va. 721, 66 S.E.2d 595.
> Rule requiring filing of notice of appeal and assignments of error within 60 days are mandatory and must be complied with.

1950—*Burton v. Russell,* 190 Va. 339, 57 S.E.2d 95.
> Party who comes before supreme court with judgment in his favor is in superior position.

1948—*Mullen v. Mullen,* 188 Va. 259, 49 S.E.2d 349.
> Supreme court, on appeal, increased amount of child support awarded and adjusted custody arrangement.

1947—*Sutton v. Menges,* 186 Va. 805, 44 S.E.2d 414.
> Though evidence was presented in this case in form of live testimony and deposition testimony, verdict cannot be disturbed unless Court's judgment was plainly wrong or without evidence to support it.

1947—*Nix v. Nix,* 186 Va. 14, 41 S.E.2d 345.
> Finding of trial court upon ore tenus hearing is equivalent to finding of jury upon conflicting evidence insofar as review by supreme court

is concerned. Factual determination reached by court upon conflicting evidence is binding upon court of appeals unless it finds that evidence is incredible and unworthy of belief.

1946—*Ring v. Ring,* 185 Va. 269, 38 S.E.2d 471.

In equity action, when evidence is heard ore tenus, case comes to supreme court with all conflicts in evidence resolved in favor of prevailing party.

1944—*Kerr v. Kerr,* 182 Va. 731, 30 S.E.2d 684.

Finding of trial court on factual matter, supported by substantial evidence is entitled to great weight, is presumed correct and will not as general rule be disturbed on appeal.

1944—*Lowdon v. Lowdon,* 183 Va. 78, 31 S.E.2d 271.

Verdict of trial court sitting as trier of fact has same effect as verdict of jury.

1943—*Francis v. Francis,* 181 Va. 373, 25 S.E.2d 253.

Jurisdiction of supreme court in relation to appeals is purely statutory.

1943—*Gray v. Gray,* 181 Va. 262, 24 S.E.2d 444.

Where question of fact is resolved by lower court, then that determination must be affirmed by supreme court if evidence is sufficient to sustain decree.

1940—*Owen v. Owen,* 175 Va. 245, 7 S.E.2d 890.

Divorce suit heard ore tenus has same effect as jury verdict and will not be overturned unless it is plainly wrong.

1938—*Jones v. Jones,* 172 Va. 14, 199 S.E. 510.

Supreme court did not have before it all of evidence on which conclusions of trial court were based and thus could not rule on assignment of errors.

1938—*Rogers v. Rogers,* 170 Va. 417, 196 S.E. 586.

Where question of court's jurisdiction to decide property rights is raised but not fully developed in brief of either party, it is not necessary for supreme court to rule on issue.

1937—*Casilear v. Casilear,* 168 Va. 46, 190 S.E. 314.

Failure to note objection to reply to answer in trial court constitutes waiver.

1936—*Allen v. Allen,* 166 Va. 303, 186 S.E. 17.

Decree of chancellor who heard evidence ore tenus has force and effect of jury verdict.

1935—*Williamson v. Johnson,* 164 Va. 632, 180 S.E. 310.

Decree of chancery court upon evidence heard in open court has same effect as jury verdict.

1933—*Nethers v. Nethers,* 160 Va. 335, 168 S.E. 428.

Appeal denied because evidence which was taken ore tenus was not authenticated and made part of record within time prescribed by law.

1932—*Craddock's Adm'r v. Craddock's Adm'r,* 158 Va. 58, 163 S.E. 387.

Appeal in chancery case results in trial de novo. Issues to be reviewed are limited to those raised in assignment of error. In determining issues of fact judgment of chancellor is given much persuasive force. Divorce suit did not abate upon death of both parties so as to render appeal unavailable to heirs, insofar as it affected property rights of parties.

1932—*Surber v. Bridges,* 159 Va. 329, 165 S.E. 508.

Where trial judge hears witnesses in open court, his finding is to be viewed as jury verdict.

1928—*Hayes v. Strauss,* 151 Va. 136, 144 S.E. 432.

Judgment of court of competent jurisdiction is presumed correct. Judgment of trial court without jury is accorded same force as jury verdict.

1926—*Hitt v. Smallwood,* 147 Va. 778, 133 S.E. 503.

Report of commissioner, sustained by trial court, where evidence taken in his presence, should not be disturbed on appeal unless clearly unsupported by evidence.

1924—*Miller v. Miller,* 140 Va. 424, 125 S.E. 220.

Conclusions of trial court upon evidence are entitled to great respect and ought not to be disturbed unless they are contrary to evidence or without evidence to support them.

1924—*Elder v. Elder,* 139 Va. 19, 123 S.E. 369.

There is presumption in favor of correctness of decree of lower court in divorce proceedings. That presumption is rebutted where greater weight of evidence is against it.

1923—*Mowles v. Mowles,* 137 Va. 274, 119 S.E. 54.

In this divorce action, supreme court noted that burden was upon complainant to prove desertion on part of wife. Although wife's account of her grievances was most appealing, Court denied divorce and noted that it resolved its doubts in favor of defendant.

1922—*Black v. Black,* 134 Va. 246, 114 S.E. 592.

In this case, husband gave testimony, first by deposition and then trial court required testimony to be given in open court. Husband testified inconsistently in those two proceedings. Trial court found that this inconsistency discredited his case and denied him decree of divorce. Trial judge, having seen and heard complaint and other witnesses, was in better position than appellate court to judge credibility of their testimony. Decision of trial court was upheld.

1922—*Chandler v. Chandler,* 132 Va. 418, 112 S.E. 856.

Where testimony is heard orally, decision of lower court upon facts is entitled to great weight.

1922—*Barnard v. Barnard,* 132 Va. 155, 111 S.E. 227.

When trial court has nothing before it but written record, it has little if any advantage over appellate court in determining correctness of cause. Case is entirely different where trial court has heard witnesses and can observe their demeanor on witness stand. Great weight should be attached to finding of tribunal charged with weighing such evidence, whether it be commissioner, jury or court.

1921—*Twohy v. Twohy,* 130 Va. 557, 107 S.E. 642.

Conclusions of trial court, based upon entire body of testimony, are entitled to great respect and are to be followed unless they are contrary to evidence or without evidence to support them.

1920—*Cumming v. Cumming,* 127 Va. 16, 102 S.E. 572.

Husband was granted divorce on fault grounds by trial court. Husband died pending appeal by wife. Since husband's death would render inoperative decree granting wife divorce or allowing her alimony, no decree was entered on those subjects by supreme court, except to reverse original decree granting husband divorce since that was in error.

1920—*Towson v. Towson,* 126 Va. 640, 102 S.E. 48.

Plaintiff cannot complain of instruction, although erroneous, where verdict is in his favor. Error is harmless, as neither party is hurt by it.

1919—*Reynolds v. Adams,* 125 Va. 295, 99 S.E. 695.

Judgment of court of competent jurisdiction will always be presumed to be right. Party before appellate court alleging error must show error, otherwise presumption of correctness will prevail.

1917—*White v. White,* 121 Va. 244, 92 S.E. 811.

In this adultery action, note that was introduced into evidence was subject of considerable testimony without any objection. It is too late to raise admissibility of that note for first time on appeal.

1915—*Hairston v. Hairston,* 117 Va. 207, 84 S.E. 15.

Failure to pay attorney's fees decreed against husband in suit for divorce is no ground for dismissal of husband's appeal. Decree for attorney's fees may be enforced by execution or other legal proceedings.

1914—*Johnston v. Johnston,* 116 Va. 678, 82 S.E. 694.

Wife contended on appeal that court erred in refusing to permit her to retake her depositions which had been suppressed because they were taken before justice of peace rather than commissioner in chancery. Court held that it would have been vain for trial court to have allowed deposition to be retaken since they could not affect result of litigation·since it was evident that there had been condonation of offense charged by wife.

1899—*Engleman v. Engleman,* 97 Va. 487, 34 S.E. 50.

> Supreme court will not reverse decree in chancery merely because incompetent and illegal evidence appears on record. It will consider only legitimate evidence and determine rights of parties based upon that.

§ 8-3. Attorneys.

(A) In General.

1957—*Daniels v. Morris,* 199 Va. 205, 98 S.E.2d 694.

> Plaintiff's wife, during her cross-examination by plaintiff's attorney in this case of criminal conversation was repeatedly contradicted by use of previously written statement made by her in attorney's office. While this procedure is not to be condoned, defendant at no time made objection. As such, objection was waived.

1932—*Inman v. Inman,* 158 Va. 597, 164 S.E.2d 382.

> Generally when counsel for party finds he is material witness he should withdraw. Exceptions to this Rule are rare.

(B) Fees.

See Va. Code § 20-71.1 as to attorney's fees for support proceedings under Va. Code § 20-71.

1982—*Carswell v. Masterson,* 224 Va. 329, 295 S.E.2d 899.

> Court of equity has power to award attorney's fees incurred incident to contempt proceedings instituted to obtain enforcement of support order of court. In this case, husband had failed to pay child support and wife was awarded attorney's fees for enforcement of that order.

1982—*Leisge v. Leisge,* 224 Va. 303, 296 S.E.2d 538.

> Trial court awarded $25,000 in expenses and attorney's fees for wife in her attempts to enforce custody order issued by court.

1982—*Greene v. Greene,* 223 Va. 210, 288 S.E.2d 447.

> Husband was awarded divorce and custody of two children. There was no award of alimony or child support. Thereafter, decree was entered in Florida granting wife custody and child support and $20,000 in counsel fees. And thereafter, Virginia trial court awarded husband $500 month child support and required wife to pay her former husband $20,000 for his counsel fees. Counsel fees, if any, must be awarded upon proper showing of what is reasonable based on evidence. In this case, there was no evidence as to nature, extent or reasonableness of services rendered, and as such, award must be reversed.

1979—*Alig v. Alig,* 220 Va. 80, 255 S.E.2d 494.

> Attorney's fees may be allowed in suit to establish and enforce foreign decree of alimony and should be allowed in this case since wife was forced to employ attorneys to establish and enforce her rights, this expense being attributable to husband's recalcitrance.

1976—*Thomas v. Thomas,* 217 Va. 502, 229 S.E.2d 887.
Where evidence indicates wife's need to have attorney's fees paid and her need and entitlement to alimony and husband's ability to pay, it was abuse of discretion to deny award of attorney's fees.

1976—*Ingram v. Ingram,* 217 Va. 27, 225 S.E.2d 362.
Court awarded attorney's fees of $4,000. This was not excessive.

1975—*Robertson v. Robertson,* 215 Va. 425, 211 S.E.2d 41.
Wife was awarded $10,000 attorney's fees. Husband's income was approximately $70,000 per year. Record was inadequate to justify or explain that award of attorney's fees. Matter was remanded for re-examination.

1974—*Rowland v. Rowland,* 215 Va. 344, 210 S.E.2d 149.
Award of attorney's fees is within discretion of trial court who had before him evidence of wife's income and expenses.

1971—*Monahan v. Monahan,* 212 Va. 406, 184 S.E.2d 812.
Amount of attorney's fees is within sound discretion of court. Award of $200, while small, does not constitute abuse of discretion as matter of law.

1973—*Wilkerson v. Wilkerson,* 214 Va. 395, 200 S.E.2d 581.
In this divorce action, husband was awarded divorce and awarded custody. It was within discretion of trial court to award attorney's fees to wife.

1971—*Rowlee v. Rowlee,* 211 Va. 689, 179 S.E.2d 461.
Where wife has no separate estate and is defendant in divorce action initiated by her husband, it is proper for her to be allowed reasonable sum to be paid by her husband for attorney's fees and suit money. In awarding such sum, court should consider financial condition of husband. Abuse of discretion will not be presumed from failure of trial court to award attorney's fees.

1970—*Moon v. Moon,* 211 Va. 575, 172 S.E.2d 778.
Attorney's fees of $150 was awarded. Supreme court refused to alter that on grounds that record before it was inadequate to say whether or not fee was improper.

1967—*George v. King,* 208 Va. 136, 156 S.E.2d 615.
In this action to annul marriage brought by husband, wife was awarded costs and attorney's fees.

1964—*Higgins v. Higgins,* 205 Va. 324, 136 S.E.2d 793.
Trial court awarded attorney's fees of $1,500 in action where husband prevailed. Award of attorney's fees to wife's attorney was decreased by court of appeals to $1,000.

1954—*Hepler v. Hepler,* 195 Va. 611, 79 S.E.2d 652.
In this appeal involving petition for change of custody wherein husband prevailed, parties were directed to bear their own costs and attorney's fees.

1948—*Williams v. Williams,* 188 Va. 543, 50 S.E.2d 277.
> Wife awarded attorney's fees and costs, even though husband prevailed on appeal.

1948—*Eddens v. Eddens,* 188 Va. 511, 50 S.E.2d 397.
> Court may enforce its decrees for payments of counsel fees and suit money through contempt.

1946—*Ring v. Ring,* 185 Va. 269, 38 S.E.2d 471.
> Attorney's fees of $1,200 awarded by trial court. Additional $500 awarded for appeal.

1946—*Taylor v. Taylor,* 185 Va. 126, 37 S.E.2d 886.
> Attorney's fees in amount of $150 in this case were deemed to be adequate.

1946—*McKeel v. McKeel,* 185 Va. 108, 37 S.E.2d 746.
> Attorney's fees awarded to wife on appeal in effort to obtain alimony payments.

1944—*Kern v. Lindsey,* 182 Va. 775, 30 S.E.2d 707.
> Court conditioned payment of attorney's fees upon execution of bond to ensure compliance with decree appealed from.

1943—*Hudgins v. Hudgins,* 181 Va. 81, 23 S.E.2d 774.
> Fees of $1,000 awarded to wife in divorce action where trial lasted four days.

1942—*McClaugherty v. McClaugherty,* 180 Va. 51, 21 S.E.2d 761.
> Suit by daughter against father for child support. Attorney's fees awarded to daughter.

1942—*Bennett v. Bennett,* 179 Va. 239, 18 S.E.2d 911.
> $100 awarded for appellate representation.

1939—*Hughes v. Hughes,* 173 Va. 293, 4 S.E.2d 402.
> Where wife has no separate estate and is defendant in divorce suit then award of attorney fees is appropriate.

1936—*Allen v. Allen,* 166 Va. 303, 186 S.E. 17.
> $100 attorney fees for representation in supreme court.

1934—*Colbert v. Colbert,* 162 Va. 393, 174 S.E. 660.
> Husband awarded divorce for desertion. Wife is usually allowed reasonable sum for attorney's fees. Income of husband was $4,000. Attorney's fees of $750 awarded for trial and appeal. Husband should be required only to pay for one attorney for wife.

1924—*Miller v. Miller,* 140 Va. 424, 125 S.E. 220.
> Court awarded attorney's fees of $100. Trial court award of $250 was reduced to that amount.

1924—*Kirn v. Kirn,* 138 Va. 132, 120 S.E. 850.
> Wife sued husband for divorce and husband countersued. Court found recrimination and therefore divorce was denied. Wife awarded $3,500 in attorney's fees.

1923—*Mowles v. Mowles,* 137 Va. 274, 119 S.E. 54.

Wife denied attorney's fees at appellate court level. Husband had sued her for desertion, but claim was denied. Wife's claim for alimony likewise was denied.

1922—*Barnard v. Barnard,* 132 Va. 155, 111 S.E. 227.

Upon affirmance of decree for divorce a mensa in favor of wife, supreme court will award reasonable fee to her counsel. Fee in this case was fixed at $100.

1921—*Twohy v. Twohy,* 130 Va. 557, 107 S.E. 642.

Supreme court commended trial court for awarding small amount of attorney's fees initially at beginning of proceedings. In final decree, after merits of controversy had been settled and husband determined to be at fault, sum of $2,500 was allowed. Husband's annual income was at least $11,500. In making allowances for attorney's fees, court should keep in mind amount of estate, difficulties of litigation, demands which it makes upon time, industry knowledge and professional skill of counsel.

1919—*McCormick v. McCormick,* 123 Va. 778, 97 S.E. 305.

Wife was denied divorce at trial court, and husband was granted divorce on grounds of desertion. On appeal, husband's claim was sustained. Wife was awarded $200 attorney's fees by supreme court.

1916—*Craig v. Craig,* 118 Va. 294, 87 S.E. 731.

Wife's suit for desertion was dismissed. She was awarded attorney's fees and suit costs in amount of $375.

1915—*Hairston v. Hairston,* 117 Va. 207, 84 S.E. 15.

Failure to pay attorney's fees decreed against husband in suit for divorce is no ground for dismissal of husband's appeal. Decree for attorney's fees may be enforced by execution or other legal proceedings.

1914—*Craig v. Craig,* 115 Va. 764, 80 S.E. 507.

Husband and wife sued each other for divorce. Both claims were denied. Wife's claim for attorney's fees was remanded to circuit court for determination.

1899—*Engleman v. Engleman,* 97 Va. 487, 34 S.E. 50.

Measure of husband's liability to pay for wife's attorney's fees depends upon his ability to meet them and, in absence of anything in record to guide this court, it will not make allowance for fees in this court but will adhere to sum fixed by trial court.

§ 8-4. Bill of Review.

1971—*Lawrence v. Lawrence,* 212 Va. 44, 181 S.E.2d 640.

Husband asked for rehearing as to divorce decree. Husband was fully cognizant of proceedings and participated in proceedings prior to his general appearance. No error in denying rehearing.

1943—*Francis v. Francis,* 181 Va. 373, 25 S.E.2d 253.

When final decree has been entered, there are two ways of reopening it in trial court; one by petition for rehearing and other by bill of review. Petition for rehearing, showing error of law or fact, or discovery of new and material evidence, must be presented while cause is still within control of trial court. If term of trial court at which final decree was entered has expired, only mode of rehearing is by bill of review.

1932—*Craddock's Adm'r v. Craddock's Adm'r,* 158 Va. 58, 163 S.E. 387.

Record for bill of review is same as on appeal. Evidence may be reviewed to determine whether there is any evidence to support decree.

1925—*Scott v. Scott,* 142 Va. 31, 128 S.E.2d 599.

Bill, which does not point out any error of law, apparent on face of record nor allege any newly discovered evidence, is not maintainable as bill of review. Claim that evidence was insufficient to support judgment can be corrected only by appeal and not by bill of review. Conclusion of court upon issues of fact is conclusive as to bill of review.

§ 8-5. Burden of Proof.

1982—*Grigg v. Commonwealth,* 224 Va. 356, 297 S.E.2d 799.

Standard of proof to be applied in civil case to compel parents to properly provide for education of their children is clear and convincing evidence. This standard is more stringent than that used in ordinary civil matters, but it is lesser burden than reasonable doubt standard.

1959—*Brooks v. Brooks,* 200 Va. 530, 106 S.E.2d 611.

Proof required for divorce must be full, clear and adequate evidence.

§ 8-6. Commissioner in Chancery.

See Appeal and Error, § 8-2.
See Supreme Court Rule 2:18.
See Va. Code § 8.01-607 et seq.

1977—*Clark v. Clark,* 217 Va. 924, 234 S.E.2d 266.

Evidence was heard orally by commissioner. Decree confirming commissioner's report, while not given same weight as jury verdict, is presumed to be correct. Decree cannot be disturbed if it is reasonably supported by substantial, competent and credible evidence.

1971—*Lawrence v. Lawrence,* 212 Va. 44, 181 S.E.2d 640.

Court is not bound by commissioner's recommendations but has duty to review evidence according to correct principles of law and arrive at its own conclusions.

1964—*Higgins v. Higgins,* 205 Va. 324, 136 S.E.2d 793.
Conclusions of chancellor should stand unless contrary to weight of evidence. In spite of that, it was duty of court on appeal to evaluate evidence to determine whether it in fact did support conclusions reached. It was duty of chancellor to weigh evidence himself since he had not delegated his function to commissioner. In this case, commissioner made certain recommendations and court simply adopted them. In light of that, court of appeals was in as good position as trial court to evaluate matter.

1960—*Plattner v. Plattner,* 202 Va. 263, 117 S.E.2d 128.
Report of commissioner may be accepted or rejected in whole or in part by trial court. Commissioners are appointed to assist court, not to supplant it.

1958—*Hoffecker v. Hoffecker,* 200 Va. 119, 104 S.E.2d 771.
Since evidence was heard by commissioner in chancery and not ore tenus by court, decree of trial court, while presumed to be correct, is not given same weight as jury verdict. Report of commissioner in chancery shall not have weight given to verdict of jury on conflicting evidence.

1958—*Green v. Green,* 199 Va. 927, 103 S.E.2d 202.
Court does not delegate its judicial functions to commissioner in chancery when he refers case to him. In final analysis, it is duty of chancellor to review evidence and arrive at its own conclusions. There is no requirement that conclusions of commissioner, when evidence is taken in his presence, should be sustained simply because they are not contrary to law or unsupported or unwarranted by unreasonable view of evidence.

1952—*Raiford v. Raiford,* 193 Va. 221, 68 S.E.2d 888.
Trial court has power to adopt rule requiring referral to commissioner in chancery of divorce actions. Practice is to accept report of commissioner as prima facie correct.

1945—*Jacobs v. Jacobs,* 184 Va. 281, 35 S.E.2d 119.
Report of commissioner in chancery is entitled to respect and to greater weight where evidence has been taken in his presence. However, it is still duty of court to review and weigh evidence and, if report is unsupported by evidence, to reject it.

1926—*Hitt v. Smallwood,* 147 Va. 778, 133 S.E. 503.
Report of commissioner does not bind trial court like jury verdict. Chancellor is presumed to be more competent to pass upon evidence and draw conclusions than is commissioner. When testimony is conflicting, commissioner has seen witnesses and his conclusions are supported by unimpeached witnesses, then his report will not be disturbed unless weight of testimony contrary to his report makes it clear he has erred. It is practice to accept report as prima facie correct unless exceptions are filed.

1926—*Pereira v. Moon,* 146 Va. 225, 135 S.E. 672.

Appellate court could not consider evidence in determining whether commissioner arrived at right conclusion since evidence was not authenticated. Trial court is therefore presumed correct.

1924—*Clevinger v. County School Bd.,* 139 Va. 444, 124 S.E. 440.

Notwithstanding weight due to commissioner's report and respect it is accorded, neither trial court nor supreme court should avoid duty of weighing evidence when its sufficiency is fairly challenged.

1922—*Barnard v. Barnard,* 132 Va. 155, 111 S.E. 227.

Though less weight is to be given to findings of commissioner than to those of jury or court, nevertheless when commissioner has seen and examined witnesses and testimony is conflicting and his conclusions are clearly supported by competent and unimpeached witnesses, court will not set aside or disturb his report unless weight of testimony which is contrary to his conclusions is such, on account of number of witnesses and nature of their evidence, as to make it clear that commissioner has erred. In this case, evidence while conflicting was abundant to support decree of trial court and therefore affirmed.

1920—*Carle v. Carle,* 127 Va. 223, 103 S.E. 699.

Where it is apparent from face of report of commissioner and from pleadings and exhibits, independent of other evidence, that commissioner's report was based on fundamental error of law, no exception to report is necessary. Questions of law are for court to decide upon evidence produced and it is not proper to refer them to commissioner. In this case, it was not proper to refer this matter to commissioner to decide question of liability of defendants. That was question of law for court to decide upon evidence produced.

1919—*Reynolds v. Adams,* 125 Va. 295, 99 S.E. 695.

Commissioner's report confirmed by decree upon conflicting evidence of depositions taken before commissioner in person is entitled to great weight and should not be disturbed unless clearly at variance with result of evidence.

1912—*Walter v. Whitacre,* 113 Va. 150, 73 S.E. 984.

Party cannot except to commissioner's report on one ground in trial court and rely upon wholly different ground in appellate court, unless objection made in appellate court is apparent upon face of report.

1911—*Howard v. Gose,* 112 Va. 552, 72 S.E. 140.

Report of commissioner is prima facie correct and where evidence is conflicting, this court will not reverse action of trial court confirming report unless finding of commissioner is clearly erroneous.

1911—*Smiley v. Smiley,* 112 Va. 490, 71 S.E. 532.

Where evidence consists of depositions taken by commissioner or in his presence and he has advantage of noting demeanor of witnesses, their intelligence and manner of testifying, then his findings of fact will not, as rule, be disturbed where evidence is conflicting.

1909—*Virginia & Kentucky Ry. Co. v. Heninger,* 110 Va. 301, 67 S.E. 185.
Objections to report of commissioner on account of errors not apparent on its face cannot be made for first time on appeal. Where evidence is conflicting, findings of commissioner approved by trial court will not be disturbed on appeal unless they are clearly wrong.

1908—*Branner v. Branner,* 108 Va. 660, 62 S.E. 952.
Objections to report of commissioner not made in trial court cannot be made for first time on appeal.

1895—*Shipman v. Fletcher,* 91 Va. 473, 22 S.E. 458.
Report of commissioner in chancery, even where evidence is conflicting, is not entitled to weight of verdict of jury. Report is prima facie correct and objection to it must be raised. Report will only be accepted as conclusive when testimony, though conflicting, is evenly balanced, and report is supported by testimony of competent and unimpeached witnesses.

1887—*Cralle v. Cralle,* 84 Va. 198, 6 S.E. 12.
Unless commissioner's report on its face shows error, exceptions will not be allowed to be made for first time on appeal.

§ 8-7. Common Law.

1984—*Weishaupt v. Commonwealth,* 227 Va. 389, 315 S.E.2d 847.
English common-law will not be applied if it is repugnant to bill of rights in constitution, if it is altered by General Assembly, if it is repugnant to nature and character of our political system or if different and varied circumstances of our country render it inapplicable.

1978—*In re: Change of Name of Miller,* 218 Va. 939, 243 S.E.2d 464.
English common law is in force in Virginia except as altered by statute. Under common law person may adopt any name he or she wishes provided it is not done for fraudulent purpose or it does not infringe upon rights of others.

1975—*In re: Strikwerda and Antell,* 216 Va. 470, 220 S.E.2d 245.
English common law, if not repugnant to bill of rights and constitution of Virginia, continues in full force except as amended by statute. Under common law person is free to adopt any name if it is not done for fraudulent purpose or in infringement of rights of others.

1944—*Brown v. Brown,* 183 Va. 353, 32 S.E.2d 79.
By statute, common law continues in full force in Virginia except as altered by General Assembly.

1930—*Gloth v. Gloth,* 154 Va. 511, 153 S.E. 879.
Law of divorce as developed in ecclesiastical courts of England was branch of common law which was inherited by Virginia.

1929—*Johnson v. Commonwealth,* 152 Va. 965, 146 S.E. 289.
Common law of England shall be rule of decision except where contrary to bill of rights and constitution of Virginia or state law.

1902—*Offield v. Davis,* 100 Va. 250, 40 S.E. 910.
Statute in question wholly abrogated common law on subject of marriages and clearly abrogated common law marriages by requiring that all marriages be under license and solemnized according to statute. Language of statute is mandatory and not directory.

1902—*Stewart v. Conrad,* 100 Va. 128, 40 S.E. 624.
In absence of evidence to contrary, common law is presumed to be in force in other states and under it contracts of married women are void.

§ 8-8. Conflicts of Law.

1962—*Doulgeris v. Bambacus,* 203 Va. 670, 127 S.E.2d 145.
Virginia court refused to recognize adoption under Greek law, because adoption was contrary to public policy of Virginia.

1962—*Calma v. Calma,* 203 Va. 880, 128 S.E.2d 440.
Supreme court found interracial marriage contracted in New Jersey to be invalid on grounds that it was contrary to public policy in Virginia.

1942—*Howe v. Howe,* 179 Va. 111, 18 S.E.2d 294.
Each state has exclusive control of matrimonial status of those domiciled within its borders.

1939—*Toler v. Oakwood Smokeless Coal Corp.,* 173 Va. 425, 4 S.E.2d 364.
General rule as to marriage is that law of place of its celebration governs as to its validity with two exceptions: (1) marriages contrary to laws of nature as generally recognized in Christian countries (2) marriages forbidden by statute because contrary to public policy.

1903—*Young v. Hart,* 101 Va. 480, 44 S.E. 703.
Contracts in this case made by married woman were valid where contracted and to be performed and, as such, they will be enforced by courts of this state in manner provided by its laws for as to remedy upon foreign contracts law of forum governs.

1885—*Greenhow v. Janes,* 80 Va. 636.
Conflicts principle as to marriage is lex loci contractus. Yet, rule which requires that marriage valid where celebrated is valid everywhere else has no application to marriage entered into that is in contravention of public policy and statutes of domicile of parties which pronounces marriage not only absolutely void but criminal. In this case, marriage was interracial.

1878—*Kinney v. Commonwealth,* 71 Va. 858.
While forms and ceremonies of marriage are governed by laws of place where marriage is celebrated, essentials of contract depend upon and are governed by laws of place where parties are domiciled at time of marriage and in which matrimonial residence is contemplated. In this case, this interracial marriage was deemed to be void even though it was performed in District of Columbia.

§ 8-9. Contempt.

See Va. Code § 20-115 indicating that court may order commitment and sentence for failure to comply with its order.

1982—*Leisge v. Leisge,* 224 Va. 303, 296 S.E.2d 538.

While disobedience to void order is not contempt, custody order issued in this case was valid. Contempt proceedings prosecuted to preserve power and vindicate dignity of court are criminal. Those prosecuted to preserve and enforce rights of private parties are civil, remedial and coercive. Character and purpose of punishment often served to determine class of contempt. In this case, fine and imprisonment imposed were remedial in nature, father having opportunity at any time to abate his contemptuous acts by complying with decree and returning child to mother as ordered by court. As such, there is no need for showing of specific intent to violate court order.

1977—*Winn v. Winn,* 218 Va. 8, 235 S.E.2d 307.

Property settlement agreement indicated that husband would maintain for period of two years present group hospitalization policy carried on wife or similar policy containing substantially same benefits. After divorce, wife filed claim under this policy which was denied on grounds that she was no longer covered under policy since she was now divorced. Wife filed petition to have husband held in contempt of court for violation of property settlement agreement which had been incorporated into final decree. As general rule, person may be held in contempt for violating court order only when order imposes duties upon person in definite terms, and command is expressed rather than implied. In this case Supreme Court found language of agreement to be ambiguous in sense technically all that was required of husband was to maintain same policy that he had previously. This he had done. It so happened that coverage was denied in light of subsequent divorce. Husband not guilty of contempt.

1954—*Hepler v. Hepler,* 195 Va. 611, 79 S.E.2d 652.

In this custody battle, husband was entitled to children during summer months. In August of 1952, mother demanded custody of all three children. Father refused and applied to court for modification of order. In applying for this modification, he was exercising right given to him under state code and was not guilty of willful disobedience of prior order.

1948—*Eddens v. Eddens,* 188 Va. 511, 50 S.E.2d 397.

To have one held in contempt of court, motion for rule to show cause must be filed. Resulting order must then be served upon alleged contemnor who then is permitted to file answer setting forth his defense. Frequently, order to show cause is issued on verbal motion of counsel for complaining party. Contempt proceedings are of two classes — those prosecuted to preserve power of court and to vindicate dignity of court are criminal and those instituted to preserve and enforce rights of private parties are civil. Imprisonment in contempt proceeding for refusal to pay alimony is not imprisonment for debt but is imprisonment for willful disobedience of court order. Fact that decree had become final does not deprive court of power to enforce it by contempt proceeding. Statute of limitations applicable to criminal contempt cases does not apply to civil contempt cases.

1932—*Lindsey v. Lindsey,* 158 Va. 647, 164 S.E. 551.
On rule to show cause to enforce payment of alimony trial court had right to consider all that had occurred prior to hearing on rule.

1932—*Gloth v. Gloth,* 158 Va. 98, 163 S.E. 351.
Two types of contempt proceedings: criminal — prosecuted to preserve power of court; civil — to enforce rights of private parties. Present case was not criminal contempt; no rule to show cause had ever been issued.

1926—*Branch v. Branch,* 144 Va. 244, 132 S.E. 303.
Proceeding for contempt is quasi-criminal and guilt of defendant must be shown beyond reasonable doubt. In this case, husband had failed to pay alimony. Prior to contempt proceeding, husband had opportunity to challenge wife's claim for alimony but he had failed to do so. Decree awarding alimony is presumed to be correct. Imprisonment for failure to pay alimony is not ordered simply to enforce payment of money but to punish for willful disobedience. Imprisonment should not be ordered except where conduct is contumacious.

§ 8-10. Continuance.

1900—*Willard v. Willard,* 98 Va. 465, 36 S.E. 518.
In suits for divorce, courts are liberal in allowing continuances and suspensions of hearings to supply defects in evidence or pleadings.

§ 8-11. Costs.

1977—*Lindsay v. Lindsay,* 218 Va. 599, 238 S.E.2d 817.
Court noted in absence of provision within order providing for payment of cost it is reasonable to infer cost were payable by losing party in accord with general rule. Losing party in this case was husband.

1964—*Higgins v. Higgins,* 205 Va. 324, 136 S.E.2d 793.
Costs were awarded to husband since he was one who substantially prevailed on appeal.

1957—*Carter v. Carter,* 199 Va. 79, 97 S.E.2d 663.
Court ordered husband to pay cost of depositions. Although he complained that they were unnecessarily long and that therefore cost should be apportioned, this condition was as much due to him as to wife.

1935—*Wright v. Wright,* 164 Va. 245, 178 S.E. 884.
Award of cost is within discretion of trial court.

1924—*Miller v. Miller,* 140 Va. 424, 125 S.E. 220.

Court, in this case, awarded full cost of printing appellate brief.

1923—*Mowles v. Mowles,* 137 Va. 274, 119 S.E. 54.

Supreme court denied wife's prayer for attorney's fees but awarded her costs, including printing costs.

1922—*Barnard v. Barnard,* 132 Va. 155, 111 S.E. 227.

Upon affirmance of decree for divorce a mensa in favor of wife, supreme court will grant appellee clerical expenses of preparation and printing of her brief.

§ 8-12. Courts.

See Va. Code § 16.1-226 as to Juvenile and Domestic Relations Court.

1983—*Deahl v. Winchester Dep't of Social Servs.,* 224 Va. 664, 299 S.E.2d 863.

Trial judge must exercise reasonable discretion to determine whether he possesses such bias or prejudice as would deny party fair trial. Mere familiarity by trial judge with party and his legal difficulties through prior judicial hearings creates no inference of bias.

1982—*Leisge v. Leisge,* 223 Va. 688, 292 S.E.2d 352.

Trial court gave father full and adequate hearing, but did avoid cumulative testimony. Due process was not denied.

1946—*Taylor v. Taylor,* 185 Va. 126, 37 S.E.2d 886.

Writ of prohibition will lie to restrain judge from proceeding in action in which he is disqualified by reason of interest, although court over which he presides may have jurisdiction of cause. Within liberal limits, judge, in determining his own qualifications, must exercise sound, judicial discretion, subject to review.

§ 8-13. Cross-Bill.

1958—*Brewer v. Brewer,* 199 Va. 626, 101 S.E.2d 516.

Cross-bill is aggressive pleading with its subject matter restricted or limited to that which is germane to or outgrowth of original bill. In this case, court held that husband had right to file cross-bill for divorce in suit for separate maintenance filed by his wife.

§ 8-14. Decree.

1981—*Dorn v. Dorn,* 222 Va. 288, 279 S.E.2d 393.

Alleged drafting error in this case is oversight, and it can be corrected by nunc pro tunc order. Va. Code § 8.01-428(B) give courts authority to enter such orders modifying support obligations in rare situation where evidence clearly supports conclusion that error covered by code has been made.

1979—*Cutshaw v. Cutshaw,* 220 Va. 638, 261 S.E.2d 52.

Although there was no court order to reduce child support payments due to oversight of counsel, this omission was not fatal. Court had authority to correct such ministerial omissions nunc pro tunc when record clearly supports correction.

1979—*Gazale v. Gazale,* 219 Va. 775, 250 S.E.2d 365.

While consent decree is court order, it is contractual in nature and should be construed as though it were contract. In this case court found that consent decree served only to amend rather than to supplant contractual provisions and that parties' contractual intent was therefore controlling.

1976—*Shank v. Dep't of Social Servs.,* 217 Va. 506, 230 S.E.2d 454.

Trial court order severing parental rights was not modified or vacated nor appealed. It was as final as if affirmed on appeal and is immune from collateral attack except upon jurisdictional grounds.

1976—*Thomas v. Thomas,* 216 Va. 741, 222 S.E.2d 557.

Where a mensa decree is merged into vinculo decree, latter subsumes former, a mensa decree loses separate identity in all of its provisions, not lawfully modified, assumes identity of vinculo decree. In this case property settlement agreement was incorporated into a mensa decree. In entering vinculo decree trial court had no jurisdiction to alter alimony terms that had been incorporated into prior decree.

1972—*Brinn v. Brinn,* 147 Va. 277, 137 S.E. 503.

Reservation of jurisdiction over part of subject of litigation should be clearly stated in decree. Court of equity has inherent power to reserve control over its decree.

1971—*Jenkins v. Jenkins,* 211 Va. 797, 180 S.E.2d 516.

Husband must pay support according to terms of decree, not influenced by any prior proceedings. His only alternative is to seek modification of decree.

1970—*Carneal v. Carneal,* 211 Va. 162, 176 S.E.2d 305.

Divorce decree was entered on April 29th, but execution was suspended on May 17th for period of 21 days. By subsequent order of June 7th, decree was made final as of June 8th. Appeal was filed as of July 29th which is within 60-day period allowed.

1967—*Fearon v. Fearon,* 207 Va. 927, 154 S.E.2d 165.

Court is without authority to modify its decree retroactively and relieve husband of obligation to pay past due support installments.

1965—*Cofer v. Cofer,* 205 Va. 834, 140 S.E.2d 663.

Husband petitioned court for reduction in amount of child support. By consent order, wife was given 10 days to answer petition. She did not do so and thereafter court entered order granting husband's petition. This order was void and should have been vacated on grounds that order was not endorsed by counsel for wife and also because notice was not given of time and place of presentation of order. Since order was void, it could not become final. Void decree is nullity and may be vacated at any time.

1961—*Newton v. Newton,* 202 Va. 515, 118 S.E.2d 656.

Husband contended that wife had violated terms of property settlement agreement which had been incorporated into final decree and as such she had forfeited payment that had been ordered. Even if this interpretation was correct, it was husband's duty to comply with order until such time as it was modified. As to any overpayments he may have made, he was not entitled to setoff as to arrears claimed by wife. His obligation was to comply with order.

1957—*Daniels v. Morris,* 199 Va. 205, 98 S.E.2d 694.

No objection to form of verdict was made for 10 days, at which time motion for new trial was filed. Under these circumstances, court committed no error in refusing to disturb verdict.

1955—*Higgins v. McFarland,* 196 Va. 889, 86 S.E.2d 168.

Judgments and decrees are contracts of highest order and especially is this so when entered by consent of parties.

1953—*Patterson v. Anderson,* 194 Va. 557, 74 S.E.2d 195.

To vitiate judgment on grounds that it was procured through fraud it must be shown that testimony at first trial was false and that fact of its falsity could not have been discovered by exercise of due diligence.

1948—*Eddens v. Eddens,* 188 Va. 511, 50 S.E.2d 397.

Fact that decree has become final does not deprive court of authority to enforce it by contempt proceeding.

1947—*Haskins v. Haskins,* 185 Va. 1001, 41 S.E.2d 25.

All judgments or decrees entered during any term of court become final at end of term or within 15 days of rendition.

1946—*Henebry v. Henebry,* 185 Va. 320, 38 S.E.2d 320.

Decree for alimony cannot be superceded by agreement of parties which court itself does not adopt or approve.

1946—*McKeel v. McKeel,* 185 Va. 108, 37 S.E.2d 746.

Florida order of alimony, even though subject to amendment, is entitled to full faith and credit enforcement in State of Virginia.

1945—*Tarr v. Tarr,* 184 Va. 443, 35 S.E.2d 401.

Remarriage of party will not present any insuperable obstacle to vacation of decree if petitioner has not been guilty of laches even though children have been born of second marriage. This is intended to restrain divorced parties from entering into new marriages too hastily.

1942—*Howe v. Howe,* 179 Va. 111, 18 S.E.2d 294.

If decree is void then no action nor inaction gives it any effect. Voidable marriage is valid for all civil purposes until annulled by competent tribunal.

1940—*Hill School v. Buchanan,* 174 Va. 281, 6 S.E.2d 622.
Judgment declared void due to lack of jurisdiction is not enforceable.

1938—*Buchanan v. Buchanan,* 170 Va. 458, 197 S.E. 426.
Successful collateral attack made upon judgment of court of general jurisdiction must show judgment to be void, not merely voidable.

1938—*Golderos v. Golderos,* 169 Va. 496, 194 S.E. 706.
Decree of divorce, which contained award of alimony became final upon adjournment of court for that term as to all matters litigated or that should have been litigated as incidental thereto. Court has no authority to modify. Fact that parties consent to modification does not bestow jurisdiction on court.

1937—*Casilear v. Casilear,* 168 Va. 46, 190 S.E. 314.
Contract between parties will not supersede provisions for support in court decree.

1935—*Capell v. Capell,* 164 Va. 45, 178 S.E. 894.
No agreement of parties has any effect on decree unless ratified and made effective by judicial sanction.

1934—*Hodnett v. Hodnett,* 163 Va. 644, 177 S.E. 106.
Wife attempted to set aside divorce decree in part. She waited almost three years and after husband had remarried. Claim barred by laches.

1932—*Taylor v. Taylor,* 159 Va. 338, 165 S.E. 414.
Remarriage of one of parties is not insuperable obstacle to vacating decree of divorce even though children have been born provided there is no laches. In this case, husband obtained divorce by fraud, knowing that wife was insane. Contest here was between first wife and second wife. Divorce vacated, although second wife was guiltless, although not diligent in knowing facts. If in righting wrong even greater injury is to be done, then court will consider this. Insanity of defendant at time of judgment is not sufficient cause to vacate judgment, although judgment may be voidable if there was fraud involved.

1932—*Sussman v. Sussman,* 158 Va. 382, 163 S.E. 69.
To constitute judgment by decree, legal terms "adjudged, ordered and decreed" must precede final action of court.

1925—*Barnes v. American Fertilizer Co.,* 144 Va. 692, 130 S.E. 902.
Settlement agreement, in this case, was approved and adopted by court and incorporated into decree. Decree is contract between parties and is binding unless secured by fraud or mistake.

1925—*Scott v. Scott,* 142 Va. 31, 128 S.E. 599.
Decree of divorce obtained by collusion cannot be attacked by either party. Wife in this case claimed that decree was obtained through duress and fraud of her husband. Evidence failed to establish that.

1919—*Shelton v. Shelton,* 125 Va. 381, 99 S.E. 557.

> There is no statute that authorizes court to grant parties indefinite time within which to move court to reinstate suit in which final decree has been rendered.

1919—*Reynolds v. Adams,* 125 Va. 295, 99 S.E. 695.

> Judgment of court of competent jurisdiction will always be presumed to be right. Party in appellate court alleging error must show error; otherwise presumption of correctness will prevail.

1917—*Gum v. Gum,* 122 Va. 32, 94 S.E. 177.

> There is no principle of law better settled than that every act of court of competent jurisdiction shall be presumed to have been rightly done until contrary appears. In present case, subject was within jurisdictional power of court, parties were before court, decree has never been reversed or annulled and therefore must conclusively be presumed to be correct and it cannot be collaterally attacked in subsequent suit.

§ 8-15. Default.

Rule 2:9 of supreme court. Allegations in bill of complaint for divorce or annulment shall not be taken for confessed.

See Va. Code § 20-99 indicating that no bill of complaint shall be taken for confessed.

1954—*Westfall v. Westfall,* 196 Va. 97, 82 S.E.2d 487.

> There are marked differences between divorce actions and other equity actions since in divorce action State has interest. In this case, defendant-wife failed to file answer to bill of complaint within prescribed time, although this failure did not delay case. She had substantial defense in that she was receiving payments for separate maintenance under order of another court. Trial court abused its discretion in permitting her to file answer only on condition that she file cross-bill for separate maintenance in this court.

1952—*Ciarochi v. Ciarochi,* 194 Va. 313, 73 S.E.2d 402.

> Though defendant failed to answer bill, it still could not be taken for confessed. In this action based upon fraud, necessity clearly to allege and prove fraud was in no way lessened by defendant's failure to appear.

1952—*Baker v. Baker,* 194 Va. 284, 72 S.E.2d 632.

> Supreme court rule dealing with bill being taken for confessed is not applicable to divorce suit, because such bill cannot be taken for confessed.

1932—*Craddock's Adm'r v. Craddock's Adm'r,* 158 Va. 58, 163 S.E. 387.

> Bill in divorce suit shall not be taken for confessed. Suit cannot be proceeded with ex parte unless there is statutory authority for it. Defendant entitled to notice of deposition even though he has not answered. There is no waiver of objections where defendant has not

appeared. Notice is likewise to be given where evidence is to be given ore tenus.

§ 8-16. Demurrer.

1947—*Haskins v. Haskins,* 185 Va. 1001, 41 S.E.2d 25.
Demurrer admits as true all facts which are properly pleaded but does not admit conclusions of law.

1945—*Griffin v. Griffin,* 183 Va. 443, 32 S.E.2d 700.
Bill of complaint which was too indefinite and uncertain is demurrable. Demurrer must go to heart of cause and, if it is sustained, it is decision on merits of cause. Special demurrers which dealt with matters of form are abolished in Virginia, and only matters of substance can be grounds for demurrer.

1940—*Eaton v. Davis,* 176 Va. 330, 10 S.E.2d 893.
Facts alleged in bill are taken as true upon demurrer.

1930—*Gloth v. Gloth,* 154 Va. 511, 153 S.E. 879.
Bill for divorce asked for construction of separation agreement and deed of trust, and for injunction as to enforcement of agreement and deed of trust. This was not demurrable.

§ 8-17. Depositions.

1962—*Mackey v. Mackey,* 203 Va. 526, 125 S.E.2d 194.
In divorce case, record should affirmatively show that each procedural step is taken properly unless waived by party for whose benefit it is provided. If procedural requirement is not followed and it is not waived, record then shows, upon its face, defect which challenges authority of court to proceed with case. In all divorce cases except where defendant is proceeded against by order of publication or its equivalent, and defendant fails to appear, notice of taking depositions is required. It should affirmatively show from record that proper notice was served, accepted or waived. Record in this case did not show that and as such this was grounds for reversal.

1956—*Owens v. Owens,* 197 Va. 681, 90 S.E.2d 776.
Taking of depositions was not premature where respondent was served on November 3 and depositions were taken on November 29. It was proper to take depositions at any time after lapse of 21 days from time of service since defendant had not appeared.

1952—*Baker v. Baker,* 194 Va. 284, 72 S.E.2d 632.
Purpose of notice requirement as to taking of deposition is to give opposing party opportunity to appear and cross-examine.

1925—*Scott v. Scott,* 142 Va. 31, 128 S.E. 599.
Where defendant in divorce suit not only personally accepted notice of deposition but was present when deposition was taken and filed her answer without objecting to notice, she thereby waived any irregularity.

§ 8-18. Discovery.

1965—*DeRyder v. Metropolitan Life,* 206 Va. 602, 145 S.E.2d 177.

Defendant responded to request for admissions by stating that facts were not within his knowledge. Plaintiff moved to strike these responses. Motion was denied. While party is required to answer, even though he has no personal knowledge of matter, if means are reasonably within his power. This was not case with most of these requests. Some of requests even went to ultimate facts at issue and as such were improper.

§ 8-19. Dismissal.

1978—*Moore v. Moore,* 218 Va. 790, 240 S.E.2d 535.

General Assembly has changed existing equity rule that complainant had absolute right to dismiss his suit at any time before final decree unless affirmative rights of defendant or others had attached and provided instead for voluntary dismissal as matter of right only up to time suit had been submitted to chancellor for decision. For submission to occur, it is necessary for both parties by counsel to yield issues to court for consideration and decision. Neither filing by commissioner of his report nor defendant's unilateral act of forwarding to court draft order is submission. In this case plaintiff had absolute right to voluntary dismissal.

§ 8-20. Equity.

1983—*Brown v. Kittle,* 225 Va. 451, 303 S.E.2d 864.

Unclean hands doctrine denying equitable relief to party guilty of inequitable conduct is applicable to family law cases except where rights of children will be prejudiced by result. In this case, father of illegitimate child sought custody and was awarded such in spite of his own prior conduct.

1981—*Pleasants v. Pleasants,* 221 Va. 1017, 277 S.E.2d 170.

Equity will decree that as done which by agreement is agreed to be done and properly effectuates fully intentions of parties concerned.

1948—*Henderson v. Henderson,* 187 Va. 121, 46 S.E.2d 10.

Equity, having once taken jurisdiction, will retain it and settle all matters in dispute.

1943—*White v. White,* 181 Va. 162, 24 S.E.2d 448.

Courts of law and courts of equity may have concurrent jurisdiction, and power of equity may be invoked whenever it appears necessary in order to give complete relief. When court of equity acquires jurisdiction for any purpose, it will retain it and do complete justice between parties, enforcing if necessary, legal rights and applying legal remedies.

1942—*McClaugherty v. McClaugherty,* 180 Va. 51, 21 S.E.2d 761.
In every well-regulated government, there must exist power of affording remedy where law affords none and this peculiarly belongs to court of equity. Equity has jurisdiction in cases of recognized rights when plain, adequate and complete remedy cannot be had at law. Therefore, jurisdiction of equity court is sometimes concurrent with that of court of law.

1941—*McNeir v. McNeir,* 178 Va. 285, 16 S.E.2d 632.
Plaintiff must come into equity with clean hands.

1941—*Pretlow v. Pretlow,* 177 Va. 524, 14 S.E.2d 381.
Equity, having once acquired jurisdiction never loses it because jurisdiction of same matter is given to law courts unless statute uses prohibitory or restrictive words.

1941—*Heflin v. Heflin,* 177 Va. 385, 14 S.E.2d 317.
Where equity has assumed jurisdiction due to lack of legal remedy, it will retain jurisdiction even though law court subsequently assumes similar jurisdiction due to change in statute.

1940—*Buchanan v. Buchanan,* 174 Va. 255, 6 S.E.2d 612.
For remedy at law to be exclusive it must be adequate. That is, it must reach end intended and compel performance of duty in question. Remedy at law must also be plain; if it be doubtful then equity will assert jurisdiction. When equity acquires jurisdiction for any reason it will retain it and do complete justice as to parties, enforcing legal rights and applying legal remedies if necessary. Courts of law and equity may have concurrent jurisdiction.

1938—*Buchanan v. Buchanan,* 170 Va. 458, 197 S.E. 426.
Equitable relief cannot be awarded in common law action. In this habeas corpus action award of money was not valid.

1927—*McCotter v. Carle,* 149 Va. 584, 140 S.E. 670.
When equity has acquired jurisdiction on any equitable ground it will grant complete relief, including legal relief.

1923—*Heflinger v. Heflinger,* 136 Va. 289, 118 S.E. 316.
Equitable doctrine of clean hands is subservient to public policy of State and cannot be invoked in contravention thereof. In this particular case, public policy of State to declare marriage void outweighed equitable maxim of clean hands. Exception to this maxim exists where State has an interest in controversy and where there are no property rights of parties involved.

§ 8-21. Estoppel.

1979—*Alig v. Alig,* 220 Va. 80, 255 S.E.2d 494.
There is no equitable estoppel of wife from recovering arrearages from past due monthly alimony payments. Husband was under clear duty to comply with terms of alimony decree until modified by court order and could not escape this duty merely by relying upon erratic statements and actions of his emotionally unstable wife.

1976—*T. . . v. T. . .,* 216 Va. 867, 224 S.E.2d 148.

To establish equitable estoppel it is not necessary to show actual fraud, but only that person to be estopped has misled another to his prejudice or that innocent party acted in reliance upon conduct or misstatements by person to be estopped. Elements then to establish equitable estoppel, absent showing fraud and deception, are representation, reliance, change of position, and detriment.

1975—*Gagliano v. Gagliano,* 215 Va. 447, 211 S.E.2d 62.

Wife having entered into agreement for payments in lieu of those fixed in decree, and having accepted those payments and used funds for purposes specified in decree, she is now estopped to deny that such payments are proper credit against payments fixed in decree.

1952—*Evans v. Asphalt Road & Materials Co.,* 194 Va. 165, 72 S.E.2d 321.

One who has participated in obtaining fraudulent divorce is estopped to deny its validity. This applies to parties and their privies.

1950—*Ballard v. Cox,* 191 Va. 654, 62 S.E.2d 1.

One of essential elements of estoppel is that person claiming it or on whose behalf it is asserted must have been misled to his injury.

1942—*McClaugherty v. McClaugherty,* 180 Va. 51, 21 S.E.2d 761.

Child support action brought by child against father. Any inconsistent positions taken by child's mother in other litigation against father cannot operate as estoppel as to child.

1941—*McNeir v. McNeir,* 178 Va. 285, 16 S.E.2d 632.

Party cannot profit from his own wrong. Wife who fraudulently obtained divorce cannot later contest divorce.

1934—*Simpson v. Simpson,* 162 Va. 621, 175 S.E. 320.

Husband deserted wife. Husband was absent for more than seven years when wife filed for divorce. Filing of suit for divorce does not estop wife from claiming that husband is dead.

1930—*Gloth v. Gloth,* 154 Va. 511, 153 S.E. 879.

Husband claimed property settlement agreement procured by duress. Failure to repudiate promptly resulted in estoppel.

1929—*Fidelity & Deposit Co. v. Anderson,* 155 Va. 535, 150 S.E. 413.

He who kept silent when he ought to have spoken, will not be heard to speak when he ought to keep silent.

1927—*McCotter v. Carle,* 149 Va. 584, 140 S.E. 670.

When subsequent case is between same parties and upon same cause of action, judgment in former case estops parties as to all matters litigated or which might have been litigated in former suit.

§ 8-22. Full Faith and Credit.

1983—*Brown v. Kittle,* 225 Va. 451, 303 S.E.2d 864.

Principles of comity in full faith and credit do not preclude relitigation of child custody issues. Here evidence of changed circumstances and of improvement and development of child while he had been with father justified review of custody situation.

1983—*Scott v. Sylvester,* 225 Va. 304, 302 S.E.2d 30.

Under comity doctrine modifiable Maryland decree, although lacking quality of finality contemplated by full faith and credit clause, may be given same force and effect as if entered in Virginia, although due process requires court to consider any questions of modification raised by either party.

1981—*Pace v. Pace,* 222 Va. 524, 281 S.E.2d 891.

Full faith and credit should be given to sister State's decree for child support arrearages, accrued support payments being entitled to full faith and credit if obligee had vested right to payments after they became due. Entry of two Virginia decrees prior to entry of 1978 Missouri order alters degree to which 1978 Missouri judgment is entitled to full faith and credit. Virginia court acquired jurisdiction over wife when she filed her petition and full faith and credit does not require giving greater effect to judgments of sister State than Virginia gives to judgments of its own court.

1981—*Ceyte v. Ceyte,* 222 Va. 11, 278 S.E.2d 791.

Entry in Virginia of pendente lite decree for spousal support does not affect question whether foreign court's final decree barring support is entitled to full faith and credit. Full faith and credit will be awarded foreign court's earlier divorce decree barring spousal support where that court has personal jurisdiction over spouse.

1980—*Oehl v. Oehl,* 221 Va. 618, 272 S.E.2d 441.

Child custody order is always subject to modification and therefore is not necessarily entitled to full faith and credit. In this case, full faith and credit does not apply because order in question is one of English court, however concept is analogous to doctrine of comity.

1979—*Alig v. Alig,* 220 Va. 80, 255 S.E.2d 494.

Foreign decree for alimony is entitled to full faith and credit as to past due installments if right to such installments is absolute and vested that is not subject to modification in state where decree was rendered. In this case Maryland decree, under Maryland law, may be modified both in respect to installments which have accrued and those not yet due. As such, decree does not possess degree of finality as to be entitled to full faith and credit. Under RURESA it is however, entitled to comity.

1978—*Newport v. Newport,* 219 Va. 48, 245 S.E.2d 134.

Husband, Nevada resident, secured ex parte divorce in Nevada. Wife, Virginia resident, sought award for support and maintenance in Virginia. Husband appeared in Virginia case, citing Nevada divorce and also filed cross-bill seeking partition of residence occupied by wife. Court gave full faith and credit to Nevada decree of divorce, but held that Nevada could not adjudicate question of alimony since court did not have jurisdiction over her.

1977—*Romeo v. Romeo,* 218 Va. 290, 237 S.E.2d 143.

New York court upon contested hearing on wife's counterclaim found marriage to be valid and awarded wife permanent separation. This makes issue of validity of marriage res judicata in New York and bars relitigation of that issue in Virginia. New York judgment is entitled to full faith and credit.

1974—*Osborne v. Osborne,* 215 Va. 205, 207 S.E.2d 875.

Husband filed for divorce in Texas and wife entered general appearance. Wife filed in Virginia, and husband was personally served. Texas judgment in 1972 was res judicata and must be given full faith and credit in Virginia as to divorce and alimony. Virginia court had entered decree pendente lite awarding custody of children and child support to wife before divorce decree was entered in Texas. Children resided in Virginia, and Virginia courts retained jurisdiction over them. As such, Virginia court may make proper child support award under Virginia law. Virginia is not required to give full faith and credit to child custody decrees of another State and declines to give full faith and credit to child support order entered in another State in uncontested proceeding. No proof of change of circumstances required before Virginia court may make child support award that differs from award of another State. Welfare of child is always primary consideration.

1969—*Addison v. Addison,* 210 Va. 104, 168 S.E.2d 281.

In determining whether to apply full faith and credit to custody decree, law of Virginia requires that court puts child's interest first. This court has never held that it would not apply full faith and credit in custody case. In this case, however, court found change in circumstances and therefore changed custody to mother.

1969—*Branham v. Raines,* 209 Va. 702, 167 S.E.2d 355.

Ohio decree granted parties divorce and custody of child was awarded to mother, with child to be surrendered to father for off-premises visitation during months of July and August. Court stated that in present case, it was not necessary to determine whether it would hold that full faith and credit clause does not apply to custody decrees. Instead, it founded its decision upon change of circumstances which justified Virginia court in modifying custody arrangement that had been ordered by Ohio court.

1968—*Falco v. Grills,* 209 Va. 115, 161 S.E.2d 713.

Parents, who were residents of New York, were killed in auto accident in Virginia while en route to Tennessee. Child was also seriously injured. Child was hospitalized in Virginia. New York relatives were appointed guardian by New York court in ex parte proceeding. Court stated that as general proposition courts throughout this country have been most reluctant to apply full faith and credit to custody cases. That was especially so here since New York court conducted simply ex parte proceeding.

1964—*Gramelspacher v. Gramelspacher,* 204 Va. 839, 134 S.E.2d 285.
Husband, at time of trial, testified that order had been entered by Mississippi court compelling support payments by him. No copy of order was produced at trial and, as such, there was no record upon which court could rule as to that issue.

1954—*Wallihan v. Hughes,* 196 Va. 117, 82 S.E.2d 553.
Property settlement agreement was approved and made part of Nevada divorce decree. Wife contended that agreement facilitated divorce and therefore was void. It was held that with regard to custody, agreement was subject to modification by Virginia court. With regard to property rights, agreement was binding. Rights under full faith and credit clause are federal rights, and effect of clause on State court proceeding is to be determined in light of U.S. Supreme Court decisions. Clause is to be given broad and generous application. In this case even though contract may have been against Virginia public policy that policy must now yield to mandate of full faith and credit.

1954—*Kessler v. Fauquier Nat'l Bank,* 195 Va. 1095, 81 S.E.2d 440.
Principles of res judicata apply to questions of jurisdiction. That is court of competent jurisdiction can litigate issue of jurisdiction as to another court.

1952—*Evans v. Asphalt Road & Materials Co.,* 194 Va. 165, 72 S.E.2d 321.
Defendant may not attack divorce decree on jurisdictional grounds in courts of sister State where there has been participation by defendant in divorce proceeding, full opportunity to contest jurisdictional issues and where decree is not susceptible to attack in courts of State rendering decree. In this workmen's compensation action, infant son was held not to have right to collaterally attack Nevada divorce decree of his father since he did not show that he would have been permitted to make collateral attack on decree in Nevada and as such he could not attack it in Virginia.

1946—*McKeel v. McKeel,* 185 Va. 108, 37 S.E.2d 746.
Although Virginia court may not be compelled to do so under full faith and credit clause, upon principles of comity they may establish as their own decree foreign decree for future payments of alimony, provided foreign decree violates no public policy of Virginia.

1942—*McFarland v. McFarland,* 179 Va. 418, 19 S.E.2d 77.
When suit is brought in State of matrimonial domicile against spouse who has left State, then refusal to recognize decree of divorce offends full faith and credit clause. That is not so when forum court is not in matrimonial State. No State is bound by comity to give effect in its courts to divorce laws of another state repugnant to its own laws and public policy. No requirement to give comity to decree falsely or fraudulently obtained. Denial of full faith and credit to North Carolina divorce decree does not render decree null and void but simply inoperative.

1942—*Howe v. Howe,* 179 Va. 111, 18 S.E.2d 294.
Decree of divorce from court lacking jurisdiction is not entitled to recognition.

1927—*Dry v. Rice,* 147 Va. 331, 137 S.E. 473.
Husband attacked jurisdiction of foreign court to award decree to wife. Positive statements of wife as to her residence overcame mere estimates by husband. Foreign court's determination that it had jurisdiction could not be ignored except upon satisfactory evidence to contrary. Court of this State has no jurisdiction to alter foreign judgment. Court may refuse to enforce foreign judgment and may inquire into jurisdiction over parties.

1924—*Humphreys v. Strong,* 139 Va. 146, 123 S.E. 554.
Foreign divorce decrees should be recognized by courts of Virginia, except when to recognize foreign divorce would be violation of morals or public policy of State. Nevada divorce decree in this case, was recognized by Virginia court, even though Nevada divorce was based upon cruelty which, in Nevada, is basis for absolute divorce. In Virginia, cruelty is basis only for divorce a mensa which may later be merged into absolute divorce. Full faith and credit clause does not compel recognition of foreign divorce obtained on constructive service upon defendant in State other than that of matrimonial domicile. However, such decree should be recognized on grounds of comity. State, such as Virginia, which itself recognizes divorces on constructive services, should recognize such divorces when granted by other states. Foreign divorce, however, based upon fraud, will not be recognized as matter of comity. In present case, there was no evidence of fraud.

1923—*Wilson v. Wilson,* 136 Va. 643, 118 S.E. 270.
Wife filed habeas corpus petition in Virginia seeking custody of children who, at that time, were living in Virginia. Court awarded custody to husband. Wife thereafter filed for divorce in Maryland and secured order granting her custody. Wife thereafter filed suit in Virginia, asking court to give full faith and credit to Maryland decree. Maryland decree was not entitled to full faith and credit in light of prior habeas corpus ruling.

1923—*Heflinger v. Heflinger,* 136 Va. 289, 118 S.E. 316.
If judgment is conclusive in State where it is rendered, it is equally conclusive elsewhere. In this case, six month remarriage rule was that decree of divorce is not operative at all as to subsequent marriage until expiration of six months from date of decree. This decree being valid and having this particular meaning must be given full faith and credit in all of other states of Union.

1921—*Corvin v. Commonwealth,* 131 Va. 649, 108 S.E. 651.
Decree of divorce obtained in non-matrimonial forum without personal service and without appearance by defendant is not binding on courts of State of original matrimonial domicile under full faith and credit clause.

1916—*Kelly v. Kelly,* 118 Va. 376, 87 S.E. 567.

Meaning of full faith and credit clause is that courts of one State must accord to judgment of another State same effect which it has in State where rendered if judgment is conclusive in that State. In this case, wife's petition for separate maintenance was granted by court of competent jurisdiction in Massachusetts, thereby authorizing her to live separate and apart from her husband. That decree, while it remains in force, is bar to proceedings by husband for divorce on grounds of desertion. Benefit of that decree is not waived by fact that wife defended on merits husband's subsequent action for desertion.

§ 8-23. Inconsistent Positions.

1942—*McClaugherty v. McClaugherty,* 180 Va. 51, 21 S.E.2d 761.

Child support action brought by child against father. Any inconsistent positions taken by child's mother in other litigation against father cannot operate as estoppel as to child.

§ 8-24. Juries.

1972—*Lam v. Lam,* 212 Va. 758, 188 S.E.2d 89.

Jury trial allowed in this divorce action to try question of jurisdiction.

1947—*Carpenter v. Commonwealth,* 186 Va. 851, 44 S.E.2d 419.

Child abuse case. Defense counsel asked in voir dire, "do you believe that man has right, as parent, to inflict proper punishment on child." Question properly refused, since it was attempt to determine personal opinions of jurors rather than inquiry to determine whether they would accept as defense that which law required as defense.

1930—*Waddy v. Grimes,* 154 Va. 615, 153 S.E. 807.

Issue of mental capacity within sound discretion of trial court to submit this issue to jury.

1920—*Towson v. Towson,* 126 Va. 640, 102 S.E. 48.

In this divorce action, court allowed question of domicile to be tried by jury. Different theories of parties were fully presented in instructions. Although instruction standing alone may have been misleading, verdict of jury will not be set aside for that reason where it appears that objection thereto was corrected by other instructions given by court. In other words, instructions are to be read as whole. Party cannot complain of error of law in instructions given at her request.

§ 8-25. Laches.

1948—*Eddens v. Eddens,* 188 Va. 511, 50 S.E.2d 397.

Statute of limitations applicable to criminal contempt cases is not applicable to civil cases.

§ 8-26. Opening Statement.

1972—*Lam v. Lam,* 212 Va. 758, 188 S.E.2d 89.

In this divorce proceeding, issue to be tried was whether court had jurisdiction. That issue was tried before jury. In opening statement, counsel should not argue questions of law. Legal propositions or contentions, however, may be properly stated. It was prejudicial error to rebuke counsel for misstating law on burden of proof and then to refuse proffered instruction which correctly stated burden of proof.

§ 8-27. Parties.

1953—*Patterson v. Anderson,* 194 Va. 557, 74 S.E.2d 195.

No valid judgment can be rendered where parties necessary to determination of issue were not before court.

1943—*Kirby v. Gilliam,* 182 Va. 111, 28 S.E.2d 40.

Infant wife who wishes to annul marriage must sue by next friend. Suit must be brought in infant's name.

1935—*Kilbourne v. Kilbourne,* 165 Va. 87, 181 S.E. 351.

Suit by minor for annulment of marriage. Case remanded for designation of next friend.

§ 8-28. Pleadings.

(A) Amendment.

See Va. Code § 20-121.02 indicating that no amended bill of complaint or cross-bill need be filed where, after finding of original bill of complaint on fault grounds, parties thereafter choose to proceed on no fault grounds.

1983—*Coe v. Coe,* 225 Va. 616, 303 S.E.2d 923.

Adultery being act most likely to frustrate and prevent reconciliation, trial court properly permitted plaintiff to amend his complaint in good faith by adding adultery to constructive desertion as grounds for divorce. He sought leave to amend as soon as he learned of specific acts of adultery. His amended bill did not state completely new case, but merely added additional ground while asking for same relief.

1982—*Roberts v. Roberts,* 223 Va. 736, 292 S.E.2d 370.

Principal purpose of supplemental bill is to bring into case new events referring to and supporting or affecting rights and interest already mentioned, which have arisen subsequent to filing of original bill. Right to file such pleadings rest in sound discretion of trial court. In this case, supplemental bill referred to acts of adultery which occurred three days after motion for leave to amend had been filed. Court properly concluded that motion to file was not made in good faith.

1969—*Rosenberg v. Rosenberg,* 210 Va. 44, 168 S.E.2d 251.

Husband filed suit seeking divorce on grounds of desertion. After commissioner's hearing and before hearing on exceptions to commissioner's report, husband sought leave to file amended and supplemental bill on grounds of adultery that occurred after commissioner's report was filed. Since adultery is highly relevant to issues of alimony, support and custody, court found that this does not state completely new case and was proper subject of amended bill. Had alleged adultery occurred at time prior to filing of original bill and been discovered afterwards, husband would clearly have been entitled to amend his suit. Such amendment should also be allowed here. Generally, amended bill states fact which was in existence at time original bill was filed, whereas supplemental bill states fact which came into existence after original bill was filed.

1943—*Kirby v. Gilliam,* 182 Va. 111, 28 S.E.2d 40.
Suit instituted in name of next friend that should have been in name of infant may not be amended so as to substitute parties but should be dismissed without prejudice.

1900—*Willard v. Willard,* 98 Va. 465, 36 S.E. 518.
In suits for divorce, courts are liberal in allowing continuances and suspensions of hearings to supply defects in evidence or pleadings. In present case, it was error to refuse to allow appellant to amend her cross-bill, charging husband with additional recent acts of adultery. Evidence does not disclose lack of proper diligence on her part.

(B) Answer.

1926—*Markley v. Markley,* 145 Va. 596, 134 S.E. 536.
Answer under oath is entitled to great weight.

1925—*Scott v. Scott,* 142 Va. 31, 128 S.E. 599.
It is entirely proper for defendant to file her answer prior to date returnable. Court thereby acquired jurisdiction of her person.

(C) Sufficiency.

1972—*Johnson v. Johnson,* 213 Va. 204, 191 S.E.2d 206.
Acts relied upon for divorce must be alleged and proved to have occurred prior to filing of pleadings. It may not be based upon some act or conduct alleged to have taken place thereafter.

1953—*Patterson v. Anderson,* 194 Va. 557, 74 S.E.2d 195.
Complaint failed to state cause of action since essential allegation of damage is not capable of proof, i.e., entirely speculative.

1952—*Ciarochi v. Ciarochi,* 194 Va. 313, 73 S.E.2d 402.
Where fraud is relied upon, bill must show specifically what fraud consists of.

1952—*Baker v. Baker,* 194 Va. 284, 72 S.E.2d 632.
Purpose of bill of complaint is to state plaintiff's case for information of defendant and to fix issues.

1951—*Alexander v. Kuykendall,* 192 Va. 8, 63 S.E.2d 746.

Even though motion for judgment may be imperfect, if it is so drafted that defendant cannot mistake true nature of claim, then trial court should overrule demurrer. If need be bill of particulars may be ordered. In this case defective as plaintiff's motion was it did inform defendant of true nature, though not particulars, of claim.

1947—*Haskins v. Haskins,* 185 Va. 1001, 41 S.E.2d 25.

Pleadings contained no charges of adultery and did not show any definite facts of cruelty or desertion. It alleged that for past two years life with other spouse had become unbearable and that wife harassed him in his employment, threw articles at him and destroyed some of his personal property in fits of temper but did not state how she harassed him, nature of articles she threw at him. Pleadings held to be insufficient.

1945—*Griffin v. Griffin,* 183 Va. 443, 32 S.E.2d 700.

Bill of complaint for divorce must be definite and certain. Otherwise, it may be demurrable.

1940—*Buchanan v. Buchanan,* 174 Va. 255, 6 S.E.2d 612.

Bill will not be regarded as multifarious where matters joined are not absolutely independent of each other and it will be more convenient to dispose of them in one suit.

1938—*Jones v. Jones,* 172 Va. 14, 199 S.E. 510.

Where bill for divorce on grounds of cruelty and constructive desertion contains necessary jurisdictional allegations but lacks specificity as to acts of misconduct then such can be cured by amendment if brought to court's attention.

1930—*Gloth v. Gloth,* 154 Va. 511, 153 S.E. 879.

Where bill for divorce does not allege that parties agreed that contract should be void for misconduct, it is not permissible to prove such.

1917—*White v. White,* 121 Va. 244, 92 S.E. 811.

Pleadings in this adultery action were held to be sufficient where they set forth, with reasonable certainty, time, place and circumstances of alleged action.

1911—*Haynor v. Haynor,* 112 Va. 123, 70 S.E. 531.

In case charging cruelty, facts constituting cruelty and not merely conclusions should be charged with reasonable certainty.

1895—*Miller v. Miller,* 92 Va. 196, 23 S.E. 232.

Bill for divorce on grounds of adultery which simply charges that defendant has been guilty of adultery on many occasions is demurrable. Bill should state time, place and circumstances so as to enable defendant to disprove charge, although it need not state name of person with whom adultery was committed.

§ 8-29. Res Judicata.

See Decree, § 8-14.

See Va. Code §§ 20-135 and 136 as to res judicata effect of custody decree.

1981—*Hosier v. Hosier,* 221 Va. 827, 273 S.E.2d 564.

Judgment is not res judicata if it does not go to merits of case. Trial judge in first case concluded that he did not have jurisdiction and dismissed suit. Since that decree was not adjudication on merits, trial court properly overruled plea of res judicata in subsequent action.

1977—*Romeo v. Romeo,* 218 Va. 290, 237 S.E.2d 143.

New York court upon contested hearing on wife's counterclaim found marriage to be valid and awarded wife permanent separation. This makes issue of validity of marriage res judicata in New York and bars relitigation of that issue in Virginia. New York judgment is entitled to full faith and credit.

1974—*Osborne v. Osborne,* 215 Va. 205, 207 S.E.2d 875.

Husband filed for divorce in Texas, and wife entered general appearance. Wife also filed in Virginia, and husband was personally served. Final judgment was entered in Texas in 1972. That would be res judicata and must be given full faith and credit in Virginia as to divorce and alimony.

1962—*Calma v. Calma,* 203 Va. 880, 128 S.E.2d 440.

In prior suit between same parties, husband had been denied divorce for cruelty on grounds that marriage itself was invalid since it was interracial. Court in second action therefore correctly concluded that issue could not be relitigated in present suit. If issue presented in subsequent suit between same parties is shown to have been determined in former one, question is res judicata, although actions are based on different grounds or tried on different theories.

1954—*Kessler v. Fauquier Nat'l Bank,* 195 Va. 1095, 81 S.E.2d 440.

Wife separated from husband in 1944 and moved to Florida. She obtained divorce in Florida in 1946. She died in 1947, making no provision for her former husband in her will. He filed suit in Virginia to establish his right to share in her estate and was adjudged to have no such right. In this suit, validity of Florida decree and jurisdiction of Florida court were expressly put in issue. In later suit in Florida, Florida court determined divorce was void for lack of domicile. Virginia court was not required to give full faith and credit to subsequent Florida decree declaring divorce invalid since this issue had already been resolved.

1953—*Patterson v. Anderson,* 194 Va. 557, 74 S.E.2d 195.

For doctrine of res judicata to apply, there must be identity of issues, identity of parties appearing in their identical capacity. In determining whether or not this doctrine applies, inquiry may extend to evidence and instructions as well as pleadings in prior action. If judgment in prior action is not valid, then there is no bar to relitigation.

1952—*Evans v. Asphalt Road & Materials Co.,* 194 Va. 165, 72 S.E.2d 321.
Parties to action are not allowed to attack collaterally judgment rendered therein, except where it is absolutely void for want of jurisdiction in court rendering it. Invalidity of divorce decree obtained in another State may not be shown on collateral attack by stranger thereto unless he shows that decree deprived him of right which existed at time it was rendered.

1948—*Haskins v. Haskins,* 188 Va. 525, 50 S.E.2d 437.
In prior action, husband charged wife with cruelty and constructive desertion. That matter was dismissed on wife's demurrer. That decision precludes husband from relying upon same grounds of divorce in this present case.

1945—*Griffin v. Griffin,* 183 Va. 443, 32 S.E.2d 700.
Demurrer of husband sustained to bill of complaint and wife given 60 days to amend. Wife does not amend within that period of time but thereafter files second suit virtually identical to first. Second suit is barred by doctrine of res judicata.

1942—*McFarland v. McFarland,* 179 Va. 418, 19 S.E.2d 77.
Virginia decree denying husband divorce is res judicata as to subsequently obtained North Carolina decree.

1940—*McDaniel v. McDaniel,* 175 Va. 402, 9 S.E.2d 360.
Issues, parties and cause of action in present case were same as in prior case. Res judicata applied.

1935—*Wright v. Wright,* 164 Va. 245, 178 S.E. 884.
Identity of parties, identity of issues and issue decided by court of competent jurisdiction. Prior judgment from Virginia court that Nevada divorce decree was valid was res judicata.

1932—*Sussman v. Sussman,* 158 Va. 382, 163 S.E. 69.
Judgment of court of competent jurisdiction upon question directly involved in one suit is conclusive as to that question in another suit between same parties. Statement of opinion by court which was not preceded by words "It is adjudged, ordered and decreed" is in fact not judgment of court.

1930—*Gloth v. Gloth,* 154 Va. 511, 153 S.E. 879.
Decree of divorce a mensa for desertion is res judicata of fact of desertion and is bar to suit by other spouse for adultery committed after first decree.

1929—*Robinette v. Robinette,* 153 Va. 342, 149 S.E. 493.
In original suit parties charged each other with desertion. Claims denied. This was res judicata as to second suit for desertion.

1927—*McCotter v. Carle,* 149 Va. 584, 140 S.E. 670.
Divorced wife sued former husband for debt owed to her. Divorce decree did not award alimony and did not address property rights of parties. No res judicata. However, estoppel may apply where matter might have been litigated in prior case.

1925—*Humphreys v. Strong,* 141 Va. 146, 126 S.E. 194.

Wife obtained Nevada divorce decree. Nevada court decided that she was justified in leaving her husband and that there was no willful desertion or abandonment on her part. Virginia Supreme Court, in prior case, recognized validity of that judgment and, as such, it was binding with regard to present matter. There is nothing to suggest that Nevada decree was obtained by fraud.

1924—*Humphreys v. Strong,* 139 Va. 146, 123 S.E. 554.

Foreign decrees of divorce, obtained without fraud, upon constructive service, where no statute or public policy would be violated thereby, had been generally recognized by courts on grounds of comity.

1920—*Towson v. Towson,* 126 Va. 640, 102 S.E. 48.

Wife brought suit in D.C. for divorce on grounds of cruelty. Court in D.C. held that conduct of husband did not entitle wife to divorce. In Virginia case, this D.C. judgment is binding on parties, and wife cannot assert that her desertion is justified because of husband's cruelty.

1919—*Dagner v. Dagner,* 125 Va. 94, 99 S.E. 567.

In first suit, bill for desertion was denied, where complainant prayed for divorce from bonds of matrimony and stated that if absolute divorce was not granted then that divorce from bed and board should be granted. Decree denying that divorce necessarily decided that there had been no desertion prior to date on which suit was instituted. First decree was bar to second suit for divorce from bonds of matrimony for desertion instituted in less than three years from date of that first decree.

1917—*Gum v. Gum,* 122 Va. 32, 94 S.E. 177.

Decree of divorce suit extinguishing any right that wife has in property of husband which has never been reversed or annulled and which is within subject matter jurisdiction of court cannot be collaterally attacked in subsequent suit.

1916—*Craig v. Craig,* 118 Va. 284, 87 S.E. 727.

Husband sued for adultery. Wife filed answer which was treated as cross-bill alleging cruelty and desertion. Both claims were dismissed for insufficient evidence. Thereafter, wife brought new suit for divorce on grounds of cruelty and desertion which she alleged to have commenced three months before institution of husband's previous suit. She also alleged that, since decision in first suit, she had sought to reconcile with husband and he had refused. In order to determine whether plea of res judicata afforded defense, it was necessary to examine entire record in original suit. Plea of res judicata applies, except in special cases, not only to all matters actually adjudicated at former hearing but to every point which properly belonged to subject of litigation or which parties exercising reasonable diligence might have brought forward at time. Fact that wife did not present evidence in support of her charge of cruelty and desertion does not give her opportunity to relitigate that when that claim has been dismissed for insufficient evidence. Defense of res judicata was sustained.

1915—*Hairston v. Hairston,* 117 Va. 207, 84 S.E. 15.

In order that judgment in one suit shall be conclusive as to second suit, it must appear, either upon face of record or by extrinsic evidence that precise question was raised and determined in former suit. While extrinsic evidence is admissible to show identity of question, if there is any uncertainty as to that issue, whole matter is open to new contention. In this case, suit for divorce on grounds of desertion was dismissed apparently due to fact that three year period had not elapsed. Complainant is not barred from subsequently bringing another suit for same cause if desertion continues. If it appears in record that several distinct matters may have been litigated, upon one or more of which judgment was rendered, whole subject matter of action will be open to new contention unless uncertainty be removed by extrinsic evidence showing precise point determined.

1913—*Isaacs v. Isaacs,* 115 Va. 562, 79 S.E. 1072.

Virginia court granted divorce from bed and board. Kentucky court granted divorce among same parties from bonds of matrimony. Supreme court held that decree for alimony rendered by court in this state having full jurisdiction over parties and subject matter of suit, insofar as it affects rights of property established by said decree, cannot in any way be affected by decree rendered by court of another state in suit between same parties.

1895—*Miller v. Miller,* 92 Va. 196, 23 S.E. 232.

Defense of res judicata, made by answer, is sufficiently supported by production of record of former suit between same parties, touching same matter and showing final decree therein on merits.

§ 8-30. Settlement.

1955—*Nash v. Nash,* 197 Va. 465, 89 S.E.2d 917.

Letters of attorneys discussing resolution of matters were put into evidence.

§ 8-31. Service.

See Supreme Court Rule 2:4. In suit for divorce, defendant may not waive process.

See Supreme Court Rule 2:9. Sui juris defendant may accept service in suit for divorce or annulment by signing proof of service before any officer authorized to administer oaths. Service of process may not be waived but substituted service may be made.

See Va. Code § 8.01-293. Persons 18 or older who are not party or otherwise interested in subject matter are not eligible to serve process which commences divorce or annulment actions unless authorized to do so by circuit court.

Va. Code § 8.01-329 deals with service of process as to persons over whom court has jurisdiction pursuant to Virginia longarm statute.

See Va. Code § 20-99 indicating that process shall be served in this Commonwealth by any of methods prescribed in Va. Code § 8.01-296. Service may be made on non-resident by any person authorized to serve process in jurisdiction where non-resident resides.

See Va. Code § 20-99.1 as to how defendant may accept service.

See Va. Code § 20-104 as to order of publication against non-resident defendant.

See Va. Code § 20-112 indicating that when support proceedings are reopened notice shall be given by service of process or order of publication.

1984—*Mitchell v. Mitchell,* 227 Va. 31, 314 S.E.2d 45.

> Wife, while residing in Hawaii, was personally served with bill of complaint for divorce and failed to appear. Final divorce entered in Virginia. Va. Code § 8.01-322 provides that party served by publication who does not appear before date of judgment, is entitled to petition for rehearing within two years after judgment or within one year after being served with copy of judgment, whichever time is shorter. That statute did not apply here because wife was not served by publication, but instead was served in person.

1965—*Davis v. Davis,* 206 Va. 381, 143 S.E.2d 835.

> Husband contended that wife's notice of claim for child support did not comply with code since there was no order entered allowing such. Court noted that there was no necessity for entry of any such order.

1965—*Cofer v. Cofer,* 205 Va. 834, 140 S.E.2d 663.

> Husband petitioned court for reduction in amount of child support. By consent order, wife was given 10 days to answer petition. She did not do so and thereafter court entered order granting husband's petition. This order was void and should have been vacated on grounds that order was not endorsed by counsel for wife and also because notice was not given of time and place of presentation of order.

1962—*Mackey v. Mackey,* 203 Va. 526, 125 S.E.2d 194.

> In divorce case, record should affirmatively show that each procedural step is taken properly unless waived by party for whose benefit it is provided. If procedural requirement is not followed and it is not waived, record then shows, upon its face, defect which challenges authority of court to proceed with case. In all divorce cases except where defendant is proceeding against by order of publication or its equivalent, and defendant fails to appear, notice of taking depositions is required. It should affirmatively show from record that proper notice was served, accepted or waived. Record in this case did not show that and as such this was grounds for reversal.

1956—*Owens v. Owens,* 197 Va. 681, 90 S.E.2d 776.

> Non-resident respondent, upon whom copy of bill has been served and who does not appear within period allowed, is not entitled to notice of depositions unless court orders notice.

1952—*Baker v. Baker,* 194 Va. 284, 72 S.E.2d 632.

Purpose of notice requirement as to taking of deposition is to give opposing party opportunity to appear and cross-examine. Notice must be clear and explicit. Unless lack of notice or irregularity in notice to take depositions in divorce suit is waived by appearance, there must be proof of service or acceptance of service of proper notice.

1936—*Watson v. Mose,* 165 Va. 661, 183 S.E. 428.

Order of publication which shows that object of suit is to obtain divorce is insufficient to apprise defendant of determination of property rights.

1934—*Simpson v. Simpson,* 162 Va. 621, 175 S.E. 320.

All decrees entered against person upon order of publication are in sense provisional. If person is dead decree is nullity.

1934—*Bray v. Landergren,* 161 Va. 699, 172 S.E. 252.

Judgment for alimony which rests upon process executed out of state upon non-resident is invalid.

1932—*Taylor v. Taylor,* 159 Va. 338, 165 S.E. 414.

If service is by publication and statute is followed, divorce so procured is just as valid as if procured by personal service.

1925—*Scott v. Scott,* 142 Va. 31, 128 S.E. 599.

Purpose of process is to apprise party of nature of proceeding. If party makes general appearance in case, that constitutes waiver of such defect. Statute that prescribes that notice of deposition should be served only by officer does not prohibit defendant in divorce case from accepting legal service of notice to take depositions.

§ 8-32. Soldiers and Sailors Act.

1981—*Lackey v. Lackey,* 222 Va. 49, 278 S.E.2d 811.

Soldiers' and Sailors' Act authorizes trial court on its own motion to grant stay to those in military service and mandates granting of such stay upon application by one in military service unless in opinion of court ability of plaintiff to prosecute action or defendant to conduct his defense is not materially affected by reason of his military service. In this case defendant was on board naval ship and was unable to leave. Trial court should have granted him stay in this custody matter.

1945—*Williams v. Williams,* 184 Va. 124, 34 S.E.2d 378.

Under this act, one in military service is not entitled to stay of judgment against him as matter of law if, in opinion of court, ability of such person to comply with judgment is not materially affected by reason of his military service. Act is to be liberally construed to protect those in military. Absence when one's rights or liabilities are being adjudged is usually prima facie prejudicial. In present case, serviceman never was served with process and had no opportunity to be heard. Therefore decree entered must be reversed.

§ 8-33. Statutes.

1981—*Dorn v. Dorn,* 222 Va. 288, 279 S.E.2d 393.
> Rule 1:1 was not intended to limit and could not limit trial court's statutory authority under Va. Code § 8.01-428B. Constitution of Virginia prohibits promulgation of any court rule in conflict with general law established by general assembly.

1979—*Scott v. Sylvester,* 220 Va. 182, 257 S.E.2d 774.
> RURESA is remedial statute and is to be liberally construed.

1976—*Shoosmith v. Scott,* 217 Va. 290, 227 S.E.2d 729.
> Provision in property settlement agreement, confirmed by court, creates vested property rights in parties that cannot be impaired by subsequent retroactive legislation.

1974—*Paul v. Paul,* 214 Va. 651, 203 S.E.2d 123.
> Law in force on date of making contract determines rights of parties. New laws, except as to matters of remedy, are usually presumed to be prospective in operation.

1972—*Lovisi v. Commonwealth,* 212 Va. 848, 188 S.E.2d 206.
> Accused is entitled to strict construction of criminal statute. Words, however, are to be given their ordinary meaning unless it is apparent that legislative intent is otherwise.

1965—*Hagen v. Hagen,* 205 Va. 791, 139 S.E.2d 821.
> Husband filed suit on no-fault grounds after passage of no-fault statute. Wife contended that three-year separation period required by statute could not begin to run until date of passage of statute. Court disagreed. It noted that there can be no doubt that legislature possesses power to enact retrospective legislation and generally it is valid if legislative intent is plainly manifest and if statute does not have effect of impairing obligation of contract and is not destructive of vested rights.

1955—*Naim v. Naim,* 197 Va. 80, 87 S.E.2d 749.
> Issue was whether miscegenation statute was valid. Inquiry must be whether, considering end in view statute passes bounds of reason and assumes character of merely arbitrary fiat. Statute valid.

1952—*Furey v. Furey,* 193 Va. 727, 71 S.E.2d 191.
> Statutes in derogation of common law are to be strictly construed and read as if common law remained unchanged unless purpose to change it appears expressly or by necessary implication.

1952—*Morris v. Henry,* 193 Va. 631, 70 S.E.2d 417.
> Remedial statutes are to be liberally construed.

1948—*Henderson v. Henderson,* 187 Va. 121, 46 S.E.2d 10.
> Statutes remedial in nature are to be liberally construed.

1946—*Fletcher v. Flanary,* 185 Va. 409, 38 S.E.2d 433.

Right to adopt children was unknown in common law and as such it is not in derogation of common law. Therefore adoption statutes are to be liberally construed.

1940—*Eaton v. Davis,* 176 Va. 330, 10 S.E.2d 893.

Retroactive legislation is valid if legislative intent is plainly manifest that statute is to have retroactive effect and if statute does not have effect of impairing obligation of contract and is not destructive of vested rights. Statutes will be construed wherever possible so as to avoid constitutional questions.

1939—*Bailey v. Bailey,* 172 Va. 18, 200 S.E. 622.

Remedial statute to be liberally construed.

1935—*Capell v. Capell,* 164 Va. 45, 178 S.E. 894.

Laws to subserve general welfare cannot be abrogated by private agreement.

1934—*Simpson v. Simpson,* 162 Va. 621, 175 S.E. 320.

Words in statute are to be given their usual meaning. Where meaning of words is doubtful then legislative intent should be looked at. Intent is to be found from content, from occasion and necessity of law, from mischief felt and remedy in view. Construction of statute must be to avoid absurd.

1933—*Indemnity Insurance Company v. Nalls,* 160 Va. 246, 168 S.E. 346.

In construing statute chief concern of court is to ascertain intention of legislature. Statute will not be construed as changing common law rule beyond what is expressly stated or necessarily implied and in doubtful cases presumption is that no change was intended.

1928—*Goodman v. Goodman,* 150 Va. 42, 142 S.E. 412.

Remedial statutes are to be liberally construed.

1923—*Heflinger v. Heflinger,* 136 Va. 289, 118 S.E. 316.

Statute in question was new one and language used in it is different from that of statutes of other states on subject, which had been construed by their appellate courts. It may be assumed that revisors of statute had some knowledge of those other statutes and of their construction and intended to propose to legislature to enact something different from statutes of those other states.

1920—*Hoover v. Hoover,* 131 Va. 522, 105 S.E. 91.

Intent of legislature is to be sought primarily in language used in statute. If this is plain then court must give effect to it.

1908—*Moreland v. Moreland,* 108 Va. 93, 60 S.E. 730.

In construing contract made in another state, if there is no proof as to what law of other State is, it will be presumed to be same as law of this State.

1902—*Offield v. Davis,* 100 Va. 250, 40 S.E. 910.

> Statute in this case abrogating common law marriages is clear and is mandatory. When strict letter of statute leaves doubt as to what is meant or intended, legislative intent is to be gathered from act read as whole, from occasion and necessity of law, from mischief felt and remedy in view.

§ 8-34. Trial.

See Va. Code § 20-106 indicating that in any suit for divorce trial court may require whole or any part of testimony to be given orally in open court and, if either party desires it, such testimony and rulings of court on exceptions thereto, if any, shall be reduced to writing, and judge shall certify that such evidence was given before him and such rulings made.

1952—*Fulton v. Fulton,* 193 Va. 255, 68 S.E.2d 485.

> Whether or not evidence in chancery cause will be heard orally before court rests is in discretion of trial court.

§ 8-35. Venue.

1983—*Rochelle v. Rochelle,* 225 Va. 387, 302 S.E.2d 59.

> Where defendant neither objects to venue within 21 days of service nor takes exception to court's venue ruling at trial, then he waives his right to object. Venue for child custody claim lies in jurisdiction where children are physically present.

1963—*Colley v. Colley,* 204 Va. 225, 129 S.E.2d 630.

> Statute which provides that suit for divorce shall be brought in county where parties last cohabited or at plaintiff's option, where defendant resides, is mandatory and jurisdictional.

Index

S

T

V

W

VIRGINIA DOMESTIC RELATIONS CASE FINDER

1990 CUMULATIVE SUPPLEMENT

Containing capsulizations of pertinent cases through
238 Va. 748, and 9 Va. App. 162 and legislative
changes effective as of July 1, 1989

Brien A. Roche

*Member of Virginia
and District of Columbia
Bars*

**Place this supplement in the pocket
of the bound volume**

THE MICHIE COMPANY
Law Publishers
CHARLOTTESVILLE, VIRGINIA

CHAPTER 1

MARRIAGE

§ 1-2. Ceremonial Marriages.

1988—*In re Application of Jack Ginsburg,* 236 Va. 165.
   Quaker clerk meets definition of minister and should have been granted license to celebrate marriage.

§ 1-4. Common Law Marriage.

1989—*Murphy v. Holland,* 237 Va. 212, 377 S.E.2d 363.
   Common law marriages contracted in this state not recognized. Offspring of such relationship, however, may be legitimate.

§ 1-8. Validity of Marriage.

1988—*Kleinfield v. Veruki,* 7 Va. App. 183.
   Validity of marriage is based on where marriage took place unless repugnant to public policy of Virginia. Marriage entered into prior to dissolution of previous marriage is void, not just voidable, irrespective of the good faith of the parties. In this case marriage was bigamous, therefore void. As such, court had no authority to award support, although court's refusal to order reimbursement for pendente lite support and attorney's fees was within discretion of trial court.

1986—*Petachenko v. Petachenko,* 232 Va. 296, 350 S.E.2d 600.
   Matrimonial cohabitation consists of more than sexual relations. It also imports continuing condition of living together and carrying out mutual responsibilities of marital relationship.

CHAPTER 2

TERMINATION OF THE MARRIAGE

§ 2-2. Corroboration.

1986—*Collier v. Collier,* 2 Va. App. 125, 341 S.E.2d 827.
Where it is apparent there is no collusion, then corroboration need only be slight.

§ 2-4. Divorce — Grounds.

(A) Adultery.

See Va. Code § 8.01-223.1 stating that exercise of constitutional protection shall not be used against civil litigant.

1989—*Cutlip v. Cutlip,* 8 Va. App. 618.
Although husband began to spend long hours away from home and lied to wife as to whereabouts on particular evening when in fact he was with his girlfriend, there was no evidence that husband was alone with girlfriend at any time during this period. Evidence is insufficient to establish adultery.

1989—*Lassen v. Lassen,* 8 Va. App. 502.
Wife contends that trial court erred in granting her divorce on grounds of desertion alone when grounds also existed for cruelty and adultery. Where multiple grounds for divorce exist, trial court can use sound discretion to select grounds upon which it will grant divorce.

1989—*Derby v. Derby,* 8 Va. App. 19, 378 S.E.2d 74.
Private investigator testified that wife and other man spent several nights together and engaged in public displays of affection, sufficient to establish adultery. Post-separation adultery may be basis for divorce. Grounds of divorce need not have caused deterioration. It need only be legal requirement which legislature has recognized.

1988—*Pommerenke v. Pommerenke,* 7 Va. App. 241.
Where there is no collusion, the corroboration need only be slight. The corroborative testimony need not be sufficient to prove the grounds for a divorce. In this case wife admitted adultery. There was no collusion. Therefore to prevail on adultery claim, husband need only present slight corroboration. This was established through evidence of topless sunbathing with lover and lover found naked in wife's home.

1988—*Thompson v. Thompson,* 6 Va. App. 277, 367 S.E.2d 747.
Investigator testified that alleged paramour entered wife's apartment in evening. Investigator taped the front door but not the back door. Investigator saw no one leave apartment from 10:10 p.m. to 6:45 a.m. the next morning. The record contains other relevant evidence: wife

3

and paramour held themselves out as husband and wife, paramour had telephone at apartment in his name and he had mailbox key. This was sufficient to justify finding of adultery.

1987—*Davis v. Davis*, 233 Va. 452, 357 S.E.2d 495.
Husband refused to testify in post-divorce proceeding between parties, asserting Fifth Amendment privilege. Because of this court struck his counterclaim. Reversed. Without citing Va. Code § 8.01-223.1, Court held that refusal to testify must be about issues pertinent to pleadings in order to justify striking those pleadings.

1987—*Seemann v. Seemann*, 233 Va. 290, 355 S.E.2d 884.
Adultery must be proved by clear and convincing evidence. Testimony of hired detective should be carefully scrutinized and acted on with great caution. Clear and convincing evidence is more than preponderance but less than beyond reasonable doubt. It does not mean clear and unequivocal. Evidence showed that wife and male companion had spent several nights together in same bedroom. They denied they had had intercourse and cited religious beliefs to confirm there had been no sex. This was credibility question and trial court believed wife. Wife was not guilty of adultery.

1986—*Dodge v. Dodge*, 2 Va. App. 238, 343 S.E.2d 363.
Evidence of adultery must be clear and convincing. In this case, wife relied on statement by husband and independent proof that husband was living with another woman. This was sufficient corroboration to prove adultery.

1985—*Wallace v. Wallace*, 1 Va. App. 183, 336 S.E.2d 27.
Wife took Fifth Amendment as to questions relating to her conduct for one-year period prior to hearing. Statute of limitation is one year. This was upheld since evidence showed that husband's fault was cause of divorce and therefore even if wife was guilty of adultery she could have successfully pled recrimination.

(B) Constructive Desertion.

(2) MISCELLANEOUS.

1986—*Byrd v. Byrd*, 232 Va. 115, 348 S.E.2d 262.
Wife not guilty of desertion in separating while divorce suit pending if suit not frivolous and was not instituted as sham to shield complainant from charge of desertion. In this case, wife was not able to prove her claim for divorce but court found suit not frivolous and not in bad faith.

1986—*Zinkhan v. Zinkhan*, 2 Va. App. 200, 342 S.E.2d 658.
Desertion may be constructive, for cruelty by one party which results in other party's enforced separation is tantamount to desertion. Desertion in this case means leaving marital relationship. The cruelty involved must be extreme and entirely subversive of family relationship.

1986—*Brawand v. Brawand*, 1 Va. App. 305, 338 S.E.2d 651.
Husband's request during arguments that wife "get out" does not support constructive desertion claim. The evidence in this case, although

showing some violent behavior by husband, does not establish cruelty amounting to constructive desertion.

(C) Cruelty.

(3) PHYSICAL ABUSE.

1989—*Davis v. Davis*, 8 Va. App. 12, 377 S.E.2d 640.
Husband shoots wife. Husband guilty of cruelty. A single act may constitute cruelty if it is so severe and atrocious as to endanger life, if it indicates intent to do serious bodily harm, if it causes reasonable apprehension of serious danger in future, or if prior or present circumstances show that acts are likely to be repeated. Conduct constituting cruelty occurring after separation may be grounds for divorce.

1986—*McLaughlin v. McLaughlin*, 2 Va. App. 463, 346 S.E.2d 535.
Wife alleged that when she mentioned divorce to husband he ordered her from bedroom; that he angrily broke chair in her presence; he physically removed her from son's bedroom; that he ripped comic pages from her hand; he broke in door; that he closed joint account; he threw her breakfast against wall when she refused to cook for him. Husband had mitigating explanation for all of these acts. Evidence supports trial court conclusion that wife did not prove cruelty.

1986—*Venable v. Venable*, 2 Va. App. 178, 342 S.E.2d 646.
Husband admitted acts of violence towards wife. Physical evidence and testimony from another witness were sufficient to establish cruelty.

(D) Desertion.

(1) ELEMENTS.

1988—*Dexter v. Dexter*, 7 Va. App. 36.
Elements: (1) actual breaking off of marital cohabitation; (2) intent to desert in mind of offender. Marital cohabitation consists of more than sexual relations. It includes the mutual responsibility of the marriage. A mere denial of sex is not desertion. Desertion may occur within home where there is wilfull breach and neglect of significant marital duties in addition to sexual relations resulting in practical destruction of home life and rendering marriage intolerable. Separation by mutual consent is not desertion.

1987—*Sprott v. Sprott*, 233 Va. 238, 355 S.E.2d 881.
Although general rule that one spouse is not justified in leaving other unless conduct of other is sufficient to establish foundation of judicial proceeding for divorce has been relaxed in other cases (cases cited, 233 Va. at 241-42, 355 S.E.2d at 822-83), gradual breakdown in relationship does not justify departure.

1987—*Jamison v. Jamison*, 3 Va. App. 644, 352 S.E.2d 719.
Parties remained under same roof. Cessation of sex for five years and wife's breach and neglect of other marital duties in this case constituted willful desertion.

1986—*Petachenko v. Petachenko,* 232 Va. 296, 350 S.E.2d 600.

Desertion is actual breaking off of matrimonial cohabitation coupled with intent to desert. Once separation and intent have been established, desertion is presumed to continue until contrary is shown. To end desertion parties must resume marital cohabitation with intent to end desertion.

1986—*Brawand v. Brawand,* 1 Va. App. 305, 338 S.E.2d 651.

Desertion consists of (1) breaking of matrimonial cohabitation, (2) an intent to desert in mind of offender. In the absence of evidence to show justification or excuse for leaving, wife would be guilty of desertion as intent would be inferred. Justification may be established even though this evidence not sufficient to award divorce to departing spouse. If wife leaves house due to reasonable belief that health or wellbeing is endangered by remaining and prior to leaving she has taken whatever measures might be expected to eliminate concern then her departure is justified. Burden of proof as to justification rests on departing spouse.

(2) In General.

1987—*Sprott v. Sprott,* 233 Va. 238, 355 S.E.2d 881.

Wife's suit for divorce on desertion and cruelty grounds was found to be attempt by wife to justify departure and not jeopardize claim for alimony. Mere filing of suit in this case did not justify departure. Wife was found guilty of desertion and alimony was barred.

1987—*Wagner v. Wagner,* 4 Va. App. 397, 358 S.E.2d 407.

When separation is by agreement or with assent, there is no desertion.

1987—*Graves v. Graves,* 4 Va. App. 326, 357 S.E.2d 554.

When wife left house, she took only purse and jacket with her. She tried to return next day and when she did, fight ensued with husband. She made statement to daughter that she may or may not return. This is insufficient to establish clear intent to desert.

1986—*Bacon v. Bacon,* 3 Va. App. 484, 351 S.E.2d 37.

Standard of proof in desertion case is preponderance of evidence.

1986—*Collier v. Collier,* 2 Va. App. 125, 341 S.E.2d 827.

Husband left home and left note saying why he was leaving. Desertion established.

1986—*Rexrode v. Rexrode,* 1 Va. App. 385, 339 S.E.2d 544.

Wife entered psychiatric hospital and while confined filed suit for divorce for constructive desertion. Court held wife guilty of desertion since no evidence that husband made hospitalization necessary. And no evidence that wife exercised reasonable efforts to eliminate undesirable conduct by husband. Wife's claim for alimony is barred.

1985—*McGinnis v. McGinnis,* 1 Va. App. 272, 338 S.E.2d 159.

Wife alleged desertion. Husband said that separation was at wife's request. He alleged abusive and assaultive behavior by wife. Trial court's determination that desertion has not been established by wife is affirmed.

(3) MARITAL HOME — CHOICE OF.

1988—*Kerr v. Kerr,* 6 Va. App. 620, 371 S.E.2d 30.
In this case wife justified in not accompanying husband when he was transferred to another city. Prior case law held that husband had right to select place of abode and wife must acquiesce. Wife's constitutional challenge is deferred because spouse may be justified in not acquiescing in some cases. Justification arises where conduct of other spouse has caused conditions to be intolerable. The outmoded expectation that wife must follow husband is no longer applicable.

(E) No Fault.

1987—*Graves v. Graves,* 4 Va. App. 326, 357 S.E.2d 554.
Commissioner's hearing took place less than one year after date of separation. No fault divorce must be denied.

1986—*Dukelow v. Dukelow,* 2 Va. App. 21, 341 S.E.2d 208.
In this case, court could find no benefit to either party to have no fault divorce awarded to wife as opposed to husband.

§ 2-5. Divorce — Jurisdiction.

(B) Subject Matter.

See Va. Code § 20-96 permitting the court where the action was commenced to, for a good cause, transfer the action to any forum in the Commonwealth in which the action could have been brought.

1988—*Rock v. Rock,* 7 Va. App. 198.
Venue is jurisdictional in divorce case. Place of last cohabitation is where parties ceased to live together as husband and wife. This is not place where they last had sex but refers to place where they last dwelled together. Domicile contemplates living in a place with intent to remain there. Domicile and cohabitation are distinctly different concepts. Cohabitation is determined solely by the location where people reside. Domicile is based on residence and intent. In this case the parties had two residences in Virginia. They last cohabited at their Richmond residence and therefore that court had jurisdiction.

1986—*Netzer v. Reynolds,* 231 Va. 444, 345 S.E.2d 291.
Venue statutes are mandatory and jurisdictional. Final decree in this case stated parties last cohabitated in another county. In fact they last cohabited in the county of forum court since the word "cohabit" carries with it idea of substantial measure of temporal continuity. Court had the authority to correct this error in decree since there was sufficient record evidence to support change.

1985—*Parra v. Parra,* 1 Va. App. 118, 335 S.E.2d 157.
In divorce suits, jurisdiction is purely statutory and cannot be acquired. Court may expressly reserve jurisdiction to address equitable distribution or modification of support after entry of final decree.

§ 2-7. Divorce — Defenses.

(B) Condonation.

1989—*Cutlip v. Cutlip,* 8 Va. App. 618.
Condonation is remission of offense of which one party knows other has committed during marriage, on condition of being continually thereafter treated by other with conjugal kindness. Conjugal kindness requires that guilty spouse shall not only refrain from repetition of offense forgiven but shall also refrain from committing any other offense which falls within cognizance of matrimonial accord. Condoned adultery is revived where guilty party resumes association with paramour. Although revival does not require strict proof of actual repetition of offense, evidence presented in this case was insufficient to revive previously forgiven act of adultery. While husband's behaviour may create suspicion of guilt, it is also not inconsistent with his innocence.

1986—*Petachenko v. Petachenko,* 232 Va. 296, 350 S.E.2d 600.
Single act of sexual intercourse after desertion does not constitute condonation. Result may be different under Va. Code § 20-94 in regards to adultery claim.

1986—*Byrd v. Byrd,* 232 Va. 115, 348 S.E.2d 262.
Condonation must be specially pleaded and proved. Single act of sex may be condonation. Where guilty party has solicited sex and thereafter shows no intent to reform, such an act may be insufficient to qualify as condonation.

(E) Justification.

1988—*Reid v. Reid,* 7 Va. App. 553.
Breaking off of cohabitation with intent to desert constitutes desertion. Gradual breakdown in marriage does not justify leaving. The gradual breakdown was evidenced by sexual inactivity, husband's excessive work, husband's failure to assist in child rearing, and lack of intimacy in the marriage. These combined factors did not justify wife in leaving.

1988—*Seehorn v. Seehorn,* 7 Va. App. 375.
Where party who leaves relies on defense of justification he has burden of going forward to show that misconduct so serious as to make marital relation intolerable. There was evidence of excessive alcohol consumption in this case but that did not justify departure.

1988—*Kerr v. Kerr,* 6 Va. App. 620, 371 S.E.2d 30.
Justification for leaving arises when conduct of other spouse has caused conditions in home to become intolerable. Party may be justified in

leaving even if grounds of divorce do not exist and may do so without committing desertion. Justification exists when spouse's conduct creates conduct so intolerable that other spouse cannot reasonably be expected to remain. This is so even if conduct of departing spouse contributed to difficulties so long as other spouse's conduct is disproportionate to any provocation.

1987—*Seemann v. Seemann,* 233 Va. 290, 355 S.E.2d 884.
Verbal and physical abuse in this case was sufficient to justify wife's departure. Even though this conduct by husband may not be sufficient basis for fault grounds, it is sufficient to justify departure.

1986—*Zinkhan v. Zinkhan,* 2 Va. App. 200, 342 S.E.2d 658.
To constitute defense to husband's prima facie showing of desertion, wife must prove misconduct of husband to constitute ground for divorce. Such conduct must be foundation of judicial proceeding for divorce. Wife's complaints in this case were that he wanted sex too frequently, fished too frequently, and he "hammered" on her asking her to get out. No specific dates or occasions were shown and there was no complaint concerning this in immediate time frame of separation. Justification not established.

1986—*D'Auria v. D'Auria,* 1 Va. App. 455, 340 S.E.2d 164.
Burden of proof rests on party asserting justification for leaving marital home. Wife is free from legal fault in leaving when she reasonably believes her health is endangered and she has unsuccessfully tried less drastic measures. Wife's doctor, in this case, testified that wife's physical problems were result of anxiety in contemplation of divorce. They were not sufficient to establish justification.

(F) Laches.

1989—*Murphy v. Holland,* 237 Va. 212, 377 S.E.2d 363.
Determination of whether laches bars claim is within sound discretion of court. To bar claim, there must be showing of intention to abandon claim and delay must be unreasonable and injurious to other party.

(I) Recrimination.

1989—*Davis v. Davis,* 8 Va. App. 12, 377 S.E.2d 640.
Recrimination exists where applicant has himself done what is grounds for divorce. Under § 20-117 grounds of divorce from bed and board will not bar any ground otherwise justifying divorce from bonds of matrimony. In this case, husband's cruelty bars wife's suit for willful desertion and wife's desertion bars her claim for cruelty. Therefore, only ground available is one year separation.

1989—*Derby v. Derby,* 8 Va. App. 19, 378 S.E.2d 74.
Fault grounds are no basis for recrimination defense to no fault divorce.

1987—*Surbey v. Surbey,* 5 Va. App. 119, 360 S.E.2d 873.
Recrimination bars plaintiff's suit founded on whatever cause, whether defendant is guilty or not. Court found both parties at fault in causing

separation and both guilty of post-separation adultery. Because of this, fault grounds for divorce were barred as to both parties. On this record, court was justified in awarding spousal support to wife.

1986—*Venable v. Venable,* 2 Va. App. 178, 342 S.E.2d 646.
Wife testified to adulterous activity on her part subsequent to separation. There was no corroboration and recrimination was not pleaded. Recrimination bars granting divorce where complainant's own conduct constitutes grounds for divorce. Recrimination is not bar in this case.

1985—*Wallace v. Wallace,* 1 Va. App. 183, 336 S.E.2d 27.
Fault of husband caused breakdown of marriage. If wife was guilty of adultery after separation she could have pleaded recrimination which would have prevented husband from obtaining fault divorce.

CHAPTER 3

CHILDREN

§ 3-1. Adoption.

1989—*NPA v. WBA*, 8 Va. App. 246, 380 S.E.2d 178.
Adoption in Virginia is solely creature of statute. Virginia does not recognize common law adoption.

1987—*Frye v. Spotte*, 4 Va. App. 530, 359 S.E.2d 315.
Stepfather attempted to adopt children of his wife. Wife joined in petition. Adoption and termination of natural father's rights found to be in best interest of children. Natural father in this case deserted family, provided little support, maintained only minimal contact, and previously neglected and abused children. Termination of parental right was found upon clear and convincing evidence to be in child's best interest. Adoption in such instance must be in best interest of child, and continuation of relationship with non-consenting parent must be detrimental to child's welfare.

1986—*Division of Social Servs. v. Unknown Father*, 2 Va. App. 420, 345 S.E.2d 533.
Parent who has not reached 18 has legal capacity to give consent to adoption. Such agreement may be revoked prior to final adoption and rights of natural parent may be restored upon proof that consent was obtained by fraud or duress.

§ 3-2. Custody.

(A) Criteria.

(1) IN GENERAL.

1985—*Roe v. Roe*, 228 Va. 722, 324 S.E.2d 691.
Child's best interests are not promoted by award of custody to parent who carries on active homosexual relationship in same residence as child. Father's continuous exposure of child to his immoral and illicit relationship renders him unfit as a matter of law.

1984—*Armistead v. Armistead*, 228 Va. 352, 322 S.E.2d 836.
In this custody dispute, court held that prior agreement as to temporary custody does not have any estoppel effect. Since relevant evidence was not considered by trial court, it would make no sense for appellate court to review evidence; instead case will be remanded.

(2) FAULT.

1986—*Venable v. Venable*, 2 Va. App. 178, 342 S.E.2d 646.
Wife admitted to adulterous conduct after separation. Wife and her lover were often in presence of children although there was no evidence of improper conduct in presence of children. Custody to wife.

1985—*Brinkley v. Brinkley*, 1 Va. App. 222, 336 S.E.2d 901.
Evidence of adultery without more evidence of improper conduct is insufficient basis to find parent unfit. Extent to which child is exposed to illicit relationship must be given most careful consideration.

(4) TENDER YEARS.

1986—*Visikides v. Derr*, 3 Va. App. 69, 348 S.E.2d 40.
As between parents there is no presumption or inference in favor of either.

(5) WISHES OF CHILD.

1985—*Patrick v. Byerly*, 228 Va. 691, 325 S.E.2d 99.
Although wishes of child are not controlling, court gave weight to his preference.

(B) Divided Custody.

See Va. Code § 20-107.2 Allowing Joint Custody.
It may be joint legal custody, joint physical custody, or both.

1986—*Box v. Talley*, 1 Va. App. 289, 338 S.E.2d 349.
Circuit court in trial de novo approved joint custody arrangement where child stayed with mother during school year and with father during summer.

(C) Grandparents.

1986—*Ferris v. Underwood*, 3 Va. App. 25, 348 S.E.2d 18.
Presumption favors natural parents. Custody had been previously given to grandparent by court order. Natural parents retained visitation rights and did not relinquish their natural parental rights. This was not an order of divestiture, therefore presumption still works to advantage of natural parents. Both mother and grandmother were found to be fit. In light of this presumption custody was given to mother.

1986—*Division of Social Servs. v. Unknown Father*, 2 Va. App. 420, 345 S.E.2d 533.
Grandparents may intervene in child custody proceedings but they may not assert that mother entered into custody agreement under duress when mother makes no such contention.

(E) Jurisdiction.

1988—*Peple v. Peple,* 5 Va. App. 414, 364 S.E.2d 232.

Filing of suit for divorce in which custody is an issue divests juvenile court of jurisdiction, although it may enforce its prior orders until circuit court enters order on custody. If circuit court asked to modify prior juvenile court order, then it need not conduct de novo hearing. Proper standard in this case is change in circumstances.

(F) Leaving Jurisdiction.

1986—*Scinaldi v. Scinaldi,* 2 Va. App. 571, 347 S.E.2d 149.

Determination of whether child may be removed from jurisdiction must be based on child's best interest. Several factors to be considered: can benefit of relationship with non-custodial parent continue if child is removed from state; likelihood non-custodial parent being transferred; children's development in new area; motivation for move. In this case mother allowed to move to New York with children to be near her parents.

1986—*Simmons v. Simmons,* 1 Va. App. 358, 339 S.E.2d 198.

Mother sought to move to Florida with four children. This move was not motivated by spite. The move offered educational and training opportunities to wife and possibility of more stable life for children. There was no question of unfitness of parents therefore primary criteria is best interest of children. Move to Florida allowed.

1985—*Gray v. Gray,* 228 Va. 696, 324 S.E.2d 677.

Before court permits custodial parent to remove child from Virginia it must determine that removal is in best interest of child.

(G) Modification of Custody.

See Va. Code § 20-108 providing that no support order may be retroactively modified, but may be modified during the period in which a petition for modification is pending.

1988—*Peple v. Peple,* 5 Va. App. 414, 364 S.E.2d 232.

Change in circumstance test is correct test for modification. It must also be shown that modification is in best interest of child. The factors: (1) circumstances of two parents as they affect children; (2) which parent better qualified to provide highest quality of care; and (3) which home will provide child with greatest opportunity to fulfill potential.

1986—*Visikides v. Derr,* 3 Va. App. 69, 348 S.E.2d 40.

Two tests: material change in circumstance, and whether change is in best interest of child. This change may take form of negative change or positive change in either parent's circumstance. In this case, there was positive change as to non-custodial wife who had since remarried and now was able to stay home with child where formerly she had not been able to do so. This satisfied first test. Since trial court applied tender years inference, case remanded.

1986—*Turner v. Turner,* 3 Va. App. 31, 348 S.E.2d 21.
Since Judge trying this case was not same one as tried the previous custody matter, he was justified in taking evidence of prior conditions so that he had adequate background information. In motion to change custody, two tests apply: change in circumstance; would change be in best interest of child. This first test has been met where non-custodial parent shows that remarriage has stabilized, child has undergone changes and has expressed prejudice to be with non-custodial parent. Best interest of child in this case was found to justify change of custody due to child's desire to live with mother and opinions of psychologists showing her psychological need to do so.

(H) Natural Parents.

1988—*Edwards v. County of Arlington,* 5 Va. App. 294, 361 S.E.2d 644.
The facts did not support finding that mother's illness was sufficiently severe to allow Department of Human Services to invoke presumption of Va. Code § 16.1-283(B)(2)(a). Circumstances are rare where termination will be allowed. Department must prove: (1) termination in best interest of child; (2) neglect or abuse presents serious and substantial threat to life, health or development; and (3) not reasonably likely that conditions can be substantially corrected or eliminated.

1988—*Rader v. Montgomery County,* 5 Va. App. 523, 365 S.E.2d 234.
Court lacked jurisdiction to terminate parental right because no custody petition had been filed.

1987—*Smith v. Pond,* 5 Va. App. 161, 360 S.E.2d 885.
Evidence in this case did not establish by clear and convincing evidence special facts and circumstances to justify granting custody to non-parent. Law presumes that best interest of child served by custody with natural parents. Presumption is rebuttable if there is clear and convincing evidence that: (1) parents are unfit; (2) court previously granted order of divestiture; (3) parents voluntarily relinquished custody; (4) abandonment has occurred; (5) special facts and circumstances constitute extraordinary reason to take child from parents. Once presumption has been rebutted, then parents have burden of proving custody with them is in best interest of child.

1986—*Lowe v. Department of Public Welfare,* 231 Va. 277, 343 S.E.2d 70.
Before parental rights can be terminated under § 16.1-283(B), court must find by clear and convincing evidence that termination is in child's best interest, neglect and abuse present serious and substantial threat to life, health or development, not reasonably likely that condition can be corrected in reasonable time. These conditions were met here.

1986—*Bailes v. Sours,* 231 Va. 96, 340 S.E.2d 824.
Presumption favoring parent over non-parent is strong but it may be overcome by clear and convincing evidence of: (1) unfitness, (2) previous

order of divestiture, (3) voluntary relinquishment, (4) abandonment, (5) finding of special facts and circumstances constituting extraordinary reason for taking child from parent. In this case, evidence showed mother was stranger to her son. The child preferred to stay with his stepmother, change of custody to mother would be harmful. Presumption is not in any way weakened in this case, but here presumption has been overcome.

1986—*Department of Social Servs. v. Unnamed Mother,* 3 Va. App. 40, 348 S.E.2d 26.
Unmarried natural father has parental rights which must be considered and dealt with by due process means. Both father and child should have opportunity to determine what, if any, relationship is desired before termination of parental rights.

1986—*Martin v. Department of Social Servs.,* 3 Va. App. 15, 348 S.E.2d 13.
Where prior order has formally divested mother of custody, burden rests on mother to show change of circumstance by clear and convincing evidence that return of child would be in child's best interests.

1986—*Barkey v. Commonwealth,* 2 Va. App. 662, 347 S.E.2d 188.
In determining best interest of child, court should consider: age and condition of parent and child; relationship between them; needs of child; role of each parent and such other factors as bear on child's best interest. Social Services in this case gave mother fair opportunity to change circumstance. Parental rights terminated.

1986—*Robinette v. Keene,* 2 Va. App. 578, 347 S.E.2d 156.
Where no question of fitness of parent and parent has not by conduct or previous legal action lost his rights to child then it must be shown that continuance of the relationship would be detrimental to child.

1986—*Banes v. Department of Social Servs.,* 1 Va. App. 463, 339 S.E.2d 902.
Burden on party seeking to terminate parental rights to prove by clear and convincing evidence that such is in best interest of child. Burden was met in this case based on consistent pattern of neglect and unwillingness to change.

1985—*James v. James,* 230 Va. 51, 334 S.E.2d 551.
Fit parent with suitable home has right to custody of his child superior to rights of others. To overcome this presumption, the evidence of unfitness must be cogent and convincing. This presumption may be overcome by proof of unfitness, voluntary relinquishment or abandonment. In this case because of open hostility of parties, trial court awarded custody to grandparents. This was insufficient basis to deprive parents of custody.

1985—*Patrick v. Byerly,* 228 Va. 691, 325 S.E.2d 99.
Child's welfare is paramount consideration. This rule subject to exception that fit parent with suitable home has right to custody superior to rights of others in which case law presumes that child's best interests will be served in custody of parent. Opposing party has burden of prov-

ing abandonment or unfitness by clear and convincing evidence. In this case, mother abandoned child and court found that best interests of child were served by awarding custody to stepmother.

(I) Visitation.

See Va. Code § 18.2-49.1 as to parental abduction in violation of custody or visitation order.

1987—*Robinson v. Robinson,* 5 Va. App. 222, 361 S.E.2d 356.
In fixing visitation court must consider those factors specifically enumerated by Va. Code § 20-107.2. Commissioner in Chancery granted mother visitation with children at her home in Arizona where she lived with other man, provided that this man was not present during visitation. Trial court then restricted visitation to Virginia. Trial court was held to be in error since it did not give consideration to statutory factors as did Commissioner.

1986—*Fariss v. Tsapel,* 3 Va. App. 439, 350 S.E.2d 670.
Termination of visitation rights was reversed due to lack of reasonable notice, insufficient evidence of change of circumstance, and improper admission of testimony as to condition of father's residence at time of entry of initial visitation decree. Making motion for first time during hearing was insufficient notice.

1986—*M.E.D. v. J.P.M.,* 3 Va. App. 391, 350 S.E.2d 215.
Best interest of child is criteria. Parental sexual abuse would indicate that visitation by that parent may not be in best interest of child. Here, there is extensive discussion of child abuse allegations and how to deal with them.

1986—*Eichelberger v. Eichelberger,* 2 Va. App. 409, 345 S.E.2d 10.
Custodial parent sought to prohibit father from allowing child to use trail bike during visitation. In absence of finding of danger to child, custodial parent has no right to restrict visitation activities when award has been liberal visitation privileges.

§ 3-4. Parent — Child.

(B) In Loco Parentis.

1989—*NPA v. WBA,* 8 Va. App. 246, 380 S.E.2d 178.
Theory of in loco parentis provides that stepparent or one who knowingly, voluntarily assumes role of parent to child may obtain certain legally recognizable rights and obligations but only so long as relationship continues to exist.

(D) Paternity.

1987—*Florence v. Roberts,* 233 Va. 297, 355 S.E.2d 316.
The standard of proof as to paternity is beyond reasonable doubt whether the proceeding is civil or criminal.

1987—*Commonwealth v. Harrison,* 5 Va. App. 8, 360 S.E.2d 212.
Result of HLA test is admissible upon being offered by properly qualified expert without testimonial identification of blood samples by person who took blood.

1986—*Marks v. Sanzo,* 231 Va. 350, 345 S.E.2d 263.
Suit by child to recover benefits under Retirement Fund. Statements by putative father acknowledging child is logical and satisfactory way of resolving issue.

1985—*Buckland v. Commonwealth,* 229 Va. 290, 329 S.E.2d 803.
Paternity established based on blood test, evidence of access, and admissions of father.

1985—*Jones v. Robinson,* 229 Va. 276, 329 S.E.2d 794.
It is unconstitutional for state to give legitimate children judicially enforceable right to support while denying such to illegitimate children. Pre-1982 § 20-61.1 is unconstitutional because it allowed illegitimate children to prove paternity only by showing father lived with mother or acknowledged child. Although it may be permissible to impose a standard of proof different than preponderance, it is impermissible to so severely restrict admissible evidence as this statute did.

1985—*Hankerson v. Moody,* 229 Va. 270, 329 S.E.2d 791.
In light of unconstitutionality of § 20-61.1, court may admit any probative evidence including results of blood grouping tests to determine paternity by a preponderance of evidence. Undisputed evidence based on blood test and mother's testimony established paternity.

1985—*Lawrence v. Bluford-Brown,* 1 Va. App. 202, 336 S.E.2d 899.
Blood grouping tests can be used to establish paternity.

1984—*Johnson v. Branson,* 228 Va. 65, 319 S.E.2d 735.
Person born out of wedlock is child of mother. Such a person is child of father if paternity is established by clear and convincing evidence as set forth in § 64.1-5.2. Alleged father's name appeared on birth certificate. Burden is on child to establish by clear and convincing evidence that father gave consent to someone other than mother that his name be placed on birth certificate. Mere listing of alleged father's name on birth certificate is not enough to establish paternity.

CHAPTER 4

SUPPORT—CHILD AND SPOUSAL

§ 4-1. In General.

(A) Criteria.

See Va. Code § 20-108.1 stating that mathematical formula for determining support may only be used as guideline.

See Va. Code § 20-108.1 which provides that guideline is rebuttably presumed correct. Gross income includes spousal support paid under pre-existing written agreement of parties or court order and amount of such support is deducted from gross income of payor.

1989—*Cutlip v. Cutlip,* 8 Va. App. 618.
Appellate court reverses trial court finding of adultery. As such, it was error for trial court to consider adultery. Award of spousal support in this matter is remanded for further consideration.

1989—*Lassen v. Lassen,* 8 Va. App. 502.
Commissioner recommended that wife be awarded $1,500.00 per month spousal support. Trial court reduced this to $1,200.00 per month which was pendente lite amount. When court awards support based upon due consideration of factors contained in § 20-107.1, it will not be disturbed except for clear abuse of discretion. One of factors to be considered is amount awarded under § 20-107.3.

1989—*Commonwealth v. Johnson,* 7 Va. App. 614, 376 S.E.2d 787.
Mother does not have same rights as child. Mother simply has right to act as conduit for payments of child support. When child is born out of wedlock, duty of support is to child not mother.

1989—*Reid v. Reid,* 7 Va. App. 553.
Once the marital wealth has been distributed then the amount of support to be ordered may be affected.

1988—*Kaufman v. Kaufman,* 7 Va. App. 488.
Absent adequate reason in the record, court should not finalize child and spousal support without considering the income which may result from a monetary award. In this case the court did not consider wife's earning capacity since she had an infant child at home to care for.

1988—*Holmes v. Holmes,* 7 Va. App. 472.
Amount of temporary support is not a factor that court must consider in awarding permanent support.

1988—*Keyser v. Keyser,* 7 Va. App. 405.
Parties married for four years. Trial court improperly ruled that due to short duration of marriage no spousal support award. Court must consider all statutory factors.

1988—*Goetz v. Goetz,* 7 Va. App. 50.
Court may decree spousal support in lump sum or periodic payment. $15,000 lump sum award to satisfy marital debt not justified based on the record since insufficient evidence as to husband's ability to pay.

1988—*Gibson v. Gibson,* 5 Va. App. 426, 364 S.E.2d 518.
Consideration of factors in Va. Code § 20-107.1 involves more than recitation that all factors have been considered.

1987—*Payne v. Payne,* 5 Va. App. 359, 363 S.E.2d 428.
Spouse has right to be maintained in manner to which accustomed during marriage. This must be balanced against other spouse's ability to pay. Award must be based on circumstances in existence at time. Husband's disposable monthly income was $1,660. Support award of $1,400 is abuse of discretion.

1987—*Ray v. Ray,* 4 Va. App. 509, 358 S.E.2d 754.
Income of party who is required to pay spousal support, regardless of how income is derived or derivable, is fund from which allowance is made. When one party is possessed of sizable estate, law does not require that party to invade estate to relieve obligation of former spouse whose actions have brought end to marriage.

1987—*Lee v. Lee,* 3 Va. App. 631, 352 S.E.2d 534.
Court must consider all of factors mandated by statute.

1986—*Rippe v. Rippe,* 3 Va. App. 506, 351 S.E.2d 181.
Custody was changed from mother to father. Trial court denied child support to father because this would aggravate relationship within family. This is not sufficient basis to deny child support.

1986—*Woolley v. Woolley,* 3 Va. App. 337, 349 S.E.2d 422.
Income of husband $88,000. Wife unemployed. Wife has no current job skills or training. In making the equitable distribution, court provided wife $15,000 more than husband. Record is devoid of whether court considered earning capacities, resources, education, training, and ability to secure training. Award of annual support was $6,500. Trial court abused its discretion for not having considered these factors.

1986—*Morris v. Morris,* 3 Va. App. 303, 349 S.E.2d 661.
In determining spousal support, court must consider provisions made as to marital property. Where this latter issue is subject to remand, then spousal support likewise must be reconsidered. Husband's gross income was $73,000. Wife unemployed at time of hearing and had only unskilled jobs during marriage. Her only source of income is $622 per month from VA. Spousal support of $850 not excessive.

1986—*Young v. Young,* 3 Va. App. 80, 348 S.E.2d 46.
There is no presumption that each parent should contribute equally to financial cost of children even if both earn same income. Where one parent provides considerable non-monetary contributions to wellbeing of child, court may require other parent to pay more than one-half of support. In this case, wife testified what it would cost to live in another

dwelling separate from her mother. Wife never testified she was actually going to obtain such quarters and that money would actually be used for this. It was reversible error for court to base its award on this.

1986—*Keyser v. Keyser,* 2 Va. App. 459, 345 S.E.2d 12.
In fixing amount of spousal support, the court may not consider funds the obligor may receive in future. Court may not include an automatic escalator.

1986—*Dodge v. Dodge,* 2 Va. App. 238, 343 S.E.2d 363.
Court must consider each factor in § 20-107.1 as to spousal support and failure to do so is reversible error. Husband had net income of $1150 per month and wife was unemployed with monthly expenses of $694.76. Alimony of $300 per month sustained.

1986—*Venable v. Venable,* 2 Va. App. 178, 342 S.E.2d 646.
The grant or denial of equitable distribution award is factor to be considered in determining spousal and child support.

1986—*Papuchis v. Papuchis,* 2 Va. App. 130, 341 S.E.2d 829.
Decision of trial court in setting spousal support should not be interfered with unless it is clear there has been some injustice.

1986—*Collier v. Collier,* 2 Va. App. 125, 341 S.E.2d 827.
When court has given due consideration to factors in § 20-107.1, then this determination will not be disturbed on appeal except for clear abuse of discretion. Marriage was of 3-year duration. Wife made $536 per month and husband $748 per month. $100 per month alimony to wife appropriate.

1986—*Dukelow v. Dukelow,* 2 Va. App. 21, 341 S.E.2d 208.
Husband's net monthly income was $2622. Wife's was $863 plus value of free residence. Alimony award of $700 per month left husband with net income of $1922 and wife with $1563.

(B) Enforcement.

1989—*Doherty v. Doherty,* 9 Va. App. 97.
Payments of spousal support must be made according to terms of decree. Spousal support payments ordered by decree become vested as they accrue and trial court is without authority to make any change as to past due installments.

1988—*Goodpasture v. Goodpasture,* 7 Va. App. 55.
District court held husband in arrears. He appealed to circuit court. Divorce decree then entered. Filing of suit divested district court of jurisdiction except to enforce order already entered. Wife authorized husband to suspend court ordered support. He continued making contributions. Wife thereafter filed motion for arrearage. Parties by waiver cannot modify court order. Husband not entitled to credit for contribution.

1988—*Martin v. Bales,* 7 Va. App. 141.
An appeal of a support order to circuit court does not suspend the juvenile court order unless a judge so orders. If a suit for divorce has

been filed and support is an issue then juvenile court only has jurisdiction to enforce its orders. In instances of support arrearage, a court is without authority to modify its decree retroactively and relieve a party of the obligation to pay past due installments.

1988—*Schmidt v. Schmidt,* 6 Va. App. 501, 370 S.E.2d 311.
With spouse's delay in pursuing enforcement, acquiescence of lesser amount will not relieve obligor of court order. When a property settlement agreement was incorporated into a decree, subsequent decree modifying amount does not necessarily supplant contract obligations.

1988—*Johns v. Johns,* 5 Va. App. 494, 364 S.E.2d 775.
Colorado support decree was properly enforced under RURESA since Colorado had personal jurisdiction.

1987—*Henderlite v. Henderlite,* 3 Va. App. 539, 351 S.E.2d 913.
Support obligations are not abated during period when non-custodial parent assumes temporary custody.

1986—*Cass v. Lassiter,* 2 Va. App. 273, 343 S.E.2d 470.
URESA is economical and expedient means of enforcing support orders rather than device for terminating or modifying child support. URESA provides that Virginia support order is not nullified by support order of another state unless specifically provided by that state. Support obligations ordered by original decree become vested as they accrue and court is without authority to make any change as to past due installments.

1986—*Acree v. Acree,* 2 Va. App. 151, 342 S.E.2d 68.
Husband by agreement of parties took over custody and total responsibility for child but sought no modification of court order. Where custodial parent has voluntarily agreed to elimination of support payments and to relinquish custody on permanent basis and such agreement has been fully performed, then inflexible rule denying credit for non-conforming payments will not be applied.

1986—*Dickers v. Commonwealth,* 2 Va. App. 72, 341 S.E.2d 392.
Circuit court affirmed paternity order of North Carolina court and ordered child support. Fact that affidavits in support of petition were more than two years old does not affect their validity.

1986—*Johnson v. Johnson,* 1 Va. App. 330, 338 S.E.2d 353.
Child support money that husband paid directly to children is simply gratuity and husband not entitled to credit for this.

1984—*Carper v. Carper,* 228 Va. 185, 319 S.E.2d 766.
Order for support may not be modified retroactively. The right to support payments becomes vested as they accrue and court has no authority to make changes in past due installments. Pendente lite order which required husband to pay mortgage on family house was ratified by final decree. House was sold to wife's parents who assumed payments. Husband not liable for ongoing payments.

(C) Jurisdiction.

1988—*Taylor v. Taylor,* 5 Va. App. 436, 364 S.E.2d 244.
During pendency of divorce, court may order one spouse to pay mortgage on home. In doing so court should make clear whether this is spousal or child support or whether it is a provision for use and possession or preservation of estate.

1987—*Morris v. Morris,* 4 Va. App. 539, 359 S.E.2d 104.
Property settlement agreement was incorporated into final decree. Husband was in arrears as to spousal support. Husband was non-resident who was then served by publication as to motion for support arrearages. Service was not by method allowed by long arm statute and therefore did not have jurisdiction. Service by publication only gave court *in rem* jurisdiction. This may produce inconsistencies where property settlement agreement has been incorporated — i.e., court may have jurisdiction to litigate divorce but not spousal support.

1987—*Smith v. Smith,* 4 Va. App. 148, 354 S.E.2d 816.
When case is dismissed, then court-ordered pendente lite support also should terminate.

1986—*Johnson v. Johnson,* 1 Va. App. 330, 338 S.E.2d 353.
Unitary support award was for $531 per month for wife and three children. Oldest child was 18 at time. Ten years later when wife seeks arrearage, husband challenges child support as to this child. This is something that should have been challenged in timely appeal from original order and not now. This provision, even if erroneous, did not cause order to be void. If court has jurisdiction over subject matter and parties, decree in usual equity form is not void, even if erroneous.

1985—*Stephens v. Stephens,* 229 Va. 610, 331 S.E.2d 484.
Personal jurisdiction cannot be transferred from one state to another simply by registration of decree under RURESA. Registration of foreign decree coupled with personal service on defendant in foreign jurisdiction does not create personal jurisdiction.

1985—*Rodriguez v. Rodriguez,* 1 Va. App. 87, 334 S.E.2d 595.
Jurisdiction of divorce court to provide for child support is purely statutory. Jurisdiction may continue beyond 18 if agreement providing for continued support is incorporated into final decree.

§ 4-2. Child Support.

(A) Education.

1986—*Harris v. Woodrum,* 3 Va. App. 428, 350 S.E.2d 667.
Under terms of property settlement agreement, husband is obliged to pay for secondary education at school which he approves, which approval will not be unreasonably withheld. Husband believed that structured home environment was what child needed, and therefore he refused to pay for boarding school. This was held to be reasonable.

1985—*Tiffany v. Tiffany,* 1 Va. App. 11, 332 S.E.2d 796.
Property Settlement Agreement by its own terms did not give husband veto power over child's choice of college. Under Agreement, husband obliged to contribute to college expenses.

(C) Modification.

See Va. Code § 20-108 stating that no support order may be retroactively modified, but may be modified with respect to any period during which there is pending petition for modification, but only from date that notice of such has been given.

1989—*Schoenwetter v. Schoenwetter,* 8 Va. App. 601.
In petition for modification of support, party must prove material change in circumstance and that this change warrants modification of support. In this instance, husband's net income had increased by $3,400.00 per month. Wife's income had increased by $840.00 per month. Although trial court did not specifically state on record that there was material change in circumstance, there was ample evidence of record to confirm that conclusion. Increase in support in this instance is upheld.

1988—*Anderson v. Van Landingham,* 236 Va. 85.
Agreement incorporated into final decree. Parties then by agreed order amended the agreement. This constituted amendment of both the original decree and agreement and barred subsequent action to enforce original agreement. Court has continuing jurisdiction to modify maintenance of minor children in spite of contract.

1987—*Yohay v. Ryan,* 4 Va. App. 559, 359 S.E.2d 320.
Moving party must: (1) prove by preponderance of evidence material change in circumstance; (2) make full and clear disclosure of ability to pay; (3) show that lack of ability to pay is not due to voluntary act or neglect; and (4) prove that material change justifies modification. Contract between husband and wife does not bar court from making modification. Moving party need not prove that modification would be in best interest of child. Trial court is not obliged to consider all factors set forth in Va. Code § 20-107.2. Mere fact that wife's financial position has improved does not justify modification.

1987—*Mayhood v. Mayhood,* 4 Va. App. 365, 358 S.E.2d 182.
Court may modify child support only if there is material change in circumstances.

1986—*Edwards v. Lowry,* 232 Va. 110, 348 S.E.2d 259.
Party whose income has declined as result of his own misconduct cannot rely on such to seek reduction of court ordered child support. Section 20-108 gives divorce court continuing jurisdiction to modify custody or support of minor children. Party seeking change must prove material change in circumstance. Party seeking reduction must make full and clear disclosure relating to his ability to pay and must show his

lack of ability is not due to his own voluntary act or neglect. Party's remarriage and subsequent increased expenses is not basis for decrease.

1986—*Hederick v. Hederick,* 3 Va. App. 452, 350 S.E.2d 526.
Child support award may be modified only on showing of material change in circumstance. Court must consider present needs and circumstances of children.

1986—*Johnson v. Johnson,* 1 Va. App. 330, 338 S.E.2d 353.
Unitary award of child support and alimony. Husband claimed that wife was obliged to seek reduction as each child turned 18. This burden was on him.

(D) Parental Duty to Support.

1989—*NPA v. WBA,* 8 Va. App. 246, 380 S.E.2d 178.
Issue in this case was whether husband who is not biological father of wife's child can be required to support child after divorce when he has reared and supported child for five years since birth under false belief he was child's father. Wife argued that support is required on one of several theories: (1) common law adoption; (2) in loco parentis; (3) implied contract or (4) equitable estoppel. Court rejected all of these theories.

1985—*Prestera v. Denny,* 1 Va. App. 103, 335 S.E.2d 169.
Mother filed petition for support of child born out of wedlock. This was civil action and therefore right of appeal to circuit court exists.

§ 4-3. Spousal Support.

(A) Fault of Wife.

See Va. Code § 20-107.1 which eliminates fault, except adultery, as absolute bar to support. The fault may be considered by the court, however. Support may be awarded to spouse who commits adultery upon finding that failure to do so would constitute manifest injustice.

1989—*Davis v. Davis,* 8 Va. App. 12, 377 S.E.2d 640.
Fault by both parties bars their respective fault divorces. Divorce awarded on basis of one year separation. This is no bar to spousal support.

1987—*Surbey v. Surbey,* 5 Va. App. 119, 360 S.E.2d 873.
Both husband and wife were at fault in causing separation and guilty of post-separation adultery. Divorce was awarded on no fault grounds. Since husband did not have grounds which legally may be used to obtain divorce, wife's claim for alimony was not barred.

1986—*Bacon v. Bacon,* 3 Va. App. 484, 351 S.E.2d 37.
Fault in break-up of marriage must be considered in making spousal support award.

1986—*Zinkhan v. Zinkhan,* 2 Va. App. 200, 342 S.E.2d 658.
Party shall not be required to pay permanent spousal support if there exists in his favor ground for divorce under § 20-91(6).

1985—*Wallace v. Wallace,* 1 Va. App. 183, 336 S.E.2d 27.
With neither party entitled to fault divorce, the obligation to support a spouse continues.

(B) Miscellaneous.

1989—*Lassen v. Lassen,* 8 Va. App. 502.
There is no statutory mandate that health care coverage be provided for spouse although physical and medical condition of parties is one fact court must consider in awarding spousal support. In this instance trial court did not abuse discretion in making no separate provision for health care coverage.

1987—*Ray v. Ray,* 4 Va. App. 509, 358 S.E.2d 754.
Trial court erred where it considered monetary award derived from wife's marital property interest as income rather than as asset from which potential income might be derived.

1986—*Collier v. Collier,* 2 Va. App. 125, 341 S.E.2d 827.
Lump-sum award to wife of $4,000 set aside. Only evidentiary basis for this was that wife had depleted savings account of this amount to pay obligation of husband. This is not appropriate consideration.

1985—*Gray v. Gray,* 228 Va. 696, 324 S.E.2d 677.
Former Code § 20-107 empowered court to award lump-sum payment based on consideration of property interest of parties. Nothing in record suggests that trial court abused its discretion in this regard and therefore decision is affirmed.

(C) Modification.

See Va. Code § 20-109 indicating that court may increase, decrease or terminate spousal support and maintenance that may thereafter accrue. However, if stipulation or contract signed by party is filed before entry of a final decree, then no decree or order directing payment of support and maintenance for spouse, suit money or counsel fee or establishing or imposing any other condition or consideration, monetary or non-monetary, shall be entered except in accordance with that stipulation or contract. Upon death or remarriage of spouse receiving support, support terminates unless otherwise provided by stipulation or contract. If stipulation or contract is filed after entry of final decree and any party so moves, the court shall modify its decree to conform to the stipulation or contract.

1988—*Hollowell v. Hollowell,* 6 Va. App. 417, 369 S.E.2d 451.
Cohabitation of ex-wife post divorce with other men is not a basis for modification. Financial need and ability are the criteria.

1986—*Bacon v. Bacon,* 3 Va. App. 484, 351 S.E.2d 37.
Reversible error for court, upon request, to fail to reserve right in decree to receive alimony in event of change of circumstance.

1986—*Hederick v. Hederick,* 3 Va. App. 452, 350 S.E.2d 526.
Foreign decree for alimony may not be modified as to past due installments if right to such is absolute and vested under state law where entered.

1986—*D'Auria v. D'Auria,* 1 Va. App. 455, 340 S.E.2d 164.
Court has power by proper reservation to change or modify its decree as to spousal support. This reservation of jurisdiction must be clear and specific. It is reversible error for court to fail to make such reservation when expressly requested to do so by party.

1985—*Parrillo v. Parrillo,* 1 Va. App. 226, 336 S.E.2d 23.
When spousal support has been agreed upon as part of unitary sum and agreement is ratified by final decree of divorce, provision of § 20-109 inhibits modification of spousal support.

1985—*Floyd v. Floyd,* 1 Va. App. 42, 333 S.E.2d 364.
Court retains jurisdiction to modify upon showing of substantial change of circumstance of need or ability to pay. Husband self-employed as accountant. Part of husband's current expenses were for support of present wife. His salary had decreased but what he was doing was to take loans from the business. Substantial change not proven.

(E) Remarriage — Effect of.

1988—*Mallery-Sayre v. Mallery,* 6 Va. App. 471, 370 S.E.2d 113.
When a lump sum spousal support award has been made, the right to the amount, whether payable immediately or in installments, is fixed and vested at time of decree and is unalterable by court order, remarriage or death.

(F) Right to.

1989—*Zipf v. Zipf,* 8 Va. App. 387, 382 S.E.2d 263.
Trial court held that wife had to exhaust her share of marital property before it would award more than nominal spousal support. This was error. Law does not require spouse who seeks support to exhaust his or her own estate in order to qualify for spousal support thereby relieving other spouse of all obligations to support until that estate is depleted. Income of party who is required to pay is fund from which allowance of spousal support is to be made and enactment of equitable distribution statute did not negate that well established rule.

1989—*Owney v. Owney,* 8 Va. App. 255, 379 S.E.2d 745.
Issue is when husband agrees in PSA to be responsible for payments of first deed of trust and wife subsequently unilaterally pays such deed of trust in full, does husband's obligation continue until original deed of trust would have been paid? Trial court answered this question affirmatively. Court of Appeals reverses and remands for further consideration noting that agreement had not been incorporated into final decree and noting further that agreement seems to disallow award of spousal sup-

port which is essentially what trial court had done by ordering husband to pay monthly payment after deed of trust had been paid off. Since agreement has not been incorporated, dispute here is purely contractual and is to be decided by trial court on pure contractual principles and not on basis of spousal support.

1987—*Collins v. Collins,* 233 Va. 245, 355 S.E.2d 332.
When divorce decree founded on Va. Code § 20-91(9) denies spousal support, it must contain findings supported by credible evidence of marital fault barring the claim or consideration of factors in Va. Code § 20-107.1.

1987—*Brown v. Brown,* 5 Va. App. 238, 361 S.E.2d 364.
Both wife and counsel stated at hearing that spousal support was not being sought. Because of this it was deemed waived.

1986—*Hayes v. Hayes,* 3 Va. App. 499, 351 S.E.2d 590.
Because divorce was granted when wife was served by publication and she did not appear, Va. Code § 8.01-322 did not bar her right to petition for award of spousal support two years after decree.

1986—*Hodges v. Hodges,* 2 Va. App. 508, 347 S.E.2d 134.
Under § 20-107.1, court may award spousal support in periodic payments or lump sum or both. When wife has shown need for support and husband's ability to pay and she is not guilty of conduct entitling husband to divorce, then court abuses discretion in refusing support.

1985—*Sawyer v. Sawyer,* 1 Va. App. 75, 335 S.E.2d 277.
Wife awarded equitable distribution out of military pension of husband plus alimony which was calculated based on pension income and other income.

1985—*Floyd v. Floyd,* 1 Va. App. 42, 333 S.E.2d 364.
Spouse, deemed entitled to support, has right to be maintained in manner to which accustomed during marriage but this must be balanced against other spouse's ability to pay.

CHAPTER 5

PROPERTY DISTRIBUTION

§ 5-1. Dower and Curtesy.

See Va. Code § 64.1-21 which provides that spouse not entitled to dower or curtesy in equitable estate of deceased spouse.

1984—*Jacobs v. Meade,* 227 Va. 284, 315 S.E.2d 383.
Surviving spouse shall not be entitled to dower in equitable separate estate of deceased spouse if such right has been expressly excluded by instrument creating same or if such instrument describes estate as sole and separate equitable estate.

§ 5-2. Equitable Distribution.

See Va. Code § 8.01-460 indicating that monetary awards shall on order of court be lien on real estate of obligor.

See Va. Code § 20-107.3 requiring court to determine value of property as of date of hearing unless at least 21 days before hearing a party makes a motion to use another date for good cause shown in order to attain the ends of justice. This same section defines marital share of pension, profit sharing, or deferred compensation plans as that portion earned during the marriage prior to separation.

See Va. Code § 20-107.3 which provides that judgment of monetary award should not be docketed unless so directed by decree.

1989—*Bosserman v. Bosserman,* 9 Va. App. 1.
Issue in this case is whether trial court when valuing marital property for purposes of making monetary award correctly valued stock of closely held corporation whose shares were subject to stock transfer restriction. Restriction indicated that stock was to be offered back to corporation at book value. Trial court determined that book value really meant fair market value under circumstances. Trial court also properly did not discount corporate debt since there is no promissory note evidencing debt and therefore IRS would treat this as capital contribution. Trial court also properly ruled that husband failed to produce credible evidence as to how value of stock should be discounted because of his minority interest. Price of stock set by buyout agreement does not control determination of value when other spouse did not consent or is not otherwise bound by its terms.

1989—*Lassen v. Lassen,* 8 Va. App. 502.
When pension is vested and payments are being made, court may infer present value of pension from evidence. Expert testimony though is most expedient and preferable method for determining valuation. In this instance, trial court rejected expert's testimony. It was improper in this instance for trial court to take judicial notice of American Juris-

prudence 2nd Desk Book compound interest and annuity tables. They were not offered into evidence and, as such, trial court erred in resorting to them. Husband had inherited substantial sum of money which he placed in certificates of deposit in his name only. During marriage, husband cashed in some of certificates and placed proceeds in checking account in his name alone. He then wrote checks to establish three other investment accounts. Because husband deposited his retirement payments into checking account during marriage, this account was marital property. Since the three new investment accounts were opened with funds from this account these new investment accounts were also marital property. Husband had made $2,000.00 loan during course of marriage. Although loan was marital property there is no evidence that it was jointly owned and therefore no basis to order partition or transfer of loan. Trial court could use monetary award to compensate wife for any interest she had in loan.

1989—*Zipf v. Zipf,* 8 Va. App. 387, 382 S.E.2d 263.
Trial court used date of filing of Bill of Complaint as date of valuation. Since wife never contended date of valuation should be date of hearing, appellate court upholds this finding of trial court. As general rule, however, date as near as practical to date of trial is most suitable valuation date. This divorce action filed after nearly thirty years of marriage and twenty-year military career of husband. Court awarded twenty-five percent of husband's pension to wife citing husband's greater contribution to acquisition of family wealth and husband's completion of his education in U.S. Naval Academy prior to marriage as primary factor which established marital standard of living. Trial court also appropriately discounted value of certain stock held by husband due to lack of voting rights. As to military pension, trial court in this case found present value of such pension to be $280,000 and awarded wife one-fourth of that; i.e., $70,000. Although that present value calculation is useful, trial court decision reversed as to method of payment since payment instead should have been on monthly basis equivalent to one-fourth of each monthly payment or if to be lump sum then record must show that wife has received benefit of adjustments to future earnings and that present value of calculation accounts for fact that lump-sum payment may not be paid immediately.

1989—*Day v. Day,* 8 Va. App. 346, 381 S.E.2d 364.
Trial court ordered husband to pay certain marital debts arising from credit card obligations and auto loan. Question whether trial court had statutory authority to order husband to pay these debts. Appellate court overruled trial court order saying that trial court had no authority to enter such order. Trial court authorized by statute to order monetary payments or awards only in form of spousal support, child support or monetary awards under equitable distribution statute. Trial court could cite no authority or rationale as to basis for its order. Order in question is void.

1989—*Dean v. Dean,* 8 Va. App. 143, 379 S.E.2d 742.
Wife waived her rights to equitable distribution, spousal support, and attorney's fees for consideration of $300,000. Court held that husband

and wife were joint owners of certain stock. Wife did not waive or give up her property rights to stock and trial court correctly held that she was entitled to have partition of jointly registered stock certificates by requiring husband to have certificates reissued. Husband was also required to account for stock dividends received after divorce.

1989—*Ellington v. Ellington,* 8 Va. App. 48, 378 S.E.2d 626.
Property must be classified as either all marital or all separate but not both. Income received from an increase in value of separate property during marriage is separate property. However, when appreciation in value of property is due to effort of parties during marriage that may convert separate property into marital property. Where property is essentially of no or of negative value it is generally inappropriate to consider it as basis for monetary award.

1988—*Reid v. Reid,* 7 Va. App. 553.
Monetary award does not flow from any legal duty but involves an adjustment of equities, rights and interests in marital property. Va. Code § 20-107.3 does not contemplate the financial needs or abilities of the parties.

1988—*Kaufman v. Kaufman,* 7 Va. App. 488.
The court may not require one party to pay a sum equal to one-half of the value of marital property given to wife when she retains ownership of the item during the marriage. Also, court cannot require one spouse to pay to the other a sum equal to one-half of value of equity in jointly owned property while allowing the other spouse to retain the one-half interest therein. If this were allowed, the effect would be that one spouse would have 100% of equity in property.

1988—*Holmes v. Holmes,* 7 Va. App. 472.
In deciding equitable distribution award of pensions, court must consider present value. Trial court properly reserved authority to reopen case in event of death of either party if at that time a balance remains to be paid.

1988—*Keyser v. Keyser,* 7 Va. App. 405.
The fact that wife's financial condition is no worse now than when she got married is no basis for denial of award. Denial of award solely because of short duration of marriage is improper. Trial court, without explanation, gave wife no interest in husband's pension and therefore cannot be upheld on appeal.

1988—*Seehorn v. Seehorn,* 7 Va. App. 375.
Parties agreed husband's pension had value of $262,000. Court approved monetary award of $100,000 to wife payable at rate of 50% of cash benefits actually received by husband.

1988—*Pommerenke v. Pommerenke,* 7 Va. App. 241.
Equitable Distribution Act does not adopt source of funds doctrine but rather has distinct definitions for separate and marital property. The source of funds is a factor to be considered. The Code does not require

reimbursement for a down payment for marital property when source of funds is separate property, although such reimbursement is allowable. In this case, husband was reimbursed for down payment on family home.

1988—*Trivett v. Trivett,* 7 Va. App. 148.
Where a party has encumbered marital property in anticipation of divorce to frustrate equitable distribution, court may include unencumbered value within pool of marital wealth from which it determines monetary award. This determination must be based on evidence of deliberate attempt to defeat monetary award and not merely fact that previously unsecured creditor is granted a security interest. In this case, the record did not disclose what the basis was for the court's decision to include property in marital wealth as if it were unencumbered.

1988—*Booth v. Booth,* 7 Va. App. 22.
Waste is dissipation of marital assets in anticipation of divorce for a purpose unrelated to marriage and in derogation of marriage. Where there is waste, then the party who last had the assets is accountable. Court ruled that wife wasted $60,000 which she lost in a speculative stock market venture. The wife used $86,000 to pay attorney and to support self and son. This was not wasted. The wasted asset should be considered in equitable distribution award. Unpaid attorney's fees are a debt and they should be considered in equitable distribution award.

1988—*Aster v. Gross,* 7 Va. App. 1.
Prior to 1988, the valuation date was to be as near as practicable to trial date, although court could exercise discretion as far as picking evaluation date. Fault in dissolution of marriage should not be used to punish economically either of the parties. In this case husband at fault for dissolution. Court award to wife of roughly 35% of marital property was affirmed. As to the issue of fault, the factors that are relevant to equitable distribution are those that affect the marriage's economic condition.

1988—*Pledger v. Pledger,* 6 Va. App. 627, 371 S.E.2d 43.
Question presented was whether interest due on pension benefits ran from date of final decree or date when payment due. Court ruled latter date applied.

1988—*Fitchett v. Fitchett,* 6 Va. App. 562, 370 S.E.2d 318.
Court has no power to order sale of real estate without first determining that partition in kind cannot conveniently be made and then determining the sale will be in best interest of the parties. The procedure for distribution of the property and/or proceeds of sale is governed by Va. Code § 8.01-81 et seq.

1988—*Gologanoff v. Gologanoff,* 6 Va. App. 340, 369 S.E.2d 446.
Claim for equitable distribution must be properly pled to be allowed. The statute makes no provision for granting monetary award based on consideration of less than all the marital assets. In this case, there was

an attempt to reserve jurisdiction for distribution of military pension only. Court refused to do so.

1988—*Lambert v. Lambert,* 6 Va. App. 94, 367 S.E.2d 184.
Gift from spouse to spouse during marriage is marital property. If interest in business is marital property, then use of funds from business to acquire another business is marital property. Transmutation may occur when there is appreciation in value of separate property due to efforts of either or both spouses. Trial court incorrectly classified three business entities as separate property in this case. Even if amount of marital property that is commingled is insubstantial, if it is significant to marital relation it is sufficient to trigger presumption.

1988—*Westbrook v. Westbrook,* 5 Va. App. 446, 364 S.E.2d 523.
Transmutation of property may be by agreement or conduct. Commingled property must be treated as marital property. In this case, residence was transmuted when wife signed second deed of trust note.

1988—*Taylor v. Taylor,* 5 Va. App. 436, 364 S.E.2d 244.
Court has no authority to transfer title to jointly owned property. Court may partition real estate. Husband had used certificates of deposit titled in his name to maintain the family during separation. Court had no authority to order him to reimburse wife for one-half of this but court should consider this as marital property when making a monetary award.

1987—*Payne v. Payne,* 5 Va. App. 359, 363 S.E.2d 428.
To satisfy award, court authorized husband to convey California property to wife with wife assuming mortgage. Court failed to consider what would be actual net proceeds from sale of property, had no authority to order assumption and therefore abused discretion. As to jointly owned household furnishings, court may give parties opportunity to mutually divide and, if unable, then to partition.

1987—*Smoot v. Smoot,* 233 Va. 435, 357 S.E.2d 728.
When spouse commingles separate property with marital property, then property becomes marital property subject to distribution. In this case, each party made contribution to marital home from separate property. Home was held to be marital property. Court rejects "source of funds" doctrine in terms of classifying property but does say that each party is entitled to credit for that party's monetary contributions for acquisition and maintenance of house. After these credits were given, remaining equity was divided fifty-fifty. Supreme Court upheld this even though husband was guilty of desertion. Although this was fault grounds for divorce, it was not cause of dissolution of marriage but was only last unhappy event in relationship.

1987—*Lowe v. Lowe,* 233 Va. 431, 357 S.E.2d 31.
Court has no authority to order husband to convey to wife his interest in jointly owned marital home.

1987—*Brown v. Brown,* 5 Va. App. 238, 361 S.E.2d 364.
Only two types of property are contemplated: marital or separate. No hybrids. If separate and marital are commingled, then court will find it

to be marital. Marital home cannot be classified as part marital and part separate. In determining monetary award, court should consider means of acquisition. Monetary award is equivalent to money judgment. If no due date is specified or if award is not satisfied by payment date in decree, then award becomes equivalent to money judgment, to be enforced as such and not through mandatory decree of payment. In this case, family farm and husband's partnership interest in farming operation were marital property.

1987—*Cousins v. Cousins,* 5 Va. App. 156, 360 S.E.2d 882.
Property jointly owned or titled is marital. Separate property is all property acquired during marriage by bequest, devise, descent, survivorship, or gift from source other than spouse. To remain separate, it must be owned by or titled to only one party. In determining amount and method for paying monetary award, court may consider how and when it was acquired. In making distribution, court may consider grounds for divorce and factors and circumstances that may have contributed to dissolution. Wife in this case maintained that family home, which was titled jointly, was actually advancement of inheritance from her parents, and therefore was separate property. Fact that it was titled jointly makes it marital although means of acquisition of house is relevant consideration.

1987—*Brinkley v. Brinkley,* 5 Va. App. 132, 361 S.E.2d 139.
Monetary award can be lump sum or periodic payments. Court must determine rights and interest in property no matter how property titled. Once amount of award has been determined, Court may direct payment of percentage of retirement benefits towards satisfaction of award. In determining amount of monetary award, Court must determine present value of pension and retirement benefits.

1987—*Bowers v. Bowers,* 4 Va. App. 610, 359 S.E.2d 546.
Wife in this case had burden of proving value of husband's pension benefits. Wife failed to meet this burden, and trial court did not abuse discretion in making monetary award without considering value of retirement benefits.

1987—*Wagner v. Wagner,* 4 Va. App. 397, 358 S.E.2d 407.
Classification of property is initially ascertained as of date of acquisition. Separate property by manner it is maintained may be commuted into marital property. Marital property in absence of valid, express agreement cannot become separate property.

1987—*Price v. Price,* 4 Va. App. 224, 355 S.E.2d 905.
Presumption that property is marital ceases on de facto dissolution of marital partnership. In most cases date for classification of marital property is date of last separation. When dealing with pension, court must make special provisions for payment of it in order to conform with payment restrictions. Bank account accumulated by parties during marriage but expended by wife after separation is marital property that must be considered for distribution.

1987—*Clayberg v. Clayberg,* 4 Va. App. 218, 355 S.E.2d 902.
Court has no authority to order one spouse to convey interest in joint property. Court has authority to order partition of property titled in both names. Award to wife of 15% of husband's military pension was error since not all statutory factors were considered.

1987—*Artis v. Artis,* 4 Va. App. 132, 354 S.E.2d 812.
Value of military pension was in issue. Trial court simply awarded wife 15% of military pension. Court must first determine value as it did in this case. It is unclear from record how court arrived at 15%, especially in light of stipulation that both parties contributed equally.

1987—*Robinette v. Robinette,* 4 Va. App. 123, 354 S.E.2d 808.
No presumption exists as to equal distribution. Statute is intended to compensate for contribution to acquisition of property without regard to title when marriage is dissolved. Statutory factors must be applied to all marital property, and no one item of marital property is to be segregated out.

1987—*Mitchell v. Mitchell,* 4 Va. App. 113, 355 S.E.2d 18.
Value of assets determined as near as practicable to trial date will usually be most accurate, but court may use date of last separation if this would be more consistent with factors in Va. Code § 20-107.3. Equitable distribution of pension benefits shall not begin until pensioner actually begins receiving benefits. In this case, wife was awarded $22,087, payable in 30 days.

1987—*Calamos v. Calamos,* 4 Va. App. 96, 354 S.E.2d 102.
Suit filed prior to effective date of Va. Code § 20-107.3. Wife filed answer prior to this date and filed Cross Bill requesting affirmative relief after effective date. Suit is governed by pre-equitable distribution law.

1987—*Williams v. Williams,* 4 Va. App. 19, 354 S.E.2d 64.
No presumption favors equal division of marital property. Hallmark of statute is monetary award which can be satisfied by conveyance of property subject to court approval. Court has no power to allot specific marital property not titled in names of both parties.

1986—*Bacon v. Bacon,* 3 Va. App. 484, 351 S.E.2d 37.
In making award court may consider circumstances and factors which contributed to dissolution.

1986—*Woolley v. Woolley,* 3 Va. App. 337, 349 S.E.2d 422.
Husband's mother contributed money to purchase family home. No basis for imposing constructive trust on this money at time of equitable distribution.

1986—*Morris v. Morris,* 3 Va. App. 303, 349 S.E.2d 661.
Wife claims that 15-acre parcel of land was separate property. Wife alleges she purchased property with proceeds from sale of stock she owned before marriage. Wife failed to prove she owned stock before marriage or acquired it by gift or inheritance. Based on presumption favoring marital property and other evidence, the court concluded this

was marital property. As to husband's law practice, wife showed that husband's anticipated gross income for 1983 was $73,000. This was insufficient to establish value. As to jointly owned property, court has no authority to order transfer as part of monetary award. Property may be allotted, partitioned in kind, sold or sold in part, and the remainder divided.

1986—*Hodges v. Hodges,* 2 Va. App. 508, 347 S.E.2d 134.
When marital property is encumbered with debt which equals or exceeds its value, then for purposes of monetary award it has no value and therefore no basis for award.

1986—*Bentz v. Bentz,* 2 Va. App. 486, 345 S.E.2d 773.
Court refused to grant husband monetary award but ruled that parties were entitled to share equally in marital property all of which was owned or titled jointly. Entire $10,000 from husband's mother used to acquire marital property was gift. There was no evidence this was not gift to both spouses.

1986—*McLaughlin v. McLaughlin,* 2 Va. App. 463, 346 S.E.2d 535.
Expert testified that present value of husband's pension was $205,293.87; $17\frac{1}{2}$ years of his 25-year Navy career were during marriage (i.e., 70%). Thus 70% of present value was considered marital property. Court awarded wife 40% of this. Monetary award of $60,000 to be paid periodically. It would be illogical to require interest on these sums before they become due. On death of husband, his pension benefits cease and therefore obligation to wife ceases.

1986—*Venable v. Venable,* 2 Va. App. 178, 342 S.E.2d 646.
Jointly owned marital property may be partitioned but it may not simply be transferred from one to another by court order. Once court makes monetary award then party against whom it is made may satisfy award by conveyance of property with court's approval.

1986—*Papuchis v. Papuchis,* 2 Va. App. 130, 341 S.E.2d 829.
Court refuses to adopt presumption of equal distribution.

1986—*Rexrode v. Rexrode,* 1 Va. App. 385, 339 S.E.2d 544.
Issue of whether credit union account was marital or separate property. On date of marriage, $13,000 in account. After marriage husband's income went into account. All property acquired during marriage is presumed marital. Part of this account was acquired during marriage. Burden is on husband to prove what part is not marital. He failed to meet this burden. Case is remanded for determination of this issue and consideration of all property of parties.

1985—*McGinnis v. McGinnis,* 1 Va. App. 272, 338 S.E.2d 159.
Trial court erred in allotting to wife personal property titled in husband's name. Trial court also allotted one-third of husband's pension to wife. This was error in this case. On remand, court should consider factors set forth in statute. Award must be specific, presently ascertainable amount and must be result of court's consideration of statutory

factors. In an appropriate case, court may direct payment of a percentage of pension in satisfaction of such award.

1985—*Shaughnessy v. Shaughnessy,* 1 Va. App. 136, 335 S.E.2d 166.
Trial court against wishes of wife reserved ruling on equitable distribution until after final decree. Because ample evidence was introduced and wife requested equitable distribution, court should have determined this issue.

1985—*Parra v. Parra,* 1 Va. App. 118, 335 S.E.2d 157.
Court retains jurisdiction as to equitable distribution where final decree expressly so provides. Parties entered into partial property settlement agreement which was not incorporated into final decree. Where parties have agreed to disposition of property, court may not decree equitable distribution that is inconsistent.

1985—*Sawyer v. Sawyer,* 1 Va. App. 75, 335 S.E.2d 277.
Pension is property acquired during marriage when it accrued and vast majority of benefits were earned during marriage. Military pension is subject to distribution provided no part of award based on present value shall be effective until benefits are received. Court determined present value of pension to be $103,700 without any expert testimony. Where pension not vested or not being collected expert testimony may be required. In this case, husband was collecting it. Court found wife entitled to $40,000 of pension to be paid $250 per month. This was in addition to alimony which was set based on husband's pension income and other income.

§ 5-3. In General.

1987—*Hausman v. Hausman,* 233 Va. 1, 353 S.E.2d 710.
Husband signed deed of trust as to property held as tenants by entirety. This was ineffective and did not have priority over subsequent child support judgment entered against husband.

1986—*Troyer v. Troyer,* 231 Va. 90, 341 S.E.2d 182.
Husband and wife signed contract for purchase of real estate. Later they separated and divorced. In divorce disposition, husband agreed to convey property to wife. This was an enforceable contract for sale of real estate and therefore husband had no rights to real estate.

1984—*Hill v. Hill,* 227 Va. 569, 318 S.E.2d 292.
Husband and wife formed corporation with each contributing start-up money and labor. No stock was issued. The issuance of certificate of incorporation is conclusive evidence that de jure corporation exists. Each party was entitled to one-half ownership of corporation, one-half of fruits and benefits, and one-half of control.

§ 5-5. Property Settlement Agreement.

(A) Ante-Nuptial.

See Va. Code § 20-147 for Premarital Agreement Act.

See Va. Code § 20-155 giving married persons same right to execute such agreements that now exists for prospective spouses.

(B) Post-Nuptial.

1989—*Derby v. Derby,* 8 Va. App. 19, 378 S.E.2d 74.
Property Settlement Agreement entered into by competent parties upon valid consideration for lawful purposes are favored and will be upheld unless their illegality is clear and certain. Trial court in this case improperly set aside agreement on constructive fraud grounds. Constructive fraud is breach of legal or equitable duty which, irrespective of moral guilt, is declared by law to be fraudulent because of its tendency to deceive others or violate confidence. In this instance, parties were each represented by counsel when wife presented proposed agreement to husband to sign. Husband signed in hope that this would bring wife back to him. Whatever fiduciary relationship may have existed between husband and wife in this instance had been terminated due to adversary nature of their relationship and they were henceforth dealing with each other at arm's length. Agreement in this case likewise was not unconscionable. Agreement is unconscionable if it is such as no man in his senses and not under delusion would make on one hand and as no honest and fair man would accept on other. Although there may have been gross disparity between value of properties that parties would receive under terms of this Agreement, court must view that in equity in light of other circumstances. In this case, wife became sole owner of bulk of parties' marital property and husband essentially gave up everything he had earned during his lifetime for ephemeral promise on part of wife to permit him to reside in one of apartment units in building if "he did not pull anything." Agreement properly found to be unconscionable. Other factors to be considered are cited along with pertinent cases.

1989—*Holmes v. Holmes,* 8 Va. App. 457, 382 S.E.2d 27.
On twenty-first day after entry of divorce decree, wife presented ex parte proof that separation agreement had been procured by fraud. Trial court should have vacated that part of final decree incorporating agreement and allow divorce decree otherwise to stand. Judgment obtained by intrinsic fraud such as perjury, forged documents, or other incidents of trial related to issues material to judgment is voidable prior to judgment becoming final. Judgment procurred by extrinsic fraud; i.e., by conduct which prevents fair submission of controversy to court is void and subject to attack at any time. Court did not decide in this instance whether fraud was intrinsic or extrinsic because motion was presented prior to judgment becoming final.

1989—*Drewry v. Drewry,* 8 Va. App. 460, 383 S.E.2d 12.
Wife challenged property settlement agreement on grounds that she was incompetent at time of execution. Her psychiatrist testified in support of that. Other lay witnesses testified that she was competent. Law presumes every adult who executes agreement is mentally competent

to enter into contract. To be competent to enter into legally binding obligation, party must simply understand nature and character of agreement and consequences of entering into it. Decision of trial court upholding agreement is supported by competent evidence. Wife also challenged agreement on grounds of fraud. Prior to agreement being signed, wife had announced her intention of leaving marriage. Husband employed independent counsel and wife was free to do so also. Generally, when spouses separate with intent to divorce and propose to divide their property interest, they have assumed adversarial roles and no longer occupy position of trust as to each other. In this instance, trial court did not err in failing to impose upon husband duty of trust and in holding that parties could negotiate at arm's length. In this case, no evidence of any material misrepresentation by husband. Fact husband sold piece of property shortly after agreement was signed for considerably more than what wife thought it was worth is not necessarily proof of fraud. Wife also contends agreement was unconscionable. When court considers this issue, adequacy of price or quality of value transferred in contract is of initial concern. If there is gross disparity, then court should consider whether oppressive influences affected agreement to extent that process was unfair and terms of resulting agreement unconscionable. Trial court in this instance found agreement not unfair.

1988—*Seehorn v. Seehorn,* 7 Va. App. 375.
Parties signed property settlement agreement after separation. Husband objected to incorporation and was awarded fault divorce. Property settlement agreement called for payment of support to be renegotiated by parties or settled by court after one year. Since parties could not agree on support after one year and since husband awarded fault decree, wife not entitled to any spousal support. In spite of this, parties retain right to bring law action to enforce contract.

1988—*Dexter v. Dexter,* 7 Va. App. 36.
Five days after marriage, parties signed agreement which required husband to pay wife $1,000 per month in the event of divorce. This was intended to replace $1,000 alimony wife had been receiving from prior husband. Court properly ruled there was no consideration since prior alimony payments ceased upon remarriage. Agreement also invalid as promoting divorce.

1988—*Pledger v. Pledger,* 6 Va. App. 627, 371 S.E.2d 43.
General contract rules of construction apply. Question presented was whether agreement called for payment of interest on pension benefits from date of final decree or date of first payment. Court of Appeals holds interest runs from first payment date. General rule is that interest is due when debt is due and payable.

1988—*Westbrook v. Westbrook,* 5 Va. App. 446, 364 S.E.2d 523.
When parties have entered into valid agreement, then court should impose no condition, monetary or non-monetary, except in accord with agreement.

1987—*Rook v. Rook,* 233 Va. 92, 353 S.E.2d 756.
Property settlement agreement was incorporated into final decree. More than 21 days later wife moved to have husband held in contempt for non-compliance with agreement. Husband defended by saying that agreement was void in that it facilitated separation and divorce. Trial court agreed. Supreme Court ruled that trial court lacked jurisdiction and as such Rule 1:1 did not apply. A judgment that is void because it was procured by extrinsic or collateral fraud is not subject to Rule 1:1.

1987—*Bragan v. Bragan,* 4 Va. App. 516, 358 S.E.2d 757.
Release of future claims in separation agreement entered into prior to passage of Va. Code § 20-107.3 barred monetary award after passage of this statute.

1987—*Fry v. Schwarting,* 4 Va. App. 173, 355 S.E.2d 342.
Decree in this case did not expressly incorporate property settlement agreement, but it did recite verbatim child support provisions. This was held to be sufficient incorporation to authorize court to order support beyond 18th birthday, as was called for in agreement.

1986—*Ross v. Caw,* 231 Va. 206, 343 S.E.2d 312.
Word "shall" is primarily mandatory in effect and "may" is primarily permissive. These interpretations have generally involved statutes. This case involves contract. Contracts must be construed as written. Merely because parties disagree as to meaning of language in contract does not mean it is ambiguous. Question of whether contract is ambiguous is one of law. Word "may" in this case was found to mean permissive.

1986—*Thompson v. Thompson,* 231 Va. 161, 343 S.E.2d 53.
There was ambiguity in agreement. Court admitted parol evidence to resolve conflict as to intent of parties. Finding of commissioner should not be disturbed unless unsupported by evidence.

1986—*Barnes v. Barnes,* 231 Va. 39, 340 S.E.2d 803.
Husband and wife signed Property Settlement Agreement. Afterwards, husband learned that wife had engaged in adulterous conduct and thereby had fraudulently induced him to sign agreement. Party is not entitled to rescind such agreement for other's concealment of material facts where confidential relationship of husband and wife has ended and parties are dealing at arm's length as they were in this case and where they were represented by independent counsel. In cases such as this, there is no duty to disclose infidelity where confidential relationship has ended and parties are dealing at arm's length. If husband had wanted support obligations to end upon discovery of prior infidelity he could have inserted this into agreement.

1986—*Smith v. Smith,* 3 Va. App. 510, 351 S.E.2d 593.
Interpretation placed on agreement by parties is entitled to greatest weight. Ambiguity exists when language admits of being understood in more than one way. Mere fact that parties attribute different meanings does not mean that ambiguity exists.

1986—*Forrest v. Forrest,* 3 Va. App. 236, 349 S.E.2d 157.

Matter of discretion for trial court to incorporate agreement into final decree. Agreement in this case called for incorporation although husband after signing agreement indicated he had changed his mind. No abuse of discretion to incorporate.

1985—*Wells v. Weston,* 229 Va. 72, 326 S.E.2d 672.

Mutual assent by parties to terms of contract is crucial to contract's validity. In evaluating party's intent, his outward expression must be examined rather than his secret unexpressed intention. Meeting of minds requires manifestation of mutual assent and party's mental reservation does not impair contract. Trial court found lack of mutuality in property settlement agreement because husband understood paragraph to have meaning different than what it said. Supreme Court held husband was bound by plain meaning of contract.

1985—*Parra v. Parra,* 1 Va. App. 118, 335 S.E.2d 157.

Agreement in this case not incorporated into final decree. Parties still bound by agreement as to issue of equitable distribution. Public policy strongly favors resolution of these disputes by agreement.

1985—*Rodriguez v. Rodriguez,* 1 Va. App. 87, 334 S.E.2d 595.

Court order did not expressly incorporate agreement but only approved, ratified, and confirmed it. Where it is incorporated then it shall be deemed term of decree and enforceable as such. Parties may agree to support children beyond minority and if incorporated into decree it is enforceable. In this case, agreement was not incorporated and therefore court lacked jurisdiction to order support payments beyond 18.

1985—*Tiffany v. Tiffany,* 1 Va. App. 11, 332 S.E.2d 796.

These agreements are contracts and will be interpreted in accord with contract law. Where agreement is unambiguous then meaning and effect are for court. Plain meaning rule will be followed. This agreement to pay college expenses by its own terms did not give husband veto power over child's choice of college.

CHAPTER 6

MISCELLANEOUS

§ 6-3. Change of Name.

1986—*Beyah v. Shelton,* 231 Va. 432, 344 S.E.2d 909.
Father of illegitimate child has standing to object to name change.
When natural father objects to name change it generally will not be
allowed unless: (1) abandonment; (2) father guilty of misconduct that
would embarrass child; (3) substantial detriment to child; (4) child of
sufficient discretion that he desires change. Change of name in this
case not in child's best interest.

§ 6-4. Duress.

1986—*Division of Social Servs. v. Unknown Father,* 2 Va. App. 420, 345
S.E.2d 533.
Duress is not readily accepted as excuse. Party alleging it must prove it
by clear and convincing evidence. Duress must have been exercised
upon him who sets it up as defense and by him who claims benefit of
contract or someone acting on his behalf or with his knowledge. Duress
means that degree of constraint or danger which is sufficient in sever-
ity or in apprehension to overcome mind and will of person of ordinary
firmness.

§ 6-5. Fraud.

1986—*Barnes v. Barnes,* 231 Va. 39, 340 S.E.2d 803.
Husband alleged fraud in inducement as to property settlement agreement since wife had not disclosed prior infidelity. No duty to disclose
infidelity where confidential relationship has ended and parties are
dealing at arm's length. Reference is made to other fraud cases involving concealment of assets.

1985—*Wells v. Weston,* 229 Va. 72, 326 S.E.2d 672.
Constructive fraud must be established by clear and convincing evidence. Constructive fraud is breach of legal or equitable duty which
irrespective of moral guilt is declared by law to be fraudulent because of
its tendency to deceive others or violate confidence. Husband, in this
case, alleged that attorney represented both he and wife and committed
constructive fraud in preparation of property settlement agreement.
Evidence did not support this.

§ 6-6. Husband — Wife.

(A) Liability.

1986—*Lewis v. House,* 232 Va. 28, 348 S.E.2d 217.
Only one-half of funds deposited in joint bank account of husband and wife is subject to garnishment by creditor of one spouse in this case. Rebuttable presumption exists that each spouse owns one-half of joint deposit. It is burden of creditor to rebut this by clear and convincing evidence.

(C) Rights.

1984—*Kizer v. Commonwealth,* 228 Va. 256, 321 S.E.2d 291.
The wife's revocation of implied consent to marital intercourse must be demonstrated beyond reasonable doubt as to her intent to terminate marital relations, i.e., wife (a) has lived separate and apart, (b) has refrained from voluntary sex with husband, (c) has acted in such manner manifesting objectively to husband that marriage is ended.

(D) Necessaries.

See Va. Code § 55-37 stating that doctrine of necessaries creates no liability between spouses as to each other.

§ 6-7. Miscellaneous.

1986—*Woolley v. Woolley,* 3 Va. App. 337, 349 S.E.2d 422.
Husband's mother contributed $27,500 to purchase of family home. At time of equitable distribution, it was improper to grant mother constructive trust as to this money from proceeds of sale of house. Mother not party to action. Constructive trusts are those which law creates independent of intent of parties to prevent fraud or injustice.

CHAPTER 7

EVIDENCE

§ 7-2. Hearsay.

1986—*Marks v. Sanzo,* 231 Va. 350, 345 S.E.2d 263.
Pedigree exception allows consideration of hearsay evidence regarding person's family relationship as proof of existence of relationship.

§ 7-5. Opinion.

1988—*Aster v. Gross,* 7 Va. App. 1.
All that is necessary for expert to testify is that he is better qualified than jury to form inference from facts.

1987—*Commonwealth v. Harrison,* 5 Va. App. 8, 360 S.E.2d 212.
Va. Code § 8.01-401.1 allows expert to render opinion based on circumstances and data made known to or perceived by him. Such facts and data need not be admissible if of type normally relied on by others in this field.

1986—*M.E.D. v. J.P.M.,* 3 Va. App. 391, 350 S.E.2d 215.
Under § 8.01-401.1, expert allowed to express opinion or draw inference from impermissible sources, i.e., hearsay.

§ 7-7. Presumptions.

1988—*Lambert v. Lambert,* 6 Va. App. 94, 367 S.E.2d 184.
A presumption is not rebutted where credible evidence for and against the presumption is balanced.

§ 7-8. Witnesses.

1984—*Burts v. Burts,* 227 Va. 618, 316 S.E.2d 745.
Trial court excluded wife from hearing on support issues. Court did not have to conduct ore tenus hearing but having decided to do so it had no right to exclude parties. This violated due process rights of wife.

PROCEDURE

§ 8-2. Appeal and Error.

1988—*Goodpasture v. Goodpasture,* 7 Va. App. 55.
No transcript or written statement of facts filed. Where transcript indispensable to determination of issues, then timely filing of transcript is jurisdictional. In this case, court ruled that record was adequate without transcript.

1988—*Thompson v. Thompson,* 6 Va. App. 277, 367 S.E.2d 747.
Decree confirming Commissioner's report presumed correct and will not be disturbed if reasonably supported by substantial, competent, credible evidence.

1986—*Hodges v. Hodges,* 2 Va. App. 508, 347 S.E.2d 134.
On appeal where chancellor has disapproved commissioner's findings, appellate court must review evidence and ascertain whether under correct application of law evidence supports findings of commissioner or conclusions of trial court.

1986—*Dodge v. Dodge,* 2 Va. App. 238, 343 S.E.2d 363.
Failure to note exceptions to commissioner's report precludes judicial review of these issues.

1986—*Collier v. Collier,* 2 Va. App. 125, 341 S.E.2d 827.
Decree based solely on depositions is not as conclusive on appeal as one based on evidence heard ore tenus, but such decree is presumed correct and will not be overturned if supported by substantial, credible evidence.

1986—*Dukelow v. Dukelow,* 2 Va. App. 21, 341 S.E.2d 208.
If exceptions are not filed to commissioner's report, then these matters may not be raised on appeal.

1986—*Rexrode v. Rexrode,* 1 Va. App. 385, 339 S.E.2d 544.
Decree based on depositions is not as conclusive as one based on evidence ore tenus, but such decree is presumed correct and will not be overturned if supported by substantial, credible evidence.

1985—*Hankerson v. Moody,* 229 Va. 270, 329 S.E.2d 791.
Generally, trial court's conclusions sitting without jury will not be set aside unless plainly wrong or without evidence to support it. However, trial court's conclusions based on evidence that is not in material conflict does not have this binding effect on appeal. In this case, trial court arbitrarily disregarded undisputed evidence which established Moody's paternity and therefore judgment is reversed.

1985—*Duckett v. Duckett,* 1 Va. App. 279, 337 S.E.2d 759.
Failure to file appeal bond is jurisdictional defect. Appeal dismissed.

§ 8-3. Attorneys.

(A) In General.

1985—*Wells v. Weston,* 229 Va. 72, 326 S.E.2d 672.
Husband alleged constructive fraud in preparation of property settlement agreement since attorney represented both he and wife. Trial court found simply an overtone of constructive fraud. Fraud must be established by clear and convincing evidence.

(B) Fees.

1989—*Ellington v. Ellington,* 8 Va. App. 48, 378 S.E.2d 626.
Wife awarded attorney's fees of $37,629.90. Given complexity of issues, quality of representation, and number of hours devoted, and result obtained, this fee award was reasonable.

1989—*Davis v. Davis,* 8 Va. App. 12, 377 S.E.2d 640.
Fees of $3,500.00 awarded. This is within sound discretion of court. It is preferred bu. not essential that counsel submit itemized billing statement for award of fees.

1988—*Kaufman v. Kaufman,* 7 Va. App. 488.
Although evidence of time expended and charges made is preferred basis for determining award, it is not only basis.

1987—*Sprott v. Sprott,* 233 Va. 238, 355 S.E.2d 881.
Husband was awarded divorce on desertion grounds, but wife was still awarded attorney's fees of $1,500.

1987—*Graves v. Graves,* 4 Va. App. 326, 357 S.E.2d 554.
Wife submitted attorney's bill to court of $4,821. Husband's income was three times wife's. Attorney's fees of $4,821 were awarded.

1987—*Price v. Price,* 4 Va. App. 224, 355 S.E.2d 905.
Wife changed attorneys three times. Denial of attorney's fees was within discretion of court.

1987—*Clayberg v. Clayberg,* 4 Va. App. 218, 355 S.E.2d 902.
It was implicit that trial court felt that each party had sufficient income and assets to pay that party's own costs and expenses. Denial of attorney's fees in this instance was not abuse of discretion.

1987—*Artis v. Artis,* 4 Va. App. 132, 354 S.E.2d 812.
Just because court has awarded alimony does not mean that award of attorney's fees is required.

1986—*Edwards v. Lowry,* 232 Va. 110, 348 S.E.2d 259.
Court of equity has power to award attorney's fees in aid of contempt proceedings especially where child's interests are at stake. Same applies to efforts to resist reduction in child support. Fees should be awarded here where wife had to make four court appearances in one year to resist husband's motion to reduce support.

1985—*McGinnis v. McGinnis,* 1 Va. App. 272, 338 S.E.2d 159.
Evidence of time expended and charges to client is preferred basis for award of attorney fees but is not only basis. Award of $1000 in this vigorously contested case was not unreasonable.

§ 8-5. Burden of Proof.

1987—*Seemann v. Seemann,* 233 Va. 290, 355 S.E.2d 884.
Clear and convincing evidence is that measure or degree of proof which will produce in mind of trier of fact firm belief or conviction as to allegations sought to be established. It is more than mere preponderance but not as much as proof beyond reasonable doubt. It does not mean clear and unequivocal.

§ 8-6. Commissioner in Chancery.

1987—*Sprott v. Sprott,* 233 Va. 238, 355 S.E.2d 881.
On appeal, decree which approves Commissioner's report will be affirmed unless plainly wrong. Where Chancellor has disapproved Commissioner's finding, this Court must review evidence and ascertain whether under correct application of law evidence supports findings of Commissioner or conclusions of court. This Court must still give due regard to Commissioner's ability, not shared by Chancellor, to hear, see, and evaluate witnesses at first hand.

1987—*Robinson v. Robinson,* 5 Va. App. 222, 361 S.E.2d 356.
Report of Commissioner is not given same weight as jury verdict; it must be sustained unless trial judge determines evidence does not support findings.

1986—*Dukelow v. Dukelow,* 2 Va. App. 21, 341 S.E.2d 208.
Circuit court is not bound by recommendations of commissioner. Court may make its own conclusions as to appropriate relief.

1984—*Hill v. Hill,* 227 Va. 569, 318 S.E.2d 292.
While report of commissioner does not carry weight of jury verdict, it should be sustained unless court concludes findings are not supported by evidence. This applies with particular force to findings of fact based on evidence taken in presence of commissioner but is not applicable to pure conclusions of law. On appeal, decree which approves commissioner's report will be affirmed unless plainly wrong. Determination of appropriate relief is responsibility of trial court and commissioner's recommendation is purely advisory.

§ 8-9. Contempt.

1986—*Frazier v. Commonwealth,* 3 Va. App. 84, 348 S.E.2d 405.
In show cause hearing, moving party must show non-compliance with order of court. Other party then has burden to show justification.

§ 8-10. Continuance.

1986—*Mills v. Mills,* 232 Va. 94, 348 S.E.2d 250.
It was abuse of discretion to refuse wife continuance in this case. On eve of hearing, conflict arose between wife and attorney. Wife could not find another attorney on short notice. No evidence that intent of wife was to evade trial.

§ 8-12. Courts.

1987—*Florence v. Roberts,* 233 Va. 297, 355 S.E.2d 316.
Either party may appeal civil paternity case to circuit court from juvenile court.

1986—*Petachenko v. Petachenko,* 232 Va. 296, 350 S.E.2d 600.
Conduct of parties does not destroy jurisdiction of trial court to adjudicate divorce proceedings. Resumption of cohabitation may require dismissal, but it does not deprive court of jurisdiction.

1986—*Box v. Talley,* 1 Va. App. 289, 338 S.E.2d 349.
Appeal from juvenile court is trial de novo. Circuit court is not court of review. Previous judgment is annulled. Burden of proof remains on plaintiff.

§ 8-14. Decree.

1989—*Holmes v. Holmes,* 8 Va. App. 457, 382 S.E.2d 27.
On twenty-first day after entry of divorce decree, wife presented ex parte proof that separation agreement had been procured by fraud. Trial court should have vacated that part of final decree incorporating agreement and allow divorce decree otherwise to stand. Judgment obtained by intrinsic fraud such as perjury, forged documents, or other incidents of trial related to issues material to judgment is voidable prior to judgment becoming final. Judgment procurred by extrinsic fraud; i.e., by conduct which prevents fair submission of controversy to court is void and subject to attack at any time. Court did not decide in this instance whether fraud was intrinsic or extrinsic because motion was presented prior to judgment becoming final.

1987—*Smith v. Smith,* 4 Va. App. 148, 354 S.E.2d 816.
When divorce proceeding has been dismissed, then court no longer has authority to order pendente lite support.

1986—*Frazier v. Commonwealth,* 3 Va. App. 84, 348 S.E.2d 405.
Erroneous order is as binding as any other order until set aside.

1986—*Division of Social Servs. v. Unknown Father,* 2 Va. App. 420, 345 S.E.2d 533.
Order which is not in compliance with Rule 1:13 as to endorsement by counsel is void. Order which is void ab initio may be vacated in spite of Rule 1:1.

1986—*Cass v. Lassiter,* 2 Va. App. 273, 343 S.E.2d 470.
Variance between settlement agreement and final decree. This evidence clearly supported conclusion that oversight had been made in decree and court has authority to correct such.

1986—*Venable v. Venable,* 2 Va. App. 178, 342 S.E.2d 646.
Husband contends that November 12 order that requires him to pay mortgage for November 1 was retroactive modification of prior decree that had ordered wife to make these payments. This not so because hearing on matter was held on October 26 and final decision had been delayed for benefit of husband.

1985—*Parrillo v. Parrillo,* 1 Va. App. 226, 336 S.E.2d 23.
If ambiguity exists in decree, primary consideration must be given to interpretation which would support facts and law of case in order to avoid result that would do violence to either.

1985—*Clephas v. Clephas,* 1 Va. App. 209, 336 S.E.2d 897.
Judgment occurs when court directs clerk to enter on court's order book not when court rules on motion or directs counsel to prepare order. Order is final if it disposes of all substantive issues even though court may not have ruled on every issue in controversy.

1984—*Hill v. Hill,* 227 Va. 569, 318 S.E.2d 292.
Court of record speaks only through its written orders. Trial court's ruling on statute of limitations was not part of final decree and was not assigned as error on appeal and therefore is law of case.

§ 8-15. Default.

Editor's Note. Rule 2:9, referred to in the bound volume, has been rescinded. Current provisions are included in Va. Code §§ 20-99, 20-99.2.

§ 8-17. Depositions.

1984—*Armistead v. Armistead,* 228 Va. 352, 322 S.E.2d 836.
Custody dispute. Refusal of trial court to admit deposition of wife into evidence or to use them for impeachment was error under Rule 4:7(a)(2) and (3).

§ 8-18. Discovery.

1986—*Johnson v. Johnson,* 1 Va. App. 330, 338 S.E.2d 353.
This action deals with delinquent support payments by husband. Court properly disallowed discovery by husband as to wife's tax returns since this was irrelevant.

§ 8-21. Estoppel.

1987—*Hausman v. Hausman,* 233 Va. 1, 353 S.E.2d 710.
Doctrine of estoppel by deed is codified in Va. Code § 55-52.

1987—*Robinette v. Robinette,* 4 Va. App. 123, 354 S.E.2d 808.
Court relies on estoppel by deed to deny creation of trust in favor of third party.

1984—*Armistead v. Armistead,* 228 Va. 352, 322 S.E.2d 836.
Custody case. Prior agreement as to temporary custody does not have any estoppel effect.

§ 8-22. Full Faith and Credit.

1988—*Gibson v. Gibson,* 5 Va. App. 426, 364 S.E.2d 518.
Husband awarded divorce in Tennessee based on wife's cruelty. Tennessee court did not have personal jurisdiction over wife, therefore that decree not entitled to full faith and credit as to issues of property and support rights.

§ 8-25. Laches.

1986—*Johnson v. Johnson,* 1 Va. App. 330, 338 S.E.2d 353.
Laches is not defense to non-compliance with lawful decree.

§ 8-28. Pleadings.

(A) Amendment.

1986—*Bentz v. Bentz,* 2 Va. App. 486, 345 S.E.2d 773.
After ore tenus hearing, husband filed motion to amend complaint to allege adultery by wife. Neither party sought spousal support. Nothing precluded husband from presenting this evidence at hearing as to issue of equitable distribution. Trial court properly denied motion.

(C) Sufficiency.

1988—*Gologanoff v. Gologanoff,* 6 Va. App. 340, 369 S.E.2d 446.
If party wishes equitable distribution award then he must file a pleading requesting the court to determine ownership and value and make a monetary award. A separate motion requesting this relief, filed in a timely fashion, was sufficient.

1986—*Boyd v. Boyd,* 2 Va. App. 16, 340 S.E.2d 578.
No request for alimony in pleading. No court can base its judgment on right which has not been pleaded. Pleading did contain general request for such further relief as may be appropriate. That was not enough.

§ 8-29. Res Judicata.

1989—*Commonwealth v. Johnson,* 7 Va. App. 614, 376 S.E.2d 787.
Doctrine of res judicata encompasses four preclusive effects: res judicata bar, merger, direct estoppel, and collateral estoppel. Res judicata bar provides that valid personal judgment on merits in favor of defen-

dant bars relitigation of same cause of action or any part thereof which could have been litigated between parties or those in privity. Privity means mutual or successor relationship to same rights of property or such identification in interest of one person with another as to represent same legal rights. Parent and child are not in privity. Therefore, child who is not party to paternity action, does not have guardian ad litem and not given adequate opportunity to litigate is not bound by judgment as to parent.

§ 8-31. Service.

Editor's Note. Rule 2:9, referred to in the bound volume, has been rescinded. Current provisions are included in Va. Code §§ 20-99, 20-99.2.

See Va. Code § 20-99 indicating that process shall be served in this Commonwealth by any method prescribed in Va. Code § 8.01-296 by any person authorized to serve process under § 8.01-293. Service may be made on non-resident by any method prescribed in § 8.01-296 by any person authorized to serve process under § 8.01-320.

See Va. Code § 20-112 indicating that no support order may be retroactively modified, but may be modified with respect to any period during which there is a pending petition for modification, but only from the date that notice of such petition has been given to the responding party.

1987—*Morris v. Morris,* 4 Va. App. 539, 359 S.E.2d 104.
Service by publication only bestows *in rem* jurisdiction.

1986—*Hayes v. Hayes,* 3 Va. App. 499, 351 S.E.2d 590.
Party served by publication is deemed to be party not served with process within meaning of Virginia Code. Right to spousal support is personal claim which may not be denied without due process. Service by publication is insufficient to bestow jurisdiction.

1985—*Lester v. Bennett,* 1 Va. App. 47, 333 S.E.2d 366.
Person attending court enjoys common-law privilege from arrest and service of process. This is not absolute. Test is whether immunity itself, if allowed, would so obstruct judicial administration in very cause for protection of which it is involved as to justify withholding it. In this case, two matters were so closely related that immunity did not apply.

§ 8-33. Statutes.

1988—*Booth v. Booth,* 7 Va. App. 22.
Statutes are generally applied prospectively. Equitable distribution statute applies to all actions filed after effective date, regardless of when cause of action arose, and applies to property acquired prior to effective date unless agreed to otherwise.

1987—*Morris v. Morris,* 4 Va. App. 539, 359 S.E.2d 104.
Where statute is subject to two interpretations, court will adopt interpretation that will harmonize statute with fundamental law.

1987—*Price v. Price,* 4 Va. App. 224, 355 S.E.2d 905.
When statute is amended while action is pending, rights of parties are to be decided in accord with law in effect when action was begun unless amended statute shows clear intention to vary such rights.

1984—*Jacobs v. Meade,* 227 Va. 284, 315 S.E.2d 383.
Every act of legislature is presumed to be constitutional. Statute will be construed in manner as to avoid constitutional question whenever possible. It is court's duty to construe statutes so as to avoid absurd results.